COLLINS
GEM

DICTIONARY OF QUOTATIONS

COLLINS
London and Glasgow

First published 1961
New Edition 1985
Reprinted 1988

ISBN 0 00 458760 10

Printed in Great Britain by Wm. Collins Sons & Co. Ltd.

PREFACE

In this volume, quotations are arranged according to authorship, in alphabetical order, except for such materials as ballads and anonymous quotations; these are placed together alphabetically under those headings. Nursery rhymes have been ommitted, and interested readers are referred to the authoritative *Oxford Dictionary of Nursery Rhymes*. Quotations from each author are presented in alphabetical order by the title of each work. With major authors, the leading mode of writing is dealt with before minor ones (thus, Milton's poems come before his prose works); where such definitions are difficult or obviously tendentious, the writings are simply presented in alphabetical order by title. These may be followed by other sources such as letters and speeches (both in chronological order), remarks, attributed quotations ('Attr.') and those found in biographical or other works, and finally, 'last words.' (In speeches, letters, etc., each quotation is drawn from a separate occasion unles 'Ib.' is employed; 'Ib.' indicates that the quotation comes from the same source as the previous one.)

Citations from the Bible, which is quoted in the King James Version, are presented in sequence under the title of each book; the Vulgate, the Prayer Book and the Latin Mass are also arranged sequentially. Quotations from foreign languages have generally been provided with recent, literal, prose translations, except where it would be a pity to omit a celebrated traditional rendition.

References have been made as compact as possible

while still allowing the reader to find the context reasonably easily in the original work. 'Ib.' appearing alone refers to the previously cited source and location, while 'Ib.' followed by a reference number refers to the last-cited title.

In the index, keywords head up an alphabetical listing of phrases in which that word appears, and each phrase is followed by the page number and the number of the relevant quotation on that page. It should be possible to find out who first uttered a well-remembered quotation by searching for the most obvious word; half-remembered quotations may be traced if one of the more striking words can be recalled; and something apposite and all the great topics of human experience can be discovered by looking up an appropriate word.

THE QUOTATIONS

Accius, Lucius (170–90 B.C.)

1 *Oderint dum metuant.* Let them hate so long as they fear. [*Atreus*]

Acheson, Dean (1893–1971)

2 Great Britain has lost an Empire and not yet found a role. [Speech, 1962]

Acton, First Baron (1834–1902)

3 Power tends to corrupt and absolute power corrupts absolutely. [Letter, *Life of Mandell Creighton*]

4 Every class is unfit to govern. [Quoted in Auden, *A Certain World*]

Adams, Sarah Flower (1805–1848)

5 Nearer, my God, to Thee, / Nearer to Thee! [Hymn]

Addison, Joseph (1672–1719)

6 And, pleas'd th' Almighty's orders to perform / Rides in the whirlwind, and directs the storm. [*The Campaign*]

7 A day, an hour of virtuous liberty / Is worth a whole eternity in bondage. [*Cato*, II]

8 The woman that deliberates is lost. [Ib. IV]

9 Music, the greatest good that mortals know, / And all of heaven we have below. ['Song for St. Cecilia's Day']

10 The truth of it is, learning, like travelling, and all other methods of improvement, as it finishes

good sense, so it makes a silly man ten thousand times more insufferable, by supplying variety of matter to his impertinence, and giving him an opportunity of abounding in absurdities. [*The Man of the Town*]

1 It was said of Socrates that he brought philosophy down from heaven to inhabit among men; and I shall be ambitious to have it said of me that I have brought philosophy out of closets and libraries, schools and colleges, to dwell in clubs and assemblies, at tea-tables and in coffee-houses. [*Spectator*, 1]

2 A perfect tragedy is the noblest production of human nature. [Ib. 39]

3 We have in England a particular bashfulness in every thing that regards religion. [Ib. 458]

4 The spacious firmament on high, / With all the blue ethereal sky, / And spangled heavens, a shining frame, / Their great Original proclaim. [Ib. 465]

5 I value my garden more for being full of blackbirds than of cherries, and very frankly give them fruit for their songs. [Ib. 477]

6 'We are always doing,' says he, 'something for Posterity, but I would fain see Posterity do something for us.' [Ib. 583]

7 When I read the several dates of the tombs, of some that died yesterday, and some six hundred years ago, I consider that great day when we shall all of us be contemporaries, and make our appearance together. [*Thoughts in Westminster Abbey*]

8 Arguments out of a pretty mouth are unanswerable. [*Women and Liberty*]

Aeschylus (525–456 B.C.)

9 The wisest of the wise may err. [*Fragments*]

1 It is always the season for the old to learn. [Ib.]

2 Words are the physicians of a mind diseased. [*Prometheus Bound*]

Agathon (c. 448–400 B.C.)

3 This only is denied to God: the power to change the past. [Aristotle, *Nicomachean Ethics*, VI]

Ainger, A. C. (1841–1919)

4 God is working His purpose out as year succeeds to year, / God is working His purpose out and the time is drawing near; / Nearer and nearer draws the time, the time that shall surely be, / When the earth shall be filled with the glory of God as the waters cover the sea. [Hymn]

Alcott, Amos Bronson (1799–1888)

5 Civilization degrades the many to exalt the few. [*Table Talk*, 'Pursuits']

Alcuin (735–804)

6 *Vox populi, vox dei.* The voice of the people is the voice of God. [Letter to Charlemagne]

Albee, Edward (1928–   )

7 Who's Afraid of Virginia Woolf? [Play title]

Aldrich, Henry (1647–1710)

8 If all be true that I do think, / There are five reasons we should drink; / Good wine — a friend — or being dry — / Or lest we should be by and by — / Or any other reason why. ['Five Reasons for Drinking']

Alexander the Great (356–323 B.C.)

9 Heaven cannot brook two suns, nor earth two masters. [Plutarch, *Apothegms*]

Alexander, Cecil Frances (1823–1895)

10 All things bright and beautiful, / All creatures

great and small, / All things wise and wonderful
− / The Lord God made them all. [Hymn]

1 Jesus calls us! O'er the tumult / Of our life's wild
restless sea. [Hymn]

2 There is a green hill far away, / Without a city
wall, / Where the dear Lord was crucified, /
Who died to save us all. [Hymn]

Alfonso X (1221–1284)

3 [On the Ptolemaic system of astronomy] If the
Lord Almighty had consulted me before
embarking upon Creation, I should have
recommended something simpler. [Attr.]

Ali, Muhamad (1942–   )

4 I am the greatest. [Catchphrase]

Alison, Richard (fl. c. 1606)

5 There cherries grow, that none can buy / Till
cherry-ripe themselves do cry. ['An Hour's
Recreation in Music']

Allainval, Léonor Jean D' (c. 1700–1753)

6 *L'Embarras de Richesse.* The embarrassment of
riches. [Title of play]

Allen, Woody (1935–   )

7 [Of masturbation] Don't knock it, it's sex with
someone you love. [*Annie Hall*]

8 I don't want to achieve immortality through my
work . . . I want to achieve it by not dying. [Attr.]

Allingham, William (1824–1889)

9 Up the airy mountain, / Down the rushy glen, /
We daren't go a-hunting, / For fear of little men.
['The Fairies']

Ambrose, St. (c. 340–397)

10 *Si fueris Romae, Romano vivito more; / Si fueri
alibi, vivito sicut ibi.* If you are in Rome, live in

the Roman way; if you are elsewhere, live as they do there. [Jeremy Taylor, *Ductor Dubitantium*]

Amiel, Henri-Frédéric (1828–1881)

1 The age of great men is going; the epoch of the ant-hill, of life in multiplicity, is beginning. [*Journal* 1851]

2 A belief is not true because it is useful. [Ib. 1876]

Amis, Kingsley (1922–)

3 More will mean worse. [*Encounter*, 1960]

Andrews, Bishop Lancelot (1555–1626)

4 A cold coming they had of it, at this time of the year; just, the worst time of the year, to take a journey, and specially a long journey, in. [Sermon]

Anonymous

5 A rainbow in the morning / Is the Shepherd's warning; / But a rainbow at night / Is the Shepherd's delight. [Old Weather Rhyme]

6 A very gallant gentleman. [Inscription on grave of Capt. Oates]

7 An army marches on its stomach. [Attr. to Napoleon]

8 An intelligent Russian once remarked to us, 'Every country has its own constitution; ours is absolutism moderated by assassination.' [Munster, *Political Sketches of Europe*]

9 Be happy while y'er leevin, / For y'er a lang time deid. [Scottish Motto]

10 Begone, dull Care! I prithee begone from me! / Begone, dull Care! Thou and I shall never agree. [Song, 17th century]

11 *Cet animal est très méchant, / Quand on láttaque il se défend. /* This animal is very wicked, /

When it is attacked it defends itself. [*La Ménagerie*, 1868]

1 [Of Bayard] *Chevalier sans peur et sans reproche*. Knight without fear and without blame. [*Chronicles*, 1476–1524]

2 Christmas is coming, the geese are getting fat, / Please to put a penny in the old man's hat; / If you haven't got a penny, a ha'penny will do, / If you haven't got a ha'penny, God bless you! [Beggar's Rhyme]

3 Dear Sir, Your astonishment's odd: / I am always about in the Quad. / And that's why the tree / Will continue to be, / Since observed by Yours faithfully, God. [Reply to Ronald Knox, 'There once was a man']

4 Difficult things take a long time; / the impossible takes a little longer. [Sometimes attr. to Nansen, and others]

5 Early one morning, just as the sun was rising, / I heard a maid sing in the valley below: / 'Oh, don't deceive me; Oh, never leave me! / How could you use a poor maiden so?' [Song, 'Early One Morning']

6 *Ein Reich, Ein Volk, Ein Führer*. One realm, one people, one leader. [Nazi Party slogan, 1934]

7 Esau selleth his birthright for a mess of potage. [*Geneva Bible* (heading to Genesis 25)]

8 *Et in Arcadia ego*. And I too in Arcadia. [Variously attr.]

9 Everyman, I will go with thee, and be thy guide, / In thy most need to go by thy side. [*Everyman*]

10 For so long as but a hundred of us remain alive, we will in no way yield ourselves to the dominion of the English. For it is not for glory, nor riches, nor honour that we fight, but for Freedom only, which no good man lays down but with his life. [Declaration of Arbroath, 1320]

1 From ghoulies and ghosties and long leggety beasties / And things that go bump in the night, / Good Lord, deliver us! [Cornish prayer]

2 *Gaudeamus igitur, / Juvenes dum sumus / Post jucundam juventutem, / Post molestam senectutem, / Nos habebit humus.* Let us be happy while we are young, for after carefree youth and careworn age, the earth will hold us also. [Students' song, traced to 1267]

3 God be in my head, / And in my understanding; / God be in my eyes, / And in my looking; / God be in my mouth, / And in my speaking; / God be in my heart, / And in my thinking; / God be at my end, / And at my departing. [Sarum Missal]

4 *Honi soit qui mal y pense.* Evil be to him who evil thinks. [Motto of the Order of the Garter]

5 Here's tae us; wha's like us? / Gey few, and they're a' deid. [Scottish toast]

6 If all the world were paper, / And all the sea were ink; / If all the trees were bread and cheese / How should we do for drink? [17th century]

7 I'll sing you twelve O / Green grow the rushes O. [Traditional song]

8 In England, justice is open to all, like the Ritz Hotel. [Variously attr.]

9 It is good to be merry and wise, / It is good to be honest and true, / It is best to be off with the old love, / Before you are on with the new. [Song]

10 It's the same the whole world over, / Ain't it all a blooming shame, / It's the rich wot gets the pleasure, / It's the poor wot gets the blame. [Song of World War I (many variants)]

11 *Laborare est orare.* Work is prayer. [Unknown origin]

8 ANONYMOUS

1 *Liberté! Egalité! Fraternité!* Liberty! Equality! Brotherhood! [Revolutionary slogan, 1793]

2 Matthew, Mark, Luke, and John, / The Bed be blest that I lie on. / Four angels to my bed, / Four angels round my head, / One to watch, and one to pray, / And two to bear my soul away. [Ady, *A Candle in the Dark*]

3 Monday's child is fair of face, / Tuesday's child is full of grace, / Wednesday's child is full of woe, / Thursday's child has far to go, / Friday's child is loving and giving, / Saturday's child works hard for its living, / And a child that's born on the Sabbath day / Is fair and wise and good and gay. [Bray, *Traditions of Devon*]

4 *Nemo me impune lacessit.* Wha daur meddle wi' me. [Motto of the Scots Crown]

5 Now I lay me down to sleep; / I pray the Lord my soul to keep. / If I should die before I wake, / I pray the Lord my soul to take. [Traditional]

6 O Death, where is thy sting-a-ling-a-ling, / O Grave, thy victoree? / The bells of Hell go ting-a-ling-a-ling / For you but not for me. [British Army song, World War I]

7 Overpaid, overfed, oversexed, and over here. [Remark on GIs in Britain during World War II]

8 Please to remember / The Fifth of November, / Gunpowder, treason and plot; / We know no reason / Why gunpowder treason / Should ever be forgot. [Rhyme]

9 *Post coitum omne animal triste.* After intercourse every animal is sad. [Traditional saying]

10 *Quidquid agas, prudenter agas, et respice finem.* Whatever you do, do it warily, and take account of the end. [*Gesta Romanorum*]

11 *Se non è vero, è molto ben trovato.* If it is not true, it is a happy invention. [16th century]

1 See the happy moron, / He doesn't give a damn, / I wish I were a moron, / My God! perhaps I am! [*Eugenics Review*, 1929]

2 [Of Ireland] She's the most distressful country that iver yet was seen / For they're hangin' men an' women there for the wearin' o' the Green. ['The Wearin' o' the Green']

3 Since wars begin in the minds of men, it is in the minds of men that the defences of peace must be constructed. [Constitution of UNESCO]

4 Summer is icumen in, / Lhude sing cuccu! / Groweth sed, and bloweth med, / And springeth the wude nu. ['Cuckoo Song', c. 1250]

5 The almighty dollar is the only object of worship. [*Philadelphia Public Ledger*, 1860]

6 The best defence against the atom bomb is not to be there when it goes off. [*The British Army Journal*, quoted in *Observer*, 'Sayings of the Week', 1949]

7 The eternal triangle. [*Daily Chronicle*, 1907]

8 The nature of God is a circle of which the centre is everywhere and the circumference is nowhere. [Attr. to Empedocles (quoted in *Roman de la Rose*)]

9 There is so much good in the worst of us, / And so much bad in the best of us, / That it hardly becomes any of us / To talk about the rest of us. [Variously attr.]

10 Time wounds all heels. [Sometimes attr. to Jane Ace]

11 Turn again, Whittington, / Lord Mayor of London. [Refrain of Bow Bells heard by Dick Whittington]

12 We hold these truths to be self-evident, that all men are created equal, that they are endowed by their Creator with certain unalienable rights, that

among these are life, liberty and the pursuit of happiness. [American Declaration of Independence, 1776 (originally drafted by Jefferson)]

1 Western wind, when wilt thou blow, / The small rain down can rain? / Christ, if my love were in my arms / And I in my bed again! [*Oxford Book of 16th-Century Verse*]

2 What did you do in the Great War, Daddy? [Caption on recruiting poster, World War I]

3 Whaur's yer Wully Shakespeare noo? [Cry from audience after opening night of Home's *Douglas*, 1756]

4 When Adam delved, and Eve span, / Who was then a gentleman? [Attr. John Ball, 1381]

5 Would you like to sin / With Elinor Glyn / On a tiger-skin? / Or would you prefer / to err / with her / on some other fur? [Quoted in A. Glyn, *Elinor Glyn*]

6 You pays your money and you takes your choice. [V. S. Lean, *Collectanea*]

7 You too can have a body like mine. [Advertising slogan for Charles Atlas body-building courses]

8 Your King and Country need you. [Caption on recruiting poster, World War I]

Arabian Nights

9 Who will change old lamps for new ones? ... New lamps for old ones? ['The History of Aladdin']

10 Open Sesame! ['The History of Ali Baba']

Arbuthnot, John (1667–1735)

11 [Biography] One of the new terrors of death. [Carruthers, *Life of Pope*]

Archimedes (287–212 B.C.)

1 Give me a firm place to stand, and I will move the earth. [Pappus Alexander, *Collectio*]

2 *Eureka!* I've got it! [Vitruvius Pollio, *De Architectura*]

Aristophanes (c. 444–380 B.C.)

3 A man may learn wisdom even from a foe. [*The Birds*]

4 How do you like 'Cloudcuckooland'? [Ib.]

5 Brekekekex, koax, koax. [*The Frogs*]

Aristotle (384–322 B.C.)

6 The roots of education are bitter, but the fruit is sweet. [Diogenes Laertius, *Life*]

7 What is a friend? A single soul dwelling in two bodies. [Ib.]

8 I count him braver who overcomes his desires than him who overcomes his enemies. [Stobaeus, *Florilegium*]

9 The whole is more than the sum of the parts. [*Metaphysics*]

10 All men by nature desire knowledge. [Ib.]

11 Piety requires us to honour truth above our friends. [*Nicomachean Ethics*, I]

12 If one way be better than another, that you may be sure is Nature's way. [Ib.]

13 Where we are free to act, we are also free to refrain from acting, and where we are able to say No, we are also able to say Yes. [Ib. III]

14 Our characters are the result of our conduct. [Ib.]

15 A tragedy, then, is the imitation of an action that is serious, has magnitude, and is complete in itself … with incidents arousing pity and fear, wherewith to accomplish its catharsis of such emotions. [*Poetics*, 6]

1 The poet's function is to describe, not the thing that has happened, but the kind of thing that might happen, i.e. what is possible as being probable or necessary. [Ib. 9]

2 Revolutions are not about trifles, but spring from trifles. [*Politics*]

3 Man is by nature a political animal. [Ib.]

Armstrong, Neil (1930–)

4 That's one small step for a man, one giant leap for mankind. [On stepping on to the moon]

Arnold, Matthew (1822–1888)

5 The Sea of Faith / Was once, too, at the full, and round earth's shore / Lay like the folds of a bright girdle furl'd. ['Dover Beach']

6 And we are here as on a darkling plain / Swept with confused alarms of struggle and flight, / Where ignorant armies clash by night. [Ib.]

7 Is it so small a thing / To have enjoy'd the sun, / To have liv'd light in the spring, / To have lov'd, to have thought, to have done? [*Empedocles on Etna*, I]

8 But as on some far northern strand, / Thinking of his own Gods, a Greek / In pity and mournful awe might stand / Before some fallen Runic stone — / For both were faiths, and both are gone. ['The Grand Chartreuse']

9 Wandering between two worlds, one dead, / The other powerless to be born. [Ib.]

10 Yes! in the sea of life enisled, / With echoing straits between us thrown, / Dotting the shoreless watery wild, / We mortal millions live *alone*. ['To Marguerite – Continued']

11 The unplumb'd, salt, estranging sea. [Ib.]

12 Friends who set forth at our side, / Falter, are

lost in the storm, / We, we only are left. ['Rugby Chapel']

1 Go, for they call you, Shepherd, from the hill. ['The Scholar-Gypsy']

2 This strange disease of modern life. [Ib.]

3 Still nursing the unconquerable hope, / Still clutching the inviolable shade. [Ib.]

4 Others abide our question. Thou art free. / We ask and ask: Thou smilest and art still, / Out-topping knowledge. ['Shakespeare']

5 Truth sits upon the lips of dying men. [*Sohrab and Rustum*]

6 Still standing for some false impossible shore. ['A Summer Night']

7 The great aim of culture is the aim of setting ourselves to ascertain what perfection is, and to make it prevail. [*Culture and Anarchy*]

8 My own definition of criticism; a disinterested endeavour to learn and propagate the best that is known and thought in the world. [*Essays in Criticism*,'Functions of Criticism at the Present Time']

9 A beautiful and ineffectual angel, beating in the void his luminous wings in vain. [Ib. 'Shelley']

Asquith, Margot (1865–1945)

10 [Of Lloyd George] He couldn't see a belt without hitting below it. [Attr.]

Astley, Sir Jacob (1579–1652)

11 O Lord, thou knowest how busy I must be this day; if I forget thee, do not thou forget me. [Prayer before Battle of Edgehill, 1642]

Attlee, Clement (1883–1967)

12 Russian Communism is the illegitimate child of Karl Marx and Catherine the Great. [*Observer*, 'Sayings of the Week', 1956]

Auden, W. H. (1907–1973)

1 When he laughed, respectable senators burst with laughter, / And when he cried the little children died in the streets. ['Epitaph on a Tyrant']

2 Lay your sleeping head, my love, / Human on my faithless arm. ['Lullaby']

3 About suffering they were never wrong, / The Old Masters. ['Musée des Beaux Arts']

4 This is the Night Mail crossing the Border / Bringing the cheque and the postal order. ['Night Mail']

5 Hunger allows no choice / To the citizen or to the police; / We must love one another or die. ['September 1, 1939']

6 History to the defeated / May say Alas but cannot help nor pardon. ['Spain 1937']

7 Most people enjoy the sight of their own handwriting as they enjoy the smell of their own farts. [*The Dyer's Hand*, 'Writing']

Augier, Emile (1820–1889)

8 *La nostalgie de la boue.* Homesickness for the gutter. [*Le Mariage d'Olympe*, I]

Augustine, St. (354–430)

9 *Da mihi castitatem et continentiam, sed noli modo.* / Give me chastity and continence, but not yet. [*Confessions*, VIII]

10 *Salus extra ecclesiam non est.* There is no salvation outside the church. [*De Bapt.*, IV]

11 *Nisi credideritis, non intelligitis.* If you don't believe it, you won't understand it. [*De Libero Arbitrio*]

12 *Ama et fac quod vis.* Love and do what you like. [*In Joannis*, VII (popular variant)]

1 *Roma locuta est; causa finita est.* Rome has spoken; the matter is settled. [*Sermons*, 1]

Austen, Jane (1775–1817)

2 Matrimony, as the origin of change, was always disagreeable. [*Emma*, 1]

3 One half of the world cannot understand the pleasures of the other. [Ib. 9]

4 Human nature is so well disposed towards those who are in interesting situations, that a young person, who either marries or dies, is sure to be kindly spoken of. [Ib. 22]

5 Why not seize the pleasure at once? How often is happiness destroyed by preparation, foolish preparation! [Ib. 30]

6 Emma denied none of it aloud, and agreed to none of it in private. [Ib. 42]

7 We all talk Shakespeare, use his similes, and describe with his descriptions. [*Mansfield Park*, 34]

8 A woman, especially if she have the misfortune of knowing anything, should conceal it as well as she can. [*Northanger Abbey*, 14]

9 One does not love a place the less for having suffered in it, unless it has all been suffering, nothing but suffering. [*Persuasion*, 20]

10 All the privilege I claim for my own sex . . . is that of loving longest, when existence or when hope is gone. [Ib. 23]

11 It is a truth universally acknowledged, that a single man in possession of a good fortune, must be in want of a wife. [*Pride and Prejudice*, 1]

12 Happiness in marriage is entirely a matter of chance. [Ib. 6]

13 A lady's imagination is very rapid; it jumps from admiration to love, from love to matrimony in a moment. [Ib.]

1 What is the difference in matrimonial affairs, between the mercenary, and the prudent motive? [*Ib.* 26]

2 Lord, how ashamed I should be of not being married before three and twenty! [*Ib.* 39]

3 For what do we live, but to make sport for our neighbours, and laugh at them in our turn? [*Ib.* 57]

4 On every formal visit a child ought to be of the party, by way of provision for discourse. [*Sense and Sensibility*, 6]

5 I do not want people to be very agreeable, as it saves me the trouble of liking them a great deal. [Letter, 1798]

6 In nine cases out of ten, a woman had better show more affection than she feels. [*Ib.*]

Babbage, Charles (1792–1871)

7 Every minute dies a man, / And one and one-sixteenth is born. [Letter to Tennyson; see Tennyson, *The Vision of Sin*]

Bacon, Francis (1561–1626)

8 If a man will begin with certainties, he shall end in doubts; but if he will be content to begin with doubts, he shall end in certainties. [*Advancement of Learning*, I]

9 [Knowledge is] a rich storehouse, for the glory of the Creator and the relief of man's estate. [*Ib.*]

10 Silence is the virtue of fools. [*Ib.*]

11 They are ill discoverers that think there is no land, when they can see nothing but sea. [*Ib.* II]

12 A man must make his opportunity, as oft as find it. [*Ib.*]

13 Hope is a good breakfast, but it is a bad supper. [*Apothegms*, 36]

14 One of the Seven was wont to say: 'That laws

were like cobwebs; where the small flies were caught, and the great brake through.' [Ib. 181]

1 What is Truth? said jesting Pilate; and would not stay for an answer. [*Essays* 1, 'Of Truth']

2 This same Truth is a naked and open daylight, that doth not show the masques and mummeries and triumphs of the world half so stately and daintily as candlelights. [Ib.]

3 The inquiry of Truth, which is the love-making, or wooing of it, the knowledge of Truth, which is the presence of it, and the belief of Truth which is the enjoying of it, is the sovereign good of human nature. [Ib.]

4 To say that a man lieth, is as much to say, as that he is brave towards God, and a coward towards Men. [Ib.]

5 It is as natural to die as to be born; and to a little infant, perhaps, the one is as painful as the other. [Ib. 2, 'Of Death']

6 All colours will agree in the dark. [Ib. 3, 'Of Unity in Religion']

7 Prosperity doth best discover Vice, but Adversity doth best discover Virtue. [Ib. 5, 'Of Adversity']

8 He that hath wife and children, hath given hostages to fortune; for they are impediments to great enterprises, either of Virtue or Mischief. [Ib. 8, 'Of Marriage and Single Life']

9 They do best who, if they cannot but admit Love, yet make it keep quarter; and sever it wholly from their serious affairs and actions of life: for if it check once with Business, it troubleth Men's Fortunes, and maketh Men, that they can no ways be true to their own ends. [Ib. 10, 'Of Love']

10 Men in Great Place are thrice Servants: Servants of the Sovereign or State; Servants of Fame; and Servants of Business ... It is a strange desire to

seek Power and to lose Liberty. [Ib. 11, 'Of Great Place']

1 All rising to Great Place is by a winding stair. [Ib.]

2 If the Hill will not come to Mahomet, Mahomet will go to the Hill. [Ib. 12, 'Boldness']

3 And Money is like muck, not good except it be spread. [Ib. 15, 'Of Seditions and Troubles']

4 It is true, that a little Philosophy inclineth Man's Mind to Atheism; but depth in Philosophy bringeth Men's Minds about to Religion. [Ib. 16, 'Atheism']

5 And he that will not apply new Remedies, must expect new Evils; For Time is the greatest innovator. [Ib. 24, 'Of Innovations']

6 Whosoever is delighted in solitude, is either a wild Beast, or a God. [Ib. 27, 'Of Friendships']

7 This communicating of a Man's Self to his Friend works two contrary effects; for it redoubleth Joys, and cutteth Griefs in halves. [Ib.]

8 Of great Riches, there is no real use, except it be in distribution; the rest is but Conceit. [Ib. 34, 'Of Riches']

9 Nature is often hidden; sometimes overcome; seldom extinguished. [Ib. 38, 'Of Nature in Men']

10 There is no Excellent Beauty, that hath not some strangeness in the proportion. [Ib. 43, 'Of Beauty']

11 God Almighty first planted a Garden. And indeed, it is the purest of human Pleasures. [Ib. 46, 'Of Gardens']

12 To spend too much Time in Studies, is Sloth; To use them too much for Ornament, is Affectation; To make Judgement wholly by their rules is the humour of a Scholar. [Ib. 50, 'Of Studies']

1 Crafty men contemn Studies; simple men admire them; and wise men use them. [Ib.]

2 Some Books are to be tasted, others to be swallowed, and some few to be chewed and digested; that is, some Books are to be read only in parts; others to be read but not curiously; and some few to be read wholly, and with Diligence and Attention. [Ib.]

3 Light gains make heavy purses. [Ib. 52, 'Of Ceremonies and Respects']

4 It was prettily devised of Aesop, 'The fly sat upon the axletree of the chariot-wheel and said, what a dust do I raise.' [Ib. 54, 'Of Vain-Glory']

5 Fame is like a river, that beareth up things light and swollen, and drowns things weighty and solid. [Ib. 53, 'Of Praise']

6 *Nam et ipsa scientia potestas est.* Knowledge itself is power. [*Religious Meditations*, 'Of Heresies']

7 The world's a bubble: and the life of man / Less than a span. ['The World']

Bagehot, Walter (1826–1877)

8 *The Times* has made many ministries. [*The English Constitution*, 1]

9 Women — one half the human race at least — care fifty times more for a marriage than a ministry. [Ib. 2]

10 The best reason why Monarchy is a strong government is, that it is an intelligible government. The mass of mankind understand it, and they hardly anywhere in the world understand any other. [Ib. 2]

11 So long as the human heart is strong and the human reason weak, Royalty will be strong. [Ib.]

12 Of all the nations in the world the English are

perhaps the least a nation of pure philosophers. [Ib.]

1 A Parliament is nothing less than a big meeting of more or less idle people. [Ib. 4]

2 A man who has not read Homer is like a man who has not seen the ocean. There is a great object of which he has no idea. [*Literary Studies*, 1]

3 Poverty is an anomaly to rich people. It is very difficult to make out why people who want dinner do not ring the bell. [Ib. 2]

4 Nothing is more unpleasant than a virtuous person with a mean mind. [Ib.]

5 So long as there are earnest believers in the world, they will always wish to punish opinions, even if their judgement tells them it is unwise, and their conscience that it is wrong. [Ib.]

6 The whole history of civilization is strewn with creeds and institutions which were invaluable at first, and deadly afterwards. [*Physics and Politics*]

7 One of the greatest pains to human nature is the pain of a new idea. [Ib.]

8 The most melancholy of human reflections, perhaps, is that, on the whole, it is a question whether the benevolence of mankind does most good or harm. [Ib.]

Ballads

N.B. Most ballads are of uncertain date and exist in many versions.

9 'But I hae dream'd a dreary dream, / Beyond the Isle of Skye; I saw a dead man win a fight, / And I think that man was I.' ['Battle of Otterbourne']

10 Ye Highlands and ye Lawlands, / O where hae ye been? / They hae slain the Earl of Murray, /

And hae laid him on the green. ['The Bonny Earl of Murray']

1 Why does your brand sae drap with bluid? / Edward! Edward! / Why does your brand sae drap with bluid, / And why sae sad gang ye, O? ['Edward! Edward!']

2 Goodman, you've spoken the foremost word! / Get up and bar the door. ['Get Up and Bar the Door']

3 'Where hae ye been hunting Lord Randal, my son? / Where hae ye been hunting, my handsome young man?' / 'In yon wild wood, O mither; so make my bed soon, / For I'm weary wi' huntin', and fain wad lie doun.' ['Lord Randal']

4 This ae nighte, this ae nighte, / — *Every nighte and alle,* / Fire and fleet and candle-lighte, / *And Christe receive thy saule.* ['Lyke-Wake Dirge']

5 When captains couragious whom death could not daunte, / Did march to the seige of the city of Gaunt. ['Mary Ambree']

6 Yestreen the Queen had four Maries, / The night she'll hae but three; / There was Marie Seaton, and Marie Beaton / And Mary Carmichael and me.
O little did my mother ken, / The day she cradled me, / The lands I was to travel in / Or the death I was to dee! ['The Queen's Maries']

7 The king sits in Dunfermline town, / Drinking the blude-red wine; / 'Oh, where will I get a gude skipper / To sail this ship of mine?' ['Sir Patrick Spens']

8 'I saw the new moon late yestreen / Wi' the auld moon in her arm; / And if we gang to sea, master, / I fear we'll come to harm.' [Ib.]

9 True Thomas lay on Huntly bank; / A ferlie he spied with his e'e; / And there he saw a ladye

bright, / Came riding down by the Eildon tree.
['Thomas the Rhymer, Part 1']

1 'O, see ye na that braid, braid road, / That lies
across the lily leven? / That is the path of
wickedness, / Tho' some call it the road to
heaven.

And see ye not yon narrow road, / Sae thick
beset with thorns and briars? / That is the path
of righteousness, / Tho' after it but few inquires.'
[Ib.]

2 As I was walking all alane, / I heard twa corbies
making a mane: / The tane unto the tither did
say, / 'Whaur sall we gang and dine the day?'

' — In behint yon auld fail dyke / I wot there lies
a new-slain knight; / And naebody kens that he
lies there / But his hawk, his hound, and his lady
fair.

'His hound is to the hunting gane, / His hawk to
fetch the wild-fowl hame, / His lady's ta'en
anither mate, / So we may make our dinner
sweet. ['The Twa Corbies']

Balzac, Honoré de (1799–1850)

3 *L'ironie est le fond du caractère de la Providence.*
Irony is the essence of the character of
Providence. [*Eugénie Grandet*]

Bangs, Edward (fl. 1775)

4 Yankee Doodle came to town / Riding on a
pony; / Stuck a feather in his cap / And called it
Macaroni. ['Yankee Doodle']

Bankhead, Tallulah (1902–1968)

5 There is less in this than meets the eye. [Attr.]

Barham, Rev. Richard Harris (1788–1845)

6 His eye so dim, / So wasted each limb, / That,
heedless of grammar, they all cried, 'That's him!'

[*The Ingoldsby Legends*, 'The Jackdaw of Rheims']

1 So put that in your pipe, my Lord Otto, and smoke it! [Ib. 'Lay of St. Odille']

Baring-Gould, Sabine (1834–1924)

2 Onward! Christian soldiers, / Marching as to war, / With the Cross of Jesus / Going on before. [Hymn]

Barnum, Phineas T. (1810–1891)

3 There's a sucker born every minute. [Attr.]

Barrie, James Matthew (1860–1937)

4 When the first baby laughed for the first time, the laugh broke into a thousand pieces and they all went skipping about, and that was the beginning of fairies. [*Peter Pan*, I]

5 Every time a child says 'I don't believe in fairies,' there is a little fairy somewhere that falls down dead. [Ib.]

6 To die will be an awfully big adventure. [Ib. III]

7 But the gladness of her gladness / And the sadness of her sadness / Are as nothing, Charles, / To the badness of her badness when she's bad. ['Rosalind']

8 [Charm] It's a sort of bloom on a woman. If you have it, you don't need to have anything else; and if you don't have it, it doesn't much matter what else you have. [*What Every Woman Knows*, I]

9 There are few more impressive sights in the world than a Scotsman on the make. [Ib. II]

Barrow, Isaac (1630–1677)

10 Poetry is a kind of ingenious nonsense. [Spence, *Anecdotes*]

Barth, John (1930–)

1 If you are a novelist of a certain type of
temperament, then what you really want to do is
re-invent the world. God wasn't too bad a
novelist, except he was a Realist. [Attr.]

Baruch, Bernard (1870–1965)

2 Let us not be deceived — we are today in the
midst of a cold war. [Speech, 1947]

Baudelaire, Charles (1821–1867)

3 *Hypocrite lecteur, — mon semblable, — mon
frère!* Hypocrite reader, my likeness, my brother.
[*Les Fleurs du Mal*, 'Au Lecteur']

4 *Là, tout n'est qu'ordre et beauté, / Luxe, calme
et volupté.* For all things there are ordered,
lovely, profuse, serene and pleasurable.
['L'Invitation au Voyage']

5 *O Mort, vieux capitaine, il est temps! levons
l'ancre!* Death, old captain, it is time, let us raise
the anchor. ['Le Voyage']

6 *Il faut épater le bourgeois.* One must shock the
bourgeois. [Attr.]

Bayly, Thomas Haynes (1797–1839)

7 Absence makes the heart grow fonder, / Isle of
Beauty, Fare thee well! ['Isle of Beauty']

8 I'm saddest when I sing. [Title of poem]

Beaumarchais, Pierre-Augustin de (1732–1799)

9 *Aujourd'hui ce qui ne vaut pas la peine d'être dit,
on le chante.* Today if something is not worth
saying, people sing it. [*Le Barbier de Seville*, I]

10 *Boire sans soif et faire l'amour en tout temps,
madame, il n'y a que ça qui nous distingue des
autres bêtes.* Drinking when we are not thirsty
and making love all year round, madam; that is

all there is to distinguish us from the other animals. [Ib. II]

1 *Tout finit par des chansons*. Everything ends in songs. [*Mariage de Figaro*, last line]

Beaumont, Francis (1584–1616) and John Fletcher (1579–1625)

2 You are no better than you should be. [*The Coxcomb*, IV]

3 Faith Sir, he went away with a flea in's ear. [*The Lover's Progress,* IV]

4 I'll put a spoke among your wheels. [*The Mad Lover*, III]

5 Kiss till the cow comes home. [*The Scornful Lady*, II]

Beauvoir, Simone de (1908–)

6 One is not born a woman, one becomes one. [*The Second Sex*]

Beckett, Samuel (1906–)

7 Nothing happens, nobody comes, nobody goes, it's awful. [*Waiting for Godot*]

Beckford, William (1759–1844)

8 He did not think with the Caliph Omar Ben Adalaziz, that it was necessary to make a hell of this world to enjoy paradise in the next. [*Vathek*]

Beecham, Sir Thomas (1879–1961)

9 A musicologist is a man who can read music but can't hear it. [Attr.]

Beerbohm, Sir Max (1872–1956)

10 Most women are not so young as they are painted. [*A Defence of Cosmetics*]

11 Undergraduates owe their happiness chiefly to the fact that they are no longer at school...The nonsense which was knocked out of them at

school is all gently put back at Oxford or Cambridge. ['Going back to school']

1 The dullard's envy of brilliant men is always assuaged by the suspicion that they will come to a bad end. [*Zuleika Dobson*, 4]

2 'I don't,' she added, 'know anything about music, really. But I know what I like.' [Ib. 16]

Beers, Ethel Lynn (1827–1879)

3 All quiet along the Potomac to-night, / No sound save the rush of the river, / While soft falls the dew on the face of the dead — / The picket's off duty forever. ['All Quiet Along the Potomac']

Beethoven, Ludwig Van (1770–1827)

4 *Muss es sein? Es muss sein.* Must it be? It must be. [Epigraph to String Quartet in F Major, Op. 135]

Behan, Brendan (1923–1964)

5 Never throw stones at your mother, / You'll be sorry for it when she's dead, / Never throw stones at your mother, / Throw bricks at your father instead. [*The Hostage*]

Behn, Aphra (1640–1689)

6 Love ceases to be a pleasure, when it ceases to be a secret. [*The Lover's Watch, Four o'clock*]

7 Faith, Sir, we are here to-day and gone tomorrow. [*The Lucky Chance*, IV]

8 Variety is the soul of pleasure. [*The Rover*, Part II, I]

9 Money speaks sense in a language all nations understand. [Ib. III]

Belloc, Hilaire (1870–1953)

10 Child! Do not throw this book about; / Refrain from the unholy pleasure / Of cutting all the pictures out! / Preserve it as your chiefest

treasure. [*Bad Child's Book of Beasts*, Dedication]

1 The chief defect of Henry King / Was chewing little bits of string. [*Cautionary Tales*, 'Henry King']

2 And always keep a hold of Nurse / For fear of finding something worse. [Ib. 'Jim']

3 Like many of the upper class / He liked the sound of broken glass. [*New Cautionary Tales*, 'About John']

4 When I am dead, I hope it may be said / 'His sins were scarlet, but his books were read.' ['On His Books']

5 The fleas that tease in the high Pyrenees. ['Tarantella']

Bellow, Saul (1915–)

6 The great enemy of progressive ideals is not the Establishment but the limitless dullness of those who take them up. [*To Jerusalem and Back*]

Benda, Julien (1867–1956)

7 *La Trahison des Clercs*. The treachery of the intellectuals. [Title of book]

Benét, Stephen (1898–1943)

8 Bury my heart at Wounded Knee. ['American Names']

Bennett, Arnold (1867–1931)

9 Pessimism, when you get used to it, is just as agreeable as optimism. [*Things That Have Interested Me*]

10 The price of justice is eternal publicity. [Ib.]

11 Journalists say a thing that they know isn't true, in the hope that if they keep on saying it long enough it *will* be true. [*The Title*]

Bentham, Jeremy (1748–1832)

1 It is with government as with medicine, its only business is the choice of evils. Every law is an evil, for every law is an infraction of liberty. [*Principles of Morals and Legislation*]

2 ... this sacred truth — that the greatest happiness of the greatest number is the foundation of morals and legislation. [*Works*, X; (quoting Francis Hutcheson)]

Bentley, Edmund Clerihew (1875–1956)

3 The art of Biography / Is different from Geography. / Geography is about Maps, / But Biography is about chaps. [*Biography for Beginners*]

4 John Stuart Mill, / By a mighty effort of will, / Overcame his natural bonhomie / And wrote 'Principles of Political Economy.' [Ib.]

Bernard of Cluny (fl. 12th century)

5 Jerusalem the golden, / With milk and honey blest. [Hymn; trans. J.M. Neale]

Bernard, William Bayle (1807–1875)

6 A Storm in a Teacup. [Title of farce, 1854]

Berryman, John (1914–1972)

7 Life, friends, is boring. We must not say so. [*Dream Songs*, 14]

Bethell, Richard, Baron Westbury (1800–1873)

8 His Lordship says he will turn it over in what he is pleased to call his mind. [Nash, *Life of Westbury*]

Betjeman, Sir John (1906–1984)

9 Come, friendly bombs, and fall on Slough / To get it ready for the plough. ['Slough']

Bevan, Aneurin (1897–1960)

1 If you carry this resolution and follow out all its
implications and do not run away from it you
will send a Foreign Secretary, whoever he may
be, naked into the conference chamber. [Speech
opposing unilateral nuclear disarmament, 1957]

Bhagavadgita

2 I am become death, the destroyer of worlds.
[Quoted by J. Robert Oppenheimer on seeing the
first nuclear explosion]

The Bible (King James Version)
N.B. for quotations from Vulgate, see under
Vulgate

GENESIS

3 In the beginning God created the heaven and the
earth.
And the earth was without form, and void; and
darkness was upon the face of the deep. And the
Spirit of God moved upon the face of the waters.
And God said, Let there be light: and there was
light. [1:1–3]

4 And God saw that it was good. [1:10]

5 And God said, Let us make man in our image,
after our likeness. [1:26]

6 Be fruitful, and multiply, and replenish the earth,
and subdue it. [1:28]

7 It is not good that the man should be alone; I
will make him an help meet for him. [2:18]

8 Now the serpent was more subtil than any beast
of the field. [3:1]

9 The woman whom thou gavest to be with me,
she gave me of the tree, and I did eat. [3:12]

10 The serpent beguiled me, and I did eat. [Ib.]

11 For dust thou art, and unto dust thou shalt
return. [3:19]

1 Am I my brother's keeper? [4:9]

2 While the earth remaineth, seedtime and harvest, and cold and heat, and summer and winter, and day and night shall not cease. [8:22]

3 But his wife looked back from behind him, and she became a pillar of salt. [19:26]

4 Behold, Esau my brother is a hairy man, and I am a smooth man. [27:11]

5 And he dreamed, and behold a ladder set upon the earth and the top of it reached to heaven: and behold the angels of God ascending and descending on it. [28:12]

6 Now Israel loved Joseph more than all his children, because he was the son of his old age; and he made him a coat of many colours. [37:3]

7 Ye shall eat the fat of the land. [45:18]

EXODUS

8 Who made thee a prince and a judge over us? [2:14]

9 I have been a stranger in a strange land. [2:22]

10 A land flowing with milk and honey. [3:8]

11 The Lord God of your fathers, the God of Abraham, the God of Isaac, and the God of Jacob. [3:15]

12 Let my people go. [7:16]

13 Thou shalt not kill. [20:13]

14 Thou shalt not commit adultery. [20:14]

15 Thou shalt not steal. [20:15]

16 Thou shalt not bear false witness against thy neighbour. [20:16]

17 Thou shalt not covet thy neighbour's house, thou shalt not covet thy neighbour's wife, nor his manservant, nor his maidservant, nor his ox, nor his ass, nor anything that is thy neighbour's. [20:17]

1 Life for life,
   Eye for eye, tooth for tooth, hand for hand, foot for foot,
   Burning for burning, wound for wound, stripe for stripe. [21:23–25]

2 Thou shalt not suffer a witch to live. [22:18]

3 Thou shalt have no other gods before me. [20:3]

4 Thou shalt not make unto thee any graven image, or any likeness of anything that is in heaven above, or that is in the earth beneath, or that is in the water under the earth:
   Thou shalt not bow down thyself to them, nor serve them: for I the Lord thy God am a jealous God, visiting the iniquity of the fathers upon the children unto the third and fourth generation of them that hate me. [20:4–5]

5 Thou shalt not take the name of the Lord thy God in vain. [20:7]

6 Honour thy father and thy mother: that thy days may be long upon the land which the Lord thy God giveth thee. [20:12]

LEVITICUS

7 Thou shalt love thy neighbour as thyself. [19:18]

NUMBERS

8 Be sure your sin will find you out. [32:23]

DEUTERONOMY

9 Man doth not live by bread only, but by every word that proceedeth out of the mouth of the Lord doth man live. [8:3]

10 A dreamer of dreams. [13:1]

JOSHUA

11 Hewers of wood and drawers of water. [9:21]

12 I am going the way of all the earth. [13:14]

JUDGES

1 Why is his chariot so long in coming? why tarry the wheels of his chariots? [5:28]

2 Faint, yet pursuing. [8:4]

3 Out of the eater came forth meat, and out of the strong came forth sweetness. [14:14]

4 From Dan even to Beer-sheba. [20:1]

I SAMUEL

5 Speak, Lord; for thy servant heareth. [3:9]

6 And she named the child I-chabod, saying, The glory is departed from Israel. [4:21]

7 God save the king. [10:24]

8 The Lord hath sought him a man after his own heart. [13:14]

9 For the Lord seeth not as man seeth: for man looketh on the outward appearance, but the Lord looketh on the heart. [16:7]

10 Go, and the Lord be with thee. [17:37]

11 Saul hath slain his thousands, and David his ten thousands. [18:7]

II SAMUEL

12 Saul and Jonathan were lovely and pleasant in their lives, and in their death they were not divided. [1:23]

13 How are the mighty fallen, and the weapons of war perished. [1:27]

14 Thou art the man. [12:7]

15 Would God I had died for thee, O Absalom, my son, my son! [18:33]

16 The sweet psalmist of Israel. [23:1]

I KINGS

17 Behold, the half was not told me. [10:7]

18 How long halt ye between two opinions? [18:21]

1 But the Lord was not in the wind: and after the wind an earthquake: but the Lord was not in the earthquake;

And after the earthquake a fire: but the Lord was not in the fire: and after the fire a still small voice. [19:11–12]

2 Hast thou found me, O mine enemy? [21:20]

II KINGS

3 Go up, thou bald head. [2:23]

I CHRONICLES

4 Let the heavens be glad, and let the earth rejoice: and let men say among the nations, The Lord reigneth. [16:31]

II CHRONICLES

5 And behold, the one half of the greatness of thy wisdom was not told me: for thou exceedest the fame that I heard. [9:6]

JOB

6 The Lord gave, and the Lord hath taken away; blessed be the name of the Lord. [1:21]

7 All that a man hath will he give for his life. [2:4]

8 Curse God, and die. [2:9]

9 Man is born unto trouble, as the sparks fly upward. [5:7]

10 I know that my redeemer liveth. [19:25]

11 I was eyes to the blind, and feet was I to the lame. [29:15]

12 Canst thou draw out leviathan with an hook? [41:1]

PSALMS

13 Why do the heathen rage, and the people imagine a vain thing? [2:1]

1 Out of the mouth of babes and sucklings hast thou ordained strength. [8:2]

2 Thou hast made him a little lower than the angels. [8:5]

3 The Lord is my shepherd; I shall not want.

He maketh me to lie down in green pastures: he leadeth me beside the still waters.

He restoreth my soul: he leadeth me in the paths of righteousness for his name's sake.

Yea, though I walk through the valley of the shadow of death, I will fear no evil: for thou art with me; thy rod and thy staff they comfort me.

Thou preparest a table before me in the presence of mine enemies: thou anointest my head with oil: my cup runneth over.

Surely goodness and mercy shall follow me all the days of my life: and I will dwell in the house of the Lord for ever. [23:1–6]

4 The earth is the Lord's, and the fulness thereof; the world, and they that dwell therein. [24:1]

5 Lift up your heads, O ye gates; and be ye lift up, ye everlasting doors; and the King of glory shall come in.

Who is this King of glory? The Lord strong and mighty, the Lord mighty in battle. [24:7–8]

6 As the hart panteth after the water brooks, so panteth my soul after thee, O God. [42:1]

7 Deep calleth unto deep at the noise of thy waterspouts. [42:7]

8 My heart is inditing a great matter: . . . my tongue is the pen of a ready writer. [45:1]

9 God is our refuge and strength, a very present help in trouble.

Therefore will not we fear, though the earth be removed, and though the mountains be carried into the midst of the sea. [46:1–2]

1 O that I had wings like a dove! [55:6]

2 O God, thou art my God; early will I seek thee:
   my soul thirsteth for thee, my flesh longeth for
   thee in a dry and thirsty land, where no water is.
   [63:1]

3 O come, let us sing unto the Lord; let us make a
   joyful noise to the rock of our salvation.
   Let us come before his presence with
   thanksgiving, and make a joyful noise unto him
   with psalms.
   For the Lord is a great God, and a great King
   above all gods.
   In his hand are the deep places of the earth: the
   strength of the hills is his also.
   The sea is his, and he made it: and his hands
   formed the dry land.
   O come, let us worship and bow down: let us
   kneel before the Lord our maker. [95:1–6]

4 O sing unto the Lord a new song: sing unto the
   Lord, all the earth.
   Sing unto the Lord, bless his name; shew forth
   his salvation from day to day.
   Declare his glory among the heathen, his
   wonders among all people.
   For the Lord is great, and greatly to be praised:
   he is to be feared above all gods. [96:1–4]

5 As for man, his days are as grass: as a flower of
   the field, so he flourisheth. [103:15]

6 They that go down to the sea in ships, that do
   business in great waters.
   These see the works of the Lord, and his
   wonders in the deep. [107:23–4]

7 The stone which the builders refused is become
   the head stone of the corner. [118:22]

8 Thy word is a lamp unto my feet, and a light
   unto my path. [119:105]

1 I will lift up mine eyes unto the hills, from whence cometh my help.
My help cometh from the Lord, which made heaven and earth.
He will not suffer thy foot to be moved: he that keepeth thee will not slumber. [121:1–3]

2 They that sow in tears, shall reap in joy. [126:5]

3 Except the Lord build the house, they labour in vain that build it: except the Lord keep the city, the watchman waketh but in vain. [127:1]

4 By the rivers of Babylon, there we sat down, yea, we wept when we remembered Zion. [137:1]

5 Put not your trust in princes, nor in the son of man, in whom there is no help. [146:3]

PROVERBS

6 Her ways are ways of pleasantness, and all her paths are peace. [3:17]

7 Wisdom is the principal thing; therefore get wisdom: and with all thy getting get understanding. [4:7]

8 The path of the just is as the shining light that shineth more and more unto the perfect day. [4:18]

9 Wisdom hath builded her house, she hath hewn out her seven pillars. [9:1]

10 Hope deferred maketh the heart sick. [13:12]

11 He that spareth his rod hateth his son. [13:24]

12 Pride goeth before destruction, and an haughty spirit before a fall. [16:18]

13 Train up a child in the way he should go: and when he is old he will not depart from it. [22:6]

14 Look not thou upon the wine when it is red. [23:31]

15 Heap coals of fire upon his head. [25:22]

16 Answer a fool according to his folly. [26:5]

1 As a dog returneth to his vomit, so a fool
returneth to his folly. [26:11]

2 Boast not thyself of to morrow; for thou knowest
not what a day may bring forth. [27:1]

3 Who can find a virtuous woman? for her price is
far above rubies. [31:10]

ECCLESIASTES

4 Vanity of vanities, saith the Preacher, vanity of
vanities; all is vanity. [1:2]

5 To everything there is a season, and a time to
every purpose under the heaven:

A time to be born and a time to die; a time to
plant and a time to pluck that which is planted;

A time to kill, and a time to heal; a time to break
down, and a time to build up;

A time to weep, and a time to laugh; a time to
mourn, and a time to dance;

A time to cast away stones, and a time to gather
stones together; a time to embrace and a time to
refrain from embracing;

A time to get, and a time to lose; a time to keep,
and a time to cast away;

A time to rend, and a time to sew; a time to
keep silence, and a time to speak;

A time to love, and a time to hate; a time of war
and a time of peace. [3:1–8]

6 God is in heaven, and thou upon earth: therefore
let thy words be few. [5:2]

7 The race is not to the swift, nor the battle to the
strong. [9:11]

8 Cast thy bread upon the waters: for thou shalt
find it after many days. [11:1]

9 Of making many books there is no end; and
much study is the weariness of the flesh. [12:12]

SONG OF SOLOMON

1   I am black, but comely, O ye daughters of
    Jerusalem. [1:15]

2   For, lo, the winter is past, the rain is over and
    gone;
    The flowers appear on the earth: the time of the
    singing of birds is come, and the voice of the
    turtle is heard in the land. [2:11–12]

3   Take us the foxes, the little foxes, that spoil the
    vines. [2:15]

ISAIAH

4   Though your sins be as scarlet, they shall be as
    white as snow. [1:18]

5   They shall beat their swords into plowshares, and
    their spears into pruninghooks: nation shall not
    lift up sword against nation, neither shall they
    learn war any more. [2:4]

6   What mean ye that ye beat my people to pieces
    and grind the faces of the poor? saith the Lord
    God of hosts. [3:15]

7   Woe is me! for I am undone; because I am a man
    of unclean lips, and I dwell in the midst of a
    people of unclean lips. [6:5]

8   The people that walked in darkness have seen a
    great light. [9:2]

9   For unto us a child is born, unto us a son is
    given: and the government shall be upon his
    shoulder; and his name shall be called
    Wonderful, Counsellor, The mighty God, The
    everlasting Father, The Prince of Peace. [9:6]

10 The wolf also shall dwell with the lamb, and the
    leopard shall lie down with the kid. [11:6]

11 Let us eat and drink; for to-morrow we shall die.
    [22:13]

12 The desert shall rejoice, and blossom as the rose.
    [35:1]

1 Set thine house in order. [38:1]

2 The voice of him that crieth in the wilderness,
Prepare ye the way of the Lord, make straight in
the desert a highway for our God.
Every valley shall be exalted, and every
mountain and hill shall be made low: and the
crooked shall be made straight, and the rough
places plain:
And the glory of the Lord shall be revealed and
all flesh shall see it together: for the mouth of
the Lord hath spoken it. [40:3–5]

3 All flesh is grass, and all the goodliness thereof is
as the flower of the field. [40:6]

4 He shall feed his flock like a shepherd: he shall
gather the lambs with his arm, and carry them in
his bosom, and shall gently lead those that are
with young. [40:11]

5 Have ye not known? Have ye not heard? Hath it
not been told you from the beginning? [40:21]

6 There is no peace, saith the Lord, unto the
wicked. [48:22]

7 How beautiful upon the mountains are the feet of
him that bringeth good tidings. [52:7]

8 He hath no form nor comeliness; and when we
shall see him, there is no beauty that we should
desire him.
He is despised and rejected of men; a man of
sorrows and acquainted with grief; and we hid as
it were our faces from him; he was despised, and
we esteemed him not.
Surely he hath borne our griefs and carried our
sorrows. [53:2–4]

9 All we like sheep have gone astray; we have
turned every one to his own way; and the Lord
hath laid on him the iniquity of us all. [53:6]

10 Seek ye the Lord while he may be found, call ye
upon him while he is near. [55:6]

JEREMIAH

1 The harvest is past, the summer is ended, and we are not saved. [8:20]

2 Is there no balm in Gilead? [8:22]

3 Can the Ethiopian change his skin, or the leopard his spots? [13:23]

4 The heart is deceitful above all things, and desperately wicked. [17:9]

EZEKIEL

5 The fathers have eaten sour grapes, and the children's teeth are set on edge. [18:2]

6 O ye dry bones, hear the word of the Lord. [37:4]

DANIEL

7 But if ye worship not, ye shall be cast the same hour into the midst of a burning fiery furnace. [3:15]

8 Thou art weighed in the balances and art found wanting. [5:27]

9 Thy kingdom is divided, and given to the Medes and the Persians. [5:28]

HOSEA

10 They have sown the wind, and they shall reap the whirlwind. [8:7]

JOEL

11 I will pour out my spirit upon all flesh; and your sons and your daughters shall prophesy, your old men shall dream dreams, and your young men shall see visions. [2:28]

JONAH

12 Jonah was in the belly of the fish three days and three nights. [1:17]

MALACHI

13 Unto you that fear my name shall the Sun of

righteousness arise with healing in his wings.
[4:2]

APOCRYPHA

1 Let us now praise famous men, and our fathers
that begat us. [*Wisdom of Solomon*, 44:1]

2 And some there be, which have no memorial. [Ib.
44:9]

3 Their bodies are buried in peace; but their name
liveth for evermore. [Ib. 44:14]

MATTHEW

4 There came wise men from the east to
Jerusalem,
Saying, Where is he that is born King of the
Jews? for we have seen his star in the east, and
are come to worship him. [2:1–2]

5 They presented unto him gifts; gold, and
frankincense, and myrrh. [2:11]

6 The voice of one crying in the wilderness,
Prepare ye the way of the Lord, make his paths
straight. [3:3]

7 This is my beloved Son, in whom I am well
pleased. [3:17]

8 Man shall not live by bread alone, but by every
word that proceedeth out of the mouth of God.
[4:4]

9 Fishers of men. [4:19]

10 Blessed are the poor in spirit: for theirs is the
kingdom of heaven.
Blessed are they that mourn: for they shall be
comforted.
Blessed are the meek: for they shall inherit the
earth.
Blessed are they which do hunger and thirst after
righteousness: for they shall be filled.

Blessed are the merciful: for they shall obtain mercy.

Blessed are the pure in heart: for they shall see God.

Blessed are the peacemakers: for they shall be called the children of God. [5:3–9]

1 Ye are the salt of the earth: but if the salt have lost his savour, wherewith shall it be salted? [5:13]

2 Love your enemies, bless them that curse you, do good to them that hate you, and pray for them which spitefully use you, and persecute you. [5:44]

3 He maketh his sun to rise on the evil and on the good, and sendeth rain on the just and on the unjust. [5:45]

4 Let not thy left hand know what thy right hand doeth. [6:3]

5 After this manner therefore pray ye: Our Father which art in heaven, Hallowed be thy name, Thy kingdom come. Thy will be done in earth, as it is in heaven.

Give us this day our daily bread.

And forgive us our debts, as we forgive our debtors.

And lead us not into temptation, but deliver us from evil: For thine is the kingdom, and the power, and the glory, for ever. Amen. [6:9–13]

6 Lay not up for yourselves treasures upon earth, where moth and rust doth corrupt, and where thieves break through and steal:

But lay up for yourselves treasures in heaven. [6:19–20]

7 No man can serve two masters: . . . Ye cannot serve God and mammon. [6:24]

8 Consider the lilies of the field, how they grow; they toil not, neither do they spin. [6:28]

1 Take therefore no thought for the morrow; for the morrow shall take thought for the things of itself. Sufficient unto the day is the evil thereof. [6:34]

2 Judge not, that ye be not judged. [7:1]

3 Neither cast ye your pearls before swine. [7:6]

4 Ask, and it shall be given you; seek, and ye shall find; knock, and it shall be opened unto you. [7:7]

5 Beware of false prophets, which come to you in sheep's clothing, but inwardly they are ravening wolves. [7:15]

6 By their fruits ye shall know them. [7:20]

7 I am not come to call the righteous, but sinners to repentance. [9:13]

8 He that findeth his life shall lose it: and he that loseth his life for my sake shall find it. [10:39]

9 He that is not with me is against me. [12:30]

10 A prophet is not without honour, save in his own country, and in his own house. [13:57]

11 Be of good cheer; it is I; be not afraid. [14:27]

12 O thou of little faith, wherefore didst thou doubt? [14:31]

13 If the blind lead the blind, both shall fall into the ditch. [15:14]

14 Thou art Peter, and upon this rock I will build my church; and the gates of hell shall not prevail against it. [16:18]

15 Get thee behind me, Satan. [16:23]

16 What is a man profited, if he shall gain the whole world, and lose his own soul? [16:26]

17 If thine eye offend thee, pluck it out. [18:9]

18 For where two or three are gathered together in my name, there am I in the midst of them. [18:20]

1 Thou shalt love thy neighbour as thyself. [19:19]

2 With men this is impossible; but with God all things are possible. [19:26]

3 But many that are first shall be last; and the last shall be first. [19:30]

4 For many are called, but few are chosen. [22:14]

5 Render therefore unto Caesar the things which are Caesar's; and unto God the things which are God's. [22:21]

6 Ye shall hear of wars and rumours of wars. [24:6]

7 Heaven and earth shall pass away, but my words shall not pass away. [24:35]

8 I was a stranger and ye took me in:
Naked and ye clothed me: I was sick, and ye visited me: I was in prison, and ye came unto me. [25:35–36]

9 If it be possible, let this cup pass from me. [26:39]

10 The spirit indeed is willing, but the flesh is weak. [26:41]

11 All they that take the sword shall perish with the sword. [26:52]

12 My God, my God, why hast thou forsaken me? [27:46]

MARK

13 If a house be divided against itself, that house cannot stand. [3:25]

14 My name is Legion: for we are many. [5:9]

15 Suffer the little children to come unto me, and forbid them not: for such is the kingdom of God. [10:14]

16 It is easier for the little children to go through the eye of a needle than for a rich man to enter into the kingdom of God. [10:25 (cf. Matthew, 19:24)]

LUKE

1 Because there was no room for them in the inn. [2:7]

2 And, lo, the angel of the Lord came upon them, and the glory of the Lord shone round about them: and they were sore afraid. [2:9]

3 Behold, I bring you good tidings of great joy. [2:10]

4 Glory to God in the highest, and on earth peace, good will toward men. [2:14]

5 Lord, now lettest thou thy servant depart in peace, according to thy word. [2:29]

6 Wist ye not that I must be about my Father's business? [2:49]

7 Physician, heal thyself. [4:23]

8 Love your enemies, do good to them which hate you. [6:27]

9 Go, and do thou likewise. [10:37]

10 The poor, and the maimed, and the halt, and the blind. [14:21]

11 Joy shall be in heaven over one sinner that repenteth, more than over ninety and nine just persons, which need no repentance. [15:7]

12 Bring hither the fatted calf, and kill it. [15:23]

13 Father, forgive them; for they know not what they do. [23:34]

14 Father, into thy hands I commend my spirit. [23:46]

JOHN

15 In the beginning was the Word, and the Word was with God, and the Word was God. [1:1]

16 The light shineth in darkness; and the darkness comprehended it not. [1:5]

17 And the Word was made flesh, and dwelt among us. [1:14]

1 God so loved the world, that he gave his only begotten Son, that whosoever believeth in him should not perish, but have everlasting life. [3:16]

2 Rise, take up thy bed, and walk. [5:8]

3 He that is without sin among you, let him first cast a stone at her. [8:7]

4 And ye shall know the truth, and the truth shall make thee free. [8:32]

5 Jesus wept. [11:35]

6 In my Father's house are many mansions. [14:2]

7 I am the way, the truth, and the life; no man cometh unto the Father, but by me. [14:6]

8 Greater love hath no man than this, that a man lay down his life for his friends. [15:13]

ACTS OF THE APOSTLES

9 It is hard for thee to kick against the pricks. [9:5]

10 God is no respecter of persons. [10:34]

11 For in him we live, and move, and have our being. [17:28]

12 It is more blessed to give than to receive. [20:35]

13 A citizen of no mean city. [21:39]

ROMANS

14 The wages of sin is death. [6:23]

15 If God be for us, who can be against us? [8:31]

16 Rejoice with them that do rejoice, and weep with them that weep. [12:15]

17 Vengeance is mine; I will repay, saith the Lord. [12:19]

I CORINTHIANS

18 I am made all things to all men. [9:22]

19 Though I speak with the tongues of men and of angels, and have not charity, I am become as sounding brass, or a tinkling cymbal.

...and though I have all faith, so that I could remove mountains, and have not charity, I am nothing.

And though I bestow all my goods to feed the poor, and though I give my body to be burned, and have not charity, it profiteth me nothing.

Charity suffereth long and is kind; charity envieth not; charity vaunteth not itself, is not puffed up,

Doth not behave itself unseemly, seeketh not her own, is not easily provoked, thinketh no evil;

Rejoiceth not in iniquity, but rejoiceth in the truth;

Beareth all things, believeth all things, hopeth all things, endureth all things.

Charity never faileth: but whether there be prophecies, they shall fail; whether they be tongues, they shall cease; whether there be knowledge, it shall vanish away. [13:2–8]

1 And now abideth faith, hope, charity, these three; but the greatest of these is charity. [13:13]

2 The last enemy that shall be destroyed is death. [15:26]

3 Behold, I shew you a mystery; We shall not all sleep, but we shall all be changed. [15:51]

4 O death, where is thy sting? O grave, where is thy victory? [15:55]

II CORINTHIANS

5 The letter killeth, but the spirit giveth life. [3:5]

6 There was given to me a thorn in the flesh, the messenger of Satan to buffet me. [12:7]

GALATIANS

7 Be not deceived; God is not mocked: for whatsoever a man soweth, that shall he also reap. [6:7]

EPHESIANS

1 We are members one of another. [4:25]

2 Be ye angry, and sin not; let not the sun go down upon your wrath. [4:26]

3 Put on the whole armour of God. [6:11]

PHILIPPIANS

4 The peace of God which passeth all understanding. [4:7]

5 I can do all things through Christ which strengtheneth me. [4:13]

I THESSALONIANS

6 Pray without ceasing. [5:17]

I TIMOTHY

7 Old wives' fables. [4:7]

8 The love of money is the root of all evil. [6:10]

9 Fight the good fight of faith. [6:12]

II TIMOTHY

10 I have fought a good fight, I have finished my course, I have kept the faith. [4:7]

TITUS

11 Unto the pure all things are pure. [1:15]

HEBREWS

12 Faith is the substance of things hoped for, the evidence of things not seen. [11:1]

13 Whom the Lord loveth he chasteneth. [12:6]

14 Let brotherly love continue. [13:1]

15 Be not forgetful to entertain strangers: for thereby some have entertained angels unawares. [13:2]

JAMES

1 But be ye doers of the word, and not hearers only. [1:22]

2 Faith without works is dead. [2:20]

PETER

3 As newborn babes, desire the sincere milk of the word. [2:2]

4 Charity shall cover the multitude of sins. [4:8]

I JOHN

5 He that loveth not knoweth not God; for God is love. [4:8]

6 Perfect love casteth out fear. [4:18]

REVELATION

7 I am Alpha and Omega, the beginning and the ending, saith the Lord. [1:8]

8 Because thou art lukewarm, and neither cold nor hot, I will spue thee out of my mouth. [3:15]

9 And I looked, and behold a pale horse: and his name that sat on him was Death. [6:8]

10 When he had opened the seventh seal, there was silence in heaven about the space of half an hour. [8:1]

11 And I saw a new heaven and a new earth: for the first heaven and the first earth were passed away; and there was no more sea. [21:1]

12 I will give unto him that is athirst of the fountain of the water of life freely. [21:6]

13 The grace of our Lord Jesus Christ be with you all. Amen. [22:21]

Bickerstaff, Isaac (c. 1735–1812)

14 Perhaps it was right to dissemble your love, / But — why did you kick me downstairs? ['An Expostulation']

Bierce, Ambrose (1842–c. 1914)

1   *Bore:* A person who talks when you wish him to listen. [*The Devil's Dictionary*]

2   *Education:* That which discloses to the wise and disguises from the foolish their lack of understanding. [Ib.]

3   *Lawsuit:* A machine which you go into as a pig and come out as a sausage. [Ib.]

Binyon, Laurence (1869–1943)

4   They shall grow not old, as we that are left grow old: / Age shall not weary them, nor the years condemn. / At the going down of the sun and in the morning / We will remember them. [*Poems for the Fallen*]

Bismarck, Otto Von (1815–1898)

5   *Die Politik ist die Lehre von Möglichen.* Politics is the art of the possible. [Remark, 1867]

6   *Sie macht sich nur durch Blut und Eisen.* It can only be done by blood and iron. [Speech, 1886]

Blackstone, William (1723–1780)

7   It is better that ten guilty persons escape than one innocent suffer. [*Commentaries*, IV]

Blake, William (1757–1827)

8   To see a World in a Grain of Sand, / And a Heaven in a Wild Flower, / Hold Infinity in the palm of your hand, / And Eternity in an hour. [*Auguries of Innocence*]

9   A truth that's told with bad intent / Beats all the lies you can invent. [Ib.]

10   Nought can deform the human race / Like to the armourer's iron brace. [Ib.]

11   A Robin Redbreast in a Cage / Puts all Heaven in a Rage. [Ib.]

1 A dog starv'd at his master's gate / Predicts the ruin of the State. [Ib.]

2 The whore and gambler, by the state / Licensed, build that nation's fate. / The harlot's cry from street to street / Shall weave old England's winding sheet. [Ib.]

3 Can Wisdom be put in a silver rod, / Or Love in a golden bowl? [*Book of Thel*]

4 Great things are done when men and mountains meet; / This is not done by jostling in the street. ['Gnomic Verses']

5 I must Create a System, or be enslaved by another Man's; / I will not Reason and Compare: my business is to Create. [*Jerusalem*]

6 I care not whether a man is Good or Evil; all that I care / Is whether he is a Wise man or a Fool. Go! put off Holiness, / And put on Intellect. [Ib.]

7 He who would do good to another must do it in Minute Particulars. / General Good is the plea of the scoundrel, hypocrite, and flatterer. [Ib.]

8 Without contraries is no progression. [*Marriage of Heaven and Hell*, 'The Argument']

9 Energy is Eternal Delight. [*Marriage of Heaven and Hell*]

10 The reason Milton wrote in fetters when he wrote of Angels and God, and at liberty when of Devils and Hell, is because he was a true Poet, and of the Devil's party without knowing it. [Ib. Note]

11 And did those feet in ancient time / Walk upon England's mountains green? / And was the holy Lamb of God / On England's pleasant pastures seen? [*Milton*, Preface]

12 And was Jerusalem builded here / Among these dark Satanic mills? [Ib.]

1 Bring me my bow of burning gold! / Bring me
  my arrows of desire! / Bring me my spear! O
  clouds, unfold! / Bring me my chariot of fire!
  [Ib.]

2 I will not cease from Mental Strife / Nor shall
  my Sword sleep in my hand / Till we have built
  Jerusalem, / In England's green and pleasant
  Land. [Ib.]

3 Mock on, mock on, Voltaire, Rousseau; / Mock
  on, mock on; 'tis all in vain! / You throw the
  sand against the wind, / And the wind blows it
  back again. ['Mock On']

4 What is it men in women do require? / The
  lineaments of gratified desire. / What is it
  women do in men require? / The lineaments of
  gratified desire. [Note-book]

5 Prisons are built with stones of Law, brothels
  with bricks of Religion. [Proverbs of Hell]

6 Prudence is a rich, ugly, old maid courted by
  incapacity. [Ib.]

7 Truth can never be told so as to be understood,
  and not be believed. [Ib.]

8 The road of excess leads to the palace of
  wisdom. [Ib.]

9 The tigers of wrath are wiser than the horses of
  instruction. [Ib.]

10 Damn braces. Bless relaxes. [Ib.]

11 If the doors of perception were cleansed
   everything would appear as it is, infinite. ['A
   Memorable Fancy']

12 Love seeketh not itself to please, / Nor for itself
   hath any care, / But for another gives its ease, /
   And builds a heaven in hell's despair. [Songs of
   Experience, 'The Clod and the Pebble']

13 Is this a holy thing to see / In a rich and fruitful

land, / Babes reduced to misery, / Fed with cold and usurous hand? [Ib. 'Holy Thursday']

1 I was angry with my friend, / I told my wrath, my wrath did end. / I was angry with my foe, / I told it not, my wrath did grow. [Ib. 'A Poison Tree']

2 Tiger! Tiger! burning bright / In the forests of the night, / What immortal hand or eye, / Could frame thy fearful symmetry? [Ib. 'The Tiger']

3 In every cry of every man, / In every infant's cry of fear, / In every voice, in every ban, / The mind-forged manacles I hear. [Ib. 'London']

4 For Mercy has a human heart, / Pity a human face, / And Love, the human form divine, / And Peace, the human dress. [*Songs of Innocence*, 'The Divine Image']

5 Little Lamb, who made thee? / Dost thou know who made thee? [Ib. 'The Lamb']

Boccaccio, Giovanni (c. 1313–1375)

6 Do as we say, and not as we do. [*Decameron*, 3]

Boethius, Anicius Manlius Severinus (A.D. c. 480–525)

7 *Nihil est miserum nisi cum putes; contraque beata sors omnis est aequanimitate tolerantis.* Nothing is miserable unless you think it so; conversely, every lot is happy if you are content with it. [*De Consolatione Philosophiae*, II]

Bogart, Humphrey (1899–1957)

8 Here's looking at you, kid. [*Casablanca*]

Bohr, Niels Henrik David (1885–1962)

9 An expert is a man who has made all the mistakes which can be made in a very narrow field. [Attr.]

Bolingbroke, Henry St. John, Viscount (1678 –1751)

1 I have read somewhere or other — in Dionysius of Halicarnassus, I think — that History is Philosophy teaching by examples. [*On the Study of History*]

2 Truth lies within a little and certain compass, but error is immense. [*Reflections upon Exile*]

3 The Idea of a Patriot King. [Title of book]

4 Plain truth will influence half a score of men at most in a nation, or an age, while mystery will lead millions by the nose. [Letter, 1721]

Boorstin, Daniel (1914–)

5 The celebrity is a person who is known for his well-knownness. [*The Image*]

Booth, General William (1829–1912)

6 This Submerged Tenth — is it, then, beyond the reach of the nine-tenths in the midst of whom they live? [*In Darkest England*]

Borgia, Cesare (1476–1507)

7 *Aut Caesar aut nihil.* Emperor or nothing. [Motto]

Borrow, George (1803–1881)

8 Youth will be served, every dog has his day, and mine has been a fine one. [*Lavengro*, 92]

Bosquet, Pierre François Joseph (1810–1861)

9 *C'est magnifique mais ce n'est pas la guerre.* It is magnificent, but it is not war. [Remark on witnessing the Charge of the Light Brigade, 1854]

Bossuet, Jacques-Bénigne (1627–1704)

10 *L'Angleterre, ah, la perfide Angleterre.* England, perfidious England. [*Sermon sur la Circoncision*]

Bowen, Lord (1835–1894)

1 The rain it raineth on the just / And also on the unjust fella: / But chiefly on the just, because / The unjust steals the just's umbrella. [Quoted in Sichel, *Sands of Time*]

Boyd, Mark Alexander (1563–1601)

2 Twa gods guides me; the ane of tham is blin', / Yea and a bairn brocht up in vanitie; / The next a wife ingenrit of the sea, / And lichter nor a dauphin with her fin. [Sonnet]

Bradford, John (?1510–1555)

3 But for the grace of God there goes John Bradford. [Remark on criminals going to the gallows]

Bradley, F.H. (1846–1924)

4 Metaphysics is the finding of bad reasons for what we believe upon instinct; but to find these reasons is no less an instinct. [*Appearance and Reality*, Preface]

Braham, John (c. 1774–1856)

5 England, home and beauty. [*The Americans*]

Brando, Marlon (1924–)

6 We'll make him an offer he can't refuse. [*The Godfather*]

7 An actor's a guy who, if you ain't talking about him, ain't listening. [*Observer*, 'Sayings of the Week', 1956]

Braxfield, Lord (1722–1799)

8 [To an eloquent culprit at the bar] Ye're a vera clever chiel, man, but ye wad be nane the waur o' a hanging. [Lockhart, *Life of Scott*]

9 [Gerald, a political prisoner, remarked that Christ had been a reformer]Muckle he made o' that; he was hanget. [Cockburn, *Memorials*]

Brecht, Bertolt (1898–1956)

1 Unhappy the land that is in need of heroes. [*Galileo*, sc.13]

2 *Erst Kommt das Fressen, dann Kommt die Moral.* Fodder comes first, then morality. [*Threepenny Opera*, II]

Bright, John (1811–1889)

3 England is the mother of Parliaments. [Speech, 1865]

4 [Of Disraeli] He is a self-made man, and worships his creator. [Remark, c. 1868]

Brillat-Savarin, Anthelme (1755–1826)

5 *Dis-moi ce que tu manges, je te dirai ce que tu es.* Tell me what you eat and I will tell you what you are. [*Physiologie du Gout*]

Bronowski, Jacob (1908–1974)

6 Science has nothing to be ashamed of, even in the ruins of Nagasaki. [*Science and Human Values*]

Brontë, Anne (1820–1849)

7 The human heart is like Indian rubber: a little swells it, but a great deal will not burst it. [*Agnes Grey*, 13]

Brontë, Charlotte (1816–1855)

8 Conventionality is not morality. Self-righteousness is not religion. To attack the first is not to assail the last. To pluck the mask from the face of the Pharisee, is not to lift an impious hand to the Crown of Thorns. [*Jane Eyre*, Preface]

9 Reader, I married him. [Mr. Rochester] [Ib. 38]

10 Novelists should never allow themselves to weary of the study of real life. [*The Professor*, 19]

11 If there is one notion I hate more than another, it

is that of marriage — I mean marriage in the vulgar, weak sense, as a mere matter of sentiment. [*Shirley*, 2]

Brontë, Emily (1818–1848)

1 Oh, for the time when I shall sleep / Without identity. ['Oh, For the Time When I Shall Sleep']

2 No coward soul is mine, / No trembler in the world's storm-troubled sphere: / I see Heaven's glories shine, / And faith shines equal, arming me from fear. ['Last Lines']

3 My love for Heathcliff resembles the eternal rocks beneath: — a source of little visible delight, but necessary. [*Wuthering Heights*, 9]

4 I lingered round them, under that benign sky: watched the moths fluttering among the heath and hare-bells; listened to the soft wind breathing through the grass; and wondered how anyone could ever imagine unquiet slumbers for the sleepers in that quiet earth. [Ib. last lines]

Brooke, Rupert (1887–1915)

5 Blow out, you bugles, over the rich Dead! ['The Dead']

6 These laid the world away; poured out the red / Sweet wine of youth. [Ib.]

7 Here tulips bloom as they are told; / Unkempt about those hedges blows / An English unofficial rose. ['Grantchester']

8 Stands the Church clock at ten to three? / And is there honey still for tea? [Ib.]

9 If I should die, think only this of me: / That there's some corner of a foreign field / That is for ever England. ['The Soldier']

10 A dust whom England bore, shaped, made aware, / Gave once, her flowers to love, her ways to roam, / A body of England's breathing English

air, / Washed by the rivers, blest by the suns of home. [Ib.]

Brougham, Lord Henry (1778–1868)

1 Education makes a people easy to lead, but difficult to drive; easy to govern, but impossible to enslave. [Attr.]

2 The great Unwashed. [Attr.]

Browne, Sir Thomas (1605–1682)

3 The created world is but a small parenthesis in eternity. [*Christian Morals*]

4 Life itself is but the shadow of death, and souls but the shadows of the living. All things fall under this name. The sun itself is but the dark *simulacrum*, and light but the shadow of God. [*The Garden of Cyrus*]

5 But the iniquity of oblivion blindly scattereth her poppy, and deals with the memory of men without distinction to merit of perpetuity. [*Hydrotaphia (Urn Burial)*]

6 Herostratus lives that burnt the Temple of Diana — he is almost lost that built it. [Ib.]

7 I am not so much afraid of death, as ashamed thereof; 'tis the very disgrace and ignominy of our natures. [*Religio Medici*]

8 There is surely a piece of divinity in us, something that was before the elements, and owes no homage unto the sun. [Ib.]

9 We all labour against our own cure, for death is the cure of all diseases. [Ib.]

Browning, Elizabeth Barrett (1806–1861)

10 Since when was genius found respectable? [*Aurora Leigh*, 6]

11 The devil's most devilish when respectable. [Ib. 7]

1 Earth's crammed with heaven, / And every common bush afire with God. [Ib.]

2 How do I love thee? Let me count the ways. [*Sonnets from the Portuguese*, 43]

Browning, Robert (1812–1889)

3 Ah, but a man's reach should exceed his grasp, / Or what's a heaven for? ['Andrea del Sarto']

4 I am grown peaceful as old age tonight. / I regret a little, I would change still less. [Ib.]

5 Truth that peeps / Over the edge when dinner's done, / And body gets its sop and holds its noise / And leaves soul free a little. ['Bishop Blougram's Apology']

6 The grand Perhaps. [Ib.]

7 Just when we are safest, there's a sunset-touch, / A fancy from a flower-bell, some one's death, / A chorus-ending from Euripides, — / And that's enough for fifty hopes and fears / As old and new at once as Nature's self, / To rap and knock and enter in our soul. [Ib.]

8 All we have gained then by our unbelief / Is a life of doubt diversified by faith, / For one of faith diversified by doubt: / We called the chess-board white, — we call it black. [Ib.]

9 I show you doubt, to prove that faith exists. [Ib.]

10 Blue as a vein o'er the Madonna's breast. ['The Bishop Orders his Tomb in St. Praxed's Church']

11 And brown Greek manuscripts, / And mistresses with great smooth marbly limbs. [Ib.]

12 For the loving worm within its clod, / Were diviner than a loveless god. ['Christmas Eve']

13 There's a world of capability / For joy, spread round about us, meant for us, / Inviting us. ['Cleon']

14 Progress, man's distinctive mark alone, / Not

God's, and not the beasts': God is, they are, /
Man partly is and wholly hopes to be. ['A Death
in the Desert']

1 Stung by the splendour of a sudden thought. [Ib.]

2 Open my heart and you will see / Graved inside
of it, 'Italy.' ['De Gustibus']

3 Where the haters meet / In the crowded city's
horrible street. ['The Flight of the Duchess']

4 When the liquor's out, why clink the cannikin?
[Ib.]

5 If you get simple beauty and nought else, / You
get about the best thing God invents. ['Fra Lippo
Lippi']

6 You should not take a fellow eight years old, /
And make him swear to never kiss the girls. [Ib.]

7 Oh, to be in England, / Now that April's there.
['Home-Thoughts from Abroad']

8 That's the wise thrush; he sings each song twice
over, / Lest you should think he never could
recapture / The first fine careless rapture! [Ib.]

9 Nobly, nobly Cape St. Vincent to the North-west
died away. ['Home-Thoughts from the Sea']

10 I sprang to the stirrup, and Joris, and he; / I
galloped, Dirck galloped, we galloped all three.
['How they brought the Good News from Ghent
to Aix.']

11 I count life just a stuff / To try the soul's
strength on, educe the man. ['In a Balcony']

12 Just for a handful of silver he left us, / Just for a
riband to stick in his coat. ['The Lost Leader']

13 One more devils'-triumph, and sorrow for angels,
/ One wrong more to man, one more insult to
God! [Ib.]

14 Never glad confident morning again! [Ib.]

15 She liked whate'er / She looked on, and her
looks went everywhere. ['My Last Duchess']

1 Never the time and the place / And the loved
   one all together! ['Never the Time and the Place']

2 Works done least rapidly, Art most cherishes.
   ['Old Pictures in Florence']

3 God be thanked, the meanest of his creatures /
   Boasts two soul-sides, one to face the world with,
   / One to show a woman when he loves her.
   ['One Word More']

4 God is the perfect poet, / Who in his person acts
   his own creations. [*Paracelsus*]

5 It was roses, roses, all the way, / With myrtle
   mixed in my path like mad. ['The Patriot']

6 Rats! / They fought the dogs and killed the cats,
   / And bit the babies in the cradles. ['The Pied
   Piper of Hamelin']

7 And the muttering grew to a grumbling / And
   the grumbling grew to a mighty rumbling / And
   out of the houses rats came tumbling. [Ib.]

8 So munch on, crunch on, take your nuncheon, /
   Breakfast, supper, dinner, luncheon! [Ib.]

9 The lark's on the wing / The snail's on the thorn
   / God's in his heaven — / All's right with the
   world. ['Pippa Passes']

10 Fear death? — to feel the fog in my throat, / The
   mist in my face. ['Prospice']

11 Irks care the crop-full bird? Frets doubt the maw-
   crammed beast? ['Rabbi Ben Ezra']

12 Everyone soon or late comes round by Rome.
   [*The Ring and the Book*, V]

13 Faultless to a fault. [Ib. IX]

14 'Tis not what man does which exalts him, but
   what a man would do! ['Saul']

15 One who never turned his back but marched
   breast forward, / Never doubted clouds would
   break, / Never dreamed, though right were
   worsted, wrong would triumph / Held we fall to

rise, are baffled to fight better, / Sleep to wake. ['Summum Bonum', epilogue]

1 What of soul was left, I wonder, when the kissing had to stop? ['A Toccata of Galuppi's']

2 Ichabod, Ichabod, / The glory is departed! [*Waring*]

Brummel, Beau (1778–1840)

3 Who's your fat friend? [Said of the Prince of Wales, 1813]

Buchan, John (1875–1940)

4 An atheist is a man who has no invisible means of support. [Variously attr.]

Buchanan, Robert Williams (1841–1901)

5 A race that binds / Its body in chains and calls them Liberty, / And calls each fresh link Progress. ['Titan and Avatar']

Buckingham, George Villiers, 2nd Duke of (1628–1687)

6 What the devil does the plot signify, except to bring in fine things? [*The Rehearsal*, III]

7 Ay, now the plot thickens very much upon us. [Ib.]

Buffon, Comte de (1707–1788)

8 *Le style est l'homme même.* Style is the man. ['Discours sur le Style']

9 *Le génie n'est qu'une plus grande aptitude à la patience.* Genius is naught but a greater aptitude for patience. [Attr.]

Bülow, Count von (1849–1929)

10 We wish to throw no one into the shade, but we demand our own place in the sun. [Speech, 1897]

Bulwer-Lytton, Edward (1803–1873)

1 In science, read, by preference, the newest works; in literature, the oldest. [*Caxtoniana*]

2 Beneath the rule of men entirely great / The pen is mightier than the sword. [*Richelieu*, II]

Buñuel, Luis (1900–1983)

3 I am still an atheist, thank God. [Attr.]

Bunyan, John (1628–1688)

4 The name of the slough was Despond. [*The Pilgrim's Progress*, I]

5 It beareth the name of Vanity-Fair, because the town where 'tis kept, is lighter than vanity. [Ib.]

6 Hanging is too good for him, said Mr. Cruelty. [Ib.]

7 Then I saw there was a way to hell, even from the gates of heaven. [Ib.]

8 One leak will sink a ship, and one sin will destroy a sinner. [Ib. II]

9 He that is down need fear no fall, / He that is low no pride. [Ib.]

10 Who would true valour see, / Let him come hither. [Ib.]

11 Then fancies flee away! / I'll fear not what men say. / I'll labour night and day / To be a pilgrim. [Ib.]

12 So he passed over, and all the trumpets sounded for him on the other side. [Ib.]

Burgess, Gelett (1866–1951)

13 Love is only chatter, / Friends are all that matter. ['Willy and the Lady']

Burgon, John William (1813–1888)

14 Match me such marvel save in Eastern clime, / A rose-red city 'half as old as Time'! ['Petra']

Burke, Edmund (1729–1797)

1 The age of chivalry is gone. That of sophisters, economists and calculators has succeeded: and the glory of Europe is extinguished for ever. [*Reflections on the Revolution in France*]

2 A state without the means of some change is without the means of its conservation. [Ib.]

3 Government is a contrivance of human wisdom to provide for human *wants*. Men have a right that these wants should be provided for by this wisdom. [Ib.]

4 Kings will be tyrants from policy, when subjects are rebels from principle. [Ib.]

5 You choose a member; but when you have chosen him, he is not member of Bristol, but he is a member of *parliament*. [Speech at Bristol, 1774]

6 It is the nature of all greatness not to be exact. [Speech (on American taxation), 1774]

7 Passion for fame; a passion which is the instinct of all great souls. [Ib.]

8 To tax and to please, no more than to love and to be wise, is not given to men. [Ib.]

9 Young man, there is America — which at this day serves for little more than to amuse you with stories of savage men, and uncouth manners; yet shall, before you taste of death, show itself equal to the whole of that commerce which now attracts the envy of the world. [Speech (on conciliation with America), 1775]

10 The use of force alone is but *temporary*. It may subdue for a moment; but it does not remove the necessity of subduing again: and a nation is not governed, which is perpetually to be conquered. [Ib.]

11 All protestantism, even the most cold and

passive, is a sort of dissent. But the religion most prevalent in our northern colonies is a refinement on the principle of resistance; it is the dissidence of dissent, and the protestantism of the Protestant religion. [Ib.]

1 The people are the masters. [Speech, 1780]

2 The people never give up their liberties but under some delusion. [Speech, 1784]

3 An event... upon which it is difficult to speak, and impossible to be silent. [Speech (on impeachment of Warren Hastings), 1789]

4 The only infallible criterion of wisdom to vulgar judgements — success. [Letter, 1791]

5 Tyrants seldom want pretexts. [Ib.]

6 The only thing necessary for the triumph of evil is for good men to do nothing. [Attr.]

Burney, Fanny (1752–1840)

7 Dancing? Oh, dreadful! How it was ever adopted in a civilized country I cannot find out; 'tis certainly a Barbarian exercise, and of savage origin. [*Cecilia*, 3]

8 Nothing is so delicate as the reputation of a woman; it is at once the most beautiful and most brittle of all human things. [*Evelina*, 39]

Burns, Robert (1759–1796)

9 O Thou! Whatever title suit thee — / Auld Hornie, Satan, Nick, or Clootie. ['Address to the Deil']

10 Then gently scan your brother man, / Still gentler sister woman; / Tho' they may gang a kennin wrang, / To step aside is human. ['Address to the Unco Guid']

11 Ae fond kiss, and then we sever; / Ae fare-weel, and then for ever! ['Ae Fond Kiss']

1 Should auld acquaintance be forgot, / And never brought to mind? ['Auld Lang Syne']

2 Freedom and whisky gang theither, / Tak aff your dram! ['Author's Earnest Cry and Prayer']

3 An' Charlie he's my darling, my darling, my darling, / Charlie he's my darling, the young Chevalier. ['Charlie he's my darling'; *see* Hogg]

4 Gin a body meet a body / Coming through the rye; / Gin a body kiss a body, / Need a body cry? ['Coming Through the Rye']

5 I wasna fou, but just had plenty. ['Death and Dr. Hornbook']

6 But ae the best dance e'er cam to the Land / Was, the de'il's awa wi' th'Exciseman. ['The De'il's awa wi' th'Exciseman']

7 Who will not sing *God Save the King* / Shall hang as high's the steeple; / But while we sing *God Save the King*, / We'll ne'er forget the People! ['Does Haughty Gaul Invasion Threat?']

8 But Facts are chiels that winna ding, / An' downa be disputed. ['A Dream']

9 The heart ay's the part ay / That makes us right or wrang. ['Epistle to Davie']

10 Gie me ae spark o' Nature's fire, / That's a' the learning I desire. ['First Epistle to Lanark']

11 Some rhyme a neebor's name to lash; / Some rhyme (vain thought!) for needfu' cash; / Some rhyme to court the countra clash, / An' raise a din; / For me, an aim I never fash: / I rhyme for fun. ['Epistle to James Smith']

12 Green grow the rashes O, / Green grow the rashes O; / The sweetest hours that e'er I spend, / Are spent among the lasses O! ['Green Grow the Rashes']

13 O, gie me the lass that has acres o' charms, / O,

gie me the lass wi' the weel-stockit farms. ['Hey for a Lass wi' a Tocher']

1 There's some are fou o' love divine, / There's some are fou o' brandy; / An monie jobs that day begin, / May end in houghmagandie / Some ither day. ['The Holy Fair']

2 O Thou that in the heavens does dwell, / Wha, as it pleases best Thysel, / Sends ane to heaven, and ten to hell, / A' for Thy glory, / And no' for ony guid or ill, / They've done afore Thee! ['Holy Willie's Prayer']

3 A man's a man for a' that. ['Is there for Honest Poverty?']

4 For a' that, an' a' that, / It's comin yet for a' that, / That man to man the world o'er / Shall brithers be for a' that. [Ib.]

5 John Anderson my jo, John, / When we were first acquent, / Your locks were like the raven, / Your bonny brow was brent. ['John Anderson My Jo']

6 Some have meat and cannot eat, / Some cannot eat that want it: / But we have meat and we can eat, / Sae let the Lord be thankit. ['The Kirkcudbright Grace']

7 But och! they catch'd him at the last, / And bound him in a dungeon fast. / My curse upon them every one — / They've hang'd my braw John Highlandman! [*Love and Liberty* (or *The Jolly Beggars*)]

8 Whistle owre the lave o't. [Ib.]

9 [Of women] Their tricks an' craft hae put me daft, / They've taen me in, an a' that; / But clear your decks, an' here's the Sex! / I like the jads for a' that. [Ib.]

10 A fig for those by law protected! / Liberty's a glorious feast! / Courts for cowards were

erected, / Churches built to please the priest!
[Ib.]

1 If I'm design'd yon lordling's slave − / By
Nature's law design'd − / Why was an
independent wish / E'er planted in my mind?
['Man was made to Mourn']

2 My heart's in the Highlands, my heart is not
here; / My heart's in the Highlands a-chasing the
deer. ['My Heart's in the Highlands']

3 O, my Luve's like a red red rose / That's newly
sprung in June: / O my Luve's like the melodie /
That's sweetly play'd in tune. ['My Love is like a
Red Red Rose']

4 Hear, Land o' Cakes, and brither Scots. ['On
Captain Grose's Peregrinations']

5 A chield's amang you taking notes, / And, faith,
he'll prent it. [Ib.]

6 An idiot race, to honour lost − / Who know
them best, despise them most. ['On Seeing the
Royal Palace at Stirling in Ruins']

7 Scots, wha hae wi' Wallace bled, / Scots, wham
Bruce has aften led, / Welcome to your gory bed,
/ Or to victorie. ['Scots, Wha Hae']

8 As Tammie glowr'd, amaz'd, and curious, / The
mirth and fun grew fast and furious; / The piper
loud and louder blew, / The dancers quick and
quicker flew, / They reel'd, they set, they cross'd,
they cleekit, / Till ilka carlin swat and reekit, /
And cost her duddies to the wark, / And linket
at it in her sark! ['Tam o' Shanter']

9 Even Satan glowr'd, and fidg'd fu' fain, / And
hotch'd and blew wi' might and main: / Till first
ae caper, syne anither, / Tam tint his reason a'
thegither, / And roars out, 'Weel done, Cutty-
sark!' [Ib.]

10 That I for poor auld Scotland's sake, / Some

usefu' plan or beuk could make, / Or sing a sang
at least. ['To the Guidwife of Wauchope House']

1 Fair fa' your honest sonsie face, / Great chieftain
o' the puddin'-race! ['To a Haggis']

2 O wad some Power the giftie gie us / To see
oursels as others see us! / It wad frae monie a
blunder free us, / An' foolish notion: / What airs
in dress an' gait wad lea'e us / An' ev'n
devotion! ['To a Louse']

3 Wee, sleekit, cow'rin', tim'rous beastie, / O what
a panic's in thy breastie! ['To a Mouse']

4 The best laid schemes o' mice an' men / Gang
aft a-gley. [Ib.]

5 Their sighin', cantin', grace-proud faces, / Their
three mile prayers, and half mile graces. ['To the
Rev. John McMath']

6 We labour soon, we labour late, / To feed the
titled knave, man, / And a' the comfort we're to
get, / Is that ayont the grave, man. ['The Tree of
Liberty']

7 But human bodies are sic fools, / For a' their
colleges and schools, / That when nae real ills
perplex them, / They mak enow themsels to vex
them. ['The Twa Dogs']

8 O whistle, and I'll come to you, my lad. ['Whistle,
and I'll come to you, my Lad']

9 We are na fou, we're nae that fou, / But just a
drappie in our e'e! / The cock may craw, the day
may daw, / And ay we'll taste the barley-bree!
['Willie Brew'd a Peck o' Maut']

10 Ye banks and braes o' bonny Doon, / How can
ye bloom sae fresh and fair? / How can ye chant,
ye little birds, / And I sae weary fu' o' care? ['Ye
Banks and Braes o' Bonny Doon']

11 Don't let the awkward squad fire over me.
[Cunningham, *Life*]

Burroughs, Edgar Rice (1875–1950)

1 Me Tarzan, you Jane. [*Tarzan of the Apes*]

Burton, Robert (1577–1640)

2 All my joys to this are folly, / Naught so sweet as Melancholy. [*Anatomy of Melancholy*]

3 All poets are mad. [Ib.]

4 *Hinc quam sit calamus saevior ense patet.* Hence it is clear how much more cruel the pen is than the sword. [Ib.]

5 One was never married, and that's his hell; another is, and that's his plague. [Ib.]

6 Tobacco, divine, rare, superexcellent tobacco, which goes far beyond all their panaceas, potable gold, and philosopher's stones, a sovereign remedy to all diseases. [Ib. II]

7 England is a paradise for women, and hell for horses: Italy a paradise for horses, hell for women. [Ib. III]

8 One religion is as true as another. [Ib.]

Bussy-Rabutin, Comte de (1618–1693)

9 *L'absence est à l'amour ce qu'est au feu le vent; il éteint le petit, il allume le grand.* Absence is to love what wind is to fire; it extinguishes the small, it inflames the great. [*Histoire amoureuse des Gaules*]

Butler, Nicholas Murray (1862–1947)

10 An expert is one who knows more and more about less and less. [Attr.]

Butler, Samuel (1612–1680)

11 For rhetoric he could not ope / His mouth, but out there flew a trope. [*Hudibras*, I]

12 And prove their doctrine orthodox / By apostolic blows and knocks. [Ib.]

1 What ever sceptic could inquire for; / For every why he had a wherefore. [Ib.]

2 She that with poetry is won / Is but a desk to write upon. [Ib. II]

3 Oaths are but words, and words but wind. [Ib.]

4 As the ancients / Say wisely, Have a care o' th' main chance, / And look before you ere you leap; / For, as you sow, you are like to reap. [Ib.]

5 For, those that fly, may fight again, / Which he can never do that's slain. [Ib. III]

Butler, Samuel (1835–1902)

6 It has been said that the love of money is the root of all evil. The want of money is so quite as truly. [*Erewhon*, 20]

7 Though God cannot alter the past, historians can. [*Erewhon Revisited*, 14]

8 An honest God's the noblest work of man. [*Further Extracts from the Notebooks*; *see* Pope, *Essay on Man*, IV]

9 A hen is only an egg's way of making another egg. [*Lie and Habit*]

10 An apology for the devil: it must be remembered that we have heard only one side of the case; God has written all the books. [*Notebooks*]

11 God is Love, I dare say. But what a mischievous devil Love is. [Ib.]

12 To live is like love, all reason is against it, and all healthy instinct for it. [Ib.]

13 Parents are the last people on earth who ought to have children. [Ib.]

14 I do not mind lying, but I hate inaccuracy. [Ib.]

15 The world will, in the end, follow only those who have despised as well as served it. [Ib.]

1 Life is the art of drawing sufficient conclusions from insufficient premises. [Ib.]

2 All progress is based upon a universal innate desire on the part of every organism to live beyond its income. [Ib.]

3 When the righteous man turneth away from his righteousness that he hath committed and doeth that which is neither quite lawful nor quite right, he will generally be found to have gained in amiability what he has lost in holiness. [Ib.]

4 To himself every one is an immortal; he may know that he is going to die, but he can never know that he is dead. [Ib.]

5 We think as we do, mainly because other people think so. [Ib.]

Bygraves, Max (1922–)

6 I've arrived, and to prove it, I'm here. [Quoted in Halliwell, *Filmgoers' Book of Quotes*]

Byrom, John (1692–1763)

7 God bless the King! — I mean the Faith's Defender; / God bless (no harm in blessing) the Pretender! / But who Pretender is, or who is King, / God bless us all! — that's quite another thing. ['To an Officer in the Army']

Byron, George Gordon, Lord (1788–1824)

8 In short, he was a perfect cavaliero, / And to his very valet seem'd a hero. [*Beppo*]

9 His heart was one of those which most enamour us, / Wax to receive, and marble to retain. [Ib.]

10 Death in the front, Destruction in the rear! [*Childe Harold*, II]

11 Since my young days of passion — joy or pain — / Perchance my heart and harp have lost a string — / And both may jar. [Ib. III]

12 Years steal / Fire from the mind as vigour from

the limb; / And Life's enchanted cup but sparkles near the brim. [Ib.]

1 On with the dance! let joy be unconfined; / No sleep till morn, when Youth and Pleasure meet / To chase the glowing Hours with flying feet. [Ib.]

2 . . . the madmen who have made men mad / By their contagion; Conquerors and Kings, / Founders of sects and systems. [Ib.]

3 To fly from, need not be to hate, mankind. [Ib.]

4 I live not in myself, but I become / Portion of that around me; and to me / High mountains are a feeling, but the hum / Of human cities torture. [Ib.]

5 There is a pleasure in the pathless woods, / There is a rapture on the lonely shore, / There is society, where none intrudes, / By the deep sea and music in its roar; / I love not man the less, but Nature more. [Ib. IV]

6 He, their sire, / Butcher'd to make a Roman holiday. [Ib.]

7 While stands the Coliseum, Rome shall stand: / When falls the Coliseum, Rome shall fall; / And when Rome falls — the World. [Ib.]

8 The Assyrian came down like the wolf on the fold. ['Destruction of Sennacherib']

9 What men call gallantry, and gods adultery, / Is much more common where the climate's sultry. [*Don Juan*, I]

10 Christians have burnt each other, quite persuaded / That all the Apostles would have done as they did. [Ib.]

11 Whether it was she did not see, or would not, / Or, like all very clever people, could not. [Ib.]

12 A little still she strove, and much repented, / And whispering 'I will ne'er consent' — consented. [Ib.]

1   Man's love is of man's life a thing apart, / 'Tis woman's whole existence. [Ib.]

2   Let us have wine and women, mirth and laughter, / Sermons and soda water the day after. [Ib. II]

3   Man, being reasonable, must get drunk; / The best of life is but intoxication: / Glory, the grape, love, gold, in these are sunk / The hopes of all men, and of every nation. [Ib.]

4   There's nought, no doubt, so much the spirit calms / As rum and true religion. [Ib.]

5   Alas! the love of women! it is known / To be a lovely and a fearful thing! [Ib.]

6   In her first passion woman loves her lover, / In all the others all she loves is love. [Ib. III]

7   Think you, if Laura had been Petrarch's wife, / He would have written sonnets all his life? [Ib. III]

8   The mountains look on Marathon — / And Marathon looks on the sea; / And musing there an hour alone, / I dream'd that Greece might still be free. [Ib.]

9   We learn from Horace, 'Homer sometimes sleeps'; / We feel without him, Wordsworth sometimes wakes. [Ib.]

10 That all-softening, overpowering knell, / The tocsin of the soul — the dinner-bell. [Ib. V]

11 There is a tide in the affairs of women, / Which, taken at the flood, leads — God knows where. [Ib. VI; see Shakespeare, *Julius Caesar*, IV.3]

12 A lady of a 'certain age,' which means / Certainly aged. [Ib.]

13 'Let there be light!' said God, 'and there was light!' / 'Let there be blood!' says man, and there's a sea! [Ib. VII]

1 And, after all, what is a lie? 'Tis but / The truth in masquerade. [Ib. XI]

2 'Tis strange the mind, that very fiery particle, / Should let itself be snuff'd out by an article. [Ib.]

3 Merely innocent flirtation. / Not quite adultery, but adulteration. [Ib. XII]

4 Now hatred is by far the longest pleasure; / Men love in haste, but they detest at leisure. [Ib. XIII]

5 The English winter — ending in July, / To recommence in August. [Ib.]

6 Society is now one polish'd horde, / Form'd of two mighty tribes, the *Bores* and *Bored*. [Ib.]

7 'Tis strange — but true; for truth is always strange; / Stranger than fiction. [Ib. XIV]

8 [Of Wordsworth] Who, both by precept and example, shows / That prose is verse, and verse is merely prose. [*English Bards and Scotch Reviewers*]

9 Who killed John Keats? / 'I,' says the Quarterly, / So savage and Tartarly; / "Twas one of my feats.' ['John Keats']

10 Maid of Athens, ere we part, / Give, oh give me back my heart! / Or, since that has left my breast, / Keep it now, and take the rest! ['Maid of Athens']

11 We are the fools of time and terror: Days / Steal on us, and steal from us; yet we live, / Loathing our life, and dreading still to die. [*Manfred*, I]

12 Knowledge is not happiness, and science / But an exchange of ignorance for that / Which is another kind of ignorance. [Ib. II]

13 She walks in beauty, like the night. ['She Walks in Beauty']

14 So we'll go no more a-roving / So late into the night / Though the heart be still as loving, / And

the moon be still as bright. ['So We'll Go No More A-Roving']

1 Oh, talk not to me of a name great in story; / The days of our youth are the days of our glory; / And the myrtle and ivy of sweet two-and-twenty / Are worth all your laurels, though ever so plenty. ['Stanzas Written on the Road between Florence and Pisa']

2 I knew it was love, and I felt it was glory. [Ib.]

3 The more I see of men, the less I like them. If I could but say so of women too, all would be well. [Journal, 1814]

4 I awoke one morning and found myself famous. [Remark on instantaneous success of Childe Harold]

Cabell, James Branch (1879–1958)

5 The optimist proclaims that we live in the best of all possible worlds; and the pessimist fears this is true. [The Silver Stallion]

Caesar, Caius Julius (c. 102–44 B.C.)

6 Gallia est omnis divisa in partas tres. All Gaul is divided into three parts. [De Bello Gallico, I]

7 Caesar's wife must be above suspicion. [Attr. by Plutarch, Life]

8 Iacta alea est. The die is cast. [Remark on crossing the Rubicon]

9 Veni, vidi, vici. I came, I saw, I conquered. [Letter, 47 B.C.]

10 Et tu Brute? You too, Brutus? [Last words]

Cagney, James (1904–   )

11 Look, Ma! Top of the world! [White Heat]

Caligula (A.D. 12–41)

12 Utinam populus Romanus unam cervicem

haberet! Would that the Roman people had only one neck! [Suetonius, *Life*]

Cameron, Simon (1789–1889)

1 An honest politician is one who, when he is bought, will stay bought. [Remark]

Campbell, Mrs. Patrick (1865–1940)

2 Marriage: the deep, deep peace of the double bed after the hurly-burly of the chaise-longue. [Quoted in Cooper and Hartman, *Violets and Vinegar*]

Campbell, Thomas (1777–1844)

3 O leave this barren spot to me! / Spare, woodman, spare the beechen tree. ['The Beech-Tree's Petition']

4 The combat deepens. On, ye brave, / Who rush to glory, or the grave! ['Hohenlinden']

5 Better be courted and jilted / Than never be courted at all. ['The Jilted Nymph']

6 'Tis distance lends enchantment to the view, / And robes the mountain in its azure hue. [*Pleasures of Hopes*, I]

7 Ye Mariners of England / That guard our native seas, / Whose flag has braved, a thousand years, / The battle and the breeze. ['Ye Mariners of England']

8 Now Barabbas was a publisher. [Also attr. to Byron]

Campion, Thomas (1567–1620)

9 There cherries grow, which none may buy / Till 'Cherry ripe' themselves do cry. [*Book of Airs*]

Canning, George (1770–1827)

10 But of all plagues, good Heaven, thy wrath can send, / Save me, oh, save me, from the candid friend. ['New Morality']

1 I called the New World into existence, to redress the balance of the Old. [Speech, 1826]

Carew, Thomas (c. 1595–c. 1639)

2 Here lies a King that rul'd, as he thought fit / The universal Monarchy of wit; / Here lie two Flamens, and both those, the best, / Apollo's first, at last, the true God's Priest. ['An Elegy upon the Death of Dr. John Donne']

3 Give me more love or more disdain; / The torrid or the frozen zone. ['Mediocrity in Love Rejected']

Carey, Henry (c. 1693–1743)

4 God save our gracious king! / Long live our noble king! ['God Save the King' (also attr. to others)]

5 Confound their politics, / Frustrate their knavish tricks. [Ib.]

6 Of all the girls that are so smart / There's none like pretty Sally, / She is the darling of my heart, / And she lives in our alley. ['Sally in our Alley']

Carlyle, Thomas (1795–1881)

7 There is no life of a man, faithfully recorded, but is a heroic poem of its sort, rhymed or unrhymed. [*Critical and Miscellaneous Essays*, 'Sir Walter Scott']

8 A witty statesman said, you might prove anything by figures. [Ib. 'Chartism']

9 The three great elements of modern civilization, Gunpowder, Printing, and the Protestant Religion. [Ib. 'State of German Literature']

10 'Genius' (which means transcendent capacity of taking trouble, first of all). [*Frederick the Great*, IV]

1 Happy the people whose annals are blank in history-books! [Ib. XVI]

2 Worship is transcendent wonder. [*Heroes and Hero Worship*, I]

3 No great man lives in vain. The history of the world is but the biography of great men. [Ib.]

4 France was long a despotism tempered by epigrams. [*History of the French Revolution*, I]

5 A whiff of grapeshot. [Ib.]

6 [Robespierre] The sea-green Incorruptible. [Ib. II]

7 Aristocracy of the Money bag. [Ib.]

8 [Economics] The Dismal Science. [*Latter-Day Pamphlets*]

9 Cash payment is not the sole nexus of man with man. [*Past and Present*, III]

10 Captains of industry. [Ib. IV]

11 No man who has once heartily and wholly laughed can be altogether irreclaimably bad. [*Sartor Resartus*]

12 Man is a tool-using animal. [Ib.]

13 The everlasting No. [Ib. II (chapter title)]

14 Man's unhappiness, as I construe, comes of his greatness; it is because there is an Infinite in him, which with all his cunning he cannot quite bury under the Finite. [Ib. II]

15 It is a mathematical fact that the casting of this pebble from my hand alters the centre of gravity of the universe. [Ib. III]

16 If Jesus Christ were to come to-day, people would not even crucify him. They would ask him to dinner, and hear what he had to say, and make fun of it. [Remark]

Carnegie, Dale (1888–1955)

17 How to Win Friends and Influence People. [Title of book]

Carroll, Lewis (1832–1898)

1 'Curiouser and curiouser!' cried Alice. [*Alice in Wonderland*, 2]

2 The Duchess! The Duchess! Oh my dear paws! / Oh my fur and whiskers! [Ib. 4]

3 'You are old, Father William,' the young man said, / 'And your hair has become very white; / And yet you incessantly stand on your head − / Do you think, at your age, it is right?' [Ib. 5]

4 Speak roughly to your little boy, / And beat him when he sneezes; / He only does it to annoy, / Because he knows it teases. [Ib. 6]

5 Twinkle, twinkle, little bat! / How I wonder what you're at! / Up above the world you fly! / Like a teatray in the sky. [Ib. 7]

6 The Queen was in a furious passion, and went stamping about, and shouting, 'Off with his head!' or 'Off with her head!' about once in a minute. [Ib. 8]

7 'A cat may look at a king,' said Alice. [Ib.]

8 'Just about as much right,' said the Duchess, 'as pigs have to fly.' [Ib. 9]

9 We called him Tortoise because he taught us. [Ib.]

10 Take care of the sense, and the sounds will take care of themselves. [Ib.]

11 'Will you walk a little faster?' said a whiting to a snail, / 'There's a porpoise close behind us, and he's treading on my tail.' [Ib. 10]

12 Will you, won't you, will you, won't you, will you join the dance? [Ib.]

13 The Queen of Hearts, she made some tarts, / All on a summer day: / The Knave of Hearts, he stole those tarts, / And took them quite away! [Ib. 11]

14 'Begin at the beginning,' the King said, gravely,

'and go on till you come to the end: then stop.' [Ib. 12]

1 'Twas brillig, and the slithy toves / Did gyre and gimble in the wabe; / All mimsy were the borogoves, / And the mome raths outgrabe. [*Alice Through the Looking-Glass,* 1]

2 'And hast thou slain the Jabberwock? / Come to my arms, my beamish boy! / O frabjous day! Callooh! Callay!' / He chortled in his joy. [Ib.]

3 'Now, *here*, you see, it takes all the running *you* can do, to keep in the same place. If you want to get somewhere else, you must run at least twice as fast as that!' [Ib. 2]

4 'Contrariwise,' continued Tweedledee, 'if it was so, it might be; and if it were so, it would be: but as it isn't, it ain't. That's logic.' [Ib. 4]

5 'The time has come,' the Walrus said, / 'To talk of many things: / Of shoes — and ships — and sealing wax — / Of cabbages — and kings — / And why the sea is boiling hot / And whether pigs have wings.' [Ib.]

6 The rule is, jam tomorrow and jam yesterday — but never jam to-day. [Ib. 5]

7 'There's no use trying,' she said: 'one *can't* believe impossible things.' 'I dare say you haven't had much practice,' said the Queen. 'When I was your age, I always did it for half an hour a day. Why, sometimes I've believed as many as six impossible things before breakfast.' [Ib.]

8 'When *I* use a word,' Humpty Dumpty said in a rather scornful tone, 'it means just what I choose it to mean, — neither more nor less.' [Ib. 6]

9 It's as large as life and twice as natural. [Ib. 7]

10 He thought he saw a Rattlesnake / That questioned him in Greek, / He looked again and found it was / The Middle of Next Week. [*Sylvie and Bruno*]

Cary, Phoebe (1824–1871)

1 And though hard be the task, / 'Keep a stiff upper lip'. ['Keep a Stiff Upper Lip']

Catechism Shorter

2 Man's chief end is to glorify God, and to enjoy him forever.

3 I should renounce the devil and all his works, the pomps and vanity of this wicked world, and all the sinful lusts of the flesh.

4 No mere man since the fall is able in this life perfectly to keep the commandments of God, but doth daily break them in thought, word, and deed.

Cato the Elder (234–149 B.C.)

5 *Delenda est Carthago.* Carthage must be destroyed. [Pliny, *Natural History*]

6 Do not buy what you want, but what you need; what you do not need is dear at a farthing. [*Reliquae*]

Catullus, Caius Valerius (87–c. 54 B.C.)

7 *Passer mortuus est meae puellae, / Passer, deliciae meae puellae.* My lady's sparrow is dead, the sparrow which was my lady's delight. [*Carmina*, 3]

8 *Vivamus, mea Lesbia, atque amemus, / Rumoresque senum severiorum / Omnes unius aestimemus assis.* Lesbia, let us live and love, and pay no heed to all the tales of grim old men. [Ib. 5]

9 *Da mi basia mille.* Give me a thousand kisses. [Ib.]

10 *Sed mulier cupido quod dicit amanti, / In vento et rapida scribere oportet aqua.* But what a woman says to her ardent lover should be written in wind and running water. [Ib. 70]

1 *Atque in perpetuum, frater, ave atque vale.* And forever, brother, hail and farewell! [Ib. 101]

Cervantes, Miguel de (1547–1616)

2 *El Caballero de la Triste Figura.* The Knight of the Sorrowful Countenance. [*Don Quixote*, I, 19]

3 *La mejor salsa del mundo es el hambre.* The best sauce in the world is hunger. [Ib. II, 5]

4 *Muchos pocos hacen un mucho.* Mony a mickle maks a muckle. [Ib.]

5 *Dos linages solos hay en el mundo, como decía una abuela mía, que son el tener y el no tener.* There are but two families in the world as my grandmother used to say, the Haves and the Have-nots. [Ib. II, 20]

6 *Los buenos pintores imitan la naturaleza, pero los malos la vomitan.* Good painters imitate nature, bad ones vomit it. [*El Licenciado Vidriera*]

Chalmers, Patrick Reginald (1872–1942)

7 What's lost upon the roundabouts we pulls up on the swings! ['Green Days and Blue Days: Roundabouts and Swings']

Chamberlain, Neville (1869–1940)

8 I believe it is peace for our time . . . peace with honour. [Speech after Munich Agreement, 1938]

Chamfort, Nicolas (1741–1794)

9 *L'amour, tel qu'il existe dans la société, n'est que l'échange de deux fantaisies et le contact de deux épidermes.* Love, as it exists in society, is nothing but the exchange of two fantasies and the contact of two skins. [*Maximes et Pensées*, 6]

10 *Les pauvres sont les nègres de l'Europe.* The poor are the blacks of Europe. [Ib. 8]

Chandler, Raymond (1888–1959)

1 Down these mean streets a man must go who is
  not himself mean. [*The Simple Art of Murder*]

Chaplin, Charles (1889–1977)

2 All I need to make a comedy is a park, a
  policeman and a pretty girl. [*My Autobiography*]

Charles II (1630–1685)

3 This is very true: for my words are my own and
  my actions are my ministers'. [Comment on
  Rochester's epitaph on him]

4 [Of Nell Gwynn] Let not poor Nelly starve.
  [Attr.]

5 He had been, he said, an unconscionable time
  dying; but he hoped that they would excuse it.
  [Macaulay, *History of England*]

Charles V, Emperor (1500–1558)

6 An iron hand in a velvet glove. [Carlyle, *Latter-
  Day Pamphlets*]

Chaucer, Geoffrey (c. 1340–1400)

7 Whan that Aprill with his shoures soote / The
  droghte of March hath perced to the roote, / And
  bathed every veyne in swich licour / Of which
  vertu engendred is the flour. [*Canterbury Tales*,
  Prologue]

8 He loved chivalrie, / Trouthe and honour, fredom
  and curteisie. [Ib. The Knight]

9 He nevere yet no vileynye ne sayde / In al his lyf
  unto no maner wight. / He was a verray, parfit
  gentil knyght. [Ib.]

10 And Frenssh she spak ful faire and fetisly, /
   After the scole of Stratford atte Bowe, / For
   Frenssh of Parys was to hire unknowe. [Ib. The
   Prioresse]

11 Sownynge in moral vertu was his speche, / And

gladly wolde he lerne and gladly teche. [Ib. The Clerk]

1 Nowher so bisy a man as he ther nas, / And yet he seemed bisier than he was. [Ib. The Sergeant of the Lawe]

2 She was a worthy womman al hir lyve: / Housbondes at chirche dore she hadde fyve, / Withouten oother coompaignye in youthe, — / But thereof nedeth nat to speke as nowthe. [Ib. The Wife of Bath]

3 But Cristes loore and his apostles twelve / He taughte, but first he folwed it hymselve. [Ib. The Parson]

4 With scalled browes blake and piled berd, / Of his visage children were aferd. [Ib. The Somnour]

5 Thanked be Fortune and hir false wheel, / That noon estaat assureth to be weel. [Ib. 'Knight's Tale']

6 Wostow nat wel the olde clerkes sawe, / That 'who shal yeve a lovere any lawe?' / Love is a gretter lawe, by my pan, / Than may be yeve to an erthely man. [Ib.]

7 A man mot nedes love, maugree his heed. [Ib.]

8 The smylere with the knyf under the cloke. [Ib.]

9 The grettest clerkes been noght the wysest man. ['Reve's Tale']

10 Wommen desiren to have sovereynetee / As wel over hir housbond as hir love, / And for to been in maistrie hym above. [Ib. 'Wife of Bath's Tale']

11 Though clerkes preise wommen but a lite, / Ther kan no man in humblesse hym acquite / As womman kan. [Ib. 'Clerkes Tale']

12 My theme is alwey oon, and evere was — / Radix malorum est cupiditas. ['Pardoner's Tale', Prologue]

1 Nay, I wol drynke licour of the vyne, / And have a joly wenche in every toun. [Ib.]

2 O wombe! O bely! O stynking cod / Fulfilled of dong and of corrupcion! [Ib.]

3 What is bettre than wisdom? Womman. And what is bettre than a good womman? No-thing. ['Tale of Melibee']

4 'By God,' quod he, 'for pleynly, at a word, / Thy drasty rymyng is nat worth a toord!' ['Sir Thopas']

5 Of al the floures in the mede, / Thanne love I most thise floures white and rede, / Swiche as men callen daysyes in our toun. [The Legend of Good Women, Prologue]

6 The lyf so short, the craft so long to lerne, / Th'assay so hard, so sharp the conquerynge. [The Parliament of Fowls]

7 For out of olde feldes, as men seith, / Cometh al this newe corn from yere to yere; / And out of olde bokes, in good feith, / Cometh al this newe science that men lere. [Ib.]

8 The tyme, that may not sojourne, / But goth, and may never retourne, / As watir that doun renneth ay, / But never drope retourne may. [Romaunt of the Rose]

9 Povert al aloon, / That not a penny had in wolde, / All though she hir clothis solde, / And though she shulde anhonged be; / For nakid as a worm was she. [Ib.]

10 O blynde world, O blynde entencioun! / How often falleth all the effect contraire / Of surquidrie and foul presumpcion; / For kaught is proud, and kaught is debonaire. [Troilus and Criseyde, I]

11 It is nought good a sleping hound to wake. [Ib. III]

1 The worst kinde of infortune is this, / A man to have ben in prosperitee, / And it remembren, when it passed is. [Ib.]

2 Oon ere it herde, at other out it wente. [Ib. IV]

Chekhov, Anton (1860–1904)

3 When a woman isn't beautiful, people always say, 'You have lovely eyes, you have lovely hair.' [*Uncle Vanya*, III]

4 He was a rationalist, but he had to confess that he liked the ringing of church bells. [Note Book]

Chesterfield, Philip Dormer Stanhope, Earl of (1694–1773)

5 In my mind, there is nothing so illiberal and so ill-bred, as audible laughter. [*Advice to his Son*, 'Graces']

6 The knowledge of the world is only to be acquired in the world, and not in a closet. [*Letters to his Son*, 1746]

7 An injury is much sooner forgotten than an insult. [Ib.]

8 There is a Spanish proverb, which says very justly, / Tell me whom you live with, and I will tell you who you are. [Ib. 1747]

9 [Of women] A man of sense only trifles with them, plays with them, humours and flatters them, as he does with a sprightly and forward child; but he neither consults them about, nor trusts them with, serious matters. [Ib. 1748]

10 Advice is seldom welcome; and those who want it the most always like it the least. [Ib.]

11 Speak of the moderns without contempt, and of the ancients without idolatry. [Ib.]

12 Wear your learning, like your watch, in a private pocket: and do not merely pull it out and strike it; merely to show that you have one. [Ib.]

1 If Shakespeare's genius had been cultivated, those beauties, which we so justly admire in him, would have been undisgraced by those extravagancies, and that nonsense, with which they are so frequently accompanied. [Ib.]

2 Women, then, are only children of a larger growth: they have an entertaining tattle, and sometimes wit; but for solid, reasoning good-sense, I never knew in my life one that had it, or who reasoned or acted consequentially for four and twenty hours together. [Ib.]

3 Due attention to the inside of books, and due contempt for the outside, is the proper relation between a man of sense and his books. [Ib. 1749]

4 Swallow all your learning in the morning, but digest it in company in the evenings. [Ib. 1751]

5 A chapter of accidents. [Ib. 1753]

6 Religion is by no means a proper subject of conversation in a mixed company. [Letter]

7 It is an undoubted truth, that the less one has to do, the less time one finds to do it in. One yawns, one procrastinates, one can do it when one will, and therefore one seldom does it at all. [Letter]

8 The pleasure is momentary, the position ridiculous and the expense damnable. [Attr.]

Chesterton, Gilbert Keith (1874–1936)

9 For the great Gaels of Ireland / Are the men that God made mad, / For all their wars are merry, / And all their songs are sad. [*Ballad of the White Horse*, II]

10 Fools! For I also had my hour; / One far fierce hour and sweet: / There was a shout about my ears, / And palms before my feet. ['The Donkey']

11 John Grubby, who was short and stout / And troubled with religious doubt, / Refused about

the age of three / To sit upon the curate's knee. ['The New Freethinker']

1 Before the Roman came to Rye or out to Severn strode, / The rolling English drunkard made the rolling English road. ['The Rolling English Road']

2 We only know the last sad squires ride slowly towards the sea, / And a new people takes the land: and still it is not we. ['The Secret People']

3 Smile at us, pay us, pass us; but do not quite forget. / For we are the people of England, that never have spoken yet. [Ib.]

4 The souls most fed with Shakespeare's flame / Still sat unconquered in a ring, / Remembering him like anything. ['The Shakespeare Memorial']

5 And Noah he often said to his wife when he sat down to dine, / 'I don't care where the water goes if it doesn't get into the wine.' ['Wine and Water']

6 'My country, right or wrong,' is a thing that no patriot would think of saying except in a desperate case. It is like saying, 'My mother, drunk or sober.' [*The Defendant*]

7 It is the supreme proof of a man being prosaic that he always insists on poetry being poetical. [*The Everlasting Man*]

8 The artistic temperament is a disease that afflicts amateurs. [*Heretics*]

9 The human race, to which so many of my readers belong... [*The Napoleon of Notting Hill*]

10 You can never have a revolution in order to establish a democracy. You must have a democracy in order to have a revolution. [*Tremendous Trifles*]

11 The Christian ideal has not been tried and found wanting. It has been found difficult; and left untried. [*What's Wrong with the World*]

1 If a thing is worth doing, it is worth doing badly. [Ib.]

2 Democracy means government by the uneducated, while aristocracy means government by the badly educated. [*New York Times*, 1931]

3 AM IN WOLVERHAMPTON STOP WHERE OUGHT I TO BE [Telegram to wife]

Churchill, Charles (1731–1764)

4 It can't be Nature, for it is not sense. ['The Farewell']

5 Just to the windward of the law. [*The Ghost*, III]

6 Wise fear, you know, / Forbids the robbing of a foe; / But what, to serve our private ends, / Forbids the cheating of our friends? [Ib.]

Churchill, Lord Randolph (1849–1894)

7 Ulster will fight; Ulster will be right. [Letter, 1886]

Churchill, Sir Winston (1874–1965)

8 It cannot in the opinion of His Majesty's Government be classified as slavery in the extreme acceptance of the word without some risk of terminological inexactitude. [Speech, House of Commons, 1906]

9 I cannot forecast to you the action of Russia. It is a riddle wrapped in a mystery inside an enigma. [Broadcast, 1939]

10 I have nothing to offer but blood, toil, tears, and sweat. [Speech, May, 1940]

11 We shall not flag or fail. We shall fight in France, we shall fight on the seas and oceans, we shall fight with growing confidence and growing strength in the air, we shall defend our island, whatever the cost may be, we shall fight on the beaches, we shall fight on the landing grounds, we shall fight in the fields and in the streets, we

shall fight in the hills; we shall never surrender.
[Ib. June, 1940]

1 Let us therefore brace ourselves to our duties,
and so bear ourselves that, if the British Empire
and its Commonwealth last for a thousand years,
men will still say, 'This was their finest hour.'
[Ib. June, 1940]

2 Never in the field of human conflict was so much
owed by so many to so few. [Ib. Aug., 1940]

3 Give us the tools, and we will finish the job.
[Broadcast, 1941]

4 Do not let us speak of darker days; let us rather
speak of sterner days. These are not dark days;
these are great days — the greatest days our
country has ever lived; and we must all thank
God that we have been allowed, each of us
according to our stations, to play a part in
making these days memorable in the history of
our race. [Speech, 1941]

5 When I warned them [the French Government]
that Britain would fight on alone whatever they
did, their Generals told their Prime Minister and
his divided Cabinet, 'In three weeks England will
have her neck wrung like a chicken.' Some
chicken! Some neck! [Speech, 1941]

6 This is not the end. It is not even the beginning
of the end. But it is, perhaps, the end of the
beginning. [Speech after El Alamein, 1942]

7 Beware, for the time may be short. A shadow
has fallen across the scenes so lately lighted by
the Allied victory. Nobody knows what Soviet
Russia and its Communist international
organization intend to do in the immediate
future. From Stettin in the Baltic to Trieste in the
Adriatic an Iron Curtain has descended across
the Continent. [Speech, 1946]

1 It is a good thing for an uneducated man to read books of quotations. [*My Early Life*, 9]

Cibber, Colley (1671–1757)

2 Off with his head — so much for Buckingham. [*Richard III* (adapted from Shakespeare), IV]

3 Stolen sweets are best. [*The Rival Fools*]

Cicero, Marcus Tullius (106–43 B.C.)

4 There is nothing so absurd but some philosopher has said it. [*De Divinatione*]

5 *Salus populi suprema est lex.* The welfare of the people is the ultimate law. [*De Legibus*]

6 *Summum bonum.* The greatest good. [*De Officiis*]

7 *Numquam se minus otiosum esse quam cum otiosus, nec minus solum quam solus esset.* Never less idle than when free from work, nor less alone than when completely alone. [Ib.]

8 *Mens cuiusque is est quisque.* Each man's mind is the man himself. [*De Republica*]

9 *O tempora! O mores!* What an age! What customs! [*In Catilinam*]

10 *Civis Romanus sum.* I am a Roman citizen. [*In Verrem*]

11 *Cui bono?* Who stands to gain? [*Pro Milone*]

12 *Neminem saltare sobrius, nisi forte insanit.* No sober man dances, unless he happens to be mad. [*Pro Murena*]

13 I would rather be wrong with Plato than right with such men as these. [*Tusculan Disputations*]

Clare, John (1793–1864)

14 Language has not the power to speak what love indites: / The soul lies buried in the ink that writes. [Attr.]

Clarendon, Edward Hyde, Earl of (1609–1674)

15 [Of Cromwell] He will be looked upon by

posterity as a brave bad man. [*History of the Rebellion*, final words]

Clarke, Arthur Charles (1917–)

1 When a distinguished but elderly scientist states that something is possible, he is almost certainly right. When he states that something is impossible, he is very probably wrong. (Clarke's First Law.) [*Profile of the Future*]

Claudius, Matthias (1740–1815)

2 We plough the fields, and scatter / The good seed on the land, / But it is fed and watered / By God's almighty hand; / He sends the snow in winter, / The warmth to swell the grain, / The breezes and the sunshine / And soft refreshing rain. [Hymn; trans. J.M. Campbell]

Clausewitz, Karl von (1780–1831)

3 War is nothing but the continuation of politics by other means. [*On War*]

Clemenceau, Georges (1841–1929)

4 It is far easier to make war than to make peace. [Speech, 1919]

5 America is the only nation in history which miraculously has gone directly from barbarism to degeneration without the usual interval of civilization. [Quoted in Peter, *Quotations for Our Time*]

6 Mr. Wilson bores me with his Fourteen Points; why, God Almighty has only ten. [Quoted in Wintle and Kenin, *Dictionary of Biographical Quotations*]

Clough, Arthur Hugh (1819–1861)

7 Whither depart the souls of the brave that die in the battle, / Die in the lost, lost fight, for the cause that perishes with them? [*Amours de Voyage*, V]

1 And almost everyone when age, / Disease, or sorrows strike him, / Inclines to think there is a God, / Or something very like Him. [*Dipsychus*]

2 Do not adultery commit; / Advantage rarely comes of it. ['The Latest Decalogue']

3 Thou shalt not kill; but need'st not strive / Officiously to keep alive. [Ib.]

4 Say not, the struggle naught availeth, / The labour and the wounds are vain, / The enemy faints not, nor faileth, / And as things have been they remain. ['Say Not, the Struggle Naught Availeth']

Cobbett, William (1762–1835)

5 To be poor and independent is very nearly an impossibility. [*Advice to Young Men*]

6 Nouns of number, or multitude, such as *Mob*, Parliament, Rabble, House of Commons, Regiment, Court of King's Bench, Den of Thieves and the like. [*English Grammar*, 'Syntax as Relating to Pronouns']

7 [Of London] But what is to be the fate of the great wen of all? The monster, called ... 'the metropolis of the empire'? [*Rural Rides*]

Cobden, Richard (1804–1865)

8 I believe it has been said that one copy of *The Times* contains more useful information than the whole of the historical works of Thucydides. [Speech, 1850]

Cochran, Charles B. (1872–1951)

9 I still prefer a good juggler to a bad Hamlet. [*Observer*, 'Sayings of the Week', 1943]

Cocteau, Jean (1891–1963)

1 The essential in daring is to know how far one can go too far. [*Le Coq et l'Arlequin*]

2 *Victor Hugo... un fou qui se croyait Victor Hugo.* Victor Hugo... a madman who thought he was Victor Hugo. [*Opium*]

3 The worst tragedy for a poet is to be admired through being misunderstood. [*Le Rappel à L'Ordre*]

4 If it has to choose who will be crucified, the crowd will always save Barabbas. [Ib.]

5 Art is science in the flesh. [Ib.]

Coke, Sir Edward (1552–1634)

6 Six hours in sleep, in law's grave study six, / Four spend in prayer, the rest on Nature fix. [*Pandects*]

7 The house of everyone is to him as his castle and fortress, as well for his defence against injury and violence, as for his repose. [*Semayne's Case*]

Coleridge, Samuel Taylor (1772–1834)

8 It is an ancient Mariner, / And he stoppeth one of three. / 'By thy long grey beard and glittering eye, / Now wherefore stopp'st thou me?' [*The Ancient Mariner*, 1]

9 The fair breeze blew, the white foam flew, / The furrow followed free; / We were the first that ever burst / Into that silent sea. [Ib. 2]

10 As idle as a painted ship / Upon a painted ocean. [Ib.]

11 Water, water, everywhere, / And all the boards did shrink; / Water, water, everywhere, / Nor any drop to drink. [Ib.]

12 Yea, slimy things did crawl with legs / Upon the slimy sea. [Ib.]

13 Alone, alone, all, all alone, / Alone on a wide,

wide sea! / And never a soul took pity on / My soul in agony. [Ib. 4]

1 Oh! Sleep it is a gentle thing / Beloved from pole to pole, / To Mary Queen the praise be given! / She sent the gentle sleep from Heaven, / That slid into my soul. [Ib. 5]

2 From his brimstone bed at break of day / A walking the Devil is gone, / To visit his snug little farm the Earth, / And see how his stock goes on. ['The Devil's Thoughts']

3 And the Devil did grin, for his darling sin / Is pride that apes humility. [Ib.]

4 What is an Epigram? a dwarfish whole, / Its body brevity, and wit its soul. ['Epigram']

5 Swans sing before they die — 'twere no bad thing / Should certain persons die before they sing. ['Epigram on a Volunteer Singer']

6 In Xanadu did Kubla Khan / A stately pleasure-dome decree: / Where Alph, the sacred river, ran / Through caverns measureless to man / Down to a sunless sea. ['Kubla Khan']

7 Woman wailing for her demon-lover. [Ib.]

8 And 'mid this tumult Kubla heard from far / Ancestral voices prophesying war! [Ib.]

9 He who begins by loving Christianity better than Truth will proceed by loving his own sect or church better than Christianity, and end by loving himself better than all. [*Aids to Reflection: Moral and Religious Aphorisms*]

10 That willing suspension of disbelief for the moment, which constitutes poetic faith. [*Biographia Literaria*]

11 Our myriad-minded Shakespeare. [Ib.]

12 No man was ever yet a great poet, without being at the same time a profound philosopher. [Ib.]

13 The dwarf sees farther than the giant, when he

has the giant's shoulder to mount on. [*The Friend*]

1 [Of Iago] The motive-hunting of motiveless malignity. [*Notes on the Tragedies of Shakespeare*, 'Othello']

2 [Of Edmund Kean] To see him act is like reading Shakespeare by flashes of lightning. [*Table-Talk*]

3 I wish our clever young poets would remember my homely definitions of prose and poetry; that is prose = words in their best order; poetry = the best words in their best order. [Ib.]

Collins, John Churton (1848–1908)

4 To ask advice is in nine cases out of ten to tout for flattery. [*Maxims and Reflections*]

Collins, Mortimer (1827–1876)

5 A man is as old as he's feeling, / A woman as old as she looks. ['The Unknown Quantity']

Collins, William (1721–1759)

6 How sleep the brave, who sink to rest, / By all their country's wishes blest! ['Ode Written in the Year 1746']

Colman, George, the Younger (1762–1836)

7 Not to be sneezed at. [*The Heir at Law*, II]

8 Says he, 'I am a handsome man, but I'm a gay deceiver.' [*Love Laughs at Locksmiths*, II]

Colton, Charles Caleb (c. 1780–1832)

9 Imitation is the sincerest form of flattery. [*Lacon*]

10 Examinations are formidable even to the best prepared, for the greatest fool may ask more than the wisest man can answer. [Ib.]

11 Man is an embodied paradox, a bundle of contradictions. [Ib.]

12 Friendship often ends in love; but love in friendship – never. [Ib.]

Confucius (c. 550–c. 478 B.C.)

1   True goodness springs from a man's own heart. All men are born good. [*Analects*]

2   An oppressive government is more to be feared than a tiger. [Ib.]

3   Things that are done, it is needless to speak about . . . Things that are past, it is needless to blame. [Ib.]

4   Virtue is not left to stand alone. He who practises it will have neighbours. [Ib.]

5   Men's natures are alike; it is their habits that carry them far apart. [Ib.]

6   The heart of the wise, like a mirror, should reflect all objects without being sullied by any. [Ib.]

7   Learning without thought is labour lost; thought without learning is perilous. [Ib.]

8   What the superior man seeks is in himself: what the small man seeks is in others. [Ib.]

9   For one word a man is often deemed to be wise, and for one word he is often deemed to be foolish. We should be careful indeed what we say. [Ib.]

10   Everything has its beauty but not everyone sees it. [Ib.]

11   They must often change who would be constant in happiness or wisdom. [Ib.]

12   Without knowing the force of words, it is impossible to know men. [Ib.]

13   To see what is right and not to do it is want of courage. [Ib.]

14   Better a diamond with a flaw than a pebble without. [Ib.]

Congreve, William (1670–1729)

1 She lays it on with a trowel. [*The Double Dealer*, III.10]

2 See how love and murder will out. [Ib. IV.6]

3 No mask like open truth to cover lies, / As to go naked is the best disguise. [Ib. V]

4 I know that's a secret, for it's whispered everywhere. [*Love for Love*, III.3]

5 Music has charms to soothe a savage breast. [*The Mourning Bride*, I.1]

6 Heav'n has no rage, like love to hatred turn'd, / Nor Hell a fury, like a woman scorn'd. [Ib. III.8]

7 Thus grief still treads upon the heels of pleasure: / Married in haste, we may repent at leisure. [Ib. V.8]

8 Courtship to marriage, as a very witty prologue to a very dull Play. [Ib. V.10]

9 Alack, he's gone the way of all flesh. ['*Squire Bickerstaff Detected* (Attr.)]

10 A little disdain is not amiss; a little scorn is alluring. [*The Way of the World*, III.5]

Connolly, Cyril (1903–1974)

11 Whom the gods wish to destroy they first call promising. [*Enemies of Promise*]

12 Imprisoned in every fat man a thin one is wildly signalling to be let out. [*The Unquiet Grave*]

Conrad, Joseph (1857–1924)

13 Mistah Kurtz — he dead. [*The Heart of Darkness*]

14 The horror! The horror! [Ib.]

15 The terrorist and the policeman both come from the same basket. [*The Secret Agent*]

Constantine, Emperor (c. A.D. 288–337)

16 *In hoc signo vinces.* In this sign thou shalt

conquer. [Attr. words of Constantine's vision, A.D. 312]

Coolidge, Calvin (1872–1933)

1 The business of America is business. [Speech, 1925]

Corneille, Pierre (1606–1684)

2 We triumph without glory when we conquer without danger. [*Le Cid*]

3 He who allows himself to be insulted, deserves to be. [*Héraclius*]

Cornfeld, Bernard (1927–   )

4 Do You Sincerely Want to be Rich? [Title of book]

Cornuel, Madame Anne Bigot de (1605–1694)

5 *Il n'y a point de grand homme pour son valet de chambre.* No man is a hero to his valet. [Attr. (Similar sentiments attr. to Antigonus Gonatas, King of Thessaly, Madame de Sévigné, Nicolas Catinat, Goethe, and Montaigne.)]

Cory, William (1823–1892)

6 Jolly boating weather, / And a hay harvest breeze / … Swing, swing together / With your body between your knees. ['Eton Boating Song']

Coué, Emile (1857–1926)

7 *Tous les jours, à tous points de vue, je vais de mieux en mieux.* Every day, in every way, I am getting better and better. [Motto]

Cousin, Victor (1792–1867)

8 *Il faut de la religion pour la religion, de la morale pour la morale, comme de l'art pour l'art.* We must have religion for religion's sake, morality for morality's sake, as with art for art's sake. [Lecture, 1818]

Coward, Sir Noël (1899–1973)

1 Everybody worships me, it's nauseating. [*Present Laughter*, I]

2 Extraordinary how potent cheap music is. [*Private Lives*, I]

3 Comedies of manners swiftly become obsolete when there are no longer any manners. [*Relative Values*, I]

4 Don't let's be beastly to the Germans. ['Don't Let's Be Beastly to the Germans']

5 Mad about the boy, / It's pretty funny but I'm mad about the boy. ['Mad about the Boy']

6 Mad dogs and Englishmen go out in the mid-day sun. ['Mad Dogs and Englishmen']

7 Don't put your daughter on the stage, Mrs. Worthington. ['Mrs. Worthington']

Cowley, Abraham (1618–1667)

8 God the first garden made, and the first city Cain. ['The Garden']

9 Life is an incurable disease. ['To Dr. Scarborough']

10 Well then; I now do plainly see / The busy world and I shall ne'er agree. ['The Wish']

Cowley, Hannah (1743–1809)

11 But what is woman? — only one of Nature's agreeable blunders. [*Who's the Dupe?*, II]

Cowper, William (1731–1800)

12 A fool must now and then be right, by chance. ['Conversation']

13 A noisy man is always in the right. [Ib.]

14 War lays a burden on the reeling state, / And peace does nothing to relieve the weight. [*Expostulation*]

1 Thousands... / Kiss the book's outside who
ne'er look within. [Ib.]

2 And diff'ring judgments serve but to declare /
That truth lies somewhere, if we knew but
where. [*Hope*]

3 Oh! for a closer walk with God. [*Olney Hymns*,
1]

4 God moves in a mysterious way / His wonders
to perform. [Ib. 35]

5 Judge not the Lord by feeble sense, / But trust
him for his grace; / Behind a frowning
providence / He hides a smiling face. [Ib.]

6 Toll for the brave — / The brave! that are no
more: / All sunk beneath the wave, / Fast by
their native shore. ['On the Loss of the Royal
George']

7 I am monarch of all I survey, / My right there is
none to dispute. ['The Solitude of Alexander
Selkirk']

8 O solitude! where are the charms / That sages
have seen in thy face? [Ib.]

9 Freedom has a thousand charms to show, / That
slaves, howe'er contented, never know. [*Table
Talk*]

10 God made the country, and man made the town.
[*The Task*, I, 'The Sofa']

11 Variety's the very spice of life, / That gives all
its flavour. [Ib. II, 'The Timepiece']

12 Slaves cannot breathe in England, if their lungs /
Receive our air, that moment they are free; /
They touch our country, and their shackles fall.
[Ib.]

13 Domestic happiness, thou only bliss / Of
Paradise that has surviv'd the fall! [Ib. III, 'The
Garden']

14 Knowledge is proud that he has learn'd so much;

/ Wisdom is humble that he knows no more. [Ib. IV]

1 Nature is but a name for an effect, / Whose cause is God. [Ib.]

Crabbe, George (1754–1832)

2 Habit with him was all the test of truth, / 'It must be right: I've done it from my youth.' [*The Borough*, 'The Vicar']

3 Secrets with girls, like loaded guns with boys, / Are never valued till they make a noise. [*Tales of the Hall*, 'The Maid's Story']

4 'The game,' he said, 'is never lost till won.' [Ib. 'Gretna Green']

Cranmer, Thomas (1489–1556)

5 This is the hand that wrote it and therefore it shall suffer first punishment. [At the stake, 1556]

Crashaw, Richard (c. 1612–1649)

6 Love, thou art absolute sole Lord / Of life and death. ['Hymn to St. Teresa']

7 ... two faithful fountains; / Two walking baths; two weeping motions; / Portable, and compendious oceans. ['The Weeper']

8 All is Caesar's; and what odds / So long as Caesar's self is God's? [*Steps to the Temple*, 'Mark 12']

9 And when life's sweet fable ends, / Soul and body part like friends; / No quarrels, murmurs, no delay; / A kiss, a sigh, and so away. ['Temperance']

10 Whoe'er she be, / That not impossible she / That shall command my heart and me. ['Wishes to His Supposed Mistress']

Cromwell, Oliver (1599–1658)

11 I beseech you, in the bowels of Christ think it

possible you may be mistaken. [Letter to the General Assembly of the Church of Scotland, 1650]

1 [Referring to the mace] What shall we do with the bauble? Take it away! [Remark on dissolving Parliament, 1653]

2 You have sat too long here for any good you have been doing. Depart, I say, and let us have done with you. In the name of God, go! [Ib.]

3 Necessity hath no law. [Speech, 1654]

4 You have accounted yourselves happy on being environed with a great ditch from all the world beside. [Ib. 1658]

5 Mr. Lely, I desire you would use all your skill to paint my picture freely like me, and not flatter me at all; but remark all these roughnesses, pimples, warts, and everything as you see me, otherwise I will never pay a farthing for it. [Remark]

Cummings, E.E. (1894–1962)

6 'next to of course god america i / love you land of the pilgrims' and so forth oh. ['next to of course god']

7 listen: there's a hell / of a good universe next door; let's go. ['pity this busy monster, manunkind']

8 who pays any attention / to the syntax of things / will never wholly kiss you. ['since feeling is first']

Cunningham, Allan (1784–1842)

9 Wha the deil hae we got for a King, / But a wee, wee German lairdie! ['The Wee, Wee German Lairdie']

Curran, John Philpot (1750–1817)

10 The condition upon which God hath given liberty

to man is eternal vigilance; which condition if he break, servitude is at once the consequence of his crime, and the punishment of his guilt. [Speech, 1790]

Cyprian, St. (d. 258)

1 *Salus extra ecclesiam non est.* There is no salvation outside the Church. [Letter]

Dali, Salvador (1904–)

2 There is only one difference between a madman and me. I am not mad. [Remark, 1956]

Dana, Charles Anderson (1819–1897)

3 When a dog bites a man that is not news, but when a man bites a dog that is news. [*New York Sun*, 1882]

Dante Alighieri (1265–1321)

4 *Lasciate ogni speranza voi ch'entrate.* Abandon hope, all ye who enter here. [*Inferno*, 3]

5 *Il gran rifiuto.* The great refusal. [Ib.]

6 *L'arte vostra quella, quanto puote, / Segue, come il maestro fa il discente, / Sì che vostr'arte a Dio quasi è nipote.* Art, as far as it can, follows nature, as a pupil imitates his master; thus your art must be, as it were, God's grandchild. [Ib. 11]

7 *Onorate l'altissimo poeta.* Honour the greatest poet. [Ib.]

8 *E'n la sua volontade e nostra pace.* In His will is our peace. [*Paradiso*, 3]

Danton, Georges (1759–1794)

9 *De l'audace, et encore de l'audace, et toujours de l'audace!* Boldness and more boldness, and always boldness! [Speech, 1792]

10 My address will soon be Annihilation. As for my name you will find it in the Pantheon of History. [Response at his trial, 1794]

Darwin, Charles (1809–1882)

1 I have called this principle, by which each slight variation, if useful, is preserved, by the term of Natural Selection. [*The Origin of Species*, 3]

2 The struggle for existence. [Ib.]

3 The expression often used by Mr. Herbert Spencer of the Survival of the Fittest is more accurate, and is sometimes equally convenient. [Ib.]

Davenant, Charles (1656–1714)

4 Custom, that unwritten law, / By which the people keep even kings in awe. [*Circe*, II]

Davenant, William (1606–1668)

5 Frail Life! in which, through Mists of human breath, / We grope for Truth, and make our Progress slow. ['The Christians Reply to the Philosopher']

6 For I must go where lazy Peace / Will hide her drowsy head; / And, for the sport of kings, increase / The number of the dead. ['The Soldier Going to the Field']

Davidson, John (1857–1909)

7 Seraphs and saints with one great voice / Welcomed the soul that knew not fear; / Amazed to find it could rejoice, / Hell raised a hoarse, half-human cheer. ['A Ballad of Hell']

Davies, Sir John (1569–1626)

8 Judge not the play before the play be done. ['Respice Finem']

Davies, William Henry (1870–1940)

9 What is this life if, full of care, / We have no time to stand and stare? ['Leisure']

Davis, Bette (1908–)

1 Fasten your seat belts, it's going to be a bumpy night. [*All About Eve*]

2 [Of a starlet]I see — she's the original good time that was had by all. [Quoted in Halliwell, *Filmgoers' Book of Quotes*]

Davis, Sammy, Junior (1925–)

3 Being a star has made it possible for me to get insulted in places where the average Negro could never hope to get insulted. [*Yes I can*]

Debs, Eugene Victor (1855–1926)

4 While there is a lower class, I am in it. While there is a criminal class I am in it. While there is a soul in prison, I am not free. [*Labor and Freedom*]

Decatur, Stephen (1779–1820)

5 Our country! In her intercourse with foreign nations, may she always be in the right; but our country, right or wrong. [Mackenzie, *Life of Decatur*]

Defoe, Daniel (c. 1661–1731)

6 The best of men cannot suspend their fate: / The good die early, and the bad die late. ['Character of the late Dr. S. Annesley']

7 Nature has left this tincture in the blood, / That all men would be tyrants if they could. ['The Kentish Petition']

8 Wherever God erects a house of prayer, / The Devil always builds a chapel there; / And 'twill be found, upon examination, / The latter has the largest congregation. [*The True-Born Englishman*, I]

9 From this amphibious, ill-born mob began / That vain, ill-natur'd thing, an Englishman. [Ib.]

1 Necessity makes an honest man a knave.
[*Serious Reflections of Robinson Crusoe*]

De Gaulle, Charles (1890–1970)

2 *Vive le Québec! Vive le Québec libre!* Long live
Quebec! Long live free Quebec! [Speech, Quebec,
1967]

Dekker, Thomas (c. 1570–c. 1641)

3 Golden slumbers kiss your eyes, / Smiles awake
you when you rise. [*Patient Grissill*, I]

De La Mare, Walter (1873–1956)

4 Nought but vast sorrow was there — / The
sweet cheat gone. ['The Ghost']

5 I met at eve the Prince of Sleep, / His was a still
and lovely face, / He wandered through a valley
steep, / Lovely in a lonely place. ['I Met at Eve']

6 It's a very odd thing — / As odd as can be — /
That whatever Miss T eats / Turns into Miss T.
['Miss T']

7 Slowly, silently, now the moon / Walks the night
in her silver shoon. ['Silver']

De Mille, Cecil B. (1881–1959)

8 The public is always right. [Quoted in Colombo,
Wit and Wisdom of the Moviemakers]

Demosthenes (385–322 B.C.)

9 The easiest thing of all is to deceive one's self;
for what a man wishes he generally believes to
be true. [*Olynthiaca*, 3]

10 There is one safeguard known generally to the
wise, which is an advantage and security to all,
but especially to democracies against despots —
suspicion. [*Philippics*, 2]

Dennis, John (1657–1734)

11 A man who could make so vile a pun, would not

scruple to pick a pocket. [*Gentleman's Magazine*, 1781]

1 See how the rascals use me! They will not let my play run and yet they steal my thunder! [Remark at a production of *Macbeth*]

De Quincey, Thomas (1785–1859)

2 Thou hast the keys of Paradise, oh just, subtle, and mighty opium! [*Confessions of an English Opium Eater*, 2, 'The Pleasures of Opium']

3 If a man once indulges himself in murder, very soon he comes to think little of robbing; and from robbing he comes next to drinking and sabbath-breaking, and from that to incivility and procrastination. [Ib.]

4 Murder Considered as One of the Fine Arts. [Title of Essay]

Descartes, René (1596–1650)

5 *Cogito, ergo sum.* I think, therefore I am. [*Le Discours de la Méthode*]

Deschamps, Eustache (c. 1345–1406)

6 *Qui pendre la sonnette au chat?* Who will bell the cat? [Ballade]

Desmoulins, Camille (1760–1794)

7 Clemency is also a revolutionary measure. [Speech, 1793]

Dewar, Lord Thomas Robert (1864–1930)

8 The road to success is filled with women pushing their husbands along. [Epigram]

Dibdins, Thomas (1771–1841)

9 Oh! what a snug little Island, / A right little, tight little Island! ['The Snug Little Island']

Dickens, Charles (1812–1870)

1 There are strings ... in the human heart that had better not be wibrated. [*Barnaby Rudge*, 22]

2 This is a London particular ... A fog, miss. [*Bleak House*, 3]

3 'God bless us every one!' said Tiny Tim. [*A Christmas Carol*, 3]

4 'In case anything turned up,' which was his [Mr. Micawber's] favourite expression. [*David Copperfield*, 11]

5 Annual income twenty pounds, annual expenditure nineteen nineteen six, result happiness. Annual income twenty pounds, annual expenditure twenty pounds ought and six, result misery. [Ib. 12]

6 We are so very 'umble. [Ib. 17]

7 'It was as true,' said Mr. Barkis, ' ... as taxes is. And nothing's truer than them.' [Ib. 21]

8 Accidents will occur in the best-regulated families. [Ib. 28]

9 Train up a fig-tree in the way it should go, and when you are old sit under the shade of it. [*Dombey and Son*, 19]

10 I had cherished a profound conviction that her bringing me up by hand, gave her no right to bring me up by jerks. [*Great Expectations*, 8]

11 You don't object to an aged parent, I hope? [Ib. 25]

12 'Now, what I want is, Facts. Teach these boys and girls nothing but Facts. Facts alone are wanted in life. Plant nothing else, and root out everything else ... Stick to Facts, sir!' [*Hard Times*, I, 1]

13 Whatever was required to be done, the Circumlocution Office was beforehand with all

the public departments in the art of perceiving —
HOW NOT TO DO IT. [*Little Dorrit*, I, 10]

1 In company with several other old ladies of both
sexes. [Ib. I, 17]

2 It was not a bosom to repose upon, but it was a
capital bosom to hang jewels upon. [Ib. I, 21]

3 Once a gentleman, and always a gentleman. [Ib.
II, 28]

4 With affection beaming in one eye, and
calculation shining out the other. [*Martin
Chuzzlewit*, 8]

5 Here's the rule, for bargains: 'Do other men, for
they would do you.' That's the true business
precept. [Ib. 11]

6 He'd make a lovely corpse. [Ib. 25]

7 He had but one eye, and the popular prejudice
runs in favour of two. [*Nicholas Nickleby*, 4]

8 There are only two styles of portrait painting; the
serious and the smirk. [Ib. 10]

9 This is all very well, Mr. Nickleby, and very
proper, so far as it goes — so far as it goes, but
it doesn't go far enough. [Ib. 16]

10 Language was not powerful enough to describe
the infant phenomenon. [Ib. 23]

11 All is gas and gaiters. [Ib. 49]

12 My life is one demd horrid grind! [Ib. 64]

13 Fan the sinking flame of hilarity with the wing of
friendship; and pass the rosy wine. [*The Old
Curiosity Shop*, 7]

14 Oliver Twist has asked for more! [*Oliver Twist*,
2]

15 Known by the *sobriquet* of 'The artful Dodger'.
[Ib.]

16 'If the law supposes that,' said Mr. Bumble . . .
'the law is a ass — a idiot.' [Ib. 51]

1 I think ... that it is the best club in London. [The House of Commons] [*Our Mutual Friend*, II, 3]

2 Queer Street is full of lodgers just at present. [Ib. III, 1]

3 I wants to make your flesh creep. [*Pickwick Papers*, 8]

4 'Suppose there are two mobs?' suggested Mr. Snodgrass. 'Shout with the largest,' replied Mr. Pickwick. [Ib. 13]

5 Poverty and oysters always seem to go together. [Ib. 22]

6 It's over, and can't be helped, and that's one consolation, as they always says in Turkey, ven they cuts the wrong man's head off. [Ib. 23]

7 Wery glad to see you, indeed, and hope our acquaintance may be a long 'un, as the gen'l'm'n said to the fi' pun' note. [Ib. 25]

8 When you're a married man, Samivel, you'll understand a good many things as you don't understand now; but vether it's worth while goin' through so much to learn so little, as the charityboy said when he got to the end of the alphabet, is a matter o' taste. [Ib. 27]

9 It's my opinion, sir, that this meeting is drunk, sir! [Ib. 33]

10 As it is, I don't think I can do with anythin' under a female markis. I might keep up with a young 'ooman o' large property as hadn't a title, if she made wery fierce love to me. Not else. [Ib.]

11 Grief never mended no broken bones, and as good people's wery scarce, what I says is, make the most on 'em. [Ib. 'Gin Shops']

12 It was the best of times, it was the worst of times, it was the age of wisdom, it was the age of foolishness, it was the epoch of belief, it was the epoch of incredulity, it was the season of

Light, it was the season of Darkness, it was the spring of hope, it was the winter of despair, we had everything before us, we had nothing before us, we were all going direct to Heaven, we were all going direct the other way. [*A Tale of Two Cities*, I, 1]

1 It is a far, far better thing that I do, than I have ever done; it is a far, far better rest that I go to, than I have ever known. [Ib. III, 15]

Dickinson, Emily (1830–1886)

2 Because I could not stop for Death − / He kindly stopped for me − / The Carriage held but just Ourselves − / And Immortality. ['Because I could not stop']

3 Parting is all we know of heaven / And all we need of hell. ['My life closed twice']

4 How dreary to be somebody! / How public, like a frog / To tell your name the livelong day / To an admiring bog! [*Poems*]

Dickinson, John (1732–1808)

5 Then join hand in hand, brave Americans all, − / By uniting we stand, by dividing we fall. ['The Liberty Song']

Diderot, Denis (1713–1784)

6 Men will never be free until the last king is strangled with the entrails of the last priest. [*Dithyrambe sur la fête des rois*]

Diogenes (the Cynic) (c. 412–323 B.C.)

7 I do not know whether there are gods, but there ought to be. [Tertullian, *Ad Nationes*]

8 [Asked by Alexander if he wanted anything] Yes, stand a little out of my sun. [Plutarch, *Life of Alexander*]

9 I am looking for an honest man. [Diogenes Laertius, *Diogenes*]

1 I am a citizen of the world [*Kosmopolites*: origin of the word 'cosmopolitan']. [Ib.]

2 I am called a dog because I fawn on those who give me anything, I yelp at those who refuse, and I set my teeth in rascals. [Ib.]

Disraeli, Benjamin (1804–1881)

3 No Government can be long secure without a formidable opposition. [*Coningsby*, II, 1]

4 Conservatism discards Prescription, shrinks from Principle, disavows Progress: having reflected all respect for antiquity, it offers no redress for the present, and makes no preparation for the future. [Ib. II, 5]

5 A sound Conservative government ... Tory men and Whig measures. [Ib. II, 6]

6 Youth is a blunder; Manhood a struggle; Old Age a regret. [Ib. III, 1]

7 When a man fell into his anecdotage it was a sign for him to retire from the world. [*Lothair*, 28]

8 I have always thought that every woman should marry — and no man. [Ib. 30]

9 I was told that the Privileged and the People formed Two Nations. [*Sybil*, IV, 8]

10 There is moderation even in excess. [*Vivian Grey*, II, 6]

11 The Continent will not suffer England to be the workshop of the world. [Speech, 1838]

12 A starving population, an absentee aristocracy, and an alien Church, and in addition the weakest executive in the world. That is the Irish question. [Speech, 1844]

13 A Conservative government is an organized hypocrisy. [Speech, 1845]

1 Finality is not the language of politics. [Speech, 1859]

2 Is man an ape or an angel? Now I am on the side of the angels. [Speech, 1864]

3 Lord Salisbury and myself have brought you back peace — but peace, I hope, with honour. [Speech, 1878]

4 [Of Gladstone] A sophistical rhetorician, inebriated with the exuberance of his own verbosity. [Speech, 1878]

5 Damn your principles! Stick to your party. [Attr.]

6 [To Queen Victoria] We authors, Ma'am. [Attr.]

7 When I want to read a novel I write one. [Attr.]

8 [Asked if Queen Victoria should visit him during his last illness] No, it is better not. She would only ask me to take a message to Albert. [Quoted in Wintle and Kenin, *Dictionary of Biographical Quotations*]

Dobson, Austin (1840–1921)

9 Fame is a food that dead men eat, — / I have no stomach for such meat. ['Fame is a Food']

10 Time goes, you say? Ah no! / Alas, Time stays, *we* go. ['The Paradox of Time']

Donatus, Aelius (fl. 4th century A.D.)

11 *Pereant, inquit, qui ante nos nostra dixerunt.* Confound those who have said our remarks before us. [St. Jerome, *Commentaries on Ecclesiastes*]

Donne, John (c. 1571–1631)

12 Twice or thrice had I loved thee, / Before I knew thy face or name; / So in a voice, so in a shapeless flame, / Angels affect us oft, and worship'd be. ['Air and Angels']

13 Just such disparity / As is 'twixt Air and Angels'

purity, / 'Twixt women's love and men's will ever be. [Ib.]

1 All other things, to their destruction draw, / Only our love hath no decay; / This, no tomorrow hath, nor yesterday, / Running it never runs from us away, / But truly keeps his first, last, everlasting day. ['The Anniversary']

2 Come live with me, and be my love, / And we will some new pleasures prove / Of golden sands, and crystal brooks, / With silken lines, and silver hooks. ['The Bait']

3 Chang'd loves are but chang'd sorts of meat, / And when he hath the kernel eat, / Who doth not fling away the shell? ['Community']

4 No man is an *Island*, entire of it self. [*Devotions*]

5 Any man's *death* diminishes *me*, because I am involved in *Mankind*; And therefore never send to know for whom the *bell* tolls; It tolls for *thee*. [Ib.]

6 Love built on beauty, soon as beauty dies. [*Elegies*, 2, 'The Anagram']

7 No Spring, nor Summer Beauty hath such grace, / As I have seen in one Autumnal face. [Ib. 9, 'The Autumnal']

8 So, if I dream I have you, I have you, / For, all our joys are but fantastical. [Ib. 10, 'The Dream']

9 And must she needs be false because she's fair? [Ib. 15, 'The Expostulation']

10 By our first strange and fatal interview / By all desires which thereof did ensue. [Ib. 16, 'On His Mistress']

11 How happy were our Sires in ancient times, / Who held plurality of loves no crime! [Ib. 17]

12 O my America! my new-found-land. [Ib. 19, 'Going to Bed']

13 So, so, break off this last lamenting kiss, /

Which sucks two souls, and vapours both away.
['The Expiration']

1 Love's mysteries in souls do grow, / But yet the body is his book. ['The Ecstasy']

2 I wonder by my troth what thou, and I / Did, till we lov'd? ['The Good-Morrow']

3 Or snorted we in the Seven Sleepers den? [Ib.]

4 I am a little world made cunningly / Of Elements, and an Angelic spright. [*Holy Sonnets*, 5]

5 Death be not proud, though some have called thee / Mighty and dreadful, for thou art not so. [Ib. 10]

6 One short sleep past, we wake eternally, / And death shall be no more; Death, thou shalt die. [Ib.]

7 What if this present were the world's last night? [Ib. 13]

8 Batter my heart, three person'd God; for, you / As yet but knock. [Ib. 14]

9 Since I am coming to that Holy room, / Where, with thy Quire of Saints for evermore, / I shall be made thy Music; As I come / I tune the Instrument here at the door, / And what I must do then, think now before. ['Hymn to God my God, in my Sickness']

10 I long to talk with some old lover's ghost, / Who died before the god of Love was born. ['Love's Deity']

11 'Tis the year's midnight, and it is the day's. ['Nocturnal upon St. Lucy's Day']

12 The world's whole sap is sunk: / The general balm th'hydroptic earth hath drunk. [Ib.]

13 A bracelet of bright hair about the bone. ['The Relic']

14 Giddy fantastic Poets of each land. [*Satyres*, 1]

1 On a huge hill, / Cragged, and steep, Truth stands, and he that will / Reach her, about must, and about must go; / And what the hill's suddenness resists, win so. ['Ib. 3]

2 Go, and catch a falling star, / Get with child a mandrake root, / Tell me, where all past years are, / Or who cleft the Devil's foot. ['Song']

3 Busy old fool, unruly Sun, / Why dost thou thus, / Through windows, and through curtains call on us? ['The Sun-Rising']

4 Love, all alike, no season knows, nor clime, / Nor hours, days, months, which are the rags of time. [Ib.]

5 I am two fools, I know, / For loving, and for saying so / In whining Poetry. ['The Triple Fool']

6 But he who loveliness within / Hath found, all outward loathes, / For he who colour loves, and skin, / Loves but their oldest clothes. ['The Undertaking']

7 Dull sublunary lovers love / (Whose soul is sense) cannot admit / Absence, because it doth remove / Those things which elemented it. ['A Valediction Forbidding Mourning']

Douglas, Lord Alfred (1870–1945)

8 I am the Love that dare not speak its name. ['Two Loves']

Dowson, Ernest (1867–1900)

9 I have forgot much, Cynara! gone with the wind. ['Non Sum Qualis Eram']

10 I cried for madder music and stronger wine, / But when the feast is finish'd and the lamps expire, / Then falls thy shadow, Cynara! . . . / I have been faithful to thee, Cynara! in my fashion. [Ib.]

11 They are not long, the days of wine and roses. ['Vitae Summa Brevis']

Doyle, Sir Arthur Conan (1859–1930)

1 'Excellent!' I [Dr. Watson] cried. 'Elementary,'
   said he [Holmes]. ['The Crooked Man']

2 [Of Moriarty] The Napoleon of crime. ['The Final
   Problem']

3 A man should keep his little brain attic stocked
   with all the furniture that he is likely to use, and
   the rest he can put away in the lumber-room of
   his library, where he can get it if he wants it.
   ['Five Orange Pips']

4 How often have I said to you that when you have
   eliminated the impossible, whatever remains,
   however improbable, must be the truth. [*The
   Sign of Four*]

5 You know my methods. Apply them. [Ib. (Also,
   with slight variations, in other stories)]

6 The vocabulary of Bradshaw is nervous and
   terse, but limited. [*The Valley of Fear*]

7 Mediocrity knows nothing higher than itself, but
   talent instantly recognizes genius. [Ib.]

Drake, Sir Francis (c. 1540–1596)

8 I remember Drake, in the vaunting style of a
   soldier, would call the Enterprise [of Cadiz, 1587]
   the singeing of the King of Spain's Beard.
   [Bacon, *Considerations touching a War with
   Spain*]

9 There is plenty of time to win this game, and to
   thrash the Spaniards too. [Attr. in *Dictionary of
   National Biography*]

Drayton, Michael (1563–1631)

10 Fair stood the wind for France / When we our
    sails advance, / Nor now to prove our chance /
    Longer will tarry. [*To the Cambro-Britons*,
    'Agincourt']

11 Neat Marlowe, bathed in the Thespian springs, /

Had in him those brave translunary things / That the first poets had; his raptures were / All air and fire, which made his verse clear, / For that fine madness still he did retain / Which rightly should possess a poet's brain. ['Of Poets and Poesy']

1 Since there's no help, come let us kiss and part. [*Sonnets*, 'Idea']

Dressler, Marie (1869–1934)

2 If ants are such busy workers, how come they find time to go to all the picnics? [Quoted in Cowan, *The Wit of Women*]

Dryden, John (1631–1700)

3 In pious times, ere priestcraft did begin, / Before polygamy was made a sin. [*Absalom and Achitophel*, Part I]

4 Gods they had tried of every shape and size / That godsmiths could produce or priests devise. [Ib.]

5 Pleased with the danger, when the waves went high / He sought the storms; but for a calm unfit, / Would steer too nigh the sands to boast his wit. / Great wits are sure to madness near alli'd, / And thin partitions do their bounds divide. [Ib.]

6 In friendship false, implacable in hate, / Resolved to ruin or to rule the state. [Ib.]

7 So easy still it proves in factious times / With public zeal to cancel private crimes. [Ib.]

8 Better one suffer than a nation grieve. [Ib.]

9 Not is the people's judgement always true: / The most may err as grossly as the few. [Ib.]

10 None but the brave deserves the fair. ['Alexander's Feast']

1 Drinking is the soldier's pleasure... / Sweet is pleasure after pain. [*Ib.*]

2 Men are but children of a larger growth. [*All for Love*, IV]

3 Our author by experience finds it true, / 'Tis much more hard to please himself than you. [*Aureng-Zebe*, Prologue]

4 When I consider life, 'tis all a cheat; / Yet, fooled with hope, men favour the deceit. [*Ib.* IV]

5 Here lies my wife: here let her lie! / Now she's at rest, and so am I. ['Epitaph intended for his wife']

6 His grandeur he derived from Heaven alone, / For he was great, ere fortune made him so. ['Heroic Stanzas after Cromwell's Funeral']

7 By education most have been misled; / So they believe, because they so were bred. / The priest continues what the nurse began, / And thus the child imposes on the man. [*The Hind and the Panther*]

8 Either be wholly slaves or wholly free. [*Ib.*]

9 And love's the noblest frailty of the mind. [*The Indian Emperor*, II]

10 All human things are subject to decay, / And, when fate summons, monarchs must obey. [*Mac Flecknoe*]

11 Thou last great Prophet of Tautology. [*Ib.*]

12 The rest to some faint meaning make pretence, / But Shadwell never deviates into sense. [*Ib.*]

13 But now the world's o'er stocked with prudent men. [*The Medal*]

14 Dim, as the borrowed beams of moon and stars / To lonely, weary, wandering travellers / Is reason to the soul. [*Religio Laici*]

15 How can the less the greater comprehend? / Or finite reason reach Infinity? [*Ib.*]

1 From harmony, from heavenly harmony / This universal frame began. ['Song for St. Cecilia's Day']

2 And Music shall untune the sky. [Ib.]

Dubček, Alexander (1921–)

3 Socialism with a human face. [Attr.]

Dudley, Sir Henry Bate (1745–1824)

4 Wonders will never cease. [Letter to Garrick, 1776]

Duffield, George (1818–1888)

5 Stand up! stand up for Jesus, / Ye soldiers of the Cross! [Hymn]

Dukes, Ashley (1885–1959)

6 The woman who runs will never lack followers. [*The Man with a Load of Mischief*, 1]

7 Men reason to strengthen their own prejudices, and not to disturb their adversary's convictions. [Ib. 2]

8 The tender passion is much overrated by the poets. They have their living to earn, poor fellows. [Ib. 3]

Dumas, Alexandre (1803–1870)

9 *Cherchez la femme.* Look for the woman. [*Les Mohicans de Paris*; also attr. Joseph Fouché (1763–1820)]

10 *Tous pour un, un pour tous.* All for one, one for all. [*Les Trois Mousquetiers*]

Du Maurier, George (1834–1896)

11 [Of a husband] Feed the brute. [*Punch*, 1886]

Dunbar, William (c. 1465–c. 1530)

12 Our plesance here is all vain glory, / This fals world is but transitory, / The flesh is bruckle, the

Feynd is slee: / *Timor Mortis conturbat me.*
['Lament for the Makaris']

Dundy, Elaine (1927–)

1 The question actors most often get asked is how
they can bear saying the same things over and
over again night after night, but God knows the
answer to *that* is, don't we all *anyway*; might as
well get paid for it. [*The Dud Avocado*, 9]

Dyer, John (fl. 18th century)

2 And he that will his health deny, / Down among
the dead men let him lie. [Toast: 'Here's a Health
to the King']

Dylan, Bob (1941–)

3 How many roads must a man walk down /
Before you call him a man? / ... The answer,
my friend, is blowin' in the wind, / The answer
is blowin' in the wind. ['Blowin' in the Wind']

4 A Hard Rain's A-Gonna Fall. [Title of song]

5 Money doesn't talk, it swears. ['It's Alright, Ma
(I'm Only Bleeding)']

6 She takes just like a woman, yes, she does / She
makes love Just like a woman, yes, she does /
And she aches just like a woman / But she
breaks just like a little girl. ['Just Like a
Woman']

7 She knows there's no success like failure / And
that failure's no success at all. ['Love Minus
Zero/No Limit']

8 Come mothers and fathers / Throughout the
land/ And don't criticize / What you can't
understand. ['The Times They Are A-Changin'']

Eban, Abba (1915–)

9 History teaches us that men and nations behave
wisely once they have exhausted all other

alternatives. [*Observer*, 'Sayings of the Week', 1970]

Eden, Anthony (1897–1977)

1 We are not at war with Egypt. We are in armed conflict. [*Observer*, 'Sayings of the Week', 1956]

Edgeworth, Maria (1767–1849)

2 Well! some people talk of morality, and some of religion, but give me a little snug property. [*The Absentee*, 2]

3 Business was his aversion; pleasure was his business. [*The Contrast*, 2]

Edison, Thomas Alva (1847–1931)

4 Genius is one per cent inspiration and ninety-nine per cent perspiration. [Newspaper interview]

Edmeston, James (1791–1867)

5 Lead us, heavenly Father, lead us / O'er the world's tempestuous sea. [Hymn]

Edward III (1312–1377)

6 [Of the Black Prince at Crécy] Let the boy win his spurs. [Froissart's *Chronicle*]

Edward VIII later Duke of Windsor (1894–1972)

7 I have found it impossible to carry the heavy burden of responsibility and to discharge my duties as King as I would wish to do without the help and support of the woman I love. [Broadcast, 1936]

Edwards, Oliver (1711–1791)

8 I have tried too in my time to be a philosopher; but, I don't know how, cheerfulness was always breaking in. [Boswell, *Life of Johnson*]

Einstein, Albert (1879–1955)

9 If my theory of relativity is proven successful,

Germany will claim me as a German and France
will declare that I am a citizen of the world.
Should my theory prove untrue, France will say
that I am a German and Germany will declare
that I am a Jew. [Address, Sorbonne, Paris]

1 I shall never believe that God plays dice with the
world. [Attr.]

2 Common sense is the collection of prejudices
acquired by age eighteen. [Attr.]

Eliot, George (1819–1880)

3 I'm not denyin' the women are foolish: God
Almighty made 'em to match the men. [*Adam
Bede*, 53]

4 A blush is no language: only a dubious flag-signal
which may mean either of two contradictories.
[*Daniel Deronda*, 35]

5 'Abroad', that large home of ruined reputations.
[*Felix Holt*, Epilogue]

6 The happiest women, like the happiest nations,
have no history. [*The Mill on the Floss*, VI, 3]

7 I should like to know what is the proper function
of women, if it is not to make reasons for
husbands to stay at home, and still stronger
reasons for bachelors to go out. [Ib. VI, 6]

8 Debasing the moral currency. [*Theophrastus
Such*, title of essay]

Eliot, T.S. (1888–1965)

9 Because I do not hope to turn again / Because I
do not hope / Because I do not hope to turn.
['Ash Wednesday']

10 You shouldn't interrupt my interruptions: /
That's really worse than interrupting. [*The
Cocktail Party*]

11 Those to whom nothing has ever happened /

Cannot understand the unimportance of events. [*The Family Reunion*]

1 Time present and time past / Are both perhaps present in time future, / And time future contained in time past. [*Four Quartets*, 'Burnt Norton']

2 Human kind / Cannot bear very much reality. [Ib.]

3 At the still point of a turning world. [Ib.]

4 Only through time time is conquered. [Ib.]

5 In my beginning is my end. [Ib. 'East Coker']

6 Each venture / Is a new beginning, a raid on the inarticulate / With shabby equipment always deteriorating / In the general mess of imprecision of feeling. [Ib.]

7 We shall not cease from exploration / And the end of all our exploring / Will be to arrive where we started / And know the place for the first time. [Ib. 'Little Gidding']

8 In the juvescence of the year / Came Christ the tiger. ['Gerontion']

9 Thoughts of a dry brain in a dry season. [Ib.]

10 This is the way the world ends / Not with a bang but a whimper. ['The Hollow Men']

11 A cold coming we had of it, / Just the worst time of the year / For a journey. ['Journey of the Magi']

12 Let us go then, you and I, / When the evening is spread out against the sky / Like a patient etherized upon a table. ['Love Song of J. Alfred Prufrock']

13 In the room the women come and go / Talking of Michelangelo. [Ib.]

14 Have known the evenings, mornings, afternoons, / I have measured out my life with coffee spoons. [Ib.]

1 I grow old ... I grow old ... / I shall wear the bottoms of my trousers rolled ... / Do I dare to eat a peach? [Ib.]

2 However certain our expectation / The moment foreseen may be unexpected / When it arrives. [*Murder in the Cathedral*]

3 The last temptation is the greatest treason: / To do the right deed for the wrong reason. [Ib.]

4 The winter evening settles down / With smells of steaks in passageways. / Six o'clock. / The burnt-out ends of smoky days. ['Preludes']

5 That's all the facts when you come to brass tacks: / Birth, and copulation and death. [*Sweeney Agonistes*]

6 April is the cruellest month, breeding / Lilacs out of the dead land. [*The Waste Land*, 'The Burial of the Dead']

7 And I will show you something different from either / Your shadow at morning striding behind you, / Or your shadow at evening rising to meet you / I will show you fear in a handful of dust. [Ib.]

8 Unreal City, / Under the brown fog of a winter dawn, / A crowd flowed over London Bridge, so many, / I had not thought death had undone so many. [Ib.]

9 'Jug Jug' to dirty ears. [Ib. 'A Game of Chess']

10 O O O O that Shakespeherian Rag — / It's so elegant / So intelligent. [Ib.]

11 These fragments have I shored against my ruins. [Ib. 'What the Thunder Said']

12 Webster was much possessed by death / And saw the skull beneath the skin / ... Daffodil bulbs instead of balls / Stared from the sockets of the eyes! ['Whispers of Immortality']

13 In the seventeenth century a dissociation of

sensibility set in from which we have never recovered. ['The Metaphysical Poets']

1 Poetry is not a turning loose of emotion, but an escape from emotion; it is not the expression of personality, but an escape from personality. ['Tradition and the Individual Talent']

Elizabeth I (1533–1603)

2 I know I have the body of a weak and feeble woman, but I have the heart and stomach of a king, and of a king of England too; and think foul scorn that Parma or Spain, or any prince of Europe, should dare to invade the borders of my realm. [Speech on the approach of the Armada, 1588]

3 Though God hath raised me high, yet this I count the glory of my crown: that I have reigned with your loves. [The Golden Speech, 1601]

4 Must! Is must a word to be addressed to princes? [Attr.]

Elliot, Jane (1727–1805)

5 I've heard them lilting, at the ewe milking. / Lasses a' lilting, before dawn of day; / But now they are moaning, on ilka green loaning; / The flowers of the forest are a' wede awae. ['The Flowers of the Forest']

Ellis, Henry Havelock (1859–1939)

6 What we call 'Progress' is the exchange of one nuisance for another nuisance. [*Impressions and Comments*]

7 The absence of flaw in beauty is itself a flaw. [Ib.]

8 The whole religious complexion of the modern world is due to the absence from Jerusalem of a lunatic asylum. [Ib.]

Eluard, Paul (1895–1952)

1 *Adieu tristesse / Bonjour tristesse / Tu es
 inscrite dans les lignes du plafond.* Farewell
 sadness, hello sadness, you are written in the
 lines of the ceiling. ['A peine défigurée']

Emerson, Ralph Waldo (1803–1882)

2 As there is use in medicine for poison, so the
 world cannot move without rogues. [*Conduct of
 Life*, 'Power']

3 Art is a jealous mistress, and if a man have a
 genius for painting, poetry, music, architecture,
 or philosophy, he makes a bad husband and an
 ill provider. [Ib. 'Wealth']

4 Adhere to your own act, and congratulate
 yourself if you have done something strange and
 extravagant, and broken the monotony of a
 decorous age. [*Essays*]

5 There is properly no history; only biography. [Ib.
 'History']

6 To believe your own thought, to believe that
 what is true for you in your private heart is true
 for all men — that is genius. [Ib. 'Self-Reliance']

7 Whoso would be a man, must be a
 nonconformist. [Ib.]

8 A foolish consistency is the hobgoblin of little
 minds, adored by little statesmen and
 philosophers and divines. With consistency a
 great soul has simply nothing to do. [Ib.]

9 What is a weed? A plant whose virtues have not
 yet been discovered. [*Fortune of the Republic*]

10 Earth laughs in flowers. [*Hamatreya*]

11 Artists must be sacrificed to their art. Like bees,
 they must put their lives into the sting they give.
 [*Letters and Social Aims*, 'Inspiration']

12 Good manners are made up of petty sacrifices.
 [Ib. 'Social Aims']

1 Light is the first of painters. There is no object so foul that intense light will not make it beautiful. [*Nature*]

2 The bitterest tragic element in life is the belief in a brute Fate or Destiny. [*Natural History of Intellect*, 'The Tragic']

3 Every hero becomes a bore at last. [*Representative Men*]

4 Now that is the wisdom of a man, in every instance of his labour, to hitch his wagon to a star, and see his chore done by the gods themselves. [*Society and Solitude*, 'Civilization']

5 Other world! There is no other world! Here or nowhere is the whole fact. [*Uncollected Lectures*, 'Natural Religion']

Engels, Friedrich (1820–1895)

6 The state is not abolished, it withers away. [*Anti-Dühring*]

7 Freedom is the recognition of necessity. [Quoted in Mackay, *The Harvest of a Quiet Eye*]

Ennius (239–169 B.C.)

8 *Quem metuunt, oderunt.* They hate whom they fear. [*Thyestes*]

Erasmus, Gerard Didier (c. 1465–1536)

9 *Scitum est inter caecos luscum regnare posse.* It is well known, that among the blind the one-eyed man is king. [*Adagia*]

Estienne, Henri (1531–1598)

10 *Si jeunesse savoit; si vieillesse pouvoit.* If youth only knew; if age only could. [*Les Prémices*]

Euclid (fl. c. 300 B.C.)

11 [To Ptolemy I] There is no royal road to geometry. [Proclus, *Commentaria in Euclidem*]

1 *Quod erat demonstrandum.* Which was to be proved. [*Elements* (Latin version)]

2 *Pons asinorum.* The bridge of asses. [Ib.]

Euripides (c. 485–406 B.C.)

3 Those whom God wishes to destroy, he first makes mad. [Fragment]

Ewer, William Norman (1885–1976)

4 I gave my life for freedom — This I know: / For those who bade me fight had told me so. ['The Souls']

5 How odd / Of God / To choose / The Jews. ['How Odd']

Fanon, Frantz (1925–1961)

6 For the black man there is only one destiny. And it is white. [*Black Skin, White Masks*]

Farquhar, George (1678–1707)

7 My Lady Bountiful. [*The Beaux Stratagem*, I.1]

8 No woman can be a beauty without a fortune. [Ib. II.2]

9 Crimes, like virtues, are their own rewards. [*The Inconstant*, IV.2]

10 Poetry's a mere drug, Sir. [*Love and a Bottle*, III.2]

Faulkner, William (1897–1962)

11 The writer's only responsibility is to his art ... If a writer has to rob his mother, he will not hesitate; the 'Ode on a Grecian Urn' is worth any number of old ladies. [Attr.]

Fawkes, Guy (1570–1606)

12 Desperate diseases require desperate remedies. [Quoted in *Dictionary of National Biography*]

Ferdinand I, Emperor (1503–1564)

1 *Fiat justitia, et pereat mundus.* Let justice be done though the world perish. [Attr.] or *Fiat justitia ruat caelum.* Let justice be done though the heavens fall.

Fergusson, Sir James (1832–1907)

2 I have heard many arguments which influenced my opinion, but never one which influenced my vote. [Attr.]

Feuerbach, Ludwig (1804–1872)

3 *Der Mensch ist, was er isst.* Man is what he eats. [*Blätter für Literarische Unterhaltung*, 1850]

Fielding, Henry (1707–1754)

4 The devil take me, if I think anything but love to be the object of love. [*Amelia*, V]

5 I am as sober as a judge. [*Don Quixote in England*, III]

6 Oh! The roast beef of England, / And old England's roast beef. [*The Grub Street Opera*, III]

7 He in a few minutes ravished this fair creature, or at least would have ravished her, if she had not, by a timely compliance, prevented him. [*Jonathan Wild*]

8 Greatness consists in bringing all manner of mischief on mankind, and goodness in removing it from them. [Ib.]

9 It hath been thought a vast commendation of a painter to say his figures seem to breathe; but surely it is much greater and nobler applause, that they appear to think. [*Joseph Andrews*]

10 Public schools are the nurseries of all vice and immorality. [Ib. III, 5]

11 Some folks rail against other folks because other folks have what some folks would be glad of. [Ib. IV, 6]

1 Love and scandal are the best sweeteners of tea. [*Love in Several Masques*, IV]

2 An amiable weakness. [*Tom Jones*, X, 8]

3 His designs were strictly honourable, as the phrase is; that is, to rob a lady of her fortune by way of marriage. [Ib. XI, 4]

Fields, W.C. (1878–1946)

4 On the whole, I'd rather be in Philadelphia. [His own epitaph]

Fitzgerald, Edward (1809–1883)

5 Awake! for Morning in the Bowl of Night / Has flung the Stone that puts the Stars to Flight: / And Lo! the Hunter of the East has caught / The Sultan's Turret in a Noose of Light. [*Rubáiyát of Omar Khayyám*, 1st Ed.]

6 Here with a Loaf of Bread beneath the Bough, / A Flask of Wine, a Book of Verse — and Thou / Beside me singing in the Wilderness — / And Wilderness is Paradise enow! [Ib.]

7 Ah, take the Cash in hand and waive the Rest; / Oh, the brave Music of a *distant* Drum! [Ib.]

8 I sometimes think that never blows so red / The Rose as where some buried Caesar bled. [Ib.]

9 ... that inverted Bowl they call the Sky. [Ib.]

10 Who *is* the Potter, pray, and who the Pot? [Ib.]

11 I often wonder what the Vintners buy / One half so precious as the Goods they sell. [Ib.]

Fitzgerald, F. Scott (1896–1940)

12 In the real dark night of the soul it is always three o'clock in the morning. [*The Crack-Up*]

13 'What'll we do with ourselves this afternoon?' cried Daisy, 'and the day after that, and the next thirty years?' [*The Great Gatsby*]

Fitzsimmons, Robert (1862–1917)

1 The bigger they come, the harder they fall.
[Remark before boxing match, 1902]

Flecker, James Elroy (1884–1915)

2 Half to forget the wandering and the pain, / Half
to remember days that have gone by, / And
dream and dream that I am home again!
['Brumana']

3 For lust of knowing what should not be known, /
We take the Golden Road to Samarkand.
[*Hassan*]

Fletcher, Andrew, of Saltoun (1655–1716)

4 Like him that lights a candle to the sun. [Letter]

Fletcher, John (1579–1625)

5 It's impossible to ravish me / I'm so willing. [*The
Faithful Shepherdess*, III.1]

6 Of all the paths lead to a woman's love / Pity's
the straightest. [*The Knight of Malta*, I.1]

Florio, John (1553–1625)

7 England is the paradise of women, the purgatory
of men, and the hell of horses. [*Second Frutes*]

Foch, Ferdinand (1851–1929)

8 *Mon centre cède, ma droite recule, situation
excellente. J'attaque!* My centre gives way, my
right retreats; situation excellent. I shall attack.
[Attr. dispatch during Battle of Marne]

Fontaine, Jean de la (1621–1695)

9 *C'est double plaisir de tromper le trompeur.* It is
double pleasing to trick the trickster. [*Fables*, 'Le
Coq et le Renard']

10 *La raison du plus fort est toujours la meilleure.*
The argument of the stronger man is always the
best. [Ib. 'Le Loup et l'Agneau']

1 *La mort ne surprend point le sage, / Il èst toujours prêt à partir.* Death does not surprise a wise man, he is always ready to leave. [Ib. 'La Mort et le Mourant']

2 *Hélas! on voit que de tout temps, / Les Petits ont pâti des sottises des Grands.* Alas, it seems that for all time the Small have suffered from the folly of the Great. [Ib. 'Les Deux Taureaux et la Grenouille']

3 *En tout chose il faut considérer la fin.* In all matters one must consider the end. [Ib. 'Le Renard et le Bouc']

Fontenelle, Bernard (1657–1757)

4 I detest war: it ruins conversation. [Quoted in Auden, *A Certain World*]

Foote, Samuel (1720–1777)

5 He is not only dull in himself but the cause of dullness in others. [Boswell, *Life of Johnson*]

6 For as the old saying is, / When house and land are gone and spent / Then learning is most excellent. [*Taste*]

Ford, Henry (1863–1947)

7 History is bunk. [Remark, 1919]

8 [Of Model-T Fords] You can have any colour, so long as it's black. [Attr.]

Ford, John (c. 1586–1639)

9 Revenge proves its own executioner. [*The Broken Heart*, IV.1]

Forgy, Howell (1908–)

10 Praise the Lord and pass the ammunition. [Attr. remark at Pearl Harbour, 1941]

Forster, E.M. (1879–1970)

11 If I had to choose between betraying my country

and betraying my friend, I hope I should have the guts to betray my country. [*Two Cheers for Democracy*, 'What I Believe']

Fourier, François Charles Marie (1772–1837)

1 Instead of by battles and Ecumenical Councils, the rival portions of humanity will one day dispute each other's excellence in the manufacture of little cakes. [Emerson, *Lectures and Biographical Sketches*]

France, Anatole (1844–1924)

2 *Le hasard c'est peut-être le pseudonyme de Dieu, quand il ne veut pas signer.* Chance is perhaps God's pseudonym when he does not want to sign. [*Le Jardin d'Epicure*]

3 The law, in its majestic equality, forbids the rich as well as the poor to sleep under bridges, to beg in the streets, and to steal bread. [Cournos, *Modern Plutarch*]

4 It is better to understand little than to misunderstand a lot. [*Revolt of the Angels*]

Franklin, Benjamin (1706–1790)

5 Remember that time is money. [*Advice to Young Tradesman*]

6 Where there's marriage without love, there will be love without marriage. [*Poor Richard's Almanac*, 1734]

7 Necessity never made a good bargain. [Ib. 1735]

8 Three may keep a secret, if two of them are dead. [Ib.]

9 At twenty years of age, the will reigns; at thirty, the wit; and at forty, the judgement. [Ib. 1741]

10 Experience keeps a dear school, but fools will learn in no other. [Ib. 1743]

11 The golden age never was the present age. [Ib. 1750]

1 Little strokes fell great oaks. [Ib.]

2 Old boys have their playthings as well as young ones; the difference is only in price. [Ib. 1752]

3 If you would know the value of money, go and try to borrow some; for he that goes a borrowing goes a sorrowing. [Ib. 1754]

4 He that lives upon hope will die fasting. [Ib. 1758, Preface]

5 A little neglect may breed mischief . . . for want of a nail, the shoe was lost; for want of a shoe, the horse was lost; and for want of a horse the rider was lost. [Ib.]

6 Early to bed and early to rise, / Makes a man healthy, wealthy and wise. [Ib. 1758]

7 Creditors have better memories than debtors. [Ib.]

8 No nation was ever ruined by trade. [*Thoughts on Commercial Subjects*]

9 Here Skugg lies snug / As a bug in a rug. [Letter to Miss Shipley, 1772]

10 In this world nothing can be said to be certain, except death and taxes. [Letter, 1789]

11 We must all hang together, or, most assuredly, we shall all hang separately. [Remark, Independence Day, 1776]

12 Man is a tool-making animal. [Boswell, *Life of Johnson*]

13 There are more old drunkards than old doctors. [Attr.]

Frederick the Great (1712–1786)

14 My people and I have come to an agreement which satisfies us both. They are to say what they please, and I am to do what I please. [Attr.]

Frost, Robert (1875–1963)

1 Earth's the right place for love: / I don't know
where it's likely to go better. ['Birches']

2 Home is the place where, when you have to go
there, / They have to take you in. ['The Death of
the Hired Man']

3 I would have written of me on my stone: / I had
a lover's quarrel with the world. ['Epitaph']

4 Some say the world will end in fire, / Some say
in ice. / From what I've tasted of desire / I hold
with those who favour fire. ['Fire and Ice']

5 I never dared be radical when young / For fear it
would make me conservative when old.
['Precaution']

6 We dance round in a ring and suppose, / But the
Secret sits in the middle and knows. ['The Secret
Sits']

7 The woods are lovely, dark, and deep, / But I
have promises to keep, / And miles to go before
I sleep, / And miles to go before I sleep.
['Stopping by Woods on a Snowy Evening']

8 A poem may be worked over once it is in being,
but may not be worried into being. ['The Figure a
Poem Makes']

9 Poetry is a way of taking life by the throat.
[*Vogue*, 1963]

Fry, Christopher (1907–   )

10 I've begun to believe that the reasonable / Is an
invention of man, altogether in opposition / To
the facts of creation. [*The Firstborn*, III]

11 What, after all, / Is a halo? It's only one more
thing to keep clean. [*The Lady's Not For Burning*,
I]

12 The Great Bear is looking so geometrical / One
would think that something or other could be
proved. [Ib. III]

1 Where in this small-talking world can I find / A longitude with no platitude? [Ib.]

2 I know an undesirable character / When I see one; I've been one myself for years. [*Venus Observed*, II]

Fuller, Thomas (1608–1661)

3 He was a very valiant man who first ventured on eating of oysters. [*History of the Worthies of England*]

4 Light (God's eldest daughter) is a principal beauty in building. [*Holy and Profane State*, 'Of Building']

5 Anger is one of the sinews of the soul; he that wants it hath a maimed mind. [Ib. 'Of Anger']

6 Learning hath gained most by those books by which the printers have lost. [Ib. 'Of Books']

Fyleman, Rose (1877–1957)

7 There are fairies at the bottom of our garden. ['Fairies']

Gable, Clark (1901–1960)

8 Frankly, my dear, I don't give a damn. [*Gone With the Wind*]

Gabor, Zsa-Zsa (?1921–)

9 Never despise what it says in the women's magazines: it may not be subtle but neither are men. [*Observer*, 'Sayings of the Week', 1976]

Galbraith, J. K. (1908–)

10 The Affluent Society [Title of book]

Galileo Galilei (1564–1642)

11 *Eppur si muove.* But it does move. [Attr. (probably apocryphal)]

Gandhi, Mahatma (1869–1948)

12 [When asked what he thought of Western

civilization] I think it would be an excellent idea. [Attr.]

Garbo, Greta (1905–   )

1 I never said, 'I want to be alone.' I only said, 'I want to be *let* alone.' There is all the difference. [Quoted in Colombo, *Wit and Wisdom of the Moviemakers*]

Gauguin, Paul (1848–1903)

2 Many excellent cooks are spoiled by going into the arts. [Cournos, *Modern Plutarch*]

3 Art is either a plagiarist or a revolutionist. [Huneker, *Pathos of Distance*]

Gautier, Théophile (1811–1872)

4 *Plutôt la barbarie que l'ennui.* Sooner barbarity than boredom. [Attr.]

Gavarni (1801–1866)

5 *Les enfants terribles. Lit.* the terrible children [i.e. people given to unconventional conduct or indiscreet remarks][Title of a series of prints]

Gay, John (1685–1732)

6 I rage, I melt, I burn, / The feeble God has stabb'd me to the heart. [*Acis and Galatea*, II]

7 O ruddier than the cherry, / O sweeter than the berry, / O nymph more bright / Than moonshine night, / Like kidlings blithe and merry. [Ib.]

8 Do you think your mother and I should have liv'd comfortably so long together, if ever we had been married? [*The Beggar's Opera*, I]

9 If with me you'd fondly stray, / Over the hills and far away. [Ib.]

10 Whence is thy learning? Hath thy toil / O'er books consum'd the midnight oil? [*Fables*, Introduction]

1 Where yet was ever found a mother, / Who'd give her booby for another? [Ib. 3]

2 Life is a jest; and all things show it. / I thought so once; but now I know it. ['My Own Epitaph']

George II (1683–1760)

3 [Of General Wolfe] Mad, is he? Then I hope he will *bite* some of my other generals. [Attr.]

George, Henry (1839–1897)

4 The man who gives me employment, which I must have or suffer, that man is my master, let me call him what I will. [*Social Problems*]

Gibbon, Edward (1737–1794)

5 [Of London] Crowds without company, dissipation without pleasure. [*Autobiography*]

6 It was at Rome, on the 15th October, 1764, as I sat musing amidst the ruins of the Capitol, while the barefooted friars were singing vespers in the Temple of Jupiter, that the idea of writing the decline and fall of the city first started to my mind. [Ib.]

7 My English text is chaste, and all licentious passages are left in the decent obscurity of a learned language. [Ib.

8 The various modes of worship, which prevailed in the Roman world, were all considered by the people as equally true; by the philosopher as equally false; and by the magistrate as equally useful. [*Decline and Fall of the Roman Empire*, 2]

9 History . . . is, indeed, little more than the register of the crimes, follies, and misfortunes of mankind. [Ib. 3]

10 Corruption, the most infallible symptom of constitutional liberty. [Ib. 21]

Gibbons, Stella (1902–)

1 Something nasty in the woodshed. [*Cold Comfort Farm, passim*]

Gide, André (1869–1951)

2 *L'acte gratuit.* The gratuitous action. [*Les Caves du Vatican, passim*]

Gilbert, William Schwenck (1836–1911)

3 The padre said, 'Whatever have you been and gone and done?' ['Gentle Alice Brown']

4 [Of the Duke of Plaza Toro] He led his regiment from behind − / He found it less exciting. [*The Gondoliers*, I]

5 Of that there is no manner of doubt − / No probable, possible shadow of doubt − / No possible doubt whatever. [Ib.]

6 When everyone is somebodee / Then no one's anybody! [Ib. II]

7 'And I'm never, never sick at sea!' / 'What, never? / 'No, never!' / 'What, *never*?' / 'Hardly ever!' [*H.M.S. Pinafore*, I]

8 I always voted at my party's call, / And I never thought of thinking for myself at all. [Ib.]

9 But in spite of all temptations / To belong to other nations, / He remains an Englishman. [Ib. II]

10 Bow, bow, ye lower middle classes! / Bow, bow, ye tradesmen, bow, ye masses. [*Iolanthe*, I]

11 I often think it's comical / How Nature always does contrive / That every boy and every gal, / That's born into this the world alive, / Is either a little Liberal, / Or else a little Conservative! [Ib.]

12 The House of Peers, throughout the war, / Did nothing in particular, / And did it very well. [Ib. II]

13 A wandering minstrel I − / A thing of shreds

and patches, / Of ballads, songs and snatches, / And dreamy lullaby! [*The Mikado*, I]

1 I can trace my ancestry back to a protoplasmal primordial atomic globule. Consequently, my family pride is something inconceivable. [Ib.]

2 I've got a little list / Of society offenders who might well be underground / And who never would be missed. [Ib.]

3 Three little maids from school are we, / Pert as a schoolgirl well can be. [Ib.]

4 Awaiting the sensation of a short, sharp shock, / From a cheap and chippy chopper on a big black block. [Ib.]

5 My object all sublime / I shall achieve in time — / To let the punishment fit the crime — / The punishment fit the crime. [Ib. II]

6 Merely corroborative detail, intended to give artistic verisimilitude to an otherwise bald and unconvincing narrative. [Ib.]

7 The flowers that bloom in the spring, / Tra la, have nothing to do with the case. [Ib.]

8 On a tree by a river a little tom-tit / Sang 'Willow, titwillow, titwillow!' / And I said to him, 'Dicky-bird, why do you sit? / Singing Willow, titwillow, titwillow?' [Ib.]

9 'Is it weakness of intellect, birdie?' I cried, / 'Or a rather tough worm in your little inside?' [Ib.]

10 But the peripatetics / Of long-haired aesthetics / Are very much more to their taste. [*Patience*, I]

11 Though the Philistines may jostle, you will rank as an apostle in the high aesthetic band, / If you walk down Piccadilly with a poppy or a lily in your medieval hand. [Ib.]

12 In short, in matters vegetable, animal, and mineral, / I am the very model of a modern Major-General. [*The Pirates of Penzance*, I]

1 A policeman's lot is not a happy one. [Ib. II]

2 She may very well pass for forty-three / In the dusk with a light behind her. [*Trial by Jury*]

3 It's a song of a merryman, moping mum, / Whose soul was sad, and whose glance was glum, / Who, sipped no sup, and who craved no crumb, / As he sighed for the love of a ladye. [*Yeoman of the Guard*, I]

Ginsberg, Alan (1926–)

4 I saw the best minds of my generation destroyed by madness, starving hysterical naked. [*Howl*, first line]

Gladstone, William Ewart (1809–1898)

5 [On Naples] This is the negation of God erected into a system of government. [*Letter to Lord Aberdeen*, 1851]

6 All the world over, I will back the masses against the classes. [Speech, 1886]

Godard, Jean-Luc (1930–)

7 Cinema is truth twenty-four times a second. [*Le Petit Soldat*]

8 Of course a film should have a beginning, a middle and an end. But not necessarily in that order. [Quoted in Halliwell, *Filmgoers' Book of Quotes*]

Goering, Hermann (1893–1946)

9 Guns will make us powerful; butter will only make us fat. [Broadcast, 1936]

10 When I hear anyone talk of Culture, I reach for my revolver. [Attr. Probably derived from Hanns Johst, *Schlageter* (1934)]

Goethe, Johann Wolfgang von (1749–1832)

11 *Wer reitet so spät durch Nacht und Wind? / Es ist der Vater mit seinem Kind.* Who rides so late

through the night and storm? It is the father with his child. ['Erlkönig']

1 *Es irrt der Mensch, so lang er strebt.* While man aspires, he errs. [*Faust*, I]

2 *Ich bin der Geist der stets verneint.* I am the spirit that forever denies. [Ib.]

3 *Grau, teuer Freund, ist alle Theorie / Und grün des Lebens goldner Baum.* All theory, dear friend, is grey; but the precious tree of life is green. [Ib.]

4 *Die Tat ist alles, nicht der Ruhm.* The act is all, the reputation nothing. [Ib. II]

5 *Sah ein Knab' ein Röslein stehn, / Röslein auf der Heiden.* In the woods a boy one day, saw a wild rose growing. ['Heidenröslein']

6 *In der Kunst ist das Beste gut genug.* In art the best is good enough. [*Italienische Reise*]

7 *Es bildet ein Talent sich in der Stille, / Sich ein Charakter in dem Strom der Welt.* Talent grows in peace, character in the current of affairs. [*Tasso*, I]

8 *Du kannst, denn du sollst.* You can, for you must. [*Xenien*]

9 Classicism is health, romanticism is sickness. [*Conversations with Eckermann*]

10 Architecture is frozen music. [Ib.]

11 *Mehr Licht!* More light! [Last words]

Goldsmith, Oliver (1728–1774)

12 On whatever side we regard the history of Europe, we shall perceive it to be a tissue of crimes, follies and misfortunes. [*The Citizen of the World*]

13 Ill fares the land, to hast'ning ills a prey, / Where wealth accumulates, and men decay. [*The Deserted Village*]

14 But a bold peasantry, their country's pride, /

When once destroyed, can never be supplied. [Ib.]

1 Trade's unfeeling train / Usurp the land and dispossess the swain. [Ib.]

2 Ye friends to truth, ye statesmen, who survey / The rich man's joys increase, the poor's decay, / 'Tis yours to judge, how wide the limits stand / Between a splendid and a happy land. [Ib.]

3 The man recover'd of the bite, / The dog it was that died. ['Elegy on the Death of a Mad Dog']

4 As for disappointing them I should not so much mind; but I can't abide to disappoint myself. [*She Stoops to Conquer*, I]

5 This is Liberty-Hall, gentlemen. [Ib. II]

6 Such is the patriot's boast, where'er we roam, / His first, best country ever is, at home. [*The Traveller*]

7 How small, of all that human hearts endure, / That part which laws or kings can cause or cure. [Ib.]

8 And honour sinks where commerce long prevails. [Ib.]

9 I chose my wife, as she did her wedding gown, not for a fine glossy surface, but such qualities as would wear well. [*The Vicar of Wakefield*, 1]

10 As ten millions of circles can never make a square, so the united voice of myriads cannot lend the smallest foundation to falsehood. [Ib. 26]

11 There is no arguing with Johnson; for if his pistol misses fire, he knocks you down with the butt end of it. [Boswell, *Life of Johnson*]

Goldwyn, Samuel (1884–1974)

12 You can include me out. [Quoted in Colombo, *Wit and Wisdom of the Moviemakers*]

13 I'll give you a definite maybe. [Ib.]

1 A verbal contract isn't worth the paper it's written on. [Ib.]

2 Why should people go out and pay money to see bad films when they can stay at home and see bad television for nothing? [*Observer*, 'Sayings of the Week', 1956]

3 Anyone who goes to see a psychiatrist ought to have his head examined. [Attr.]

4 Messages are for Western Union. [Quoted in Halliwell, *Filmgoers' Book of Quotes*]

Goschen, George, Lord (1831–1907)

5 We have stood alone in that which is called isolation — our splendid isolation, as one of our colonial friends was good enough to call it. [Speech, 1896]

Grade, Lord (1906–)

6 All my shows are great. Some of them are bad. But they are all great. [*Observer*, 'Sayings of the Week', 1975]

Grafton, Richard (d. 1572?)

7 Thirty days hath November, / April, June, and September, / February hath twenty-eight alone, / And all the rest have thirty-one. [*Abridgement of the Chronicles of England*, Introduction]

Graham, Billy (1918–)

8 May the Lord bless you real good. [Benediction]

Grahame, Kenneth (1859–1932)

9 Believe me, my young friend, there is *nothing* — absolutely nothing — half so much worth doing as simply messing about in boats. [*The Wind in the Willows*, 1]

Grant, Ulysses S. (1822–1885)

10 I know no method to secure the repeal of bad or

obnoxious laws so effective as their stringent execution. [Inaugural Address, 1869]

Grass, Günter (1927–)

1 The trend is towards the bourgeois-smug. [*The Tin Drum*]

Graves, John Woodcock (1795–1886)

2 D'ye ken John Peel with his coat so gay? / D'ye ken John Peel at the break of day? / D'ye ken John Peel when he's far away / With his hounds and his horn in the morning? ['John Peel']

Gray, Thomas (1716–1771)

3 The curfew tolls the knell of parting day, / The lowing herd wind slowly o'er the lea, / The ploughman homeward plods his weary way, / And leaves the world to darkness and to me. ['Elegy Written in a Country Churchyard']

4 Some village-Hampden, that with dauntless breast / The little tyrant of his fields withstood; / Some mute inglorious Milton here may rest, / Some Cromwell guiltless of his country's blood. [Ib.]

5 The paths of glory lead but to the grave. [Ib.]

6 Far from the madding crowd's ignoble strife. [Ib.]

7 Where ignorance is bliss, / 'Tis folly to be wise.' ['Ode on a Distant Prospect of Eton College']

Greeley, Horace (1811–1872)

8 Go West, young man, and grow up with the country. [*Hints toward Reform*]

Gregory I (540–604)

9 *Responsum est, quod Angli vocarentur. At ille: 'Bene,' inquit, 'nam et angelicam habent faciem, et tales angelorum in caelis decet esse coheredes.'* They replied that they were called Angles. But he said, 'It is good; for they have the

countenance of angels, and such should be the co-heirs of the angels in heaven.' [Bede, *Historia Ecclesiastica*]

Greville, Fulke, First Baron Brooke (1554–1628)

1 Fire and people do in this agree, / They both good servants, both ill masters be. ['Inquisition upon Fame']

Grey, Edward, Viscount of Falloden (1862–1933)

2 The lamps are going out all over Europe; we shall not see them lit again in our lifetime. [August, 1914]

Griffiths, Trevor (1935–)

3 Comedy is medicine. [*Comedians*, I]

Guedalla, Philip (1889–1944)

4 The work of Henry James has always seemed divisible by a simple dynastic arrangement into three reigns: James I, James II, and the Old Pretender. [*Collected Essays*, IV]

5 People who jump to conclusions rarely alight on them. [*Observer*, 'Sayings of the Week', 1924]

Guinan, Texas (1884–1933)

6 Fifty million Frenchmen can't be wrong. [Attr.]

Gunn, Thom (1929–)

7 You know I know you know I know you know. 'Carnal Knowledge'

Gurney, Dorothy (1858–1932)

8 One is nearer God's Heart in a garden / Than anywhere else on earth. ['God's Garden']

Gwyn, Nell (c. 1650–1687)

9 Good people, let me pass. I am the *Protestant* whore. [Said during the Popish Terror, 1681]

Hadrian (A.D. 76–138)

1 *Animula vagula blandula, / Hospes comesque
corporis, / Quae nunc abibis in loca / Pallidula
rigida nudula, / Nec ut soles dabis iocos!* Ah
fleeting Spirit! wand'ring Fire, / That long hast
warm'd my tender Breast, / Must thou no more
this Frame inspire? / No more a pleasing,
cheerful Guest? / Whither, ah whither art thou
flying! / To what dark, undiscover'd Shore? /
Thou seem'st all trembling, shivr'ing, dying, /
And Wit and Humour are no more! ['Ad Animam
Suam'; trans. Pope]

Hale, Sir Matthew (1609–1676)

2 Christianity is part of the Common Law of
England. [Blackstone, *Commentaries*]

Halifax, George Savile, Marquis of (1633–1695)

3 Men are not hanged for stealing horses, but that
horses may not be stolen. [*Political ... Thoughts
and Reflections*]

4 When the people contend for their Liberty, they
seldom get anything by their Victory but new
masters. [Ib.]

5 Halifax said he had known many kicked down
stairs, but never knew any kicked up stairs
before. [Burnet, *History of My Own Times*]

Hancock, John (1737–1793)

6 There, I guess King George will be able to read
that. [Remark on signing American Declaration
of Independence]

Haraucourt, Edmond (1856–1941)

7 *Partir c'est mourir un peu.* To depart is to die a
little. [*Seul*]

Hardy, Oliver (1892–1957)

1 Here's another fine mess you've gotten me into.
[Quoted in Colombo, *Wit and Wisdom of the Moviemakers*]

Hardy, Thomas (1840–1928)

2 Yet saw he something in the lives / Of those who ceased to live / That rounded them with majesty, / Which living failed to give. ['The Casterbridge Captains']

3 Till the Spinner of the Years / Said 'Now!' And each one hears, / And consummation comes, and jars two hemispheres. ['The Convergence of the Twain' (on the sinking of the *Titanic*)]

4 When shall the softer, saner politics, / Whereof we dream, have play in each proud land? ['Departures']

5 Yet portion of that unknown plain / Will Hodge for ever be. ['Drummer Hodge']

6 A local cult called Christianity. [*The Dynasts*, I]

7 My argument is that War makes rattling good history; but Peace is poor reading. [Ib. II]

8 Well, World, you have kept faith with me, / Kept faith with me; / Upon the whole you have proved to be / Much as you said you were. ['He Never Expected Much']

9 Yonder a maid and her wight / Come whispering by: / War's annals will cloud into night / Ere their story die. ['In Time of "The Breaking of Nations" ']

10 If someone said on Christmas Eve, / 'Come; see the oxen kneel, / In the lonely barton by yonder coomb / Our childhood used to know', / I should go with him in the gloom, / Hoping it might be so. ['The Oxen']

11 'Justice' was done, and the President of the

Immortals (in Aeschylean phrase) had ended his sport with Tess. [*Tess of the D'Urbervilles*, 59]

1 Good, but not religious good. [*Under the Greenwood Tree*, 2]

2 That man's silence is wonderful to listen to. [Ib. 14]

Hare, Maurice Evan (1886-1967)

3 There once was a man who said, 'Damn! / It is borne in upon me I am / An engine that moves / In predestinate grooves, / I'm not even a bus, I'm a tram.' [Limerick]

Harington, Sir John (1561-1612)

4 Treason doth never prosper, what's the reason? / For if it prosper, none dare call it treason. [*Epigrams*, IV]

Harlow, Jean (1911-1937)

5 Excuse me while I slip into something more comfortable. [*Hell's Angels*, quoted in Colombo, *Wit and Wisdom of the Moviemakers*]

Harris, Joel Chandler (1848-1908)

6 De wimmin, dey does de talkin' en de flyin', en de mens, dey does de walkin' en de pryin', en betwixt en betweenst um, dey ain't much dat don't come out. [*Brother Rabbit and His Famous Foot*]

7 Bred en bawn in a brier-patch! [*Legends of the Old Plantation*]

8 Tar-baby ain't sayin' nuthin', en Brer Fox, he lay low. [Ib.]

9 Licker talks mighty loud w'en it git loose from de jug. [*Uncle Remus*, Plantation Proverbs]

10 Hongry rooster don't cackle w'en he fine a wum. [Ib.]

11 Lazy fokes' stummucks don't git tired. [Ib.]

Hartley, L.P. (1895–1972)

1 The past is a foreign country: they do things differently there. [*The Go-Between*, first sentence]

Harvey, William (1578–1657)

2 *Ex ovo omnia.* Everything from an egg. [*De Generatione Animalium*]

Haskins, Minnie Louise (1875–1957)

3 I said to a man who stood at the gate of the year: 'Give me a light that I may tread safely into the unknown.' And he replied: 'Go out into the darkness and put your hand into the hand of God. That shall be to you better than a light, and safer than a known way.' [*God Knows*]

Hawker, Robert Stephen (1803–1875)

4 And have they fixed the where and when? / And shall Trelawney die? / Here's twenty thousand Cornishmen / Will know the reason why! ['Song of the Western Men']

Hay, Ian (1876–1952)

5 Funny-peculiar or funny-ha-ha? [*The Housemaster*, III]

Hayes, J. Milton (fl. 1911)

6 There's a one-eyed yellow idol to the north of Khatmandu, / There's a little marble cross below the town, / There's a broken-hearted woman tends the grave of Mad Carew, / And the Yellow God forever gazes down. ['The Green Eye of the Yellow God']

Hazlitt, William (1778–1830)

7 You will hear more good things on the outside of a stagecoach from London to Oxford than if you were to pass a twelvemonth with the undergraduates, or heads of colleges, of that famous city. ['The Ignorance of the Learned']

1 Sir Walter Scott (when all's said and done) is an inspired butler. ['Mrs. Siddons']

2 There is nothing good to be had in the country, or if there is, they will not let you have it. ['Observations on Mr. Wordsworth's *Excursion*']

3 Without the aid of prejudice and custom, I should not be able to find my way across the room. ['On Prejudice']

4 The art of pleasing consists in being pleased. [*Round Table*, 'On Manner']

5 [Scott] would make a bad hand of a description of the *Millennium*, unless he could lay the scene in Scotland five hundred years ago, and then he would want facts and worm-eaten parchments to support his drooping style. [*The Spirit of the Age*]

6 Violent antipathies are always suspicious, and betray a secret affinity. [*Table Talk*]

7 The love of liberty is the love of others; the love of power is the love of ourselves. ['The Times Newspaper']

Hearst, William Randolph (1863–1951)

8 You furnish the pictures and I'll furnish the war. [Attr. instruction to news photographer reporting from peaceful foreign country]

Heath, Edward (1916–   )

9 This would, at a stroke, reduce the rise of prices. [Press release of campaign speech, 1970]

10 The unacceptable face of capitalism. [Speech, 1973]

Heber, Reginald (1783–1826)

11 From Greenland's icy mountains, / From India's coral strand, / Where Afric's sunny fountains / Roll down their golden sand. / From many an ancient river, / From many a palmy plain, /

They call us to deliver / Their land from error's
chain. [Hymn]

1 Though every prospect pleases, / And only man
is vile. [Ib.]

Hegel, Georg Wilhelm (1770–1831)

2 *Was vernünftig ist, das ist wirklich: und was
wirklich ist, das ist vernünftig.* What is
reasonable is true, and what is true is reasonable.
[*Rechtsphilosophie*]

Heine, Heinrich (1797–1856)

3 *Ich weiss nicht, was soll es bedeuten / Das ich
so traurig bin, / Ein Märchen aus alten Zeiten, /
Dass kommt mir nicht aus dem Sinn.* I do not
know why I am so sad; there is an old fairy tale
that I cannot get out of my mind. ['Die Lorelei']

4 Wherever books are burned, men too are
eventually burned. [Attr.]

5 *Dieu me pardonnera. C'est son métier.* God will
pardon me. It is his profession. [Last words]

Heller, Joseph (1923–)

6 There was only one catch and that was Catch-22,
which specified that a concern for one's own
safety in the face of dangers that were real and
immediate was the process of a rational mind:
[*Catch-22*, 5]

Helpman, Robert (1909–   )

7 The trouble with nude dancing is that not
everything stops when the music stops.
[Comment on *Oh! Calcutta!*]

Helps, Sir Arthur (1813–1875)

8 Reading is sometimes an ingenious device for
avoiding thought. [*Friends in Council*]

Hemans, Felicia Dorothea (1793–1835)

9 The boy stood on the burning deck / Whence all

but he had fled; / The flame that lit the battle's
wreck / Shone round him o'er the dead.
['Casabianca']

1 The stately homes of England, / How beautiful
they stand! ['The Homes of England']

Hemingway, Ernest (1898–1961)

2 [Courage] Grace under pressure. [Attr.]

Henley, William Ernest (1849–1903)

3 In the fell clutch of circumstance, / I have not
winced nor cried aloud: / Under the bludgeonings
of chance / My head is bloody, but unbowed.
[*Echoes*, 'Invictus']

4 I am the master of my fate: / I am the captain of
my soul. [Ib.]

5 Madam Life's a piece in bloom / Death goes
dogging everywhere; / She's the tenant of the
room, / He's the ruffian on the stair. [Ib. 'To
W.R.']

Henri IV of France (1553–1610)

6 [Of James VI and I] The wisest fool in
Christendom. [Attr. Also attr. to Sully]

7 *Paris vaut bien une messe.* Paris is well worth a
mass. [Attr.]

8 In my kingdom I want there to be no peasant so
poor that he cannot have a chicken in his pot
every Sunday. [Attr.]

Henry II (1133–1189)

9 [Of Becket] Will no one free me of this turbulent
priest? [Attr.]

Henry VIII (1491–1547)

10 I perceive that that man [Cranmer] hath the right
sow by the ear. [Letter, 1529]

Henry, Matthew (1662–1714)

1 All this and heaven too. [Attr.]

Henry, O. (1862–1910)

2 Turn up the lights, I don't want to go home in the dark. [Last words]

Henry, Patrick (1736–1799)

3 Caesar had his Brutus — Charles the First, his Cromwell and George the Third — ['Treason,' cried the Speaker] ... *may profit by their example. If this be treason, make the most of it.* [Speech in the Virginia Convention, 1765]

4 Give me liberty, or give me death! [Speech, 1775]

Henryson, Robert (c. 1425–1506)

5 Nocht is your fairness bot ane fading flour, /
Nocht is your famous laud and high honour /
Bot wind inflate in other mennis eiris; /
Your rosing reid to rotting sall retour. [*The Testament of Cresseid*]

Henshaw, Bishop Joseph (1603–1679)

6 One doth but breakfast here, another dines, he that liveth longest doth but sup; we must all go to bed in another world. [*Horae Succisivae*]

Hepburn, Katharine (1909–)

7 I don't care what is written about me as long as it isn't true. [Quoted in Cooper and Hartman, *Violets and Vinegar*]

Heraclitus (fl. 6th century B.C.)

8 All things flow; nothing abides. [Quoted by Plato]

9 It is impossible to step twice into the same river. [Ib.]

Herbert, Sir A.P. (1890–1971)

10 A highbrow is the kind of person who looks at a sausage and thinks of Picasso. ['The Highbrow']

1 Let's find out what everyone is doing, / And then stop everyone from doing it. ['Let's Stop Somebody']

2 Once people start on all this Art / Goodbye, moralitee! ['Lines for a Worthy Person']

3 People must not do things for fun. We are not here for fun. There is no reference to fun in any Act of Parliament. [Ib.]

Herbert, George (1593–1633)

4 Let all the world in ev'ry corner sing / My God and King. [*The Temple*, 'Antiphon']

5 Wit's an unruly engine, wildly striking / Sometimes a friend, sometimes the engineer. [Ib. 'The Church Porch']

6 The stormy working soul spits lies and froth. [Ib.]

7 I struck the board, and cry'd, 'No more; / I will abroad.' / What, shall I ever sigh and pine? / My lines and life are free; free as the road, / Loose as the wind. [Ib. 'The Collar']

8 Death is still working like a mole, / And digs my grave at each remove. [Ib. 'Grace']

9 Who says that fictions only and false hair / Become a verse? Is there in truth no beauty? / Is all good structure in a winding stair? [Ib. 'Jordan']

10 Love bade me welcome; yet my soul drew back, / Guilty of dust and sin. [Ib. 'Love']

11 If goodness lead him not, yet weariness / May toss him to My breast. [Ib. 'The Pulley']

12 Was ever grief like mine? [Ib. 'The Sacrifice']

13 Only a sweet and virtuous soul, / Like season'd timber, never gives; / But though the whole world turn to coal, / Then chiefly lives. [Ib. 'Virtue']

1 The God of Love my Shepherd is, / And He that doth me feed, / While He is mine, and I am His, / What can I want or need? [Ib. '23rd Psalm']

2 A cheerful look makes a dish a feast. [*Jacula Prudentum*]

3 Music helps not the toothache. [Ib.]

Herford, Oliver (1863–1935)

4 The bubble winked at me and said, / 'You'll miss me brother, when you're dead.' [Toast: 'The Bubble Winked']

Herrick, Robert (1591–1674)

5 Cherry-ripe, ripe, ripe I cry, / Full and fair ones; come and buy. [*Hesperides*, 'Cherry-Ripe']

6 A sweet disorder in the dress / Kindles in clothes a wantonness. [Ib. 'Delight in Disorder']

7 Fain would I kiss my Julia's dainty leg, / Which is as white and hairless as an egg. [Ib. 'On Julia's Legs']

8 Sweet, be not proud of those two eyes, / Which star-like sparkle in their skies. [Ib. 'To Dianeme']

9 Gather ye rose-buds while ye may, / Old Time is still a-flying: / And this same flower that smiles to-day, / To-morrow will be dying. [Ib. 'To the Virgins, to Make Much of Time']

10 Whenas in silks my Julia goes, / Then, then (methinks) how sweetly flows / The liquefaction of her clothes. [Ib. 'Upon Julia's Clothes']

Hervey, Lord (1696–1743)

11 Whoever would lie usefully should lie seldom. [*Memoirs of the Reign of George II*]

Heywood, John (c. 1497–c. 1580)

12 All a green willow, willow; / All a green willow is my garland. ['The Green Willow']

Hickson, William Edward (1803–1870)

1 If at first you don't succeed, / Try, try, again. ['Try and Try Again']

Hill, Aaron (1685–1750)

2 Tender-hearted stroke a nettle, / And it stings you for your pains; / Grasp it like a man of mettle, / And it soft as silk remains. ['Verses Written on a Window in Scotland']

Hill, Joe (1879–1914)

3 You'll get pie in the sky when you die. ['The Preacher and the Slave']

Hill, Rowland (1744–1833)

4 He did not see any reason why the devil should have all the good tunes. [E.W. Broome, *Rev. Rowland Hill*]

Hindenburg, Paul von (1847–1934)

5 As an English General has very truly said, 'The German army was stabbed in the back.' [Statement in Reichstag, 1919]

Hippocrates (c. 460–357 B.C.)

6 [Of medicine] The life so short, the art so long to learn, opportunity fleeting, experience treacherous, judgement difficult. [*Aphorisms*, 1] The opening phrases are often quoted in Latin as *Ars longa, vita brevis*.

7 For extreme illnesses extreme remedies are most fitting. [Ib. 6]

Hitchcock, Alfred (1899–1980)

8 Drama is life with the dull bits cut out. [*Observer*, 'Sayings of the Week', 1960]

9 Television has brought murder back into the home — where it belongs. [Quoted in Colombo, *Wit and Wisdom of the Moviemakers*]

Hitler, Adolf (1889–1945)

1 The great mass of the people ... will more easily fall victim to a big lie than to a small one. [*Mein Kampf*]

2 It is the last territorial claim which I have to make in Europe [Sudetenland]. [Speech, 1938]

Hobbes, Thomas (1588–1679)

3 Words are wise men's counters, they do but reckon with them: but they are the money of fools. [*Leviathan*, I, 4]

4 During the time men live without a common power to keep them all in awe, they are in that condition which is called war; and such a war as is of every man against every man. [Ib. I, 13]

5 No arts; no letters; no society; and which is worst of all, continual fear and danger of violent death; and the life of man, solitary, poor, nasty, brutish, and short. [Ib.]

6 Covenants without the sword are but words and of no strength to secure a man at all. [Ib.]

7 The praise of ancient authors proceeds not from the reverence of the dead, but from the competition and mutual envy of the living. [Ib.]

8 I am about to take my last voyage, a great leap in the dark. [Last words]

Hoffmann, Heinrich (1809–1874)

9 Look at little Johnny there, / Little Johnny Head-In-Air! [*Struwwelpeter*, 'Johnny Head-in-Air']

10 'Ah!' said Mamma. 'I knew he'd come / To naughty little Suck-a-Thumb.' [Ib. 'The Little Suck-a-Thumb']

Hogg, James (1770–1835)

11 Where the pools are bright and deep, / Where the grey trout lies asleep, / Up the river and o'er

the lea / That's the way for Billy and me. ['A Boy's Song']

1 And Charlie is my darling, / The young Chevalier. [*Jacobite Relics of Scotland*; *see* Burns]

2 Better lo'ed ye canna be, / Will ye no come back again? [Ib.]

Holmes, Rev. John H. (1879–1964)

3 The universe is not hostile, nor yet is it friendly. It is indifferent. [*A Sensible Man's View of Religion*]

Holmes, Oliver Wendell (1809–1894)

4 Man has his will, — but woman has her way. [*The Autocrat of the Breakfast Table*]

5 Lean, hungry, savage anti-everythings. ['A Modest Request']

6 To be seventy years young is sometimes far more cheerful and hopeful than to be forty years old. ['On the Seventieth Birthday of Julia Ward Howe']

Homer (fl. c. 8th century B.C.)

7 Achilles' wrath, to Greece the direful spring / Of woes unnumber'd, heavenly goddess, sing. [*Iliad*, I, opening lines, in Pope's translation]

8 Rosy-fingered dawn. [Ib. and *passim*]

9 Winged words. [Ib. and *passim*]

10 The wine-dark sea. [Ib. and *passim*]

11 As the generation of leaves, so is that of men. [Ib. VI]

Hood, Thomas (1799–1845)

12 Ben Battle was a soldier bold, / And used to war's alarms: / But a cannon-ball took off his legs, / So he laid down his arms! ['Faithless Nellie Gray']

1 They went and told the sexton, and / The sexton toll'd the bell. ['Faithless Sally Brown']

2 I remember, I remember, / The house where I was born, / The little window where the sun / Came peeping in at morn. ['I Remember']

3 When Eve upon the first of Men / The apple press'd with specious cant, / Oh! what a thousand pities then / That Adam was not Adamant! ['A Reflection']

4 Holland . . . lies so low they're only saved by being dammed. [*Up the Rhine*]

Hooker, Richard (c. 1554–1600)

5 He that goeth about to persuade a multitude, that they are not so well governed as they ought to be, shall never want attentive and favourable hearers. [*Ecclesiastical Polity*]

6 Change is not made without inconvenience, even from worse to better. [Quoted by Dr. Johnson, Preface to his *Dictionary*]

Hoover, Herbert Clark (1874–1964)

7 Rugged individualism. [Speech, 1928]

Hope, Anthony (1863–1933)

8 Economy is going without something you do want in case you should, some day, want something you probably won't want. [*The Dolly Dialogues*, 12]

9 'You oughtn't to yield to temptation.' 'Well, somebody must, or the thing becomes absurd.' [Ib. 14]

10 'Boys will be boys—'
'And even that . . . wouldn't matter if we could only prevent girls from being girls.' [Ib. 16]

Hopkins, Gerald Manley (1844–1889)

1 The world is charged with the grandeur of God. ['God's Grandeur']

2 O the mind, mind has mountains; cliffs of fall / Frightful, sheer, no-man-fathomed. ['No Worst, there is None']

3 Glory be to God for dappled things. ['Pied Beauty']

4 I caught this morning morning's minion, kingdom of daylight's dauphin, dapple-dawn-drawn Falcon. ['The Windhover']

5 My heart in hiding / Stirred for a bird, — the achieve of, the mastery of the thing! [Ib.]

Hopkins, Jane Ellice (1836–1904)

6 Gift, like genius, I often think, only means an infinite capacity for taking pains. [*Work amongst Working Men*; see Carlyle, *Frederick the Great*]

Horace (65–8 B.C.)

7 *Difficile est proprie communia dicere.* It is hard to say common things in an original way. [*Ars Poetica*]

8 *In medias res.* To the heart of the matter. [Ib.]

9 *Indignor quandoque bonus dormitat Homerus.* When worthy Homer nods, I am offended. [Ib.]

10 *Ut pictura poesis.* Poetry is like painting. [Ib.]

11 *Ira furor brevis est.* Anger is a brief madness. [*Epistles*, I, 2]

12 *Naturam expellas furca, tamen usque recurret.* Though you drive away Nature with a pitchfork she always returns. [Ib. I, 10]

13 *Concordia discors.* Harmony in discord. [Ib. I, 12]

14 *Volat irrevocabile verbum.* The word flies and cannot be recalled. [Ib. I, 18]

15 *Atque inter silvas Academi quaerere verum.* And

seek after truth in the groves of Academe. [Ib. II, 2]

1 *Pallida Mors, aequo pulsat pede pauperum tabernas / Regumque turris.* Pale Death, with impartial foot, strikes at poor men's hovels and the towers of kings. [*Odes*, I, 4]

2 *Vitae summa brevis spem nos vetat incohare longam.* Life's short span forbids us to set out after far-reaching hopes. [Ib.]

3 *Nil desperandum Teucro duce et auspice Teucro.* No need to despair under Teucer's leadership and protection. [Ib. I, 7]

4 *Carpe diem, quam minimum credula postero.* Snatch at today and trust as little as you can in tomorrow. [Ib. I, 11]

5 *Dulce et decorum est pro patria mori.* It is a fine and seemly thing to die for one's country. [Ib. III, 2]

6 *Non omnis moriar.* I shall not altogether die. [Ib. III, 30]

7 *Non sum qualis eram bonae / Sub regno Cinarae.* I am not what I was when dear Cinara was my queen. [Ib. IV, 1]

Horsley, Bishop Samuel (1733–1806)

8 The mass of the people have nothing to do with the laws but to obey them. [Speech, 1795]

Housman, Alfred Edward (1859–1936)

9 The chestnut casts his flambeaux. [*Last Poems*, 9]

10 The cuckoo shouts all day at nothing / In leafy dells alone. [Ib. 40]

11 Life, to be sure, is nothing much to lose; / But young men think it is, and we were young. [*More Poems*, 36]

12 O, God will save her, fear you not: / Be you the

men you've been, / Get you the sons your
fathers got, / And God will save the Queen. [*A
Shropshire Lad*, 1]

1 The man that runs away / Lives to die another
day. [Ib. 'The Day of Battle']

2 O many a peer of England brews / Livelier liquor
than the Muse, / And malt does more than
Milton can / To justify God's ways to man. [Ib.
62]

Howe, Julia Ward (1819–1910)

3 Mine eyes have seen the glory of the coming of
the Lord: / He is trampling out the vintage
where the grapes of wrath are stored. ['Battle
Hymn of the Republic']

Howell, James (c. 1594–1666)

4 One hair of a woman can draw more than a
hundred pair of oxen. [*Familiar Letters*, II, 4]

5 This life at best is but an inn, / And we the
passengers. [Ib. II, 73]

Howitt, Mary (1799–1888)

6 'Will you walk into my parlour?' said a spider to
a fly. ['The Spider and the Fly']

Hubbard, Elbert 1859–1915)

7 Life is just one damned thing after another. [*A
Thousand and One Epigrams*]

8 Editor: a person employed by a newspaper whose
business it is to separate the wheat from the
chaff and to see that the chaff is printed. [Ib.]

Hughes, Thomas (1822–1896)

9 Life isn't all beer and skittles. [*Tom Brown's
Schooldays*, I]

Hugo, Victor (1802–1885)

10 *Le mot, c'est le Verbe, et le Verbe, c'est Dieu.*

The word is the Verb, and the Verb is God.
[*Contemplations*]

1 *On résiste à l'invasion des armées; on ne résiste pas à l'invasion des idées.* The invasion of armies is resisted; the invasion of ideas is not. [*Histoire d'un Crime*]

2 *Le beau est aussi utile que l'utile. Plus peut-être.* The beautiful is as useful as the useful. Perhaps more so. [*Les Misérables*]

3 Jesus wept; Voltaire smiled. [Oration on Voltaire, 1878]

4 England has two books: the Bible and Shakespeare. England made Shakespeare but the Bible made England. [Quoted in Simcox, *Treasury of Quotations on Christian Themes*]

Hume, David (1711–1776)

5 Nothing appears more surprising to those who consider human affairs with a philosophical eye, than the ease with which the many are governed by the few. [*First Principles of Government*]

6 Avarice, the spur of industry. ['Of Civil Liberty']

7 Beauty in things exists in the mind which contemplates them. ['Of Tragedy']

8 No testimony is sufficient to establish a miracle, unless the testimony be of such a kind that its falsehood would be more miraculous than the fact which it endeavours to establish. ['Of Miracles']

Hunt, G.W. (1829–1904)

9 We don't want to fight, but, by jingo if we do, / We've got the ships, we've got the men, we've got the money too. [Music hall song, 1878]

Huss, Jan (c. 1370–1415)

10 *O sancta simplicitas!* O holy simplicity! [Attr. On

seeing a peasant bringing a faggot to Huss's own stake]

Hutcheson, Francis (1694–1746)

1 That action is best which procures the greatest happiness of the greatest number. [*Inquiry into the Original of our Ideas of Beauty and Virtue*, II]

Huxley, Aldous (1894–1963)

2 The proper study of mankind is books. [*Chrome Yellow*]

3 It is far easier to write ten passably effective sonnets, good enough to take in the not too inquiring critic, than one effective advertisement that will take in a few thousand of the uncritical buying public. [*On the Margin*]

4 Silence is as full of potential wisdom and wit as the unhewn marble of great sculpture. [*Point Counter Point*]

5 Those who believe that they are exclusively in the right are generally those who achieve something. [*Proper Studies*]

6 Facts do not cease to exist because they are ignored. [Ib.]

7 To his dog, every man is Napoleon; hence the constant popularity of dogs. [Attr.]

Huxley, Thomas Henry (1825–1895)

8 The great tragedy of Science — the slaying of a beautiful hypothesis by an ugly fact. ['Biogenesis and Abiogenesis']

9 Science is nothing but trained and organized common sense. ['The Method of Zadig']

10 If a little knowledge is dangerous, where is the man who has so much as to be out of danger? [*Science and Culture*]

11 History warns us that it is the customary fate of

new truths to begin as heresies and to end as superstitions. [Ib.]

1 I am too much of a sceptic to deny the possibility of anything. [Letter, 1886]

2 Try to learn something about everything and everything about something. [Memorial stone]

Ibárruri, Dolores ['La Pasionaria'] (1895–)

3 *No pasarán!* They shall not pass. [Spanish Republican slogan]

Ibsen, Henrik (1828–1906)

4 The minority is always right. [*An Enemy of the People*, IV]

5 Take the saving lie from the average man and you take his happiness away, too. [*The Wild Duck*, III]

Illich, Ivan (1926–)

6 Man must choose whether to be rich in things or in the freedom to use them. [*Deschooling Society*]

Ingersoll, Robert Greene (1833–1899)

7 In nature there are neither rewards nor punishments — there are consequences. [*Lectures and Essays*]

Irving, Washington (1783–1859)

8 A sharp tongue is the only edged tool that grows keener with constant use. [*The Sketch Book*, 'Rip Van Winkle']

9 The almighty dollar, that great object of universal devotion throughout our land . . . [*Wolfert's Roost*, 'The Creole Village']

Isherwood, Christopher (1904–)

10 I am a camera with its shutter open, quite

passive, recording, not thinking. [*Goodbye to Berlin*]

James V of Scotland (1512–1542)

1 It cam' wi' a lass, and it'll gang wi' a lass. [Remark on rule of Stuart dynasty in Scotland, 1542]

James VI of Scotland and I of England (1566–1625)

2 I will govern according to the common weal, but not according to the common will. [Remark, 1621]

3 Dr. Donne's verses are like the peace of God; they pass all understanding. [Attr.]

James, Henry (1843–1916)

4 The only obligation to which in advance we may hold a novel, without incurring the accusation of being arbitrary, is that it be interesting. [*The Art of Fiction*]

5 We must grant the artist his subject, his idea, his *donnée*: our criticism is applied only to what he makes of it. [Ib.]

6 It takes a great deal of history to produce a little literature. [*Life of Nathaniel Hawthorne*]

7 [Of his own death] So here it is at last, the distinguished thing. [Attr.]

James, William (1842–1910)

8 The bitch-goddess, Success. [Quoted by Aldous Huxley, *Proper Studies*]

9 A great many people think they are thinking when they are merely rearranging their prejudices. [Attr.]

Jefferson, Thomas (1743–1826)

10 A little rebellion now and then is a good thing. [Letter, 1787]

1 The tree of liberty must be refreshed from time
to time with the blood of patriots and tyrants. It
is its natural manure. [Letter, 1787]

2 Advertisements contain the only truths to be
relied on in a newspaper. [Letter, 1819]

Jerome, Jerome K. (1859-1927)

3 I like work; it fascinates me. I can sit and look at
it for hours. I love to keep it by me: the idea of
getting rid of it nearly breaks my heart. [*Three
Men in a Boat*, 3]

Jerome, St. (c. 342-420)

4 *Cur ergo haec ipse non facis?* Why do you not
practise what you preach? [*Letters*, 48]

5 *Venerationi mihi semper fuit non verbosa
rusticas, sed sancta simplicitas.* My reverence has
always been for holy simplicity rather than
wordy vulgarity. [Ib. 57]

6 *Noli equi dentes inspicere donati.* Never look a
gift horse in the mouth. [*On the Epistle to the
Ephesians*]

Jerrold, Douglas William (1803-1857)

7 Love's like the measles   all the worse when it
comes late in life. [*Wit and Opinions of Douglas
Jerrold*]

8 We love peace, as we abhor pusillanimity; but
not peace at any price. [Ib.]

Johnson, Hiram (1866-1945)

9 The first casualty when war comes is truth.
[Speech, 1917]

Johnson, Lyndon Baines (1908-1973)

10 [Of J. Edgar Hoover, chief of the FBI] I'd much
rather have that fellow inside the tent pissing
out, than outside pissing in. [Attr.]

Johnson, Samuel (1709–1784)

1 *Net.* Anything reticulated or decussated at equal distances, with interstices between the intersections. [*Dictionary*]

2 *Oats.* A grain, which in England is generally given to horses, but in Scotland supports the people. [Ib.]

3 A Scotchman must be a very sturdy moralist who does not love Scotland better than truth. [*Journey to the Western Isles*]

4 That man is little to be envied whose patriotism would not gain force upon the plain of Marathon, or whose piety would not grow warmer among the ruins of Iona. [Ib.]

5 Language is the dress of thought. [*Lives of the English Poets*, Cowley]

6 [Of Garrick's death] That stroke of death, which has eclipsed the gaiety of nations, and impoverished the public stock of harmless pleasure. [Ib. Edmund Smith]

7 Human life is everywhere a state in which much is to be endured, and little to be enjoyed. [*Rasselas*, 11]

8 Marriage has many pains, but celibacy has no pleasures. [Ib. 26]

9 Nothing can please many, and please long, but just representations of general nature. [Preface to Shakespeare]

10 His fall was destined to a barren strand, / A petty fortress, and a dubious hand; / He left the name, at which the world grew pale, / To point a moral, or adorn a tale. [*The Vanity of Human Wishes*]

11 The only end of writing is to enable the readers better to enjoy life, or better to endure it. [*Works*, X]

1 A man may write at any time, if he will set himself doggedly to it. [Boswell, *Life*, I]

2 Is not a Patron, my Lord, one who looks with unconcern on a man struggling for life in the water, and, when he has reached ground, encumbers him with help? [Ib.]

3 [Of Chesterfield's *Letters*] They teach the morals of a whore, and the manners of a dancing master. [Ib.]

4 A man, Sir, should keep his friendship in constant repair. [Ib.]

5 [Of literary criticism] You may scold a carpenter who has made you a bad table, though you cannot make a table. It is not your trade to make tables. [Ib.]

6 But, Sir, let me tell you, the noblest prospect which a Scotchman ever sees, is the high road that leads him to England! [Ib.]

7 Sir, a woman's preaching is like a dog's walking on his hinder legs. It is not done well; but you are surprised to find it done at all. [Ib.]

8 Lexicographer: a writer of dictionaries, a harmless drudge. [Ib.]

9 A man ought to read just as inclination leads him; for what he reads as a task will do him little good. [Ib.]

10 Truth, Sir, is a cow which will yield such people no more milk, and so they are gone to milk the bull. [Ib.]

11 Your levellers wish to level *down* as far as themselves; but they cannot bear levelling *up* to themselves. [Ib.]

12 [Kicking a stone in order to disprove Berkeley's theory of the nonexistence of matter] I refute it *thus*. [Ib.]

1 We *know* our will is free, and *there's* an end on't. [Ib. II]

2 A gentleman who had been very unhappy in marriage married immediately after his wife died. Dr. Johnson said, it was the triumph of hope over experience. [Ib.]

3 Much may be made of a Scotchman, if he be *caught* young. [Ib.]

4 Read over your compositions, and where ever you meet with a passage which you think is particularly fine, strike it out. [Ib.]

5 There are few ways in which a man can be more innocently employed than in getting money. [Ib.]

6 Patriotism is the last refuge of a scoundrel. [Ib.]

7 In lapidary inscriptions a man is not upon oath. [Ib.]

8 Knowledge is of two kinds. We know a subject ourselves, or we know where we can find information upon it. [Ib.]

9 There is nothing which has yet been contrived by man, by which so much happiness is produced as by a good tavern or inn. [Ib.]

10 No man but a blockhead ever wrote, except for money. [Ib. III]

11 Depend upon it, Sir, when a man knows he is to be hanged in a fortnight, it concentrates his mind wonderfully. [Ib.]

12 When a man is tired of London, he is tired of life; for there is in London all that life can afford. [Ib.]

13 [Of ghosts] All argument is against it; but all belief is for it. [Ib.]

14 Were it not for imagination, Sir, a man would be as happy in the arms of a chambermaid as of a Duchess. [Ib.]

1 Claret is the liquor for boys; port for men; but he who aspires to be a hero must drink brandy. [*Ib.*]

2 Sir, I look upon every day to be lost in which I do not make a new acquaintance. [*Ib.* IV]

3 The man who is asked by an author what he thinks of his work, is put to the torture, and is not obliged to speak the truth. [*Ib.*]

4 There are people whom one should like very well to drop, but would not wish to be dropt by. [*Ib.*]

5 No man is a hypocrite in his pleasures. [*Ib.*]

6 [On his deathbed] I will be conquered; I will not capitulate. [*Ib.*]

7 It is very strange, and very melancholy, that the paucity of human pleasures should persuade us ever to call hunting one of them. [*Johnsonian Miscellanies*, I]

8 [On a celebrated violinist's performance] Difficult do you call it, Sir? I wish it were impossible. [*Ib.* II]

9 A man is in general better pleased when he has a good dinner upon his table, than when his wife talks Greek. [*Ib.*]

10 What is written without effort is in general read without pleasure. [*Ib.*]

11 Love is the wisdom of the fool and the folly of the wise. [*Ib.*]

Jolson, Al (1886–1950)

12 You ain't heard nothin' yet, folks! [*The Jazz Singer*]

Jonson, Ben (1572–1637)

13 Where it concerns himself, / Who's angry at a slander makes it true. [*Catiline his Conspiracy*, III.1]

14 So they be ill men, / If they spake worse, 'twere

better: for of such / To be dispraised, is the most perfect praise. [*Cynthia's Revels*, III.2]

1 If he were / To be made honest by an act of parliament, / I should not alter in my faith of him. [*The Devil is an Ass*, IV.1]

2 Alas, all the castles I have, are built with air, thou know'st. [*Eastward Ho*, II.2]

3 I do honour the very flea of his dog. [*Every Man in His Humour*, IV.2]

4 Drink to me only with thine eyes, / And I will pledge with mine; / Or leave a kiss but in the cup, / And I'll not look for wine. ['To Celia']

5 He was not of an age, but for all time! ['To the Memory of . . . Shakespeare']

6 Sweet Swan of Avon. [Ib.]

7 Good morning to the day: and next, my gold! / Open the shrine that I may see my saint. [*Volpone*, I.1]

8 I remember the players have often mentioned it as an honour to Shakespeare that in his writing (whatsoever he penned) he never blotted out a line. My answer hath been, 'Would that he had blotted a thousand.' Which they thought a malevolent speech. I had not told posterity this, but for their ignorance, who chose that circumstance to commend their friend by wherein he most faulted; and to justify mine own candour; for I loved the man, and do honour his memory, on this side idolatry, as much as any. [*Discoveries*]

Jordan, Thomas (c. 1612–1685)

9 Our God and soldier we alike adore, / Just at the brink of ruin, not before: / The danger past, both are alike requited; / God is forgotten, and our soldier slighted. [Epigram]

Jowett, Benjamin (1817–1893)

1 One man is as good as another until he has written a book. [*Letters*, I]

2 My dear child, you must believe in God in spite of what the clergy tell you. [Attr.]

Joyce, James (1882–1941)

3 riverrun, past Eve and Adam's, from swerve of shore to bend of bay, brings us by a commodius vicus of recirculation back to Howth Castle and Environs. [*Finnegans Wake*, first words]

4 Ireland is the old sow that eats her farrow. [*A Portrait of the Artist as a Young Man*]

5 Welcome, O life! I go to encounter for the millionth time the reality of experience and to forge in the smithy of my soul the uncreated conscience of my race. [Ib.]

6 Stately, plump Buck Mulligan came from the stairhead, bearing a bowl of lather on which a mirror and a razor lay crossed. [*Ulysses*, I, first sentence]

7 The snotgreen sea. The scrotumtightening sea. [Ib.]

8 When I makes tea I makes tea, as old mother Grogan said. And when I makes water I makes water... Begob, ma'am, says Mrs. Cahill, God send you don't make them in the one pot. [Ib.]

9 History is a nightmare from which I am trying to awake. [Ib. II]

10 I put my arms around him yes and drew him down to me so he could feel my breasts all perfume yes and his heart was going like mad and yes I said yes I will Yes. [Ib. III, final words]

Julian the Apostate (A.D. 332–363)

11 *Vicisti, Galilaee.* You have conquered, Galilean. [Last words]

Juliana of Norwich (1343–1443)

1 Sin is behovely, but all shall be well and all shall
be well and all manner of things shall be well.
[*Revelations of Divine Love*, 27]

Junius (fl. 1769)

2 The liberty of the press is the *Palladium* of all
the civil, political, and religious rights of an
Englishman. [*Letters*, Dedication]

3 There is a holy mistaken zeal in politics as well
as in religion. By persuading others, we convince
ourselves. [Ib. 35]

Juvenal (c. A.D. 60–130)

4 *Rara avis in terris nigroque similima cycno.* A
rare bird upon the earth, and very like a black
swan. [*Satires*, VI]

5 *Sed quis custodiet ipsos / Custodes?* But who is
to guard the guards themselves? [Ib.]

6 *Scribendi cacoethes.* The itch to write. [Ib. VII]

7 *Duas tantum res anxius optat, / Panem et
circenses.* The troubled [Roman people] long for
two things only: bread and circuses. [Ib. X]

8 *Orandum est ut sit mens sana in corpore sano.*
You should pray for a healthy mind in a healthy
body. [Ib.]

Kafka, Franz (1883–1924)

9 In the fight between you and the world, back the
world. [Attr.]

Kant, Immanuel (1724–1804)

10 I am never to act without willing that the maxim
by which I act should become a universal law.
[*Critique of Practical Reason*]

Karr, Alphonse (1808–1890)

11 *Plus ça change, plus c'est la même chose.* The

more things change the more they are the same. [*Les Guêpes*, 1849]

1 Every man has three characters: that which he exhibits, that which he has, and that which he thinks he has. [Attr.]

Kaufmann, Christoph (1753–1795)

2 *Sturm und Drang*. Storm and stress [Name invented in connection with Maximilien Klinger's play *Die Wirrwarr* (1775)]

Kearney, Denis (1847–1907)

3 Horny-handed sons of toil. [Speech, c. 1878]

Keats, John (1795–1821)

4 Season of mists and mellow fruitfulness. ['To Autumn']

5 O what can ail thee, Knight-at-arms / Alone and palely loitering; / The sedge has wither'd from the lake, / And no birds sing. ['La Belle Dame Sans Merci']

6 A thing of beauty is a joy for ever: / Its loveliness increases; it will never / Pass into nothingness. [*Endymion*, I]

7 A hope beyond the shadow of a dream. [Ib.]

8 St. Agnes' Eve — Ah, bitter chill it was! / The owl, for all his feathers, was a-cold. [*The Eve of St. Agnes*]

9 The silver, snarling trumpets 'gan to chide. [Ib.]

10 The music, yearning like a God in pain. [Ib.]

11 By degrees / Her rich attire creeps rustling to her knees. [Ib.]

12 Sudden a thought came like a full-blown rose, / Flushing his brow. [Ib.]

13 Full on this casement shone the wintry moon, / And threw warm gules on Madeline's fair breast. [Ib.]

1 Fanatics have their dreams, wherewith they
   weave / A paradise for a sect; the savage too /
   From forth the loftiest fashion of his sleep /
   Guesses at Heaven. [*The Fall of Hyperion*, I]

2 Every man whose soul is not a clod / Hath
   visions. [Ib.]

3 The poet and the dreamer are distinct, / Diverse,
   sheer opposite, antipodes. / The one pours out a
   balm upon the world, / The other vexes it. [Ib.]

4 Deep in the shady sadness of a vale / Far
   sunken from the healthy breath of morn, / Far
   from the fiery noon, and eve's one star, / Sat
   gray-hair'd Saturn, quiet as a stone. [*Hyperion.
   A Fragment*, I]

5 O aching time! O moments big as years. [Ib.]

6 Real are the dreams of Gods, and smoothly pass
   / Their pleasures in a long immortal dream.
   [*Lamia*, I]

7 Do not all charms fly / At the mere touch of cold
   philosophy? [Ib. II]

8 But vain is now the burning and the strife, /
   Pangs are in vain, until I grow high-rife / With
   old Philosophy. ['Lines on Seeing a Lock of
   Milton's Hair']

9 Thou still unravish'd bride of quietness, / Thou
   foster-child of silence and slow time. ['Ode on a
   Grecian Urn']

10 Heard melodies are sweet, but those unheard /
   Are sweeter. [Ib.]

11 For ever wilt thou love, and she be fair! [Ib.]

12 For ever warm and still to be enjoy'd, / For ever
   panting and for ever young. [Ib.]

13 Thou, silent form, dost tease us out of thought /
   As doth eternity: Cold Pastoral! [Ib.]

14 'Beauty is truth, truth beauty,' — that is all / Ye
   know on earth, and all ye need to know. [Ib.]

1 And evenings steep'd in honied indolence. ['Ode on Indolence']

2 For I would not be dieted with praise, / A pet-lamb in a sentimental farce. [Ib.]

3 No, no, go not to Lethe, neither twist / Wolf's-bane, tight-rooted, for its poisonous wine. ['Ode on Melancholy']

4 But when the melancholy fit shall fall / Sudden from heaven like a weeping cloud, / ... Then glut thy sorrow on a morning rose, / ... Or on the wealth of globèd peonies; / Or if thy mistress some rich anger shows, / Emprison her soft hand, and let her rave, / And feed deep, deep upon her peerless eyes. [Ib.]

5 Ay, in the very temple of Delight / Veil'd Melancholy has her sovran shrine. [Ib.]

6 My heart aches, and a drowsy numbness pains / My sense, as though of hemlock I had drunk. ['Ode to a Nightingale']

7 O for a draught of vintage! that hath been / Cool'd a long age in the deep-delved earth. [Ib.]

8 Full of the true, the blushful Hippocrene, / With beaded bubbles winking at the brim. [Ib.]

9 Fade far away, dissolve, and quite forget / What thou among the leaves hast never known, / The weariness, the fever and the fret / Here, where men sit and hear each other groan. [Ib.]

10 Where youth grows pale, and spectre-thin, and dies. [Ib.]

11 Away! away! for I will fly to thee, / Not charioted by Bacchus and his pards, / But on the viewless wings of Poesy. [Ib.]

12 Already with thee! tender is the night. [Ib.]

13 Darkling I listen; and, for many a time / I have been half in love with easeful Death. [Ib.]

14 Thou wast not born for death, immortal Bird! /

No hungry generations tread thee down; / The voice I hear this passing night was heard / In ancient days by emperor and clown: / Perhaps the self-same song that found a path / Through the sad heart of Ruth, when, sick for home, / She stood in tears amid the alien corn; / The same that oft-times hath / Charm'd magic casements, opening on the foam / Of perilous seas, in faery lands forlorn. [Ib.]

1 Was it a vision, or a waking dream? / Fled is that music: — / Do I wake or sleep? [Ib.]

2 O latest born and loveliest vision far / Of all Olympus' faded hierarchy. ['Ode to Psyche']

3 Stop and consider! life is but a day; / A fragile dewdrop on its perilous way / From a tree's summit. ['Sleep and Poetry']

4 A drainless shower / Of light is poesy; 'tis the supreme of power; / 'Tis might half slumb'ring on its own right arm. [Ib.]

5 Bright star, would I were steadfast as thou art — / Not in lone splendour hung aloft the night / And watching, with eternal lids apart, / Like nature's patient, sleepless Eremite, / The moving waters at their priestlike task / Of pure ablution round earth's human shores. [*Sonnets*, 'Bright Star']

6 Fame, like a wayward girl, will still be coy / To those who woo her with too slavish knees. [Ib. 'On Fame']

7 Much have I travell'd in the realms of gold, / And many goodly states and kingdoms seen. [Ib. 'On First Looking into Chapman's Homer']

8 Then felt I like some watcher of the skies / When a new planet swims into his ken; / Or like stout Cortez when with eagle eyes / He star'd at the Pacific — and all his men / Look'd at each

other with a wild surmise — / Silent, upon a peak in Darien. [Ib.]

1 To one who has been long in city pent, / 'Tis very sweet to look into the fair / And open face of heaven. [Ib. 'To One Who Has Been Long']

2 When I have fears that I may cease to be / Before my pen has glean'd my teeming brain. [Ib. 'When I have Fears']

3 Then on the shore / Of the wide world I stand alone, and think / Till love and fame to nothingness do sink. [Ib.]

4 Negative Capability, that is, when a man is capable of being in uncertainties, mysteries, doubts, without any irritable reaching after fact and reason. [Letter to George and Tom Keats, 1817]

5 I am certain of nothing but the holiness of the heart's affections and the truth of imagination — what the imagination seizes as beauty must be truth — whether it existed before or not. [Letter to Benjamin Bailey, 1817]

6 O for a life of sensations rather than of thoughts! [Letter to Benjamin Bailey, 1817]

7 Scenery is fine — but human nature is finer. [Letter to Benjamin Bailey, 1818]

8 Axioms in philosophy are not axioms until they are proved upon our pulses. [Letter to J.H. Reynolds, 1818]

9 We hate poetry that has a palpable design upon us — and if we do not agree, seems to put its hand in its breeches pocket. [Letter to J.H. Reynolds, 1818]

10 Poetry should surprise by a fine excess, and not by singularity; it should strike the reader as a wording of his own highest thoughts, and appear almost a remembrance. [Letter to John Taylor, 1818]

1 If poetry comes not naturally as leaves to a tree it had better not come at all. [Ib.]

2 Shakespeare led a life of allegory: his works are the comments on it. [Letter to George and Georgiana Keats, 1819]

3 I have met with women whom I really think would like to be married to a poem, and to be given away by a novel. [Letter to Fanny Brawne, 1819]

4 Load every rift of your subject with ore. [Letter to Shelley, 1820]

5 Here lies one whose name was writ in water. [Epitaph for himself]

Kempis, Thomas à (c. 1380–1471)

6 Verily, when the day of judgement comes, we shall not be asked what we have read, but what we have done. [*De Imitatione Christi*, 1]

7 Man proposes, but God disposes. [Ib.]

8 *Sic transit gloria mundi.* Thus the glory of the world passes away. [Ib. 3]

Kennedy, John F. (1917–1963)

9 We stand today on the edge of a new frontier. [Speech, 1960]

10 As a free man, I take pride in the words *Ich bin ein Berliner.* [Speech to West Berliners, 1963]

Kennedy, Robert F. (1925–1968)

11 One fifth of the people are against everything all the time. [*Observer*, 'Sayings of the Week', 1964]

Kepler, Johannes (1571–1630)

12 O God, I am thinking Thy thoughts after Thee. [Remark (while studying astronomy)]

Kethe, William (fl. 1593)

13 All people that on earth do dwell, / Sing to the Lord with cheerful voice. / Him serve with mirth,

His praise forth tell; / Come ye before him and rejoice. [Hymn]

Key, Francis Scott (1779–1843)

1 'Tis the star-spangled banner; O long may it wave / O'er the land of the free, and the home of the brave! ['The Star-Spangled Banner']

Keynes, J.M. (1883–1946)

2 Whenever you save five shillings you put a man out of work for a day. [*Observer*, 'Sayings of the Week', 1931]

Khruschev, Nikita (1894–1971)

3 Whether you like it or not, history is on our side. We will bury you! [Speech to Western ambassadors, 1956]

Kierkegaard, Sören (1813–1855)

4 Life can only be understood backwards; but it must be lived forwards. [*Life*]

King, Martin Luther (1929–1968)

5 I have a dream. [Various Speeches, 1963]

6 Riots are the language of the unheard. [Attr.]

7 I want to be the white man's brother, not his brother-in-law. [Attr.]

Kingsley, Charles (1819–1875)

8 He did not know that a keeper is only a poacher turned outside in, and a poacher a keeper turned inside out. [*The Water Babies*, 1]

9 As thorough an Englishman as ever coveted his neighbour's goods. [Ib. 4]

Kingsmill, Hugh (1889–1949)

10 What, still alive at twenty-two, / A clean upstanding lad like you? / Sure, if your throat 'tis hard to slit, / Slit your girl's, and swing for it. ['Poem after A.E. Housman']

Kipling, Rudyard (1865–1936)

1 Oh, East is East, and West is West, and never the twain shall meet. ['The Ballad of East and West']

2 And a woman is only a woman but a good cigar is a Smoke. ['The Betrothed']

3 O where are you going to, all you Big Steamers, / With England's own coal, up and down the salt seas.? ['Big Steamers']

4 (Boots — boots — boots — boots — movin' up an' down again!) / There's no discharge in the war! ['Boots']

5 But the Devil whoops, as he whooped of old: / 'It's clever, but is it Art?' ['The Conundrum of the Workshops']

6 The 'eathen in 'is blindness must end where 'e began, / But the backbone of the Army is the Non-commissioned man! ['The 'Eathen']

7 And what should they know of England who only England know? ['The English Flag']

8 For the female of the species is more deadly than the male. ['The Female of the Species']

9 We're poor little lambs who've lost our way, / Baa! Baa! Baa! / We're little black sheep who've gone astray, / Baa-aa-aa! / Gentleman-Rankers out on the spree, / Damned from here to Eternity, / God ha' mercy on such as we, / Baa! Yah! Bah! ['Gentleman-Rankers']

10 You're a better man than I am, Gunga Din! ['Gunga Din']

11 There are nine and sixty ways of constructing tribal lays, / And — every — single — one — of — them — is — right! ['In the Neolithic Age']

12 If you can keep your head when all about you / Are losing theirs and blaming it on you. ['If']

1 If you can dream — and not make dreams your master. [Ib.]

2 The great, grey-green, greasy Limpopo River, all set about with fever-trees. [*Just So Stories*, 'The Elephant's Child']

3 'Nice,' said the small 'stute Fish. 'Nice but nubbly,' [Ib. 'How the Whale Got his Throat']

4 A man of infinite-resource-and-sagacity. [Ib.]

5 On the road to Mandalay, / Where the flyin'-fishes play, / An' the dawn comes up like thunder outer China 'crost the Bay! ['Mandalay']

6 The tumult and the shouting dies; / The Captains and the Kings depart. ['Recessional']

7 Lest we forget — lest we forget! [Ib.]

8 Them that asks no questions isn't told a lie. / Watch the wall, my darling, while the Gentlemen go by! ['A Smuggler's Song']

9 Being kissed by a man who didn't wax his moustache was — like eating an egg without salt. [*Soldiers Three*, 'The Gadsbys, Poor Dear Mamma']

10 Take my word for it, the silliest woman can manage a clever man; but it needs a very clever woman to manage a fool. ['Three and — an Extra']

11 It's Tommy this, an' Tommy that, an' 'Chuck him out, the brute!' / But it's 'Saviour of 'is country' when the guns begin to shoot. ['Tommy']

12 When 'Omer smote 'is bloomin' lyre, / 'E'd 'eard men sing by land an' sea; / An' what 'e thought 'e might require, / 'E went an' took — the same as me! ['When 'Omer Smote 'is Bloomin' Lyre']

13 The White Man's Burden [Title of poem]

14 He travels the fastest who travels alone. ['The Winners']

15 [Of newspaper barons] Power without

responsibility — the prerogative of the harlot
throughout the ages. [Quoted by Baldwin in
speech, 1931]

Kissinger, Henry (1923–)

1 Power is the ultimate aphrodisiac. [Attr.]

Klee, Paul (1879–1940)

2 Art does not reproduce what we see; rather, it
makes us see. ['Creative Credo']

Klopstock, Friedrich (1724–1803)

3 [Of one of his poems] God and I both knew what
it meant once; now God alone knows. [Attr. Also
attr. to Browning]

Knopf, Edwin H. (1899–)

4 The son-in-law also rises. [Quoted in Colombo,
Wit and Wisdom of the Moviemakers]

Knox, John (?1505–1572)

5 The First Blast of the Trumpet Against the
Monstrous Regiment of Women [Title of
pamphlet]

Knox, Ronald (1888–1957)

6 There was once a man who said 'God / Must
think it exceedingly odd / If he finds that this
tree / Continues to be / When there's no one
about in the Quad.' [Attr.; for reply *see* Anon.,
'Dear Sir, your astonishment's odd']

Kyd, Thomas (1558-1594)

7 Why then I'll fit you. [*The Spanish Tragedy*, IV.1]

8 Hieronymo's mad againe. [Ib. Quoted by T.S.
Eliot, *The Waste Land*]

La Bruyère, Jean de (1645–1696)

9 *Le commencement et le déclin de l'amour se font
sentir par l'embarras où l'on est de se trouver
seuls.* The beginning and the decline of love make

themselves felt in the embarrassment on being left alone together. [*Les Caractères*, 'Du Coeur']

1 The pleasure of criticizing takes away from us the pleasure of being moved by some very fine things. [Ib. 'Des ouvrages de l'esprit']

Lamb, Lady Caroline (1785–1828)

2 [Of Byron] Mad, bad, and dangerous to know. [Journal, 1812]

Lamb, Charles (1775–1834)

3 I am, in plainer words, a bundle of prejudices — made up of likings and dislikings. [*Essays of Elia*, 'Imperfect Sympathies']

4 I have been trying all my life to like Scotchmen, and am obliged to desist from the experiment in despair. [Ib.]

5 Not many sounds in life, and I include all urban and all rural sounds, exceed in interest a knock at the door. [Ib. 'Valentine's Day']

6 I love to lose myself in other men's minds. When I am not walking, I am reading; I cannot sit and think. Books think for me. [*Last Essays of Elia*, 'Detached Thoughts on Books and Reading']

7 All, all are gone, the old familiar faces. ['The Old Familiar Faces']

8 Cultivate simplicity, Coleridge. [Letter, 1796]

9 I came home . . . hungry as a hunter. [Letter, 1800]

10 Nothing puzzles me more than time and space; and yet nothing troubles me less, as I never think about them. [Letter, 1810]

11 May my last breath be drawn through a pipe and exhaled in a pun. [Quoted in Wintle and Kenin, *Dictionary of Biographical Quotations*]

Landor, Walter Savage (1775–1864)

12 George the First was always reckoned / Vile, but

viler George the Second; / And what mortal ever heard / Any good of George the Third? / When from earth the Fourth descended / God be praised, the Georges ended! [Epigram]

1 I strove with none; for none was worth my strife; / Nature I loved, and next to Nature, Art; / I warmed both hands before the fire of life; / It sinks, and I am ready to depart. ['Finis']

2 Prose on certain occasions can bear a great deal of poetry: on the other hand, poetry sinks and swoons under a moderate weight of prose. [*Imaginary Conversations*, 'Archdeacon Hare and Walter Landor']

Langbridge, Frederick (1849–1923)

3 Two men look out through the same bars: / One sees the mud, and one the stars. ['A Cluster of Quiet Thoughts']

Langland, William (c. 1330–c. 1400)

4 In a somer seson whan soft was the sonne. [*Piers Plowman*, Prologue (B Text)]

5 A glotoun of wordes. [Ib.]

6 Grammere, that grounde is of alle. [Ib. (C Text)]

Lao-tze (fl. c. 550 B.C.)

7 Acting without design, occupying oneself without making a business of it, finding the great in what is small and the many in the few, repaying injury with kindness, effecting difficult things while they are easy, and managing great things in their beginnings: this is the method of Tao. [*Tao Te Ching*]

8 Heaven and Earth have no pity; they regard all things as straw dogs. [Ib.]

9 A journey of a thousand miles must begin with a single step. [Ib.]

La Rochefoucauld, François, Duc de (1613–1680)

1 *On n'est jamais si heureux ni si malheureux qu'on s'imagine.* One is never so happy or so unhappy as one thinks. [*Maximes*, 49]

2 *On peut trouver des femmes qui n'ont jamais eu de galanterie, mais il est rare d'en trouver qui n'en aient jamais eu qu'une.* One can find women who have never had a love affair, but it is rare to find a woman who has had only one. [Ib. 73]

3 *La gloire des grands hommes se doit toujours mesurer aux moyens dont ils se sont servis pour l'acquérir.* The glory of great men must always be measured by the means they have used to obtain it. [Ib. 157]

4 *L'hypocrisie est un hommage que le vice rend à la vertu.* Hypocrisy is the homage that vice pays to virtue. [Ib. 218]

5 Everyone complains of his memory; nobody of his judgment. [Attr.]

La Rochefoucauld-Liancourt, Duc de (1747–1827)

6 *Non, Sire, c'est une révolution.* No, Sire, it is a revolution. [In reply to Louis XVI's question '*C'est une révolte?*' on hearing of the fall of the Bastille]

Larkin, Philip (1922–)

7 Why should I let the toad *work* / Squat on my life? ['Toads']

Latimer, Bishop Hugh (c. 1485–1555)

8 Be of good comfort, Master Ridley, and play the man. We shall this day light such a candle by God's grace in England, as (I trust) shall never be put out. [Foxe, *Actes and Monuments*]

Lawrence, D. H. (1885–1930)

1 How beastly the bourgeois is / especially the
male of the species. ['How Beastly the Bourgeois
Is']

2 Have you built your ship of death, O have you? /
O build your ship of death, for you will need it.
['The Ship of Death']

3 Loud peace propaganda makes war seem
imminent. ['Peace and War']

4 To the Puritan all things are impure, as
somebody says. [*Etruscan Places*, 'Cerveteri']

5 Pornography is the attempt to insult sex, to do
dirt on it. ['Pornography and Obscenity']

6 Never trust the artist. Trust the tale. [*Studies in
Classic American Literature*, 'The Spirit of Place']

7 The novel is the one bright book of life. ['Why
the Novel Matters']

Lazarus, Emma (1849–1887)

8 Give me your tired, your poor, / Your huddled
masses yearning to breathe free. [Verse inscribed
on Statue of Liberty]

Leacock, Stephen Butler (1869–1944)

9 Lord Ronald said nothing; he flung himself from
the room, flung himself upon his horse and rode
madly off in all directions. ['Gertrude the
Governess']

10 I detest life-insurance agents; they always argue
that I shall someday die, which is not so.
[*Literary Lapses*, 'Insurance Up to Date']

Lear, Edward (1812–1888)

11 'How pleasant to know Mr. Lear!' / Who has
written such volumes of stuff! / Some think him
ill-tempered and queer, / But a few think him
pleasant enough. [*Nonsense Songs*, Preface]

12 The Dong! — the Dong! / The Dong with the

Luminous Nose! [Ib. 'The Dong with the
Luminous Nose']

1 Far and few, far and few, / Are the lands where
the Jumblies live; / Their heads are green, and
their hands are blue, / And they went to sea in a
Sieve. [Ib. 'The Jumblies']

2 The Owl and the Pussy-Cat went to sea / In a
beautiful pea-green boat. / They took some
honey, and plenty of money, / Wrapped up in a
five-pound note. / The Owl looked up to the
Stars above / And sang to a small guitar, / 'Oh
lovely Pussy! — O Pussy, my love, / What a
beautiful Pussy you are.' [Ib. 'The Owl and the
Pussy-Cat']

3 They dined on mince, and slices of quince, /
Which they ate with a runcible spoon; / And
hand in hand, on the edge of the sand, / They
danced by the light of the moon. [Ib.]

Leary, Timothy (1920–   )

4 Turn on, tune in, and drop out. [*The Politics of
Ecstasy*]

Le Corbusier (1887–1965)

5 *Une maison est une machine-à-habiter.* A house
is a machine for living in. [*Vers une architecture*]

Lee, Robert E. (1807–1870)

6 It is well that war is so terrible — we would
grow too fond of it. [Remark, 1862]

Lennon, John (1940–1980)

7 We're more popular than Jesus Christ now.
[Remark in interview]

L'Estrange, Sir Roger (1616–1704)

8 It is with our passions as it is with fire and
water, they are good servants, but bad masters.
[*Aesop's Fables*, 38]

Levant, Oscar (1906–)

1 Strip the phony tinsel off Hollywood and you'll find the real tinsel underneath. [Quoted in Halliwell, *Filmgoer's Book of Quotes*]

Lévis, Duc de (1764–1830)

2 *Noblesse oblige.* Nobility has obligations. [*Maximes et réflexions*]

Lévi-Strauss, Claude (1908–)

3 *La langue est une raison humaine qui a ses raisons, et que l'homme ne connaît pas.* Language is a kind of human reason, which has its internal logic of which man knows nothing. [*La Pensée Sauvage*; see Pascal, *Pensées*, IV, 277]

Lewes, G. H. (1817–1878)

4 Murder, like talent, seems occasionally to run in families. [*Physiology of Common Life*, 12]

Lewis, C.S. (1898–1963)

5 She's the sort of woman who lives for others — you can tell the others by their hunted expression. [*The Screwtape Letters*, 26]

Leybourne, George (?–1884)

6 He flies through the air with the greatest of ease, / This daring young man on the flying trapeze. ['The Man on the Flying Trapeze']

Liberace, Wlaziu Valentino (1920–)

7 I cried all the way to the bank. [*Autobiography*]

Lichtenberg, Georg Cristoph (1742–1799)

8 There can hardly be a stranger commodity in the world than books. Printed by people who don't understand them; sold by people who don't understand them; bound, criticized and read by people who don't understand them, and now even

written by people who don't understand them. [*A Doctrine of Scattered Occasions*]

Lincoln, Abraham (1809–1865)

1 You can fool some of the people all of the time, and all of the people some of the time, but you cannot fool all of the people all the time. [Attr. Speech, 1856]

2 The ballot is stronger than the bullet. [Speech, 1856]

3 I leave you, hoping that the lamp of liberty will burn in your bosoms, until there shall be no longer be a doubt that all men are created free and equal. [Speech, 1858]

4 In giving freedom to the slave, we assure freedom to the free — honourable alike in what we give and what we preserve. [Speech, 1862]

5 Fourscore and seven years ago, our fathers brought forth upon this continent a new nation conceived in liberty, and dedicated to the proposition that all men are created equal. [Address, Gettysburg, 1863]

6 The world will little note nor long remember what we say here, but it can never forget what they did here ... It is rather for us to be here dedicated to the great task remaining before us — that from these honoured dead we take increased devotion to that cause for which they gave the last full measure of devotion; that we here highly resolve that these dead shall not have died in vain; that this nation, under God, shall have a new birth of freedom; and that government of the people, by the people, for the people, shall not perish from the earth. [Ib.]

7 He reminds me of the man who murdered both his parents, and then, when sentence was about to be pronounced, pleaded for mercy on the

grounds that he was an orphan. [Gross, *Lincoln's Own Stories*]

1 Better to remain silent and be thought a fool than to speak out and remove all doubt. [Attr.]

2 [On losing an election] Like a little boy who has stubbed his toe in the dark . . . too old to cry, but it hurt too much to laugh. [Attr. by Adlai Stevenson]

Linnaeus, Carl (1707–1778)

3 *Natura non facit saltus.* Nature does not make jumps. [*Philosophia Botanica*]

Litvinoff, Maxim (1876–1951)

4 Peace is indivisible. [Speech to League of Nations, 1936]

Livy (59 B.C.–A.D. 17)

5 *Vae victis.* Woe to the vanquished. [*History*, V]

Lloyd, Marie (1870–1922)

6 I'm one of the ruins Cromwell knocked about a bit. [Music hall song]

7 A little of what you fancy does you good. [Music hall song]

Lloyd George, David (1863–1945)

8 A fully equipped duke costs as much to keep up as two Dreadnoughts; and dukes are just as great a terror and they last longer. [Speech, 1909]

9 What is our task? To make Britain a fit country for heroes to live in. [Speech, 1918]

10 Love your neighbour is not merely sound Christianity; it is good business. [*Observer*, 'Sayings of the Week', 1921]

Locke, John (1632–1704)

11 No man's knowledge here can go beyond his

experience. [*Essay concerning Human Understanding*, II]

1 Wherever Law ends, Tyranny begins. [*Second Treatise of Government*]

Locker-Lampson, Frederick (1821–1895)

2 The world's as ugly, ay, as sin, / And almost as delightful. ['The Jester's Plea']

Lodge, David (1935–)

3 Literature is mostly about having sex and not much about having children; life is the other way round. [*The British Museum is Falling Down*, 4]

Logau, Friedrich von (1605–1655)

4 *Gottesmühlen mahlen langsam, mahlen aber trefflich klein.* The mills of God grind slow, but they grind exceeding small. [*Sinngedichte*, III]

London, Jack (1876–1916)

5 The Call of the Wild [Book title]

Longfellow, Henry Wadsworth (1807–1882)

6 The cares that infest the day / Shall fold their tents, like the Arabs, / And as silently steal away. ['The Day is Done']

7 The shades of night were falling fast, / As through an Alpine village passed / A youth, who bore, 'mid snow and ice, / A banner with the strange device, / Excelsior! ['Excelsior']

8 A boy's will is the wind's will, / And the thoughts of youth are long, long thoughts. ['My Lost Youth']

9 Not in the clamour of the crowded street, / Not in the shouts and plaudits of the throng, / But in ourselves, are triumph and defeat. ['The Poets']

10 Lives of great men all remind us / We can make our lives sublime, / And, departing, leave behind

us / Footprints on the sands of time. ['A Psalm of Life']

1 By the shores of Gitche Gumee, / By the shining Big-Sea-Water, / Stood the wigwam of Nokomis, / Daughter of the Moon, Nokomis. [*The Song of Hiawatha*, 'Hiawatha's Childhood']

2 Ships that pass in the night, and speak each other in passing. [*Tales of a Wayside Inn*, 'The Theologian's Tale']

3 It was the schooner Hesperus, / That sailed the wintry sea; / And the skipper had taken his little daughter, / To bear him company. ['The Wreck of the Hesperus']

Loos, Anita (1893–1981)

4 Gentlemen Prefer Blondes [Title of book]

5 Kissing your hand may make you feel very very good but a diamond and safire bracelet lasts forever. [*Gentlemen Prefer Blondes*]

Louis XIV of France (1638–1715)

6 *L'Etat c'est moi.* I am the State. [Attr.]

Louis XVIII of France (1755–1824)

7 *L'exactitude est la politesse des rois.* Punctuality is the politeness of kings. [Attr.]

Lovelace, Richard (1618–1658)

8 When thirsty grief in wine we steep, / When healths and draughts go free, / Fishes, that tipple in the deep, / Know no such liberty. ['To Althea, from Prison']

9 Stone Walls do not a Prison make / Nor Iron bars a Cage; / Minds innocent and quiet take / That for an hermitage. [Ib.]

Lovell, Maria (1803–1877)

10 Two souls with but a single thought, / Two

hearts that beat as one. [*Ingomar the Barbarian*, II]

Lowell, Robert (1917–1977)

1 This is death, / To die and know it. This is the Black Widow, death. ['Mr. Edwards and the Spider']

2 The Lord survives the rainbow of His will. ['The Quaker Graveyard in Nantucket', VII]

Lucretius (c. 95–55 B.C.)

3 *Inque brevi spatio mutantur saecla animantum / Et quasi cursores vitai lampada tradunt.* In a short while the generations of the living are changed and like runners pass on the torch of life. [*De Rerum Natura*, II]

4 *Ut quod ali cibus est aliis fuat acre venenum.* What is food to one is to others bitter poison. [Ib. IV]

Luther, Martin (1483–1546)

5 *Ein feste Burg ist unser Gott, / Ein gute Wehr und Waffen.* A safe stronghold our God is still, / A trusty shield and weapon. [Hymn; trans. Carlyle]

6 *Hier stehe ich. Ich kann nicht anders.* Here I stand. I can do no other. [Speech at Diet of Worms]

7 *Esto peccator et pecca fortiter, sed fortius fide et gaude in Christo.* Be a sinner and sin strongly, but believe and rejoice in Christ even more strongly. [Letter to Melanchthon]

Lyte, Henry Francis (1793–1847)

8 Abide with me: fast falls the eventide; / The darkness deepens; Lord, with me abide. [Hymn]

McArthur, Douglas (1880–1964)

1 I shall return. [Message on leaving the Philippines, 1942]

Macaulay, Thomas Babington, Lord (1800–1859)

2 Lars Porsena of Clusium / By the nine gods he swore / That the great house of Tarquin / Should suffer wrong no more. [*Lays of Ancient Rome*, 'Horatius', 1]

3 But those behind cried 'Forward!' / And those before cried 'Back!' [Ib. 50]

4 O Tiber! father Tiber! / To whom the Romans pray, / A Roman's life, a Roman's arms, / Take thou in charge this day! [Ib. 59]

5 And even the ranks of Tuscany / Could scarce forbear to cheer. [Ib. 60]

6 The gallery in which the reporters sit has become a fourth estate of the realm. [*Historical Essays (Edinburgh Review*, 1828)]

7 Thus our democracy was, from an early period, the most aristocratic, and our aristocracy the most democratic in the world. [*History of England*, I]

8 The Puritan hated bear-baiting, not because it gave pain to the bear, but because it gave pleasure to the spectators. [Ib.]

9 Perhaps no person can be a poet, or can even enjoy poetry, without a certain unsoundness of mind. [*Literary Essays*, 'Milton']

10 Nothing is so useless as a general maxim. [Ib. 'Machiavelli']

11 We know of no spectacle so ridiculous as the British public in one of its periodical fits of morality. [Ib. 'Moore's Life of Byron']

12 From the poetry of Lord Byron they drew a system of ethics, compounded of misanthropy

and voluptuousness, a system in which the two great commandments were, to hate your neighbour, and to love your neighbour's wife. [Ib.]

McClellan, George (1826–1885)

1 All quiet along the Potomac. [Attr. in American Civil War; *see* E.L. Beers, 'The Picket Guard']

McCrae, John (1872–1918)

2 Take up our quarrel with the foe: / To you from failing hands we throw / The torch; be yours to hold it high. / If ye break faith with us who die / We shall not sleep, though poppies grow / In Flanders fields. ['In Flanders Fields']

MacDiarmid, Hugh (1892–1978)

3 Earth, thou bonnie broukit bairn! / — But greet, an' in your tears ye'll droun / The haill clanjamfrie! ['The Bonnie Broukit Bairn']

4 Fegs, God's no blate gin he stirs up / The men o' Crowdieknowe! ['Crowdieknowe']

5 I'll ha'e nae hauf-way hoose, but aye be whaur / Extremes meet — it's the only way I ken / To dodge the curst conceit o' bein' richt / That damns the vast majority o' men. [*A Drunk Man Looks at the Thistle*]

6 Nae doot they're sober, as a Scot ne'er was, / Each tethered to a punctual snorin' missus, / Whilst I, pure fule, owre continents unkent / And wine-dark oceans waunder like Ulysses. [Ib.]

7 And on my lips ye'll heed nae mair, / And in my hair forget, / The seed o' a' the men that in / My virgin womb ha'e met. [Ib.]

8 And as at sicna times ane I, / I wad ha'e Scotland to my eye / Until I saw a timeless flame / Tak' Auchtermuchty for a name, / And kent that Ecclefechan stood / As pairt o' an eternal mood. [Ib.]

1 The wee reliefs we ha'e in booze, / Or wun at times in carnal states, / May hide frae us but canna cheenge / The silly horrors o' oor fates. [Ib.]

2 And Jesus and a nameless ape / Collide and share the selfsame shape / That nocht terrestrial can escape. [Ib.]

3 What happens to us / Is irrelevant to the world's geology / But what happens to the world's geology / Is not irrelevant to us. ['On a Raised Beach']

4 And I lo'e love / Wi' a scunner in't. ['Scunner']

MacDonald, George (1824–1905)

5 Here lie I, Martin Elginbrodde: / Hae mercy o' my soul, Lord God; / As I wad do, were I Lord God, / And you were Martin Elginbrodde. [*David Elginbrod*, I]

MacDonald, Ramsay (1866–1937)

6 We hear war called murder. It is not: it is suicide. [*Observer*, 'Sayings of the Week', 1930]

McGonagall, William (1825–1902)

7 Beautiful Railway Bridge of the Silv'ry Tay! / Alas, I am very sorry to say / That ninety lives have been taken away / On the last Sabbath day of 1879, / Which will be remember'd for a very long time. ['The Tay Bridge Disaster']

Machiavelli, Niccolo di Bernardo dei (1469–1527)

8 Fortune is a woman, and therefore friendly to the young, who command her with audacity. [*Il Principe*, 25]

Mackintosh, Sir James (1765–1832)

9 The Commons, faithful to their system, remained

in a wise and masterly inactivity. [*Vindiciae Gallicae*]

MacLeod, Norman (1812–1872)

1 Courage, brother! do not stumble, / Though thy path be dark as night. [Hymn]

McLuhan, Marshall (1911–1980)

2 The new electronic interdependence recreates the world in the image of a global village. [*The Gutenberg Galaxy*]

3 The medium is the message. [*Understanding Media*]

MacMillan, Harold (1894–   )

4 Most of our people have never had it so good. [Speech, 1957]

5 The wind of change is blowing through this continent [Africa]. [Speech, 1960]

MacNeice, Louis (1907–1963)

6 It's no go the merrygoround, it's no go the rickshaw, / All we want is a limousine and a ticket for the peep show. ['Bagpipe Music']

Madariaga, Salvador de (1886–1979)

7 First, the sweetheart of the nation, then her aunt, woman governs America because America is a land where boys refuse to grow up. ['Americans are Boys']

Magna Carta (1215)

8 Except by the lawful judgment of his peers and by the law of the land. [39]

9 To no one will we sell, or deny, or delay, right or justice. [40]

Maistre, Joseph de (1753–1821)

10 Every country has the government it deserves. [Letter, 1811]

Mallory, George Leigh (1886–1924)

1 [Asked why he wished to climb Mt. Everest] Because it is there.

Malory, Sir Thomas (d. 1471)

2 Whoso pulleth out this sword of this stone and anvil is rightwise King born of all England. [*Le Morte D'Arthur*, I, 4]

Mann, Horace (1796–1859)

3 Lost, yesterday, somewhere between Sunrise and Sunset, two golden hours, each set with sixty diamond minutes. No reward is offered, for they are gone for ever. ['Lost, Two Golden Hours']

Mansfield, Katherine (1888–1923)

4 England is merely an island of beef flesh swimming in a warm gulf stream of gravy. ['The Modern Soul']

Mao Tse-Tung (1893–1976)

5 Political power grows out of the barrel of a gun. [*Quotations from Chairman Mao*]

6 Imperialism is a paper tiger. [Ib.]

Marie-Antoinette (1755–1793)

7 *Qu'ils mangent de la brioche*. Let them eat cake. [Attr. (but much older)]

Marlowe, Christopher (1564–1593)

8 Sweet Analytics, 'tis thou hast ravished me. [*Doctor Faustus*, I.1]

9 What doctrine call you this, *Che sera, sera*, What will be, shall be? [Ib.]

10 Why this is hell, nor am I out of it: / Thinkst thou that I who saw the face of God, / And tasted the eternal joys of heaven, / Am not tormented with ten thousand hells / In being deprived of everlasting bliss? [Ib. I.3]

1 Hell hath no limits nor is circumscrib'd / In one self place, where we are is Hell, / And where Hell is, there must we ever be. [Ib. II.1]

2 Was this the face that launch'd a thousand ships / And burnt the topless towers of Ilium? / Sweet Helen, make me immortal with a kiss! / Her lips suck forth my soul: see, where it flies! [Ib. V.1]

3 Now thou hast but one bare hour to live, / And then thou must be damned perpetually. / Stand still you ever-moving spheres of heaven, / That time may cease, and midnight never come. [Ib. V.2]

4 O lente, lente currite, noctis equi: The stars move still, time runs, the clock will strike, / The devil will come, and Faustus must be damn'd. [Ib.]

5 See see where Christ's blood streams in the firmament. / One drop would save my soul, half a drop, ah my Christ. [Ib.]

6 Cut is the branch that might have grown full straight, / And burnèd is Apollo's laurel bough, / That some time grew within this learnèd man. [Ib. Epilogue]

7 Fair blows the wind for France. [Edward II, I]

8 My men, like satyrs grazing on the lawns, / Shall with their goat feet dance the antic hay. [Ib.]

9 Where both deliberate, the love is slight; / Whoever loved that loved not at first sight? [Hero and Leander, I]

10 Like untun'd golden strings all women are / Which long time lie untouch'd, will harshly jar. [Ib.]

11 I count religion but a childish toy, / And hold there is no sin but ignorance. [The Jew of Malta, Prologue]

12 Infinite riches in a little room. [Ib. I.1]

13 Here come two religious caterpillars. [Ib. IV.1]

1 *Barnadine:* Thou hast committed —
Barabas: Fornication: but that was in another country; / And besides, the wench is dead. [Ib.]

2 Come live with me, and be my love, / And we will all the pleasures prove, / That hills and valleys, dales and fields, / Woods or steepy mountain yields. ['The Passionate Shepherd to his Love']

3 Is it not passing brave to be a King, / And ride in triumph through Persepolis? [*Tamburlaine the Great,* I]

4 Until we reach the ripest fruit of all, / That perfect bliss and sole felicity, / The sweet fruition of an earthly crown. [Ib.]

5 Ah fair Zenocrate, divine Zenocrate, / Fair is too foul an epithet for thee. [Ib.]

6 Holla, ye pampered jades of Asia! / What, can ye draw but twenty miles a-day? [Ib. II]

7 Tamburlaine, the Scourge of God, must die. [Ib.]

Marquis, Don (1878–1937)

8 but wotthehell wotthehell / oh I should worry and fret / death and I will coquette / there s a dance in the old dame yet / toujours gai toujours gai. [*archy and mehitabel*, 'the song of mehitabel']

Marryat, Frederick (1792–1848)

9 We always took care of number one. [*Frank Mildmay*, 19]

10 As savage as a bear with a sore head. [*King's Own*, 26]

11 [Of an illegitimate baby] If you please, ma'am, it was a very little one. [*Mr. Midshipman Easy*, 3]

12 It's just six of one and half-a-dozen of the other. [*The Pirate*, 4]

1 Every man paddle his own canoe. [*Settlers in Canada*, 8]

Marshall, Thomas (1854–1925)

2 What this country needs is a good five-cent cigar. [Remark to Chief Clerk of U.S. Senate]

Martial (c. A.D. 43–c. 104)

3 *Lasciva est nobis pagina, vita proba.* My poems are licentious, but my life is pure. [*Epigrams*, I]

4 *Rus in urbe.* The country in town. [Ib. XII]

Marvell, Andrew (1621–1678)

5 My Love is of a birth as rare / As 'tis for object strange and high: / It was begotten by despair / Upon Impossibility. ['The Definition of Love']

6 As Lines so Loves *oblique* may well / Themselves in every Angle greet: / But ours so truly *Parallel*, / Though infinite can never meet. [Ib.]

7 Earth cannot shew so brave a Sight / As when a single Soul does fence / The Batteries of alluring Sense, / And Heaven views it with delight. ['A Dialogue between the Resolved Soul and Created Pleasure']

8 But all resistance against her is vain, / Who has the advantage both of Eyes and Voice. / And all my Forces needs must be undone, / She having gained both the Wind and Sun. ['The Fair Singer']

9 Engines more keen than ever yet / Adorned Tyrants Cabinet; / Of which the most tormenting are / Black Eyes, red Lips, and curled Hair. ['The Gallery']

10 Meanwhile the Mind, from pleasure less, / Withdraws into its happiness: / The Mind, that Ocean where each kind / Does straight its own resemblance find. ['The Garden']

1 Annihilating all that's made / To a green Thought in a green Shade. [Ib.]

2 Had we but world enough, and time, / This coyness, Lady, were no crime. ['To His Coy Mistress']

3 My vegetable love should grow / Vaster than empires, and more slow. [Ib.]

4 But at my back I always hear / Times wingèd Chariot hurrying near. [Ib.]

5 The Grave's a fine and private place / But none I think do there embrace. [Ib.]

6 Let us roll all our strength and all / Our sweetness up into one ball, / And tear our pleasures with rough strife / Thorough the iron gates of life. [Ib.]

Marx, Groucho (1895–1977)

7 Either he's dead or my watch has stopped. [*A Day at the Races*]

8 Remember, men, we're fighting for this woman's honour; which is probably more than she ever did. [*Duck Soup*]

9 I resign. I wouldn't want to belong to any club that would have me as a member. [Attr.]

Marx, Karl (1818–1883)

10 The workers have nothing to lose but their chains in this. They have a world to win. Workers of the world, unite! [*Communist Manifesto*]

11 From each according to his abilities, to each according to his needs. [*Critique of the Gotha Programme*]

12 Religion . . . is the opium of the people. [*Critique of Hegel's Philosophy of Right*]

13 The philosophers have only interpreted the world

in various ways; the point, however, is to change it. [*Theses on Feuerbach*, 11]

1 The class struggle necessarily leads to the dictatorship of the proletariat. [*Letter*, 1852]

Mary Queen of Scots (1542–1587)

2 England is not all the world. [Said at her trial, 1586]

Mary Tudor (1516–1558)

3 When I am dead and opened, you shall find 'Calais' lying in my heart. [Attr.]

Masefield, John (1878–1966)

4 Quinquireme of Nineveh from distant Ophir / Rowing home to haven in sunny Palestine, / With a cargo of ivory, / And apes and peacocks, / Sandalwood, cedarwood and sweet white wine. ['Cargoes']

5 I must down to the seas again, to the lonely sea and the sky, / And all I ask is a tall ship and a star to steer her by. ['Sea Fever']

6 I must down to the seas again, to the vagrant gypsy life, / To the gull's way and the whale's way where the wind's like a whetted knife; / And all I ask is a merry yarn from a laughing fellow rover, / And a quiet sleep and a sweet dream when the long trick's over. [Ib.]

7 I never hear the west wind but tears are in my eyes, / For it comes from the west lands, the old brown hills, / And April's in the west wind, and daffodils. ['The West Wind']

Mass

8 *Dominus vobiscum.* / *Et cum spiritu tuo.* The Lord be with you. / And with thy spirit.

9 *Mea culpa, mea culpa, mea maxima culpa.* Through my fault, my fault, my most grievous fault.

1 *Requiem aeternam dona eis, Domine: et lux perpetua luceat eis.* Grant them eternal rest, O Lord; and let perpetual light shine on them. [At Requiem Masses]

2 *Agnus Dei, qui tollis peccata mundi, miserere nobis.* Lamb of God, who takest away the sins of the world, have mercy upon us.

3 *Requiescant in pace.* May they rest in peace. [At Requiem Masses]

Massinger, Philip (1583–1640)

4 Death has a thousand doors to let out life: / I shall find one. [*A Very Woman*, V.4]

Maugham, William Somerset (1874–1965)

5 People ask you for criticism, but they only want praise. [*Of Human Bondage*]

6 Like all weak men he laid an exaggerated stress on not changing one's mind. [Ib.]

7 It's no use crying over spilt milk, because all the forces of the universe were bent on spilling it. [Ib.]

8 Impropriety is the soul of wit. [*The Moon and Sixpence*]

Mearns, Hughes (1875–1965)

9 As I was going up the stair / I met a man who wasn't there. / He wasn't there again to-day. / I wish, I wish he'd stay away. ['The Psychoed']

Melbourne, William Lamb, Viscount (1779–1848)

10 Things have come to a pretty pass when religion is allowed to invade the sphere of private life. [Remark]

11 Damn it all, another Bishop dead — I verily believe they die to vex me. [Attr.]

1 Nobody ever did anything very foolish except from some strong principle. [Attr.]

2 While I cannot be regarded as a pillar, I must be regarded as a buttress of the church, because I support it from the outside. [Attr.]

Melville, Herman (1819–1891)

3 Call me Ishmael. [*Moby Dick*, 1, first words]

Menander (c. 342–292 B.C.)

4 Whom the gods love dies young. [*The Double Deceiver*]

Mencken, H. L. (1880–1956)

5 Every normal man must be tempted, at times, to spit on his hands, hoist the black flag, and begin slitting throats. [*Prejudices*]

6 Women hate revolutions and revolutionists. They like men who are docile, and well-regarded at the bank, and never late at meals. [Ib.]

7 Poetry is a comforting piece of fiction set to more or less lascivious music. [Ib.]

8 Faith may be defined briefly as an illogical belief in the occurrence of the improbable. [Ib.]

Meredith, George (1828–1909)

9 Ah, what a dusty answer gets the soul / When hot for certainties in this our life! [*Modern Love*]

10 I expect that Woman will be the last thing civilized by Man. [*The Ordeal of Richard Feverel*, 1]

11 Kissing don't last: cookery do! [Ib. 28]

12 Speech is the small change of silence. [Ib. 34]

13 Cynicism is intellectual dandyism. [*The Egoist*, 7]

Meredith, Owen Lord Lytton (1831–1891)

14 Genius does what it must, and Talent does what

it can. ['Last Words of a Sensitive Second-Rate Poet']

Merritt, Dixon Lanier (1879-1954)

1 A wonderful bird is the pelican, / His bill will hold more than his belican. / He can take in his beak / Food enough for a week, / But I'm damned if I see how the helican. ['The Pelican']

Metternich, Prince Clement (1773-1859)

2 When Paris sneezes, Europe catches cold. [Remark, 1830]

3 Italy is a geographical expression. [Letter, 1849]

Mill, John Stuart (1806-1873)

4 Ask yourself whether you are happy, and you cease to be so. [*Autobiography*, 5]

5 The Conservatives ... being by the law of their existence the stupidest party. [*Considerations on Representative Government*, 7 (footnote)]

6 The sole end for which mankind are warranted, individually or collectively, in interfering with the liberty of action of any of their number, is self-protection. [*On Liberty*, Introduction]

7 If all mankind minus one, were of one opinion, and only one person were of the contrary opinion, mankind would be no more justified in silencing that one person, than he, if he had the power, would be justified in silencing mankind. [Ib. 2]

8 History teems with instances of truth put down by persecution ... It is a piece of idle sentimentality that truth, merely as truth, has any inherent power denied to error, of prevailing against the dungeon and the stake. [Ib.]

9 Whatever crushes individuality is despotism, by whatever name it may be called. [Ib. 3]

1 I am not aware that any community has a right to force another to be civilized. [Ib. 4]

2 The worth of a State, in the long run, is the worth of the individuals composing it. [Ib. 5]

3 The principle which regulates the existing social relations between the two sexes — the legal subordination of one sex to the other — is wrong in itself, and now one of the chief hindrances to human improvement. [*The Subjection of Women*, 1]

Miller, William (1810–1872)

4 Wee Willie Winkie / Rins through the toon; / Upstairs an' doonstairs / In his nicht goon. ['Wee Willie Winkie']

Milman, H.H. (1791–1868)

5 Ride on! ride on in majesty! / In lowly pomp ride on to die. [Hymn]

Milne, A.A. (1882–1956)

6 And nobody knows / (Tiddely pom), / How cold my toes / (Tiddely pom), / How cold my toes / (Tiddely pom), / Are growing. [*The House at Pooh Corner*, 1]

7 Isn't it funny / How a bear likes honey? / Buzz! Buzz! Buzz! / I wonder why he does? [*Winnie-the-Pooh*, 1]

8 I am a Bear of Very Little Brain, and long words Bother me. [Ib. 4]

9 Time for a little something. [Ib. 6]

10 They're changing guard at Buckingham Palace — / Christopher Robin went down with Alice. [*When We Were Very Young*, 'Buckingham Palace']

11 I do like a little bit of butter to my bread! [Ib. 'The King's Breakfast']

12 Little Boy kneels at the foot of the bed, / Droops

on the little hands, little gold head; / Hush!
Hush! Whisper who dares! / Christopher Robin is
saying his prayers. [Ib. 'Vespers']

Milton, John (1608–1674)

1 Blest pair of Sirens, pledges of Heaven's joy, /
Sphere-born harmonious sisters, Voice and Verse.
['At a Solemn Music']

2 Come, knit hands, and beat the ground, / In a
light fantastic round. [*Comus*]

3 Hence vain, deluding joys, / The brood of folly
without father bred. ['Il Penseroso']

4 Hail divinest Melancholy. [Ib.]

5 Far from all resort of mirth, / Save the cricket
on the hearth. [Ib.]

6 Or let my Lamp at midnight hour, / Be seen in
some high lonely Tower, / Where I may oft
outwatch the Bear, / With thrice great Hermes.
[Ib.]

7 ...th'unseen Genius of the Wood. [Ib.]

8 Hence, loathed Melancholy, / Of Cerberus, the
blackest midnight born. ['L'Allegro']

9 Sport that wrinkled Care derides, / And Laughter
holding both his sides. / Come, and trip it as ye
go / On the light fantastic toe. [Ib.]

10 And if I give thee honour due, / Mirth, admit me
of thy crew / To live with her, and live with
thee, / In unreproved pleasures free. [Ib.]

11 ...many a youth, and many a maid, / Dancing
in the Chequer'd shade; / And young and old
come forth to play / On a Sunshine Holyday, /
Till the live-long daylight fail, / Then to the
Spicy Nut-brown Ale. [Ib.]

12 Or sweetest Shakespeare, fancy's child, / Warble
his native Wood-notes wild. [Ib.]

13 The melting voice through mazes running. [Ib.]

1 Yet once more, O ye Laurels, and once more /
Ye Myrtles brown, with Ivy never-sear, / I come
to pluck your Berries, harsh and crude.
['Lycidas']

2 For Lycidas is dead, dead ere his prime / Young
Lycidas, and hath not left his peer. [Ib.]

3 Were it not better done as others use, / To sport
with Amaryllis in the shade, / Or with the
tangles of Neaera's hair? [Ib.]

4 Fame is the spur that the clear spirit doth raise /
(That last infirmity of Noble mind) / To scorn
delights, and live laborious days. [Ib.]

5 The Pilot of the Galilean lake, / Two massey
Keys he bore of metals twain; / (The Golden
opes, the Iron shuts amain). [Ib.]

6 Look homeward, Angel, now, and melt with ruth.
[Ib.]

7 At last he rose, and twitch'd his Mantle blue: /
Tomorrow to fresh Woods, and Pastures new.
[Ib.]

8 It was the Winter wild, / While the Heav'n-borne
child, / All meanly wrapt in the rude manger
lies. ['On the Morning of Christ's Nativity']

9 Ring out ye Crystal spheres, / Once bless our
human ears. [Ib.]

10 Time will run back, and fetch the age of gold, /
And speckl'd vanity / Will sicken soon and die.
[Ib.]

11 Of Man's First Disobedience, and the Fruit / Of
that Forbidden Tree, whose mortal taste /
Brought Death into the World, and all our woe.
[*Paradise Lost*, I]

12 I may assert Eternal Providence, / And justify
the ways of God to men. [Ib.]

13 No light, but rather darkness visible. [Ib.]

14 But O how fall'n! how chang'd / From him who

in the happy Realms of Light / Cloth'd with transcendent brightness didst outshine / Myriads though bright. [Ib.]

1 What though the field be lost? / All is not lost; the unconquerable Will, / And study of revenge, immortal hate, / And courage never to submit or yield. [Ib.]

2 The mind is its own place, and in itself / Can make a Heav'n of Hell, a Hell of Heav'n. [Ib.]

3 To reign is worth ambition though in Hell: / Better to reign in Hell, than serve in Heav'n. [Ib.]

4 The reign of Chaos and old Night. [Ib.]

5 To Noon he fell, from Noon to dewy Eve, / A Summer's day; and with the setting Sun / Dropt from the Zenith like a falling Star. [Ib.]

6 High on a Throne of Royal State, which far / Outshone the wealth of Ormus and of Ind, / Or where the gorgeous East with richest hand / Showers on her Kings Barbaric Pearl and Gold, / Satan exalted sat. [Ib. II]

7 His trust was with th'Eternal to be deem'd / Equal in strength, and rather than be less / Car'd not to be at all. [Ib.]

8 For who would lose, / Though full of pain, this intellectual being, / Those thoughts that wander through Eternity? [Ib.]

9 ... preferring / Hard liberty before the easy yoke / Of servile Pomp. [Ib.]

10 Advise if this be worth / Attempting, or to sit in darkness here / Hatching vain Empires. [Ib.]

11 O shame to men! Devil with Devil damn'd / Firm concord holds: men only disagree / Of Creatures rational, though under hope / Of heavenly Grace; and God proclaiming peace, / Yet live in hatred, enmity, and strife / Among themselves, and levy

cruel wars, / Wasting the Earth, each other to destroy. [Ib.]

1 Long is the way / And hard, that out of Hell leads up to Light. [Ib.]

2 I fled, and cry'd out Death; / Hell trembl'd at the hideous Name, and sigh'd / From all her Caves, and back resounded Death. [Ib.]

3 Confusion worse confounded. [Ib.]

4 Which way I fly is Hell; myself am Hell. [Ib. IV]

5 Imparadis'd in one another's arms. [Ib.]

6 Evil be thou my Good. [Ib.]

7 Yielded with coy submission, modest pride, / And sweet reluctant amorous delay. [Ib.]

8 Best Image of my self and dearer half. [Ib. V]

9 But what if better counsels might erect / Our minds and teach us to cast off this Yoke? / Will ye submit your necks, and choose to bend / The supple knee? [Ib.]

10 Headlong themselves they threw / Down from the verge of Heav'n, eternal wrath / Burnt after them to the bottomless pit. [Ib. VI]

11 ...the sum of earthly bliss. [Ib. VIII]

12 The serpent subtlest beast of all the field. [Ib. IX]

13 As one who long in populous City pent, / Where Houses thick and Sewers annoy the Air. [Ib.]

14 Earth felt the wound, and Nature from her seat / Sighing through all her Works gave signs of woe, / That all was lost. [Ib.]

15 Yet I shall temper so / Justice with Mercy. [Ib. X]

16 On all sides, from innumerable tongues / A dismal universal hiss, the sound / Of public scorn. [Ib.]

17 Destruction with destruction to destroy. [Ib.]

18 The World was all before them, where to choose

/ Their place of rest, and Providence their guide:
/ They hand in hand with wand'ring steps and
slow, / Through Eden took their solitary way.
[Ib. XII]

1 I who ere while the happy Garden sung, / By
one man's disobedience lost, now sing /
Recover'd Paradise to all mankind. [*Paradise
Regained*, I]

2 The childhood shews the man, / As morning
shews the day. [Ib. IV]

3 The first and wisest of them all profess'd / To
know this only, that he nothing knew. [Ib.]

4 But headlong joy is ever on the wing, / In
Wintry solstice like the shortn'd light / Soon
swallow'd up in dark and long out-living night.
['The Passion']

5 Ask for this great Deliverer now, and find him /
Eyeless in Gaza, at the Mill with slaves. [*Samson
Agonistes*]

6 O dark, dark, dark, amid the blaze of noon, /
Irrecoverably dark, total Eclipse / Without all
hope of day! [Ib.]

7 And calm of mind all passion spent. [Ib.]

8 Now the bright morning Star, Day's harbinger, /
Comes dancing from the East, and leads with her
/ The Flow'ry May ['Song on May Morning']

9 Time, the subtle thief of youth. [*Sonnets*, 7]

10 Licence they mean when they cry liberty. [Ib. 12]

11 Avenge, O Lord, thy slaughtered Saints, whose
bones / Lie scattered on the Alpine mountains
cold; / Ev'n them who kept thy truth so pure of
old, / When all our Fathers worshipped Stocks
and Stones. [Ib. 15, 'On the late Massacre at
Piedmont']

12 Thousands at his bidding speed / And post o'er
Land and Ocean without rest: / They also serve

who only stand and wait. [Ib. 16, 'On His Blindness']

1 As good almost kill a man as kill a good book: who kills a man kills a reasonable creature, God's image; but he who destroys a good book, kills reason itself, kills the image of God, as it were in the eye. [*Areopagitica*]

Mirabeau, Comte de (1749–1791)

2 War is the national industry of Prussia. [Attr.]

Missal

3 *O felix culpa, quae talem ac tantum meruit habere Redemptorum.* O happy fault, which has earned such and so great a Redeemer. ['Exsultet' on Holy Saturday]

Mola, Emilio (1887–1937)

4 *La quinta columna.* The fifth column. [Comment on hopes of civilian uprising in Madrid, 1937]

Molière (1622–1673)

5 *Il faut manger pour vivre et non pas vivre pour manger.* One should eat to live, not live to eat. [*L'Avare*, III.5]

6 *Par ma foi! il y a plus de quarante ans que je dis de la prose sans que j'en susse rien.* Good Heavens! For more than forty years I have been speaking prose without knowing it. [*Le Bourgeois Gentilhomme*, II.4]

7 *Le mariage, Agnès, n'est pas un badinage.* Marriage, Agnès, is not a joke. [*L'Ecole des Femmes*, III]

8 *Je vis de bonne soupe et non de beau langage.* I live on good food, not fine words. [*Les Femmes Savantes*, II.7]

9 *Ils commencent ici par faire pendre un homme et puis ils lui font son procès.* Here they hang a

man first, and try him afterwards. [*Monsieur de Pourceaugnac*, III.2]

1 *Le ciel défend, de vrai, certains contentements / Mais on trouve avec lui des accommodements.* It is true that Heaven forbids certain pleasures, but one finds certain compromises. [*Tartuffe*, IV.5]

2 *L'homme est, je vous l'avoue, un méchant animal.* Man, I can assure you, is a wicked creature. [Ib. V]

Monroe, Marilyn (1926–1962)

3 [To the question 'Did you have anything on?'] I had the radio on. [Attr.]

Monsell, J.S.B. (1811–1875)

4 Fight the good fight / With all thy might. [Hymn]

Montagu, Lady Mary Wortley (1689–1762)

5 Satire should, like a polished razor keen, / Wound with a touch that's scarcely felt or seen. ['To the Imitator of ... Horace']

Montaigne, Michel de (1533–1592)

6 *Il se faut réserver une arrière boutique ... en laquelle nous établissions notre vraie liberté.* We must keep a little back shop ... where we may establish our own true liberty. [*Essai*, I, 39]

7 *Mon métier et mon art, c'est vivre.* To know how to live is all my calling and all my art. [Ib. II, 6]

8 *Que sais-je?* What do I know? [Ib. II, 12]

9 [Of marriage] It happens as with cages: the birds without are desperate to get in, and those within despair of getting out. [Ib. III, 5]

10 Women are not altogether in the wrong when they refuse the rules of life prescribed in the world, forsomuch as only men have established them without their consent. [Ib.]

11 Science without conscience is but death of the

soul. [Quoted in Simcox, *Treasury of Quotations on Christian Themes*]

Montesquieu, Charles, Baron de (1689–1755)

1 Liberty is the right of doing whatever the laws permit. [*De l'Esprit des Lois*, XI, 3]

Montrose, James Graham, Marquis of (1612–1650)

2 He either fears his fate too much, / Or his deserts are small, / That dare not put it to the touch, / To win or lose it all. ['My Dear and Only Love']

Moore, Clement C. (1779–1863)

3 'Twas the night before Christmas, when all through the house / Not a creature was stirring, not even a mouse. ['A Visit from St. Nicholas']

Moore, Edward (1712–1757)

4 This is adding insult to injuries. [*The Foundling*, V]

Moore, George (1852–1933)

5 Art must be parochial in the beginning to be cosmopolitan in the end. [*Hail and Farewell*]

6 The lot of critics is to be remembered by what they failed to understand. [*Impressions and Opinions*]

Moore, Thomas (1779–1852)

7 The harp that once through Tara's halls / The soul of music shed, / Now hangs as mute on Tara's walls / As if that soul were fled. [*Irish Melodies*, 'The Harp that Once']

8 No, there's nothing half so sweet in life / As love's young dream. [Ib. 'Love's Young Dream']

9 'Tis the last rose of summer / Left blooming alone; / All her lovely companions / Are faded and gone. [Ib. ''Tis the Last Rose']

1 Oft, in the stilly night. [*National Airs*, 'Oft in the Stilly Night']

Mordaunt, Thomas Osbert (1730–1809)

2 Sound, sound the clarion, fill the fife, / Throughout the sensual world proclaim, / One crowded hour of glorious life / Is worth an age without a name. ['Verses written during the War, 1756–63']

More, Sir Thomas (1478–1535)

3 I pray you, Master Lieutenant, see me safe up, and for my coming down let me shift for myself. [On ascending the scaffold]

Morell, Thomas (1703–1784)

4 See, the conquering hero comes! / Sound the trumpets, beat the drums! [*Joshua*]

Morgan, Charles (1894–1958)

5 One cannot shut one's eyes to things not seen with eyes. [*The River Line*, 3]

Morris, Desmond (1928–   )

6 The Naked Ape [i.e. *Homo sapiens*] [Title of book]

Morris, George Pope (1745–1838)

7 Woodman, spare that tree! / Touch not a single bough! / In youth it sheltered me, / And I'll protect it now. ['Woodman, Spare That Tree']

Morris, William (1834–1896)

8 Dreamer of dreams, born out of my due time, / Why should I strive to set the crooked straight? [*The Earthly Paradise*, 'An Apology']

9 All their devices for cheapening labour simply resulted in increasing the burden of labour. [*News from Nowhere*]

Morton, J.B. ['Beachcomber'] (1893–1979)

1 SIXTY HORSES WEDGED IN A CHIMNEY The story to fit this sensational headline has not turned up yet. [*The Best of Beachcomber*]

Motley, John Lothrop (1814–1877)

2 [Of William of Orange] As long as he lived, he was the guiding-star of a whole brave nation, and when he died the little children cried in the streets. [*Rise of the Dutch Republic*, VI, 7]

3 Give us the luxuries of life, and we will dispense with its necessities. [Attr.]

Mourie, Graham (1952–   )

4 Nobody ever beats Wales at rugby, they just score more points. [Quoted in Keating, *Caught by Keating*]

Mumford, Ethel (1878–1940)

5 Don't take the will for the deed; get the deed. [Quoted in Cowan, *The Wit of Women*]

6 Knowledge is power if you know it about the right person. [Ib.]

Napier, Charles James (1782–1853)

7 *Peccavi!* I have sinned. [Despatch after occupation of Sind, 1843]

Napoleon I (1769–1821)

8 France has more need of me than I have need of France. [Speech, 1813]

9 *Tout soldat français porte dans sa giberne le bâton de maréchal de France.* Every French soldier carries a French marshal's baton in his knapsack. [E. Blaze, *La Vie Militaire sous l'Empire*]

10 *L'Angleterre est une nation de boutiquiers.* England is a nation of shopkeepers. [Attr.]

11 *Du sublime au ridicule il n'y a qu'un pas.* It is

but a step from the sublime to the ridiculous.
[Attr.]

Nash, Ogden (1902–1971)

1 If I could but spot a conclusion, I should race to it. ['All, All Are Gone']

2 To be an Englishman is to belong to the most exclusive club there is. ['England Expects']

3 I am a conscientious man, when I throw rocks at seabirds I leave no tern unstoned. ['Everybody's Mind to Me a Kingdom Is']

4 Any kiddie in school can love like a fool, / But hating, my boy, is an art. ['Plea for Less Malice Toward None']

5 Candy / Is dandy / But liquor / Is quicker. ['Reflection on Ice-Breaking']

6 When Ah itchez, Ah scratchez. ['Requiem']

Nashe, Thomas (1567–1601)

7 Brightness falls from the air; / Queens have died young and fair; / Dust hath closed Helen's eye. / I am sick, I must die. / Lord, have mercy on us. ['In Time of Pestilence']

8 From winter, plague and pestilence, good Lord, deliver us! [*Summer's Last Will and Testament*, 'Autumn']

Nelson, Horatio, Viscount Nelson (1758–1805)

9 Before this time tomorrow I shall have gained a peerage, or Westminster Abbey. [Remark at Battle of the Nile, 1798]

10 I have only one eye — I have a right to be blind sometimes . . . I really do not see the signal. [Remark at Battle of Copenhagen, 1801]

11 This is too warm work, Hardy, to last long. [Remark at Battle of Trafalgar, 1805]

12 England expects every man will do his duty. [Ib.]

1 Kiss me, Hardy. [Ib.]

Nero (A.D. 37–68)

2 *Qualis artifex pereo!* What an artist dies with me! [Attr.]

Nerval, Gérard de (1808–1855)

3 *Dieu est mort! le ciel est vide − / Pleurez! enfants, vous n'avez plus de père.* God is dead! Heaven is empty − Weep, children, you no longer have a father. [Epigraph to 'Le Christ aux Oliviers']

4 *Je suis le ténébreux, − le veuf, − l'inconsolé, / Le prince d'Aquitaine à la tour abolie.* I am the shadowy one − the bereaved − the disconsolate − the prince of Aquitaine with the ruined tower. ['El Desdichado']

Newbolt, Sir Henry (1862–1938)

5 Drake he's in his hammock an' a thousand mile away / (Capten, art tha' sleepin' there below?). ['Drake's Drum']

6 There's a breathless hush in the Close tonight − / Ten to make and the match to win. ['Vitai Lampada']

7 'Play up! play up! and play the game!' [Ib.]

Newman, John Henry, Cardinal (1801–1890)

8 It would be a gain to the country were it vastly more superstitious, more bigoted, more gloomy, more fierce in its religion than at present it shows itself to be. [*Apologia pro Vita Sua*]

9 Ten thousand difficulties do not make one doubt. [Ib.]

10 It is as absurd to argue men, as to torture them, into believing. [Sermon, 1831]

11 When men understand what each other mean, they see, for the most part, that controversy is either superfluous or hopeless. [Sermon, 1839]

1 Lead, kindly Light, amid the encircling gloom, / Lead Thou me on. [Hymn]

News of the World

2 All human life is there. [Slogan]

Newton, Isaac (1642–1727)

3 I do not know what I may appear to the world, but to myself I seem to have been only a boy playing on the seashore, and diverting myself in now and then finding a smoother pebble or a prettier shell than ordinary, whilst the great ocean of truth lay all undiscovered before me. [Brewster, *Memoirs of Newton*]

4 If I have seen further it is by standing on the shoulders of giants. [Letter, 1676]

Nicholas I, Emperor of Russia (1796–1855)

5 Russia has two generals in whom she can confide — Generals Janvier and Février. [*Punch*, 1853]

6 [Of Turkey] We have on our hands a sick man — a seriously sick man. [Attr.]

Nietzsche, Friedrich Wilhelm (1844–1900)

7 If you gaze for long into an abyss, the abyss gazes also into you. [*Beyond Good and Evil*, IV]

8 *Herren-Moral und Sklaven-Moral.* Master morality and slave morality. [Ib.]

9 My time has not yet come either; some are born posthumously. [*Ecce Homo*]

10 *Gott ist tot; aber so wie die Art der Menschen ist, wird es vielleicht noch jahrtausendlang Höhlen geben, in denen man seinen Schatten zeigt.* God is dead; but looking at the way Man is, there will probably be caves for thousands of years to come in which his shadow will be seen. [*The Gay Science*, III]

11 *Moralität ist Herden-Instinkt in Einzelnen.* Morality is the herd-instinct in individuals. [Ib.]

1 *Gefährlich leben!* Live dangerously! [Ib. IV]

2 *Ich lehre euch den Übermenschen. Der Mensch ist etwas, das überwunden werden soll.* I teach you the superman. Man is something to be surpassed. [*Thus Spake Zarathustra*]

3 Sleeping is no mean art; for its sake one must stay awake all day. [Ib.]

4 Is man only a blunder of God, or God only a blunder of man? [*The Twilight of the Idols*]

Nivelle, General Robert (1856–1924)

5 *Ils ne passeront pas.* They shall not pass. [Statement at Battle of Verdun, 1916; often attr. Pétain]

Nixon, Richard (1913–)

6 It is time for the great silent majority of Americans to stand up and be counted. [Speech, 1970]

7 There can be no whitewash at the White House. [*Observer*, 'Sayings of the Week', 1973]

North, Christopher (1785–1854)

8 Minds like ours, my dear James, must always be above national prejudices, and in all companies it gives me true pleasure to declare, that, as a people, the English are very little indeed inferior to the Scotch. [*Noctes Ambrosianae*, 9]

9 His Majesty's dominions, on which the sun never sets. [Ib. 20]

10 Laws were made to be broken. [Ib. 24]

Northcote, Sir Stafford (1818–1887)

11 [Of Gladstone] That grand old man. [Speech, 1882]

Norton, Caroline (1808–1877)

12 All our calm is in that balm — / Not lost but gone before. ['Not Lost but Gone Before']

Novalis (1772-1801)

1 Fate and character are the same thing. [*Heinrich von Ofterdingen*, II. Often quoted as 'Character is destiny']

Noyes, Alfred (1880-1958)

2 And you shall wander hand in hand with love in summer's wonderland; / Go down to Kew in lilac-time (it isn't far from London!) ['Barrel Organ']

Oates, Captain L.E.G. (1880-1912)

3 I am just going outside, and may be some time. [Last words, quoted in Captain Scott's diary]

O'Casey, Sean (1884-1964)

4 I am going where life is more like life than it is here. [*Cock-a-Doodle Dandy*, III]

5 Th' whole worl's . . . in a terr . . . ible state o' . . . chassis! [*Juno and the Paycock*, I]

Ochs, Adolph S. (1858-1935)

6 All the news that's fit to print. [Motto of the *New York Times*]

Ogilvy, James, Earl of Seafield (1664-1730)

7 Now there's an end of ane old song. [On signing the Act of Union, 1707]

Oppenheimer, J. Robert (1904-1967)

8 The physicists have known sin; and this is a knowledge which they cannot lose. [Lecture, 1947]

Orczy, Baroness (1864-1947)

9 We seek him here, we seek him there, / Those Frenchies seek him everywhere. / Is he in heaven? — Is he in hell? / That demmed, elusive Pimpernel? [*The Scarlet Pimpernel*, 12]

OVID 229

Orwell, George (1903–1950)

1 Four legs good, two legs bad. [*Animal Farm*, 3]

2 All animals are equal, but some animals are more equal than others. [Ib. 10]

3 Big Brother is watching you. [*1984*]

4 *Doublethink* means the power of holding two contradictory beliefs in one's mind simultaneously, and accepting both of them. [Ib.]

5 Newspeak was the official language of Oceania. [Ib.]

6 If you want a picture of the future, imagine a boot stamping on a human face — for ever. [Ib.]

7 The quickest way of ending a war is to lose it. [*Shooting an Elephant*]

Osborne, John (1929–)

8 There aren't any good, brave causes left. If the big bang does come, and we all get killed off, it won't be in aid of the old-fashioned, grand design. It'll just be for the Brave New-nothing-very-much-thank-you. [*Look Back in Anger*, III]

Otis, James (1725–1783)

9 Taxation without representation is tyranny. [Attr.]

Otway, Thomas (1652–1685)

10 No praying, it spoils business. [*Venice Preserv'd*, II]

Ovid (43 B.C.–A.D. 18)

11 *Quae dant, quaeque negant, gaudent tamen esse rogatae.* Whether they give or refuse, women are glad to have been asked. [*Ars Amatoria*, I]

12 *Iam seges est ubi Troia fuit.* There is now a cornfield where Troy once was. [*Heroides*, I]

13 *Tempus edax rerum.* Time the devourer of all things. [*Metamorphoses*, XV]

Owen, Robert (1771–1858)

1 All the world is queer save thee and me, and even thou art a little queer. [Attr. remark on dissolving business partnership]

Owen, Wilfred (1893–1918)

2 What passing-bells for these who die as cattle? / Only the monstrous anger of the guns. / Only the stuttering rifles' rapid rattle / Can patter out their hasty orisons. ['Anthem for Doomed Youth']

3 The old Lie: *Dulce et decorum est / Pro patria mori.* ['Dulce et decorum est']

4 It seemed that out of battle I escaped / Down some profound dull tunnel, long since scooped / Through granites which titanic wars had groined. ['Strange Meeting']

5 I am the enemy you killed, my friend. [Ib.]

6 My subject is War, and the pity of War. The Poetry is in the pity. [*Poems*, 'Preface']

Paine, Thomas (1737–1809)

7 The sublime and the ridiculous are often so nearly related, that it is difficult to class them separately. [*The Age of Reason*, II]

8 These are the times that try men's souls. [*The American Crisis*, 1776]

9 Government, even in its best state, is but a necessary evil; in its worst state, an intolerable one. [*Common Sense*, 1]

10 [Of Burke] As he rose like a rocket, he fell like the stick. [*Letter to His Addressers*, 1792]

11 [Of Burke's *Reflections on the Revolution in France*] He pities the plumage, but forgets the dying bird. [*Rights of Man*, I]

12 Man is not the enemy of Man, but through the medium of a false system of government. [Ib.]

1 My country is the world, and my religion is to do good. [Ib. II]

Palafox, José de (1780–1847)

2 War to the knife. [Attr. reply to demand for surrender at siege of Saragossa, 1808]

Palmer, H.R. (1834–1907)

3 Yield not to temptation, for yielding is sin; / Each victory will help you some other to win. [Hymn]

Palmerston, Henry John Temple, Viscount (1784–1865)

4 [Of the Schleswig-Holstein question] There are only three men who have ever understood it: one was Prince Albert, who is dead; the second was a German professor, who became mad. I am the third — and I have forgotten all about it. [Attr. Quoted in Palmer, *Quotations in History*]

5 Die, my dear Doctor, that's the last thing I shall do! [Attr. last words]

Pankhurst, Emmeline (1858–1928)

6 The argument of the broken pane of glass is the most valuable argument in modern politics. [*Votes for Women*]

Papprill, Ross F. (1908–1975)

7 There are two kinds of people in the world: those who believe there are two kinds of people in the world, and those who don't. [Attr.]

Parker, Dorothy (1893–1967)

8 Men seldom make passes / At girls who wear glasses. ['News Item']

9 Why is it no one ever sent me yet / One perfect limousine, do you suppose? / Ah no, it's always just my luck to get / One perfect rose. ['One Perfect Rose']

232 PARKER

1 Razors pain you; / Rivers are damp; / Acids stain you; / And drugs cause cramp. ['Resumé']

2 She ran the whole gamut of the emotions from A to B. [Attr. remark on a performance by Katharine Hepburn]

3 How could they tell? [Attr. remark on hearing that President Coolidge had died]

Parker, Ross (1914–   ) and Charles, Hughie (1907–   )

4 There'll always be an England / While there's a country lane. ['There'll Always Be an England']

Parkinson, Cyril Northcote (1909–   )

5 Work expands so as to fill the time available for its completion. [*Parkinson's Law*]

Pascal, Blaise (1623–1662)

6 *Tout le malheur des hommes vient d'une seule chose, qui est de ne savoir pas demeurer en repos dans une chambre.* All the troubles of men are caused by one single thing, which is their inability to stay quietly in a room. [*Pensées*, II, 139]

7 *Le nez de Cléopâtre: s'il eût été plus court, toute la face de la terre aurait changé.* If Cleopatra's nose had been shorter the whole history of the world would have been different. [Ib. II, 162]

8 *Le silence éternel de ces espaces infinis m'effraie.* The eternal silence of these infinite spaces terrifies me. [Ib. III, 206]

9 *On mourra seul.* We shall die alone. [Ib. III, 211]

10 *Le coeur a ses raisons que la raison ne connaît point.* The heart has its reasons which the mind knows nothing of. [Ib. IV, 277]

11 *L'homme n'est qu'un roseau, le plus faible de la nature; mais c'est un roseau pensant.* Man is only

a reed, the feeblest thing in nature; but he is a thinking reed. [Ib. VI, 347]

1 *Se moquer de la philosophie, c'est vraiment philosopher.* To ridicule philosophy is really to philosophize. [Ib. 430]

Pater, Walter (1839–1894)

2 All art constantly aspires towards the condition of music. [*Studies in the History of the Renaissance*, 'Giorgione']

3 To burn always with this hard, gemlike flame, to maintain this ecstasy, is success in life. [Ib. 'Conclusion']

4 The love of art for art's sake. [Ib.]

Paterson, Andrew (1864–1941)

5 Once a jolly swagman camped by a billabong, / Under the shade of a kulibar tree, / And he sang as he sat and waited for his billy-boil, / You'll come a-waltzing, Matilda, with me.' ['Waltzing Matilda']

Patmore, Coventry (1823–1896)

6 'I saw you take his kiss!' ''Tis true.' / 'O modesty!' ''Twas strictly kept: / He thought me asleep; at least, I knew / He thought I thought he thought I slept.' [*The Angel in the House*, II, 'The Kiss']

7 For want of me the world's course will not fail: / When all its work is done, the lie shall rot; / The truth is great, and shall prevail, / When none cares whether it prevail or not. [*The Unknown Eros*, I, 12]

Payn, James (1830–1898)

8 I have never a piece of toast / Particularly long and wide, / But fell upon the sanded floor, / And always on the buttered side. [*Chamber's Journal*, 1884]

Payne, J.H. (1792–1852)

1 Mid pleasures and palaces though we may roam, / Be it never so humble, there's no place like home. ['Home, Sweet Home']

Peacock, Thomas Love (1785–1866)

2 Respectable means rich, and decent means poor. I should die if I heard my family called decent. [*Crotchet Castle*, 3]

3 A book that furnishes no quotations is, *me judice*, no book — it is a plaything. [Ib. 9]

4 I almost think it is the ultimate destiny of science to exterminate the human race. [*Gryll Grange*]

5 If ifs and ands were pots and pans / There'd be no work for the tinkers. ['Manley']

6 The mountain sheep are sweeter, / But the valley sheep are fatter; / We therefore deemed it meeter / To carry off the latter. [*The Misfortunes of Elphin*, 'The War-Song of Dinas Vawr']

Penn, William (1644–1718)

7 It is a reproach to religion and government to suffer so much poverty and excess. [*Reflections and Maxims*]

8 Men are generally more careful of the breed of their horses and dogs than of their children. [Ib.]

Pepys, Samuel (1633–1703)

9 And so to bed. [*Diary*, 1660]

10 Strange to say what delight we married people have to see these poor fools decoyed into our condition. [Ib. 1665]

11 Music and women I cannot but give way to, whatever my business is. [Ib. 1666]

12 But it is pretty to see what money will do. [Ib. 1668]

Pericles (c. 495–429 B.C.)

1 Wait for that wisest of counsellors, Time.
[Plutarch, *Life*]

Petronius Arbiter (?–A.D. 66)

2 *Cave canem.* Beware of the dog. [*Satyricon*]

Phelps, E.J. (1822–1900)

3 The man who makes no mistakes does not
usually make anything. [Speech, 1899]

Phillips, Wendell (1811–1884)

4 Every man meets his Waterloo at last. [Lecture,
1859]

5 One, on God's side, is a majority. [Ib.]

Picasso, Pablo (1881–1973)

6 *Je ne cherche pas; je trouve.* I do not search; I
find. [Attr.]

Pindar (518–438 B.C.)

7 My soul, do not search for immortal life, but
exhaust the boundaries of possibility. [*Pythian
Odes*, III]

Pindar, Peter (1738–1819)

8 What rage for fame attends both great and small!
/ Better be damned than mentioned not at all!
['To the Royal Academicians']

Pinero, Sir Arthur Wing (1855–1934)

9 While there's tea there's hope. [*The Second Mrs.
Tanqueray*, I]

10 From forty to fifty a man is at heart either a
stoic or a satyr. [Ib.]

Pinter, Harold (1930–)

11 [Asked what his plays are about] The weasel
under the cocktail cabinet. [J. Russell Taylor,
Anger and After]

Pitt, William, Earl of Chatham (1708–1778)

1 The atrocious crime of being a young man ... I shall neither attempt to palliate nor deny. [Speech, House of Commons, 1741]

2 Where law ends, there tyranny begins. [Speech, 1770]

3 I invoke the genius of the Constitution. [Speech, 1777]

Pitt, William (1759–1806)

4 Necessity is the plea for every infringement of human freedom. It is the argument of tyrants; it is the creed of slaves. [Speech, 1783]

5 England has saved herself by her exertions, and will, as I trust, save Europe by her example. [Speech, 1805]

6 Roll up that map; it will not be wanted these ten years. [Remark, on map of Europe, after hearing report of Battle of Austerlitz]

Plath, Sylvia (1932–1963)

7 Every woman adores a Fascist, / The boot in the face, the brute / Brute heart of a brute like you. ['Daddy']

8 Daddy, daddy, you bastard, I'm through. [Ib.]

9 Dying / Is an art, like everything else. / I do it exceptionally well. ['Lady Lazarus']

Plato (c. 429–347 B.C.)

10 That man is wisest who, like Socrates, realizes that his wisdom is worthless. [*Apologia of Socrates*]

11 The good is the beautiful. [*Lysis*]

12 Poets utter great and wise things which they do not themselves understand. [*Republic*, II]

13 The rulers of the State are the only ones who should have the privilege of lying, either at home

or abroad; they may be allowed to lie for the good of the State. [Ib. III]

1 Our object in the construction of the state is the greatest happiness of the whole, and not that of any one class. [Ib. IV]

2 Nothing in the affairs of men is worthy of great anxiety. [Ib. X]

3 Every king springs from a race of slaves, and every slave has had kings among his ancestors. [*Theaetetus*]

Plautus, Titus Maccius (c. 254–184 B.C.)

4 *Lupus est homo homini.* Man is a wolf to man. [*Asinaria*]

Pliny the Elder (A.D. 23–79)

5 *Ex Africa semper aliquid novi.* There is always something new out of Africa. [*Natural History*, VIII (altered)]

6 *In vino veritas.* Truth is in wine. [Ib. XIV]

7 *Cum grano salis.* With a grain of salt. [Ib. XXIII]

Plutarch (c. A.D. 46–120)

8 The great god Pan is dead. [*Morals*, 'Of Isis and Osiris']

9 Alexander wept when he heard from Anaxarchus that there was an infinite number of worlds ... he said: 'Do you not think it lamentable that with such a vast multitude of worlds, we have not yet conquered one?' [*On the Tranquillity of the Mind*]

10 It is indeed desirable to be well descended, but the glory belongs to our ancestors. [*On the Training of Children*]

Poe, Edgar Allan (1809–1849)

11 But we loved with a love which was more than love − / I and my Annabel Lee. ['Annabel Lee']

12 Keeping time, time, time, / In a sort of Runic

rhyme, / To the tintinnabulation that so musically wells / From the bells, bells, bells, bells. ['The Bells']

1 The play is the tragedy, 'Man,' / And its hero the Conqueror Worm. ['The Conqueror Worm']

2 The fever call'd 'Living' / Is conquered at last. ['For Annie']

3 Take thy beak from out my heart, and take thy form from off my door! / Quoth the Raven, 'Nevermore'. ['The Raven']

4 The glory that was Greece / And the grandeur that was Rome. ['To Helen']

Polybius (c. 204–c. 122 B.C.)

5 On any occasion when one can discover the cause of events, one should not resort to the gods. [Attr.]

Pomfret, John (1667–1702)

6 We live and learn, but not the wiser grow. [*Reason*]

Pompadour, Madame de (1721–1764)

7 *Après nous le déluge.* After us the flood. [Remark after Battle of Rossbach, 1757]

Pope, Alexander (1688–1744)

8 Books and the Man I sing, the first who brings / The Smithfield Muses to the Ear of Kings. [*The Dunciad*, I, first lines]

9 Maggots half-form'd in rhyme exactly meet, / And learn to crawl upon poetic feet. [Ib.]

10 While pensive Poets painful vigils keep, / Sleepless themselves, to give their readers sleep. [Ib.]

11 Some Daemon stole my pen (forgive th' offence) / And once betray'd me into common sense. [Ib.]

12 Stretch'd on the rack of a too easy chair. [Ib. IV]

1 Turn what they will to Verse, their toil is vain, /
   Critics like me shall make it Prose again. [Ib.]

2 All Classic learning lost on Classic ground. [Ib.]

3 Lo! thy dread Empire, Chaos! is restor'd; /
   Light dies before thy uncreating word: / Thy hand,
   great Anarch! lets the curtain fall; / And
   Universal Darkness buries All. [Ib. last lines]

4 Is it, in heav'n, a crime to love too well? ['Elegy
   to the Memory of an Unfortunate Lady']

5 A heap of dust alone remains of thee; / 'Tis all
   thou art, and all the proud shall be! [Ib.]

6 The world forgetting, by the world forgot. [Eloisa
   to Abelard]

7 Chaste to her Husband, frank to all beside, / A
   teeming Mistress, but a barren Bride. [Epistle to
   a Lady]

8 Virtue she finds too painful an endeavour, /
   Content to dwell in Decencies for ever. [Ib.]

9 In men, we various ruling passions find, / In
   women, two almost divide the kind; / Those,
   only fix'd, they first or last obey, / The love of
   pleasure, and the love of sway. [Ib.]

10 Men, some to Bus'ness, some to Pleasure take; /
   But every woman is at heart a Rake: / Men,
   some to Quiet, some to public Strife; / But ev'ry
   Lady would be Queen for life. [Ib.]

11 As yet a child, nor yet a fool to fame, / I lisp'd
   in numbers, for the numbers came. [Epistle to
   Dr. Arbuthnot]

12 And he, whose fustian's so sublimely bad, / It is
   not poetry, but prose run mad. [Ib.]

13 Damn with faint praise, assent with civil leer, /
   And without sneering, teach the rest to sneer; /
   Willing to wound, and yet afraid to strike, / Just
   hint a fault, and hesitate dislike. [Ib.]

14 Let Sporus tremble — 'What? that thing of silk, /

Sporus, that mere white curd of ass's milk? /
Satire or sense, alas! can Sporus feel? / Who
breaks a butterfly upon a wheel?' [Ib.]

1 Yet let me flap this bug with gilded wings − /
This painted child of dirt, that stinks and stings.
[Ib.]

2 The ruling Passion, be it what it will, / The
ruling Passion conquers Reason still. [*Epistle to
Lord Bathurst*]

3 Where London's column, pointing at the skies, /
Like a tall bully, lifts the head, and lies. [Ib.]

4 Consult the genius of the place in all. [*Epistle to
Lord Burlington*]

5 Another age shall see the golden ear / Imbrown
the slope, and nod on the parterre, / Deep
harvest bury all his pride had plann'd, / And
laughing Ceres reassume the land. [Ib.]

6 I am his Highness' dog at Kew; / Pray, tell me
sir, whose dog are you? [Epigram for a royal dog
collar]

7 Nature, and Nature's laws lay hid in night: / God
said, *Let Newton be!* and all was light. [Epitaph
for Sir Isaac Newton]

8 'Tis with our judgements as our watches, none /
Go just alike, yet each believes his own. [*Essay
on Criticism*]

9 Some have at first for Wits then Poets past, /
Turn'd Critics next, and prov'd plain fools at last.
[Ib.]

10 A *little learning* is a dang'rous thing; / Drink
deep, or taste not the Pierian spring; / There
shallow draughts intoxicate the brain, / And
drinking largely sobers us again. [Ib.]

11 True Wit is Nature to advantage dress'd, / What
oft was thought, but ne'er so well express'd. [Ib.]

12 Words are like leaves; and where they most

abound, / Much fruit of sense beneath is rarely found. [Ib.]

1 As some to church repair, / Not for the doctrine but the music there. [Ib.]

2 True ease in writing comes from art, not chance, / As those move easiest who have learn'd to dance. / 'Tis not enough no harshness gives offence, / The sound must seem an echo to the sense. [Ib.]

3 Good-nature and good-sense must ever join; / To err is human, to forgive, divine. [Ib.]

4 The bookful blockhead, ignorantly read, / With loads of learned lumber in his head. [Ib.]

5 For Fools rush in where Angels fear to tread. [Ib.]

6 Let us (since Life can little more supply / Than just to look about us and to die) / Expatiate free o'er all this scene of man; / A mighty maze! but not without a plan. [*Essay on Man*, I]

7 Laugh where we must, be candid where we can; / But vindicate the ways of God to man. [Ib.]

8 Who sees with equal eye as God of all, / A hero perish or a sparrow fall, / Atoms or systems into ruin hurl'd, / And now a bubble burst, and now a world. [Ib.]

9 Hope springs eternal in the human breast: / Man never is, but always to be blest. [Ib.]

10 Why has not man a microscopic eye? / For this plain reason, man is not a fly. [Ib.]

11 All nature is but art unknown to thee; / All chance, direction which thou canst not see; / All discord, harmony not understood; / All partial evil, universal good; / And, spite of pride, in erring reason's spite, / One truth is clear, 'Whatever IS, is RIGHT.' [Ib.]

1 Know then thyself, presume not God to scan; /
The proper study of Mankind is Man. [Ib. II]

2 Nor God alone in the still calm we find, / He
mounts the storm, and walks upon the wind. [Ib.]

3 A Wit's a feather, and a Chief a rod; / An honest
Man's the noblest work of God. [Ib. IV]

4 Thou wert my guide, philosopher, and friend.
[Ib.]

5 That virtue only makes our bliss below; / And all
our knowledge is ourselves to know. [Ib. last
lines]

6 The people's voice is odd, / It is, and it is not,
the voice of God. [*Imitations of Horace, Epistle
II*, 1]

7 Yes, I am proud; I must be proud to see / Men
not afraid of God, afraid of me. [Ib. *Epilogue to
the Satires*, II]

8 True friendship's laws are by this rule express'd,
/ Welcome the coming, speed the parting guest.
[*Odyssey*, XV]

9 What dire offence from am'rous causes springs, /
What mighty contests rise from trivial things, / I
sing. [*The Rape of the Lock*, I]

10 If to her share some female errors fall, / Look on
her face, and you'll forget 'em all. [Ib. II]

11 Here thou, great Anna! whom three realms obey,
/ Dost sometimes counsel take — and sometimes
Tea. [Ib. III]

12 The hungry judges soon the sentence sign, / And
wretches hang that jury-men may dine. [Ib.]

13 Not louder shrieks to pitying heav'n are cast, /
When husbands, or when lap-dogs breathe their
last. [Ib.]

14 Not Chaos-like together crush'd and bruis'd, /
But as the world, harmoniously confus'd: /

Where order in variety we see, / And where tho'
all things differ, all agree. [*Windsor Forest*]

1 The fox obscene to gaping tombs retires, / And
savage howlings fill the sacred quires. [Ib.]

2 Here am I, dying of a hundred good symptoms.
[Spence, *Anecdotes*]

Potter, Stephen (1900–1971)

3 Gamesmanship or, The Art of Winning Games
without actually Cheating [Title of book]

4 *How to be one up* — how to make the other man
feel that something has gone wrong, however
slightly. [*Lifemanship*]

Pound, Ezra (1885–1972)

5 Winter is icummen in, / Lhude sing Goddamn, /
Raineth drop and staineth slop / And how the
wind doth ramm! / Sing: Goddamn. ['Ancient
Music'; *see* Anon., 'Summer is icummen in']

6 Pull down thy vanity / Thou art a beaten dog
beneath the hail, / A swollen magpie in a fitful
sun, / Half black half white / Not knowst'ou
wing from tail / Pull down thy vanity [*Cantos*,
LXXXI]

7 Bah! I have sung women in three cities, / But it
is all the same; / And I will sing of the sun.
['Cino']

8 For an old bitch gone in the teeth, / For a
botched civilization. [*Hugh Selwyn Mauberley*]

9 The apparition of these faces in the crowd; /
Petals on a wet, black bough. ['In a Station of
the Metro']

10 When I carefully consider the curious habits of
dogs / I am compelled to conclude / That man is
the superior animal. / When I consider the
curious habits of man / I confess, my friend, I
am puzzled. ['Meditatio']

1 So many thousand fair are gone down to
Avernus, / Ye might let one remain above with
us. ['Prayer for his Lady's Life']

2 Come, my songs, let us speak of perfection — /
We shall get ourselves rather disliked.
['Salvationists']

3 Literature is news that STAYS news. [*ABC of
Reading*]

4 Great Literature is simply language charged with
meaning to the utmost possible degree. [*How to
Read*]

Prayer, Book of Common

5 We have erred and strayed from thy ways like
lost sheep . . . We have left undone those things
which we ought to have done; And we have done
those things which we ought not to have done;
And there is no health in us . . . A godly,
righteous and sober life. [General Confession]

6 And forgive us our trespasses, As we forgive
them that trespass against us. [The Lord's
Prayer]

7 As it was in the beginning, is now, and ever shall
be; world without end. Amen. [Gloria]

8 O let the Earth bless the Lord: yea, let it praise
him, and magnify him for ever. [Benedicite]

9 I believe in God the Father Almighty, Maker of
heaven and earth: And in Jesus Christ his only
Son our Lord, Who was conceived by the Holy
Ghost, Born of the Virgin Mary, Suffered under
Pontius Pilate, Was crucified, dead and buried,
He descended into hell; The third day he rose
again from the dead, He ascended into heaven,
And sitteth on the right hand of God the Father
Almighty; From thence he shall come to judge
the quick and the dead. [The Apostles' Creed]

10 Give peace in our time, O Lord. / Because there

is none other that fighteth for us, but only thou,
O God. [Versicles]

1 That peace which the world cannot give.
[Evening Prayer, Second Collect]

2 Lighten our darkness, we beseech thee, O Lord;
and by thy great mercy defend us from all perils
and dangers of this night. [Third Collect]

3 Deceits of the world, the flesh and the devil. [The
Litany]

4 The fruits of the Spirit. [Ib.]

5 All sorts and conditions of men ... all who
profess and call themselves Christians. [Prayers
and Thanksgivings upon Several Occasions]

6 Give us grace that we may cast away the works
of darkness, and put upon us the armour of light.
[Collects, 1st Sunday in Advent]

7 Hear them, read, mark, learn and inwardly digest
them. [Ib. 2nd Sunday in Advent]

8 The peace of God, which passeth all
understanding. [Nicene Creed, The Blessing]

9 If any of you know cause, or just impediment,
why these two persons should not be joined
together in holy Matrimony, ye are to declare it.
This is the first time of asking. [Solemnization of
Matrimony, The Banns]

10 Dearly beloved, we are gathered together here in
the sight of God, and in the face of this
congregation, to join together this Man and this
Woman in holy Matrimony. [Ib. Exhortation]

11 Let him now speak, or else hereafter forever hold
his peace. [Ib.]

12 Wilt thou love her, comfort her, honour, and
keep her in sickness and in health; and, forsaking
all other, keep thee only unto her, so long as ye
both shall live? [Ib. Betrothal]

13 To have and to hold from this day forward, for

better for worse, for richer for poorer, in
sickness and in health, to love and to cherish, till
death us do part, according to God's holy
ordinance; and thereto I plight thee my troth.
[Ib.]

1 To love, cherish and to obey. [Ib.]

2 With this Ring I thee wed, with my body I thee
worship, and with all my worldly goods I thee
endow. [Ib. Wedding]

3 Those whom God hath joined together let no
man put asunder. [Ib. The Prayer]

4 Consented together in holy wedlock. [Ib. Priest's
Declaration]

5 Peace be to this house, and to all that dwell in it.
[Visitation of the Sick]

6 In the midst of life we are in death. [Burial of the
Dead, First Anthem]

7 We therefore commit his body to the ground;
earth to earth, ashes to ashes, dust to dust; in
sure and certain hope of the Resurrection to
eternal life. [Ib. Interment]

8 We therefore commit his body to the deep, to be
turned into corruption, looking for the
resurrection of the body (when the sea shall give
up her dead). [Forms of Prayer to be Used at
Sea. At the Burial of their Dead at Sea]

Preston, Keith (1884–1927)

9 [Of democracy] An institution in which the whole
is equal to the scum of all the parts. [Pot Shots
from Pegasus]

Prior, Matthew (1664–1721)

10 No, no, for my virginity, / When I lose that, says
Rose, I'll die; / Behind the elms last night, cry'd
Dick, / Rose, were you not extremely sick? ['A
True Mind']

Procter, Adelaide (1825–1864)

1 But I struck one chord of music, / Like the sound of a great Amen. ['A Lost Chord']

Protagoras (c. 485–c. 410 B.C.)

2 Man is the measure of all things. [Fragment]

Proudhon, Pierre-Joseph (1809–1865)

3 If I were asked to answer the following question: 'What is slavery?' and I should answer in one word, 'Murder!' my meaning would be understood at once. No further argument would be required to show that the power to take from a man his thought, his will, his personality, is a power of life and death, and that to enslave a man is to kill him. Why, then, to this other question: 'What is property?' may I not likewise answer 'Theft'? [*Qu'est-ce que la Propriété?*]

Proust, Marcel (1871–1922)

4 For a long time I used to go to bed early. [*A la Recherche du Temps Perdu, Du côté de chez Swann*, I, 1, first sentence; trans. Scott-Moncrieff]

5 The true paradises are paradises we have lost. [Ib. *Le Temps Retrouvé*, I, 1]

6 *Impossible venir, mensonge suit.* Cannot come, lie follows. [Ib.]

Punch

7 Advice to persons about to marry — 'Don't!' [1845]

8 What is better than presence of mind in a railway accident? Absence of body. [1849]

9 Never do to-day what you can put off till tomorrow. [1849]

10 Cats is 'dogs' and rabbits is 'dogs' and so's Parrats, but this 'ere 'Tortis' is an insect, and there ain't no charge for it. [1869]

1 Go directly — see what she's doing, and tell her she mustn't. [1872]

2 It's worse than wicked, my dear, it's vulgar. [1876]

3 I used your soap two years ago; since then I have used no other. [1884]

4 'I'm afraid you've got a bad egg, Mr. Jones.' 'Oh no, my Lord, I assure you!' Parts of it are excellent! [1895]

Putnam, Israel (1718–1790)

5 Men, you are all marksmen — don't one of you fire until you see the whites of their eyes. [At the Battle of Bunker Hill, 1775]

Quarles, Francis (1592–1644)

6 Be wisely worldly, not worldly wise. [*Emblems*, II, 2]

7 Physicians of all men are most happy; what success soever they have, the world proclaimeth, and what faults they commit, the earth covereth. [*Hieroglyphics of the Life of Man*]

Quesnay, François (1694–1774)

8 [Of government interference] *Laissez faire, laissez passer.* Leave it alone, and let it happen. [Attr.]

Quiller-Couch, Sir Arthur (1863–1944)

9 The lion is the beast to fight: / He leaps along the plain, / And if you run with all your might, / He runs with all his mane. ['Sage Counsel']

10 The best is the best, though a hundred judges have declared it so. [*Oxford Book of English Verse*, Preface]

Quintilian (A.D. 42–118)

11 A liar should have a good memory. [*De Institutio Oratoria*]

Rabelais, François (c. 1494–1553)

1 *Natura vacuum abhorret.* Nature abhors a vacuum. [*Gargantua*]

2 *Tirez le rideau, la farce est jouée.* Draw the curtain, the farce is over. [Attr. last words]

3 *Je m'en vais chercher un grand peut-être.* I go to seek a great perhaps. [Attr. last words]

Racine, Jean (1639–1699)

4 *Elle s'endormit du sommeil des justes.* She slept the sleep of the just. [*Abrégé de l'Histoire de Port Royal*]

5 *Elle flotte, elle hésite; en un mot, elle est femme.* She wavers, she hesitates, in a word, she is a woman. [*Athalie*, III]

Raleigh, Sir Walter (c. 1552–1618)

6 If all the world and love were young, / And truth in every shepherd's tongue, / These pretty pleasures might me move / To live with thee, and be thy love. ['The Nymph's Reply to the Shepherd']

7 Only we die in earnest, that's no jest. ['On the Life of Man']

8 Fain would I climb, yet fear I to fall. [Written on a window-pane]

Raleigh, Sir Walter A. (1861–1922)

9 I wish I loved the Human Race; / I wish I loved its silly face; / I wish I liked the way it walks; / I wish I liked the way it talks; / And when I'm introduced to one, / I wish I thought *What Jolly Fun!* ['Wishes of an Elderly Man']

Reed, John (1887–1920)

10 Ten Days that Shook the World [Title of book on October Revolution in Russia]

Remarque, Erich Maria (1898–1970)

1 *Im Westen nichts Neues.* All Quiet on the Western Front [Title of book]

Renan, J. Ernest (1823–1892)

2 O Lord, if there is a Lord, save my soul, if I have a soul. ['A Sceptic's Prayer']

Rendall, Montague John (1862–1950)

3 Nation shall speak peace unto nation. [Motto of BBC]

Reuben, David (1933–   )

4 Everything You've Always Wanted to Know About Sex, But Were Afraid to Ask. [Title of book and film]

Reynolds, Sir Joshua (1723–1792)

5 If you have great talents, industry will improve them: if you have but moderate abilities, industry will supply their deficiency. [*Discourses*, 2]

6 A mere copier of nature can never produce anything great. [Ib. 3]

Rhondda, Viscountess (1883–1958)

7 Women must come off the pedestal. Men put us up there to get us out of the way. [*Observer*, 'Sayings of the Week', 1920]

Richard I (1157–1199)

8 *Dieu et mon droit.* God and my right. [Attr. 1198]

Richardson, Samuel (1689–1761)

9 Desert and reward, I can assure her, seldom keep company. [*Clarissa*, IV]

10 Pity is but one remove from love. [*Sir Charles Grandison*, I]

Ripley, R.L. (1893–1949)

11 Believe it or not. [Title of newspaper feature]

Rochester, John Wilmot, Earl of (1647–1680)

1 Here lies our sovereign lord the King / Whose word no man relies on, / Who never said a foolish thing, / Nor ever did a wise one. [Epitaph written for Charles II; *see* Charles II, 'This is very true . . .']

2 A merry monarch, scandalous and poor. ['Satire on King Charles II']

Rogers, Samuel (1763–1855)

3 Many a temple half as old as time. [*Italy. A Farewell*]

4 When a new book is published, read an old one. [Attr.]

Rogers, Will (1879–1935)

5 You can't say civilization don't advance, however, for in every war they kill you a new way. [*Autobiography*]

6 Half our life is spent trying to find something to do with the time we have rushed through life trying to save. [Ib.]

7 Everything is funny as long as it is happening to someone else. [*The Illiterate Digest*]

8 So live that you wouldn't be ashamed to sell the family parrot to the town gossip. [Attr.]

9 I don't make jokes — I just watch the government and report the facts. [Attr.]

Roland, Madame (1754–1793)

10 *O liberté! que de crimes on commet en ton nom!* O liberty! what crimes are committed in thy name! [Remark on mounting the scaffold]

Ronsard, Pierre (1524–1585)

11 *Quand vous serez bien vieille, au soir à la chandelle, / Assise auprès du feu, dévidant et filant, / Direz, chantant mes vers, en vous*

émerveillant, / Ronsard me célébrait du temps
que j'étais belle. When you are very old, and sit
in the candle-light at evening, spinning by the
fire, you will say, as you murmur my verses,
wonder in your eyes, 'Ronsard sang of me in the
days when I was fair.' [*Sonnets pour Hélène*]

Roosevelt, Franklin Delano (1882–1945)

1 I pledge you — I pledge myself — to a new deal
for the American people. [Speech, 1932]

2 The only thing we have to fear is fear itself.
[First Inaugural Address, 1933]

3 We have always known that heedless self-interest
was bad morals; we know now that it is bad
economics. [Ib.]

4 I would dedicate this nation to the policy of the
good neighbour. [Ib.]

5 A radical is a man with both feet firmly planted
in the air. [Radio broadcast, 1939]

6 We must be the great arsenal of democracy.
[Radio broadcast, 1940]

Roosevelt, Theodore (1858–1919)

7 Men who form the lunatic fringe in all reform
movements. [*Autobiography*]

8 There can be no fifty-fifty Americanism in this
country. There is room here for only hundred per
cent Americanism, only for those who are
Americans and nothing else. [Speech, Saratoga]

9 Don't hit at all if it is honourably possible to
avoid hitting; but *never* hit soft! [J.B. Bishop,
Theodore Roosevelt]

10 The most successful politician is he who says
what everybody is thinking most often and in the
loudest voice. [Quoted in Andrews, *Treasury of
Humorous Quotations*]

11 Speak softly and carry a big stick. [Attr.]

Roscommon, Earl of (1633–1685)

1 Choose an author as you choose a friend. [*Essay on Translated Verse*]

2 Immodest words admit of no defence, / For want of decency is want of sense. [Ib.]

Rosebery, Earl of (1847–1929)

3 It is beginning to be hinted that we are a nation of amateurs. [Speech, 1900]

Ross, Alan C. (1907–)

4 U and Non-U. [Title of essay]

Rossetti, Christina Georgina (1830–1894)

5 'Come cheer up, my lads, 'tis to glory we steer' — / As the soldier remarked whose post lay in the rear. ['Couplet']

6 In the bleak mid-winter / Frosty wind made moan / . . . In the bleak mid-winter, / Long ago. ['Mid-Winter']

7 Remember me when I am gone away, / Gone far away into the silent land. ['Remember']

8 Better by far you should forget and smile / Than you should remember and be sad. [Ib.]

9 Does the road wind up-hill all the way? / Yes, to the very end. / Will the day's journey take the whole long day? / From morn to night, my friend. ['Up-Hill']

Rossetti, Dante Gabriel (1828–1882)

10 I do not see them here; but after death / God knows I know the faces I shall see, / Each one a murdered self. [*The House of Life*, II, 'Lost Days']

11 I have been here before, / But when or how I cannot tell: / I know the grass beyond the door, / The sweet keen smell, / The sighing sound, the lights around the shore. ['Sudden Light']

12 The worst moment for the atheist is when he is

really thankful and has nobody to thank. [Attr. Also attr. to Wendy Ward]

Rossini, Gioacchino (1792–1868)

1 Wagner has lovely moments but awful quarters of an hour. [Remark, 1867]

Roth, Philip (1933–)

2 So (said the doctor). Now vee may perhaps to begin. Yes? [*Portnoy's Complaint*, last words]

Rouget de Lisle, Claude-Joseph (1760–1836)

3 *Allons, enfants de la patrie, / Le jour de gloire est arrivé.* Come, children of this country, the day of glory is here. ['La Marseillaise']

Rousseau, Jean-Jacques (1712–1778)

4 *L'homme est né libre, et partout il est dans les fers.* Man is born free, and everywhere is in chains. [*Du Contrat Social*]

Roux, Joseph (1834–1886)

5 Science is for those who learn; poetry, for those who know. [*Meditations of a Parish Priest*, 1]

Rowe, Nicholas (1674–1718)

6 Is this that haughty, gallant, gay Lothario? [*The Fair Penitent*, V.1]

7 Death is the privilege of human nature, / And life without it were not worth our taking. [Ib.]

Rowland, Helen (1875–1950)

8 Before marriage, a man will lie awake thinking about something you said; after marriage, he'll fall asleep before you finish saying it. [Quoted in Cowan, *The Wit of Women*]

Runyon, Damon (1884–1946)

9 Nicely-Nicely is known far and wide as a character who dearly loves to commit eating. ['Lonely Heart']

1 Always try to rub up against money, for if you rub up against money long enough, some of it may rub off on you. ['A Very Honourable Guy']

Rusk, Dean (1909–)

2 We're eye-ball to eye-ball and the other fellow just blinked. [Remark on Cuban crisis, 1962]

Ruskin, John (1819–1900)

3 [Of a painting by Whistler] I have seen, and heard, much of Cockney impudence before now; but never expected to hear a coxcomb ask two hundred guineas for flinging a pot of paint in the public's face. [*Fors Clavigera*, 79]

4 Mountains are the beginning and the end of all natural scenery. [*Modern Painters*, IV]

5 How long most people would look at the best book before they would give the price of a large turbot for it! [*Sesame and Lilies*]

6 When we build, let us think that we build for ever. [*The Seven Lamps of Architecture*, 6]

7 Government and cooperation are in all things the laws of life; anarchy and competition, the laws of death. [*Unto this Last*, 3]

8 There is really no such thing as bad weather, only different kinds of good weather. [Attr.]

Russell, Bertrand (1872–1970)

9 America . . . where law and custom alike are based upon the dreams of spinsters. [*Marriage and Morals*]

10 Machines are worshipped because they are beautiful, and valued because they confer power; they are hated because they are hideous, and loathed because they impose slavery. [*Sceptical Essays*]

Russell, Lord John (1792–1878)

1 If peace cannot be maintained with honour, it is no longer peace. [Speech, 1853]

2 Among the defects of the Bill, which were numerous, one provision was conspicuous by its presence and another by its absence. [Speech, 1859]

Russell, Sir William Howard (1820–1907)

3 [Of the 93rd Highlanders at the Battle of Balaclava] That thin red line tipped with steel. [*The British Expedition to the Crimea*]

Ryle, Gilbert (1900–1976)

4 The dogma of the Ghost in the Machine. [*The Concept of Mind*]

Sainte-Beuve, Charles-Augustin (1804–1869)

5 *Le silence seul est le souverain mépris.* Silence is the supreme contempt. ['Mes Poisons']

6 *Et Vigny plus secret, / Comme en sa tour d'ivoire, avant midi rentrait.* And Vigny more secretive, as if in his ivory tower, returned before noon. ['Pensées d'Août']

Saki (1870–1916)

7 A little inaccuracy sometimes saves tons of explanation. ['The Comments of Maung Ka']

8 Waldo is one of those people who would be enormously improved by death. ['The Feast of Nemesis']

9 Oysters are more beautiful than any religion . . . There's nothing in Christianity or Buddhism that quite matches the sympathetic unselfishness of an oyster. ['The Match-Maker']

10 People may say what they like about the decay of Christianity; the religious system that produced green Chartreuse can never really die. ['Reginald on Christmas Presents']

1 The cook was a good cook, as cooks go; and as cooks go she went. ['Reginald on Besetting Sins']

2 Women and elephants never forget an injury. [Ib.]

Sallust (86–34 B.C.)

3 *Punica fide.* With Carthaginian faith [i.e. treachery]. [*Jugurtha*, 35]

Sandburg, Carl (1878–1967)

4 Sometime they'll give a war and nobody will come. ['The People, Yes']

Santayana, George (1863–1952)

5 Fanaticism consists in redoubling your effort when you have forgotten your aim. [*The Life of Reason*, I]

6 Nothing is so poor and melancholy as art that is interested in itself and not in its subject. [Ib. IV]

7 Music is essentially useless, as life is. [*Little Essays*]

8 There is no cure for birth and death save to enjoy the interval. [*Soliloquies in England*]

9 It is a great advantage for a system of philosophy to be substantially true. [*The Unknowable*]

Sargent, John Singer (1856–1925)

10 Every time I paint a portrait I lose a friend. [Attr.]

Sartre, Jean-Paul (1905–1980)

11 *Mauvaise foi.* Bad faith. [*Sketch for a Theory of the Emotions*]

12 Man is condemned to be free. [*Existentialism and Humanism*]

13 Hell is other people. [*Huis clos*]

Sassoon, Siegfried (1886–1967)

1 If I were fierce and bald and short of breath, / I'd live with scarlet Majors at the Base, / And speed glum heroes up the line to death. ['Base Details']

2 Does it matter? — losing your legs? / ... For people will always be kind. ['Does it Matter?']

3 You are too young to fall asleep for ever; / And when you sleep you remind me of the dead. ['The Dug-Out']

4 'He's a cheery old card,' grunted Harry to Jack / As they slogged up to Arras with rifle and pack ... / But he did for them both with his plan of attack. ['The General']

Schiller, Friedrich von (1759–1805)

5 *Freude, schöner Götterfunken, / Tochter aus Elysium, / Wir betreten feuertrunken, / Himmlische, dein Heiligtum.* O Joy, lovely gift of the gods, daughter of Paradise, divinity, we are inspired as we approach your sanctuary. ['An die Freude' (set to music by Beethoven in the last movement of his Ninth Symphony)]

6 *Alle Menschen werden Brüder, / Wo dein sanfter Flügel weilt.* In the shade of your soft wings, all men will be brothers. [Ib.]

7 *Mit der Dummheit kämpfen Götter selbst vergebens.* With stupidity the very gods contend in vain. [*Die Jungfrau von Orleans*, III.6]

8 *Time consecrates; / And what is grey with age becomes religion.* [*Die Piccolomini*, IV]

9 *Die Weltgeschichte ist das Weltgericht.* The world's history is the world's judgement. [Lecture, 1789]

10 *Und siegt Natur, so muss die Kunst entweichen.* When Nature conquers, Art must then give way. [Remark to Goethe]

Schumacher, E.F. (1911–1977)

1 Small is Beautiful [Title of book]

Scott, Charles Prestwich (1846–1932)

2 Comment is free but facts are sacred.
[*Manchester Guardian*, 1926]

Scott, Robert Falcon (1868–1912)

3 Great God! this is an awful place [the South
Pole]. [*Journal*, 17 Jan. 1912]

4 For God's sake look after our people. [Ib. 25
Mar. 1912]

5 Had we lived, I should have had a tale to tell of
the hardihood, endurance, and courage of my
companions which would have stirred the heart
of every Englishman. These rough notes and our
dead bodies must tell the tale. [Message to the
Public]

Scott, Sir Walter (1771–1832)

6 To the Lords of Convention 'twas Claver'se who
spoke, / 'Ere the King's crown shall fall there are
crowns to be broke; / So let each cavalier who
loves honour and me, / Come follow the bonnet
of Bonny Dundee. / Come fill up my cup, come
fill up my can, / Come saddle your horses, and
call up your men; / Come open the West Port,
and let me gang free, / And it's room for the
bonnets of Bonny Dundee!' ['Bonny Dundee']

7 But answer came there none. [*The Bridal of
Triermain*]

8 The stern joy which warriors feel / In foemen
worthy of their steel. [*The Lady of the Lake*, V]

9 For ne'er / Was flattery lost on poet's ear: / A
simple race! they waste their toil / For the vain
tribute of a smile. [*The Lay of the Last Minstrel*,
IV]

10 Breathes there the man, with soul so dead, /

Who never to himself hath said, / This is my
own, my native land! / Whose heart hath ne'er
within him burned / As home his footsteps he
hath turned / From wandering on a foreign
strand! [Ib. VI]

1 The wretch, concentred all in self, / Living, shall
forfeit fair renown, / And, doubly dying, shall go
down / To the vile dust, from whence he sprung, /
Unwept, unhonour'd, and unsung. [Ib.]

2 O Caledonia! stern and wild, / Meet nurse for a
poetic child! / Land of brown heath and shaggy
wood, / Land of the mountain and the flood. [Ib.]

3 Thus, then, my noble foe I greet: / Health and
high fortune till we meet / And then — what
pleases Heaven. [Lord of the Isles, III]

4 To that dark inn, the grave! [Ib. VI]

5 But search the land of living men, / Where wilt
thou find their like agen? [Marmion, I]

6 And come he slow, or come he fast, / It is but
Death who comes at last. [Ib. II]

7 O young Lochinvar is come out of the West /
Through all the wide border his steed was the
best; / And save his good broadsword, he
weapons had none. / He rode all unarm'd, and
he rode all alone. / So faithful in love, and so
dauntless in war, / There never was knight like
the young Lochinvar. [Ib. V]

8 O what a tangled web we weave, / When first
we practise to deceive. [Ib. VI]

9 And such a yell was there, / Of sudden and
portentous birth, / As if men fought upon the
earth, / And fiends in upper air. [Ib.]

10 O Woman! in our hours of ease, / Uncertain,
coy, and hard to please, / And variable as the
shade. [Ib.]

11 Look not thou on beauty's charming, — / Sit

thou still when kings are arming, — / Taste not
when the wine-cup glistens, — / Speak not when
the people listens, — / Stop thine ear against the
singer, — / From the red gold keep thy finger, —
/ Vacant heart and hand, and eye, — / Easy live
and quiet die. [*The Bride of Lammermoor*, 3]

1 Touch not the cat but [i.e. without] a glove. [*The
Fair Maid of Perth*, 34; the motto of Clan
Chattan]

2 The hour is come, but not the man. [*The Heart of
Midlothian*, 4]

3 When we had a king, and a chancellor, and
parliament men o' our ain, we could aye pebble
them wi stanes when they werena guid bairns;
but naebody's nails can reach the length o'
Lunnon. [*Malachi Malagrowther*]

4 The ae half of the warld thinks the tither daft.
[*Redgauntlet*, 7]

5 Speak out, sir, and do not Maister or Campbell
me — my foot is on my native heath, and my
name is Macgregor! [*Rob Roy*, 34]

6 A man may drink and not be drunk; / A man
may fight and not be slain; / A man may kiss a
bonny lass, / And yet be welcome home again.
[*Woodstock*, 27]

7 We shall never learn to feel and respect our real
calling and destiny, unless we have taught
ourselves to consider every thing as moonshine,
compared with the education of the heart.
[Letter, 1825]

Scriven, Joseph (1820–1886)

8 What a Friend we have in Jesus, / All our sins
and griefs to bear! / What a privilege to carry /
Everything to God in prayer! [Hymn]

Seaman, Sir Owen (1861–1936)

9 She must know all the needs of a rational being,

/ Be skilled to keep counsel, to comfort, to coax / And, above all things else, be accomplished at seeing / My jokes. ['A Plea for Trigamy']

Sedley, Sir Charles (c. 1639–1701)

1 Love still has something of the sea / From whence his mother rose. ['Love still has Something']

Seeger, Alan (1888–1916)

2 I have a rendezvous with Death, / At some disputed barricade, / At midnight in some flaming town. ['I Have a Rendezvous with Death']

Seeley, Sir John Robert (1834–1895)

3 We [the English] seem as it were to have conquered and peopled half the world in a fit of absence of mind. [*The Expansion of England*]

Segal, Erich (1937–   )

4 Love means never having to say you're sorry. [*Love Story*]

Selden, John (1584–1654)

5 Ignorance of the law excuses no man; not that all men know the law, but because 'tis an excuse every man will plead, and no man can tell how to confute him. [*Table Talk*, 'Law']

6 There never was a merry world since the fairies left off dancing, and the Parson left off conjuring. [Ib. 'Parson']

7 There is not anything in the world so much abused as this sentence, *Salus populi suprema lex esto*. [Let public safety be the supreme law] [Ib. 'People']

8 Philosophy is nothing but discretion. [Ib. 'Philosophy']

1 Preachers say, Do as I say, not as I do. [Ib. 'Preaching']

Selfridge, H. Gordon (1858–1947)

2 The customer is always right. [Shop slogan]

Sellar, Walter Carruthers (1898–1951) and Yeatman, Robert Julian (1897–1968)

3 1066, And All That. [Title of book]

4 The Roman Conquest was, however, a *Good Thing*. [*1066, And All That*]

5 The Venomous Bead (author of *The Rosary*). [Ib.]

6 The Cavaliers (Wrong but Wromantic) and the Roundheads (Right but Repulsive). [Ib.]

7 The National Debt is a very Good Thing and it would be dangerous to pay it off for fear of Political Economy. [Ib.]

8 Napoleon's armies always used to march on their stomachs, shouting: 'Vive l'Intérieur!' [Ib.]

9 A Bad Thing: America was thus clearly top nation, and History came to a [Ib.]

Seneca (c. 4 B.C.–A.D. 65)

10 There can be slain / No sacrifice to God more acceptable / Than an unjust and wicked king. [*Hercules Furens*; trans. Milton]

11 *Illi mors gravis incubat / Qui notus nimis omnibus / Ignotus moritur sibi.* On him does death lie heavily who, but too well known to all, dies to himself unknown. [*Thyestes*, II, Chorus; trans. Miller]

Service, Robert W. (1874–1958)

12 This is the Law of the Yukon, that only the Strong shall thrive; / That surely the Weak shall perish, and only the Fit survive. ['The Law of the Yukon']

Seward, William (1801–1872)

1 There is a higher law than the Constitution. [Speech against Fugitive Slave Law, 1850]

Shacklock, Richard (fl. 1575)

2 Proud as peacocks. [*Hatchet of Heresies*]

Shadwell, Thomas (c. 1642–1692)

3 Words may be false and full of art, / Sighs are the natural language of the heart. [*Psyche*, III]

4 'Tis the way of all flesh. [*The Sullen Lovers*, V]

5 And wit's the noblest frailty of the mind. [*A True Widow*, II]

6 I am, out of the ladies' company, like a fish out of the water. [Ib. III]

Shakespeare, William (1564–1616)

ALL'S WELL THAT ENDS WELL

7 Mine eyes smell onions; I shall weep soon. [V.3]

ANTONY AND CLEOPATRA

8 The triple pillar of the world transformed / Into a strumpet's fool. [I.1]

9 There's beggary in the love that can be reckoned. [Ib.]

10 Let Rome in Tiber melt. [Ib.]

11 I love long life better than figs. [I.2]

12 Where's my serpent of old Nile? [I.5]

13 My salad days, / When I was green in judgement, cold in blood. [Ib.]

14 For her person, it beggar'd all description. [II.2]

15 Age cannot wither her, nor custom stale / Her infinite variety; other women cloy / The appetites they feed, but she makes hungry / Where most she satisfies. [Ib.]

16 Let's have one other gaudy night; call to me / All my sad captains. [III.11]

1 I am dying, Egypt, dying. [IV.13]

2 He words me, girls, he words me. [V.2]

3 I shall see some squeaking Cleopatra boy my greatness. [Ib.]

4 His biting is immortal; those that do die of it do seldom or never recover. [Ib.]

5 I wish you joy o' the worm. [Ib.]

6 Give me my robe, put on my crown; I have / Immortal longings in me. [Ib.]

7 Peace! peace! / Dost thou not see my baby at my breast, / That sucks the nurse asleep. [Ib.]

8 A lass unparallel'd. [Ib.]

AS YOU LIKE IT

9 Fleet the time carelessly, as they did in the golden world. [I.1]

10 Sweet are the uses of adversity, / Which like the toad, ugly and venomous, / Wears yet a precious jewel in his head. [II.1]

11 Sweep on, you fat and greasy citizens! [Ib.]

12 Under the greenwood tree / Who loves to lie with me / . . . Here shall he see / No enemy / But winter and rough weather. [II.5]

13 I can suck melancholy out of a song, as a weasel sucks eggs. [Ib.]

14 And so, from hour to hour we ripe and ripe, / And then from hour to hour we rot and rot, / And thereby hangs a tale. [II.7]

15 All the world's a stage, / And all the men and women merely players: / They have their exits and their entrances; / And one man in his time plays many parts, / His acts being seven ages. At first the infant, / Mewling and puking in the nurse's arms. / And then the whining schoolboy, with his satchel, / And shining morning face, creeping like snail / Unwillingly to school. [Ib.]

1 Then a soldier / ... Seeking the bubble reputation / Even in the cannon's mouth. [Ib.]

2 The lean and slipper'd pantaloon. [Ib.]

3 Second childishness and mere oblivion, / Sans teeth, sans eyes, sans taste, sans everything. [Ib.]

4 Blow, blow, thou winter wind, / Thou art not so unkind / As man's ingratitude. [III.2]

5 O wonderful, wonderful, and most wonderful! and yet again wonderful, and after that, out of all whooping! [III.2]

6 Men have died from time to time, and worms have eaten them, but not for love. [IV.1]

7 O coz, coz, coz, my pretty little coz, that thou didst know how many fathom deep I am in love! [Ib.]

8 It was a lover and his lass, With a hey, and a ho, and a hey nonino. [V.3]

9 An ill-favoured thing, sir, but mine own. [V.4]

10 Your 'if' is the only peace-maker; much virtue in 'if'. [Ib.]

CORIOLANUS

11 You common cry of curs! whose breath I hate / As reek o' the rotten fens, whose loves I prize / As the dead carcasses of unburied men / That do corrupt my air, — I banish you. [III.3]

CYMBELINE

12 Hark! hark! the lark at heaven's gate sings, / And Phoebus 'gins arise. [II.3]

13 He that sleeps feels not the toothache. [V.4]

HAMLET

14 But look, the morn, in russet mantle clad, / Walks o'er the dew of yon high eastward hill. [I.1]

15 A little more than kin, and less than kind. [I.2]

1 Seems, madam! Nay, it is; I know not 'seems'. [Ib.]

2 O! that this too too solid flesh would melt, / Thaw, and resolve itself into a dew. [Ib.]

3 How weary, stale, flat, and unprofitable / Seem to me all the uses of this world. / Fie on't! O fie! 'tis an unweeded garden. [Ib.]

4 Frailty, thy name is woman! [Ib.]

5 He was a man, take him for all in all, / I shall not look upon his like again. [Ib.]

6 Costly thy habit as thy purse can buy / ...For the apparel oft proclaims the man. [I.3]

7 Neither a borrower, nor a lender be. [Ib.]

8 This above all: to thine own self be true. [Ib.]

9 It is a custom / More honoured in the breach than the observance. [I.4]

10 Something is rotten in the state of Denmark. [Ib.]

11 Murder most foul. [I.5]

12 There are more things in heaven and earth, Horatio, / Than are dreamt of in your philosophy. [Ib.]

13 To put an antic disposition on. [Ib.]

14 The time is out of joint; O cursed spite, / That ever I was born to set it right. [Ib.]

15 Brevity is the soul of wit. [II.2]

16 Though this be madness, yet there is method in it. [Ib.]

17 There is nothing either good or bad, but thinking makes it so. [Ib.]

18 What a piece of work is a man! [Ib.]

19 Use every man after his desert and who would 'scape whipping? [Ib.]

20 O! what a rogue and peasant slave am I. [Ib.]

21 The play's the thing / Wherein I'll catch the conscience of the king. [Ib.]

1 To be, or not to be: that is the question: / Whether 'tis nobler in the mind to suffer / The slings and arrows of outrageous fortune, / Or to take arms against a sea of troubles, / And by opposing end them? To die: to sleep; / No more; and, by a sleep to say we end / The heart-ache and the thousand natural shocks / That flesh is heir to, 'tis a consummation / Devoutly to be wish'd. To die, to sleep; / To sleep: perchance to dream: ay, there's the rub; / For in that sleep of death what dreams may come / When we have shuffled off this mortal coil, / Must give us pause. [III.1]

2 He himself might his quietus make / With a bare bodkin. [Ib.]

3 The undiscover'd country from whose bourn / No traveller returns. [Ib.]

4 Thus conscience doth make cowards of us all; / And thus the native hue of resolution / Is sicklied o'er with the pale cast of thought. [Ib.]

5 Get thee to a nunnery. [Ib.]

6 O, what a noble mind is here o'erthrown. [Ib.]

7 Speak the speech, I pray you, as I pronounced it to you, trippingly on the tongue. [III.2]

8 O! it offends me to the soul to hear a robustious periwig-pated fellow tear a passion to tatters, to very rags, to split the ears of the groundlings, who for the most part are capable of nothing but inexplicable dumb-shows and noise. [Ib.]

9 It out-herods Herod. [Ib.]

10 The purpose of playing, whose end, both at the first and now, was and is, to hold, as 'twere, the mirror up to nature. [Ib.]

11 The lady doth protest too much, methinks. [Ib.]

12 Now I might do it pat, now he is praying. [III.3]

13 How now! a rat? Dead for a ducat, dead! [III.4]

1 A king of shreds and patches. [Ib.]

2 I must be cruel, only to be kind. [Ib.]

3 For 'tis the sport to have the engineer / Hoist with his own petar. [Ib.]

4 There's such divinity doth hedge a king, / That treason doth but peep to what it would. [IV.5]

5 Alas! poor Yorick. I knew him, Horatio; a fellow of infinite jest. [V.1]

6 Now get you to my lady's chamber, and tell her, let her paint an inch thick, to this favour she must come. [Ib.]

7 There's a divinity that shapes our ends, / Rough-hew them how we will. [V.2]

8 Not a whit, we defy augury; there's a special providence in the fall of a sparrow ... The readiness is all. [Ib.]

9 A hit, a very palpable hit. [Ib.]

10 This fell sergeant, death, / Is strict in his arrest. [Ib.]

11 Absent thee from felicity awhile. [Ib.]

12 The rest is silence. [Ib.]

13 Rosencrantz and Guildenstern are dead. [Ib.]

HENRY IV, Part 1

14 If all the year were playing holidays, / To sport would be as tedious as to work. [I.2]

15 By heaven methinks it were an easy leap / To pluck bright honour from the pale-faced moon. [I.3]

16 [Falstaff] lards the lean earth as he walks along. [II.2]

17 Out of this nettle, danger, we pluck this flower, safety. [II.3]

18 Instinct is a great matter, I was a coward on instinct. [II.4]

1 A plague of sighing and grief! It blows a man up like a bladder. [Ib.]

2 Shall I not take mine ease at mine inn? [III.3]

3 Rebellion lay in his way, and he found it. [V.1]

4 Honour pricks me on. Yea, but how if honour prick me off when I come on? [Ib.]

5 When that this body did contain a spirit, / A kingdom for it was too small a bound; / But now two paces of the vilest earth / Is room enough. [V.3]

HENRY IV, Part 2

6 I am not only witty in myself, but the cause that wit is in other men. [I.2]

7 I was born about three of the clock in the afternoon, with a white head, and something of a round belly. [Ib.]

8 I can get no remedy against this consumption of the purse: borrowing only lingers and lingers it out, but the disease is incurable. [Ib.]

9 Is it not strange that desire should so many years outlive performance? [II.4]

10 Uneasy lies the head that wears a crown. [III.1]

11 There is a history in all men's lives, / Figuring the nature of the times deceas'd. [Ib.]

12 We have heard the chimes at midnight. [III.2]

13 Thy wish was father, Harry, to that thought. [IV.5]

14 I know thee not, old man: fall to thy prayers; / How ill white hairs become a fool and jester! [V.5]

HENRY V

15 O! for a Muse of fire. [I, Chorus]

16 This wooden O. [Ib.]

1 Now all the youth of England are on fire, / And silken dalliance in the wardrobe lies. [II, Chorus]

2 Once more unto the breach, dear friends, once more; / Or close the wall up with our English dead. / In peace there's nothing so becomes a man / As modest stillness and humility; / But when the blast of war blows in our ears, / Then imitate the action of the tiger: / Stiffen the sinews, summon up the blood, / Disguise fair nature with hard-favour'd rage. [III.1]

3 I see you stand like greyhounds in the slips, / Straining upon the start. [Ib.]

4 Cry 'God for Harry! England and Saint George!' [Ib.]

5 O! that we now had here / But one ten thousand of those men in England / That do no work today. [IV.3]

6 But if it be a sin to covet honour / I am the most offending soul alive. [Ib.]

7 We few, we happy few, we band of brothers. [Ib.]

8 And gentlemen in England now a-bed / Shall think themselves accursed they were not here, / And hold their manhoods cheap whiles any speaks / That fought with us upon Saint Crispin's Day. [Ib.]

9 The naked, poor, and mangled Peace, / Dear nurse of arts, plenties, and joyful births. [V.1]

HENRY VI, Part 1

10 Hung be the heavens with black, yield day to night! [I.1]

11 Saint Martin's summer, halcyon days. [Ib.]

12 She's beautiful and therefore to be woo'd; / She is a woman, therefore to be won. [V.3]

HENRY VI, Part 2

1 And Adam was a gardener. [IV.2]

HENRY VI, Part 3

2 O tiger's heart wrapped in a woman's hide! [I.4]

HENRY VIII

3 Farewell! a long farewell, to all my greatness! [III.2]

4 I have ventured, / Like little wanton boys that swim on bladders, / This many summers in a sea of glory, / But far beyond my depth. [Ib.]

5 Had I but served my God with half the zeal / I served my king, he would not in mine age / Have left me naked to mine enemies. [Ib.]

JULIUS CAESAR

6 Beware the Ides of March. [I.1]

7 Why, man, he doth bestride the narrow world / Like a Colossus; and we petty men / Walk under his huge legs. [Ib.]

8 The fault, dear Brutus, is not in our stars, / But in ourselves, that we are underlings. [Ib.]

9 Let me have men about me that are fat; / Sleek-headed men and such as sleep o' nights; / Yond' Cassius has a lean and hungry look; / He thinks too much: such men are dangerous. [Ib.]

10 For mine own part, it was Greek to me. [Ib.]

11 But men may construe things after their own fashion, / Clean from the purpose of the things themselves. [I.3]

12 Between the acting of a dreadful thing / And the first motion, all the interim is / Like a phantasma or a hideous dream. [II.1]

13 Lowliness is young ambition's ladder, / Whereto the climber-upward turns his face; / But when he once attains the upmost round, / He then unto

the ladder turns his back, / Looks in the clouds, scorning the base degrees / By which he did ascend. [Ib.]

1 Cowards die many times before their deaths, / The valiant never taste of death but once. [II.2]

2 Et tu, Brute? [III.1]

3 Cry, 'Havoc!' and let slip the dogs of war. [Ib.]

4 Not that I loved Caesar less, but that I loved Rome more. [III.2]

5 Friends, Romans, countrymen, lend me your ears; / I come to bury Caesar, not to praise him. / The evil that men do lives after them / The good is oft interred with their bones. [Ib.]

6 For Brutus is an honourable man; / So are they all, all honourable men. [Ib.]

7 Ambition should be made of sterner stuff. [Ib.]

8 If you have tears, prepare to shed them now. [Ib.]

9 This was the most unkindest cut of all. [Ib.]

10 There is a tide in the affairs of men, / Which taken at the flood, leads on to fortune; / Omitted, all the voyage of their life / Is bound in shallows and in miseries. [IV.3]

11 This was the noblest Roman of them all. [V.5]

12 His life was gentle, and the elements / So mix'd in him that Nature might stand up, / And say to all the world, 'This was a man!' [Ib.]

KING JOHN

13 Bell, book, and candle shall not drive me back, / When gold and silver becks me to come on. [III.3]

14 To gild refined gold, to paint the lily, / To throw a perfume on the violet. [IV.2]

15 I beg cold comfort. [V.7]

KING LEAR

1 Nothing will come of nothing: speak again. [I.1]

2 Now, gods, stand up for bastards. [I.2]

3 We make guilty of our disasters the sun, the moon, and the stars; as if we were villains by necessity, fools by heavenly compulsion. [Ib.]

4 Pat he comes, like the catastrophe of the old comedy. [Ib.]

5 O! Let me not be mad, not mad, sweet heaven. [I.5]

6 Blow, winds, and crack your cheeks! [III.2]

7 I am a man / More sinned against than sinning. [Ib.]

8 O! that way madness lies. [III.4]

9 Take physic, pomp. [Ib.]

10 Unaccommodated man is no more but such a poor, bare, forked animal as thou art. [Ib.]

11 The prince of darkness is a gentleman. [Ib.]

12 Child Roland to the dark tower came, / His word was still, Fie, foh, and fum, / I smell the blood of a British man. [Ib.]

13 Out, vile jelly! [III.7]

14 The worst is not; / So long as we can say, 'This is the worst.' [IV.1]

15 As flies to wanton boys, are we to the gods; / They kill us for their sport. [Ib.]

16 Let copulation thrive. [IV.6]

17 Give me an ounce of civet, good apothecary, to sweeten my imagination. [Ib.]

18 *Gloucester:* O! Let me kiss that hand.
Lear: Let me wipe it first, it smells of mortality. [Ib.]

19 When we are born, we cry that we are come / To this great stage of fools. [Ib.]

1 I am bound / Upon a wheel of fire. [IV.7]

2 Men must endure / Their going hence, even as their coming hither: / Ripeness is all. [V.2]

3 The gods are just, and of our pleasant vices / Make instruments to plague us. [V.3]

4 The weight of this sad time we must obey, / Speak what we feel; not what we ought to say. / The oldest hath borne most: we that are young / Shall never see so much, nor live so long. [Ib.]

LOVE'S LABOUR'S LOST

5 Spite of cormorant devouring Time. [I.1]

6 They have been at a great feast of learning, and stolen the scraps. [V.1]

7 He draweth out the thread of his verbosity finer than the staple of his argument. [Ib.]

8 A jest's prosperity lies in the ear / Of him that hears it, never in the tongue / Of him that makes it. [V.2]

9 Cuckoo, / Cuckoo, cuckoo: O word of fear, / Unpleasing to a married ear. [Ib.]

10 Then nightly sings the staring owl / Tu-who; / Tu-whit, tu-who — a merry note, / While greasy Joan doth keel the pot. [Ib.]

11 The words of Mercury are harsh after the songs of Apollo. [Ib.]

MACBETH

12 When shall we three meet again / In thunder, lightning, or in rain? [I.1]

13 Fair is foul, and foul is fair. [Ib.]

14 Nothing in his life / Became him like the leaving it. [I.3]

15 Yet do I fear thy nature; / It is too full o' the milk of human kindness / To catch the nearest way. [Ib.]

1 Unsex me here, / And fill me from the crown to
  the toe top full / Of direst cruelty. [I.5]

2 This castle hath a pleasant seat. [I.6]

3 If it were done when 'tis done, then 'twere well /
  It were done quickly. [I.7]

4 That but this blow / Might be the be-all and the
  end-all here, / But here, upon this bank and
  shoal of time, / We'd jump the life to come. [Ib.]

5 I have no spur / To prick the sides of my intent,
  but only / Vaulting ambition, which o'erleaps
  itself / And falls on the other. [Ib.]

6 I dare do all that may become a man; / Who
  dares do more is none. [Ib.]

7 But screw your courage to the sticking-place, /
  And we'll not fail. [Ib.]

8 Is this a dagger which I see before me / The
  handle toward my hand? [II.1]

9 Methought I heard a voice cry, 'Sleep no more! /
  Macbeth does murder sleep,' the innocent sleep,
  / Sleep that knits up the ravelled sleave of care.
  [II.2]

10 Will all great Neptune's ocean wash this blood /
  Clean from my hand? No, this my hand will
  rather / The multitudinous seas incarnadine, /
  Making the green one red. [Ib.]

11 A little water clears us of this deed. [Ib.]

12 Wake Duncan with thy knocking! I would thou
  couldst! [Ib.]

13 The primrose way to the everlasting bonfire.
  [II.3]

14 Confusion now hath made his masterpiece! [Ib.]

15 There's nothing serious in mortality, / All is but
  toys. [Ib.]

16 To be thus is nothing; / But to be safely thus.
  [III.1]

1 After life's fitful fever he sleeps well. [III.2]

2 Stand not upon the order of your going, / But go at once. [III.4]

3 Double, double, toil and trouble; / Fire burn and cauldron bubble. [IV.1]

4 By the pricking of my thumbs, / Something wicked this way comes. [Ib.]

5 A deed without a name. [Ib.]

6 What! will the line stretch out to the crack of doom? [Ib.]

7 Out, damned spot! out, I say! [V.1]

8 Yet who would have thought the old man had so much blood in him? [Ib.]

9 All the perfumes of Arabia will not sweeten this little hand. [Ib.]

10 The devil damn thee black, thou cream-fac'd loon! [V.3]

11 My way of life / Is fall'n into the sear, the yellow leaf. [Ib.]

12 Canst thou not minister to a mind diseased? [Ib.]

13 She should have died hereafter; / There would have been a time for such a word, / To-morrow, and to-morrow, and to-morrow, / Creeps in this petty pace from day to day, / To the last syllable of recorded time; / And all our yesterdays have lighted fools / The way to dusty death. Out, out, brief candle! / Life's but a walking shadow, a poor player, / That struts and frets his hour upon the stage, / And then is heard no more; it is a tale / Told by an idiot, full of sound and fury, / Signifying nothing. [V.5]

14 Fear not, till Birnam wood / Do come to Dunsinane. [V.7]

15 Macduff was from his mother's womb / Untimely ripp'd. [Ib.]

MEASURE FOR MEASURE

1 Condemn the fault and not the actor of it? [II.2]

2 Man, proud man, / Drest in a little brief authority. [Ib.]

3 Be absolute for death; either death or life / Shall thereby be the sweeter. [III.1]

4 If I must die, / I will encounter darkness as a bride, / And hug it in my arms. [Ib.]

5 Ay, but to die, and go we know not where; / To lie in cold obstruction and to rot. [Ib.]

THE MERCHANT OF VENICE

6 Sometimes from her eyes / I did receive fair speechless messages. [I.1]

7 They are as sick that surfeit with too much, as they that starve with nothing. [I.2]

8 If to do were as easy as to know what were good to do, chapels had been churches, and poor men's cottages princes' palaces. [Ib.]

9 God made him, and therefore let him pass for a man. [Ib.]

10 The devil can cite Scripture for his purpose. [I.3]

11 Mislike me not for my complexion, / The shadowed livery of the burnished sun. [II.1]

12 It is a wise father that knows his own child. [Ib.]

13 All that glisters is not gold, / Often have you heard that told. [II.6]

14 My daughter! O my ducats! O my daughter! [II.8]

15 Hath not a Jew eyes? hath not a Jew hands, organs, dimensions, senses, affections, passions? [III.1]

16 If you prick us, do we not bleed? if you tickle us, do we not laugh? if you poison us, do we not die? and if you wrong us, shall we not revenge? [Ib.]

17 So may the outward shows be least themselves:

/ The world is still deceived with ornament. [III.2]

1 The pound of flesh which I demand of him / Is dearly bought, 'tis mine, and I will have it. [IV.1]

2 I am a tainted wether of the flock. [Ib.]

3 The quality of mercy is not strained, / It droppeth as the gentle rain from heaven / Upon the place beneath: it is twice blessed; / It blesseth him that gives and him that takes. [Ib.]

4 A Daniel come to judgement. [Ib.]

5 How sweet the moonlight sleeps upon this bank! / Here we will sit, and let the sounds of music / Creep in our ears. [V.1]

6 Such harmony is in immortal souls; / But whilst this muddy vesture of decay / Doth grossly close it in, we cannot hear it. [Ib.]

7 I am never merry when I hear sweet music. [Ib.]

8 How far that little candle throws his beams! / So shines a good deed in a naughty world. [Ib.]

THE MERRY WIVES OF WINDSOR

9 Why, then the world's mine oyster. [II.1]

10 Marry, this is the short and long of it. [Ib.]

11 I cannot tell what the dickens his name is. [III.2]

12 A man of my kidney. [III.5]

13 There is a divinity in odd numbers, either in nativity, chance or death. [V.1]

A MIDSUMMER NIGHT'S DREAM

14 The course of true love never did run smooth. [I.1]

15 Love looks not with the eyes, but with the mind, / And therefore is wing'd Cupid painted blind. [Ib.]

16 I will roar you as gently as any sucking dove. [I.2]

1 Ill met by moonlight, proud Titania. [II.1]

2 I'll put a girdle round about the earth / In forty minutes. [Ib.]

3 I have a reasonable good ear in music: let us have the tongs and bones. [IV.1]

4 I have had a dream, past the wit of man to say what dream it was. [Ib.]

5 The lunatic, the lover, and the poet, / Are of imagination all compact. [Ib.]

6 The poet's eye, in a fine frenzy rolling, / Doth glance from heaven to earth, from earth to heaven; / And, as imagination bodies forth / The forms of things unknown, the poet's pen / Turns them to shapes, and gives to airy nothing / A local habitation and a name. [Ib.]

7 A tedious brief scene of young Pyramus / And his love Thisbe: very tragical mirth. [Ib.]

8 The best in this kind are but shadows, and the worst are no worse, if imagination amend them. [Ib.]

MUCH ADO ABOUT NOTHING

9 Is it not strange that sheep's guts should hale souls out of men's bodies? [II.3]

10 Sigh no more, ladies, sigh no more, / Men were deceivers ever. [Ib.]

11 Sits the wind in that corner? [Ib.]

12 Comparisons are odorous. [III.5]

13 Patch grief with proverbs. [V.1]

OTHELLO

14 Your daughter and the Moor are now making the beast with two backs. [I.1]

15 I will a round unvarnished tale deliver. [I.3]

16 The Anthropophagi, and men whose heads / Do grow beneath their shoulders. [Ib.]

1 Virtue! a fig! 'tis in ourselves that we are thus, or thus. [Ib.]

2 Put money in thy purse. [Ib.]

3 I am nothing if not critical. [II.1]

4 Excellent wretch! Perdition catch my soul / But I do love thee! and when I love thee not, / Chaos is come again. [III.3]

5 Who steals my purse steals trash; 'tis something, nothing; / 'Twas mine, 'tis his, and has been slave to thousands; / But he that filches from me my good name / Robs me of that which not enriches him, / And makes me poor indeed. [Ib.]

6 O! beware, my lord, of jealousy; / It is the green-ey'd monster which doth mock / The meat it feeds on. [Ib.]

7 For I am declined / Into the vale of years. [Ib.]

8 Othello's occupation's gone! [Ib.]

9 Be sure of it; give me the ocular proof. [Ib.]

10 But yet the pity of it, Iago! O! Iago, the pity of it, Iago! [IV.1]

11 Goats and monkeys! [Ib.]

12 He hath a daily beauty in his life / That makes me ugly. [V.1]

13 It is the cause, it is the cause, my soul. [V.2]

14 Put out the light and then put out the light. [Ib.]

15 Then, must you speak / Of one that lov'd not wisely but too well. [Ib.]

16 One whose hand, / Like the base Indian, threw a pearl away / Richer than all his tribe. [Ib.]

PERICLES

17 *3rd Fisherman:* I marvel how the fishes live in the sea.
1st Fisherman: Why, as the men do a-land; the great ones eat up the little ones. [II.1]

RICHARD II

1 Things sweet to taste prove in digestion sour.
   [I.3]

2 Teach thy necessity to reason thus; / There is no
   virtue like necessity. [Ib.]

3 This royal throne of kings, this scepter'd isle, /
   This earth of majesty, this seat of Mars, / This
   other Eden, demi-Paradise. [II.1]

4 This happy breed of men, this little world, / This
   precious stone set in the silver sea. [Ib.]

5 This blessed plot, this earth, this realm, this
   England, / This nurse, this teeming womb of
   royal kings. [Ib.]

6 Let's talk of graves, of worms and epitaphs.
   [III.2]

7 For God's sake let us sit upon the ground / And
   tell sad stories of the death of kings. [Ib.]

8 What must the king do now? Must he submit? /
   The king shall do it. [III.3]

9 I have been studying how I may compare / The
   prison where I live unto the world. [V.5]

RICHARD III

10 Now is the winter of our discontent / Made
    glorious summer by this sun of York. [I.1]

11 In this weak piping time of peace. [Ib.]

12 And therefore, since I cannot prove a lover, ... /
    I am determined to prove a villain. [Ib.]

13 Thou art a traitor: / Off with his head! [III.4]

14 A horse! a horse! my kingdom for a horse! [V.4]

ROMEO AND JULIET

15 A pair of star-crossed lovers. [Prologue]

16 The two hours' traffic of our stage. [Ib.]

17 O! then I see Queen Mab hath been with you.
    [I.4]

1 O! she doth teach the torches to burn bright. [I.5]

2 He jests at scars that never felt a wound. / But, soft! what light through yonder window breaks? / It is the east, and Juliet is the sun. [II.2]

3 O Romeo, Romeo! wherefore art thou Romeo? [Ib.]

4 What's in a name? that which we call a rose / By any other name would smell as sweet. [Ib.]

5 O swear not by the moon, the inconstant moon, / That monthly changes in her circled orb, / Lest that thy love prove likewise variable. [Ib.]

6 Good-night, good-night! parting is such sweet sorrow / That I shall say good-night till it be morrow. [Ib.]

7 A plague o' both your houses! / They have made worms' meat of me. [III.1]

8 Adversity's sweet milk, philosophy. [III.3]

9 Night's candles are burnt out, and jocund day / Stands tiptoe on the misty mountain tops. [III.5]

THE TAMING OF THE SHREW

10 Love in idleness. [I.1]

11 Kiss me, Kate. [II.1]

12 This is the way to kill a wife with kindness. [IV.1]

13 Such duty as the subject owes the prince, / Even such a woman oweth to her husband. [V.2]

THE TEMPEST

14 The dark backward and abysm of time. [I.2]

15 You taught me language; and my profit on't / Is, I know how to curse. [Ib.]

16 Come unto these yellow sands, / And then take hands; / Curtsied when you have, and kissed, — / The wild waves whist. [Ib.]

1 Full fathom five thy father lies; / Of his bones are coral made. [Ib.]

2 Misery acquaints a man with strange bedfellows. [II.2]

3 Be not afeard: the isle is full of noises, / Sounds and sweet airs, that give delight and hurt not. [Ib.]

4 Our revels now are ended. These our actors, / As I foretold you, were all spirits and / Are melted into air, into thin air: / And, like the baseless fabric of this vision, / The cloud-capped towers, the gorgeous palaces, / The solemn temples, the great globe itself, / Yea, all which it inherit, shall dissolve / And, like this insubstantial pageant faded, / Leave not a rack behind. We are such stuff / As dreams are made on, and our little life / Is rounded with a sleep! [IV.2]

5 The rarer action is / In virtue than in vengeance. [V.1]

6 This rough magic / I here abjure. [Ib.]

7 Where the bee sucks, there suck I: / In a cowslip's bell I lie; / There I couch when owls do cry. [Ib.]

8 O brave new world, / That has such people in't. [Ib.]

TIMON OF ATHENS

9 He that loves to be flattered is worthy o' the flatterer. [I.1]

10 The strain of man's bred out / Into baboon and monkey. [I.2]

TITUS ANDRONICUS

11 What, man! more water glideth by the mill / Than wots the miller of. [I.2]

12 If one good deed in all my life I did, / I do repent it from my very soul. [V.3]

TROILUS AND CRESSIDA

1 Men prize the thing ungained more than it is.
[I.2]

2 Take but degree away, untune that string, / And
hark what discord follows. [I.3]

3 All the argument is a whore and a cuckold. [II.3]

4 This is the monstruosity in love, lady, that the
will is infinite and the execution confined; that
the desire is boundless, and the act a slave to
limit. [III.2]

5 Time hath, my lord, a wallet at his back, /
Wherein he puts alms for oblivion. [III.3]

6 One touch of nature makes the whole world kin.
[Ib.]

7 There's language in her eye, her cheek, her lip, /
Nay, her foot speaks. [IV.5]

8 Lechery, lechery; still wars and lechery; nothing
else holds fashion. [V.2]

TWELFTH NIGHT

9 If music be the food of love, play on; / Give me
excess of it, that, surfeiting, / The appetite may
sicken, and so die. [I.1]

10 That strain again! it had a dying fall. [Ib.]

11 Many a good hanging prevents a bad marriage.
[I.5]

12 Not to be a-bed after midnight is to be up
betimes. [II.3]

13 Journeys end in lovers meeting, / Every wise
man's son doth know. [Ib.]

14 Youth's a stuff will not endure. [Ib.]

15 Dost thou think, because thou art virtuous, there
shall be no more cakes and ale? [Ib.]

16 Come away, come away, death, / And in sad
cypress let me be laid. [II.4]

17 Be not afraid of greatness: some are born great,

some achieve greatness, and some have greatness thrust upon them. [II.5]

1 Why this is very midsummer madness. [III.4]

2 If this were played upon a stage now, / I could condemn it as an improbable fiction. [Ib.]

3 And thus the whirligig of time brings in his revenges. [V.1]

4 I'll be revenged on the whole pack of you. [Ib.]

THE WINTER'S TALE

5 A sad tale's best for winter. [II.1]

6 Exit, pursued by a bear. [III.3 (stage direction)]

7 A snapper-up of unconsidered trifles. [IV.2]

8 This is an art / Which does mend nature — change it rather; but / The art itself is nature. [IV.4]

9 Good sooth, she is / The queen of curds and cream. [Ib.]

10 The self-same sun that shines upon his court / Hides not his visage from our cottage, but / Looks on alike. [Ib.]

THE PASSIONATE PILGRIM

11 Crabbed age and youth cannot live together: / Youth is full of pleasance, age is full of care.

SONNETS

12 To the only begetter of these ensuing sonnets, Mr. W.H. [Dedication]

13 Shall I compare thee to a summer's day? / Thou art more lovely and more temperate. / Rough winds do shake the darling buds of May / And summer's lease hath all too short a date. [18]

14 For the sweet love remembered such wealth brings / That then I scorn to change my state with kings. [29]

1 When to the sessions of sweet silent thought / I summon up remembrance of things past. [30]

2 Full many a glorious morning have I seen. [33]

3 Like as the waves make towards the pebbled shore, / So do our minutes hasten to their end. [60]

4 No longer mourn for me when I am dead / Than you shall hear the surly sullen bell. [71]

5 That time of year thou mayst in me behold / When yellow leaves, or none, or few, do hang / Upon those boughs which shake against the cold, / Bare ruined choirs, where late the sweet birds sang. [73]

6 The chronicle of wasted time. [106]

7 For we, which now behold these present days, / Have eyes to wonder, but lack tongues to praise. [Ib.]

8 Let me not to the marriage of true minds / Admit impediments. Love is not love / Which alters when it alteration finds. [116]

9 Love's not Time's fool. [Ib.]

10 The expense of spirit in a waste of shame / Is lust in action. [Ib. 129]

11 My mistress' eyes are nothing like the sun. [130]

Shankly, Bill (1914–1981)

12 Some people think football is a matter of life and death. I don't like that attitude. I can assure them it is much more serious than that. [Remark on BBC T.V.]

Shaw, George Bernard (1856–1950)

13 You can always tell an old soldier by the inside of his holsters and cartridge boxes. The young ones carry pistols and cartridges: the old ones, grub. [*Arms and the Man*, I]

1 He who has never hoped can never despair.
   [*Caesar and Cleopatra*, IV]

2 We have no more right to consume happiness
   without producing it than to consume wealth
   without producing it. [*Candida*, I]

3 I'm only a beer teetotaller, not a champagne
   teetotaller. [*Ib.* III]

4 The British soldier can stand up to anything —
   except the British War Office. [*The Devil's
   Disciple*, III]

5 All professions are conspiracies against the laity.
   [*The Doctor's Dilemma*, I]

6 With the single exception of Homer, there is no
   eminent writer, not even Sir Walter Scott, whom
   I can despise so entirely as I despise Shakespeare
   when I measure my mind against his. [*Dramatic
   Opinions and Essays*]

7 It's all that the young can do for the old, to
   shock them and keep them up to date. [*Fanny's
   First Play*]

8 If you will only take the trouble always to do the
   perfectly correct thing, and to say the perfectly
   correct thing, you can do just what you like.
   [*Heartbreak House*, I]

9 Money is indeed the most important thing in the
   world; and all sound and successful personal and
   national morality should have this fact for its
   basis. [*The Irrational Knot*, Preface]

10 Reminiscences make one feel so deliciously aged
   and sad. [*Ib.*14]

11 What really flatters a man is that you think him
   worth flattering. [*John Bull's Other Island*, IV]

12 I am a Millionaire. That is my religion. [*Major
   Barbara*, II]

13 Nothing is ever done in this world until men are

prepared to kill one another if it is not done. [Ib. III].

1 The more things a man is ashamed of, the more respectable he is. [*Man and Superman*, I]

2 The true artist will let his wife starve, his children go barefoot, his mother drudge for his living at seventy, sooner than work at anything but his art. [Ib.]

3 There is no love sincerer than the love of food. [Ib.]

4 A lifetime of happiness! No man alive could bear it: it would be hell on earth. [Ib.]

5 It is a woman's business to get married as soon as possible, and a man's to keep unmarried as long as he can. [Ib.]

6 Hell is full of musical amateurs: music is the brandy of the damned. [Ib. III]

7 I am a gentleman: I live by robbing the poor. [Ib.]

8 An Englishman thinks he is moral when he is only uncomfortable. [Ib.]

9 This creature man, who in his own selfish affairs is a coward to the backbone, will fight for an idea like a hero. [Ib.]

10 There are two tragedies in life. One is not to get your heart's desire. The other is to get it. [Ib. IV]

11 Beware of the man whose god is in the skies. ['Maxims for Revolutionists']

12 Do not do unto others as you would they should do unto you. Their tastes may not be the same. [Ib.]

13 Marriage is popular because it combines the maximum of temptation with the maximum of opportunity. [Ib.]

14 Democracy substitutes election by the

incompetent many for appointment by the corrupt few. [Ib.]

1 The reasonable man adapts himself to the world: the unreasonable one persists in trying to adapt the world to himself. Therefore all progress depends on the unreasonable man. [Ib.]

2 Youth, which is forgiven everything, forgives itself nothing: age, which forgives itself anything, is forgiven nothing. [Ib.]

3 He who can, does. He who cannot teaches. [Ib.]

4 The golden rule is that there are no golden rules. [Ib.]

5 Every man over forty is a scoundrel. [Ib.]

6 Titles distinguish the mediocre, embarrass the superior, and are disgraced by the inferior. [Ib.]

7 In heaven an angel is nobody in particular. [Ib.]

8 Life levels all men: death reveals the eminent. [Ib.]

9 Decency is Indecency's Conspiracy of Silence. [Ib.]

10 Liberty means responsibility. That is why most men dread it. [Ib.]

11 There is only one universal passion: fear. [*The Man of Destiny*]

12 There is nothing so bad or so good that you will not find Englishmen doing it; but you will never find an Englishman in the wrong. He does everything on principle. He fights you on patriotic principles; he robs you on business principles; he enslaves you on imperial principles; he supports his king on royal principles and cuts off his king's head on republican principles. [Ib.]

13 There is only one religion, though there are a hundred versions of it. [*Plays Unpleasant*, Preface]

14 The English have no respect for their language,

and will not teach their children to speak it ... It is impossible for an Englishman to open his mouth, without making some other Englishman despise him. [*Pygmalion*, Preface]

1 *Pickering:* Have you no morals, man?
 Doolittle: Can't afford them, Governor. [Ib. II]

2 I have never sneered in my life. Sneering doesn't become either the human face or the human soul. [Ib. V]

3 Assassination is the extreme form of censorship. [*The Rejected Statement*]

4 An all-night sitting in a theatre would be at least as enjoyable as an all-night sitting in the House of Commons, and much more useful. [*St. Joan*, Preface]

5 The trouble is that you are only interested in art, and I am only interested in money. [Remark to Sam Goldwyn, quoted in Halliwell, *Filmgoers' Book of Quotes*]

Shawcross, Lord (1902–)

6 We are the masters at the moment, and not only at the moment, but for a very long time to come. [Speech, 1946]

Shelley, Percy Bysshe (1792–1822)

7 It might make one in love with death, to think that one should be buried in so sweet a place. [*Adonais*, Preface]

8 To that high Capital, where kingly Death / Keeps his pale court in beauty and decay. [Ib. 7]

9 From the contagion of the world's slow stain / He is secure. [Ib. 40]

10 He is a portion of the loveliness / Which once he made more lovely. [Ib. 43]

11 The One remains, the many change and pass; / Heaven's light forever shines, Earth's shadows

fly; / Life, like a dome of many-coloured glass, / Stains the white radiance of Eternity, / Until Death tramples it to fragments. [Ib. 52]

1 England, farewell! thou, who hast been my cradle, / Shalt never be my dungeon or my grave! [*Charles the First* (Hampden's speech)]

2 That orbèd maiden with white fire laden, / Whom mortals call the Moon. ['The Cloud']

3 I silently laugh at my own cenotaph, / And out of the caverns of rain, / Like a child from the womb, like a ghost from the tomb, / I arise and unbuild it again. [Ib.]

4 How wonderful is Death, / Death and his brother Sleep! [*The Daemon of the World*, I (also the opening of *Queen Mab*)]

5 We — are we not formed, as notes of music are, / For one another, though dissimilar? [*Epipsychidion*, 8]

6 I never was attached to that great sect, / Whose doctrine is, that each one should select / Out of the crowd a mistress or a friend, / And all the rest, though fair and wise, commend / To cold oblivion. [Ib. 9]

7 The breath of her false mouth was like faint flowers, / Her touch was as electric poison. [Ib. 13]

8 One Heaven, one Hell, one immortality / And one annihilation. [Ib. 19]

9 Virtue owns a more eternal foe / Than Force or Fraud: old Custom, legal Crime, / And bloody Faith the foulest birth of Time. ['Feelings of a Republican on the Fall of Bonaparte']

10 Good-night? ah! no; the hour is ill / Which severs those it should unite; / Let us remain together still, / Then it will be *good* night. ['Good Night']

11 Let there be light! said Liberty, / And like

sunrise from the sea, / Athens arose! [*Hellas*,
'The Voices of War']

1 Heaven smiles, and faiths and empires gleam, /
Like wrecks of a dissolving dream. [Ib. 'The
Future']

2 Another Athens shall arise, / And to remoter
time / Bequeath, like sunset to the skies, / The
splendour of its prime. [Ib.]

3 Oh, cease! must hate and death return? / Cease!
must men kill and die? / Cease! drain not to its
dregs the urn / Of bitter prophecy. / The world
is weary of the past, / Oh, might it die or rest at
last! [Ib.]

4 The awful shadow of some unseen Power /
Floats though unseen among us. ['Hymn to
Intellectual Beauty']

5 While yet a boy I sought for ghosts, and sped /
Through many a listening chamber, cave and
ruin, / And starlight wood, with fearful steps
pursuing / Hopes of high talk with the departed
dead. [Ib.]

6 Thou Paradise of exiles, Italy! [*Julian and
Maddalo*]

7 Most wretched men / Are cradled into poetry by
wrong: / They learn in suffering what they teach
in song. [Ib.]

8 London, that great sea, whose ebb and flow / At
once is deaf and loud, and on the shore / Vomits
its wrecks, and still howls on for more. ['Letter
to Maria Gisborne']

9 When the lamp is shattered / The light in the
dust lies dead. ['Lines: When the Lamp']

10 I met Murder on the way — / He had a mask
like Castlereagh. [*The Mask of Anarchy*]

11 His big tears, for he wept well, / Turned to mill-
stones as they fell. / And the little children, who

/ Round his feet played to and fro, / Thinking every tear a gem, / Had their brains knocked out by them. [Ib.]

1 Some say that gleams of a remoter world / Visit the soul in sleep, — that death is slumber. ['Mont Blanc']

2 Power dwells apart in its tranquillity, / Remote, serene, and inaccessible. [Ib.]

3 O wild West Wind, thou breath of Autumn's being, / Thou, from whose unseen presence the leaves dead / Are driven, like ghosts from an enchanter fleeing. ['Ode to the West Wind']

4 Wild Spirit, which art moving every- where; / Destroyer and preserver; hear, oh, hear. [Ib.]

5 Oh, lift me as a wave, a leaf, a cloud! / I fall upon the thorns of life! I bleed! [Ib.]

6 My name is Ozymandias, king of kings: / Look on my works, ye Mighty, and despair! ['Ozymandias']

7 Hell is a city much like London — / A populous and a smoky city. [Peter Bell the Third]

8 Things whose trade is, over ladies / To lean, and flirt, and stare, and simper, / Till all that is divine in woman / Grows cruel, courteous, smooth, inhuman, / Crucified 'twixt a smile and whimper. [Ib.]

9 The heaven around, the earth below / Was peopled with thick shapes of human death, / All horrible, and wrought by human hands, / And some appeared the work of human hearts, / For men were slowly killed by frowns and smiles. [Prometheus Unbound, I]

10 The good want power, but to weep barren tears. / The powerful goodness want: worse need for them. / The wise want love; and those who love want wisdom; / And all best things are thus confused to ill. [Ib.]

1 Peace is in the grave. / The grave hides all things beautiful and good: / I am a God and cannot find it there. [Ib.]

2 From the dust of creeds outworn. [Ib.]

3 The soul of man, like unextinguished fire, / Yet burns towards heaven with fierce reproach. [Ib. III.1]

4 Death is the veil which those who live call life: / They sleep, and it is lifted. [Ib. III.3]

5 Many faint with toil, / That few may know the cares and woe of sloth. [*Queen Mab*, 3]

6 Yet every heart contains perfection's germ. [Ib. 5]

7 Earth groans beneath religion's iron age, / And priests dare babble of a God of peace / Even whilst their hands are red with guiltless blood. [Ib. 7]

8 Rarely, rarely, comest thou, / Spirit of Delight! ['Song']

9 Lift not the painted veil which those who live / Call Life. ['Sonnet']

10 [Of George III] An old, mad, blind, despised, and dying king. ['Sonnet: England in 1819']

11 The worm beneath the sod / May lift itself in worship to the God. ['To Byron']

12 Music, when soft voices die, / Vibrates in the memory. ['To —:' 'Music When Soft Voices']

13 One word is too often profaned / For me to profane it, / One feeling too falsely disdained / For thee to disdain it. ['To —:' 'One Word is too often Profaned']

14 Hail to thee, blithe Spirit! / Bird thou never wert. ['To a Skylark']

15 And singing still dost soar, and soaring ever singest. [Ib.]

1 Poets are the unacknowledged legislators of the world. [*A Defence of Poetry*]

2 Poetry is the record of the best and happiest moments of the happiest and best minds. [Ib.]

Shenstone, William (1714–1763)

3 A fool and his words are soon parted; a man of genius and his money. [*Essays on Men and Manners*, 'On Reserve']

Sheridan, Philip Henry (1831–1888)

4 The only good Indian is a dead Indian. [Attr.]

Sheridan, Richard Brinsley (1751–1816)

5 I open with a clock striking, to beget an awful attention in the audience: it also marks the time, which is four o'clock in the morning, and saves a description of the rising sun, and a great deal about gilding the eastern hemisphere. [*The Critic*, II.2]

6 I wish, sir, you would practise this without me. I can't stay dying here all night. [Ib. III.1]

7 O Lord, sir, when a heroine goes mad she always goes into white satin. [Ib.]

8 'Tis safest in matrimony to begin with a little aversion. [*The Rivals*, I.2]

9 Madam, a circulating library in a town is as an evergreen tree of diabolical knowledge! It blossoms through the year! [Ib.]

10 If I reprehend anything in this world, it is the use of my oracular tongue, and a nice derangement of epitaphs! [Ib. III.3]

11 She's as headstrong as an allegory on the banks of the Nile. [Ib.]

12 Our ancestors are very good kind of folks; but they are the last people I should choose to have a visiting acquaintance with. [Ib. IV.1]

1 No caparisons, miss, if you please. Caparisons don't become a young woman. [Ib. IV.2]

2 Here's to the maiden of bashful fifteen; / Here's to the widow of fifty; / Here's to the flaunting, extravagant quean; / And here's to the housewife that's thrifty. [*The School for Scandal*, III.3]

3 An unforgiving eye, and a damned disinheriting countenance. [Ib. IV.1]

4 The Right Honourable gentleman is indebted to his memory for his jests, and to his imagination for his facts. [Speech in House of Commons]

Sherman, William Tecumseh (1820–1891)

5 There is many a boy here to-day who looks on war as all glory, but, boys, it is all hell. [Speech, 1880]

Sickert, Walter (1860–1942)

6 Nothing links man to man like the frequent passage from hand to hand of cash. [Quoted in Auden, *A Certain World*]

Sidgwick, Henry (1838–1900)

7 We think so because other people think so, / Or because – or because – after all we do think so, / Or because we were told so, and think we must think so, / Or because we once thought so, and think we still think so, / Or because having thought so, we think we will think so. ['Lines Composed in his Sleep']

Sidney, Sir Philip (1554–1586)

8 Who shoots at the mid-day sun, though he be sure he shall never hit the mark; yet as sure he is he shall shoot higher than who aims but at a bush. [*The Arcadia*, 2]

9 Come, Sleep! O Sleep, the certain knot of peace, / The baiting-place of wit, the balm of woe, / The poor man's wealth, the prisoner's release, /

Th'indifferent judge between the high and low.
[*Astrophel and Stella*, 39]

1 Nature never set forth the earth in so rich
tapestry as divers poets have done; . . . her world
is brazen, the poets only deliver a golden. [*The
Defence of Poesy*]

2 Thy necessity is greater than mine. [On giving his
water-bottle to a dying soldier on the battlefield
of Zutphen, 1586]

Sieyès, Abbé Emmanuel Joseph (1748–1836)

3 *J'ai vécu.* I survived. [Reply when asked what he
did during the French Revolution]

Simonides (c. 556–468 B.C.)

4 Go, tell the Spartans, thou who passeth by, /
That here, obedient to their laws, we lie.
[Herodotus, *Histories*]

Simpson, N.F. (1919–)

5 Each of us as he receives his private trouncings
at the hands of fate is kept in good heart by the
moth in his brother's parachute, and the scorpion
in his neighbour's underwear. [*A Resounding
Tinkle*]

Sims, George R. (1847–1922)

6 It is Christmas Day in the Workhouse. [*Dagonet
Ballads*]

Sitwell, Edith (1887–1964)

7 Still falls the Rain — / Dark as the world of
man, black as our loss — / Blind as the nineteen
hundred and forty nails / Upon the Cross. ['Still
Falls the Rain']

Sitwell, Sir Osbert (1892–1969)

8 The British Bourgeoisie / Is not born, / And does
not die, / But, if it is ill, / It has a frightened
look in its eyes. ['At the House of Mrs. Kinfoot']

Skinner, B.F. (1904–   )

1 Education is what survives when what has been learnt has been forgotten. [*New Scientist*, 1964]

Smart, Christopher (1722–1771)

2 For I will consider my Cat Jeoffry. / For he is the servant of the Living God, duly and daily serving Him. / For at the first glance of the glory of God in the East he worships in his way. / For this is done by wreathing his body seven times round with elegant quickness. [*Jubilate Agno*, 19]

Smedley, Francis Edward (1818–1864)

3 You are looking as fresh as paint. [*Frank Fairleigh*]

Smiles, Samuel (1812–1904)

4 The shortest way to do many things is to do only one thing at once. [*Self-Help*, 9]

5 A place for everything, and everything in its place. [*Thrift*, 5]

Smith, Adam (1723–1790)

6 [Of the rich] They are led by an invisible hand to make nearly the same distribution of the necessities of life which would have been made, had the earth been divided into equal portions among all its inhabitants. [*Theory of Moral Sentiments*, IV]

7 With the greater part of rich people, the chief enjoyment of riches consists in the parade of riches. [*Wealth of Nations*, I, 11]

8 To found a great empire for the sole purpose of raising up a people of customers, may at first sight appear a project fit only for a nation of shopkeepers. It is, however, a project altogether unfit for a nation of shopkeepers; but extremely fit for a nation that is governed by shopkeepers. [Ib. II, 4]

Smith, Alfred Emanuel (1873–1944)

1 The kiss of death. [Speech, 1926]

2 No matter how thin you slice it, it's still baloney. [Speech, 1936]

Smith, Logan Pearsall (1865–1946)

3 Most people sell their souls and live with a good conscience on the proceeds. [*All Trivia*]

4 People say that life is the thing, but I prefer reading. [Ib.]

5 How often my Soul visits the National Gallery, and how seldom I go there myself! [Ib.]

6 Married women are kept women, and they are beginning to find it out. [Ib.]

7 I cannot forgive my friends for dying: I do not find these vanishing acts of theirs at all amusing. [Ib.]

8 I love money; just to be in the room with a millionaire makes me less forlorn. [Ib.]

9 Thank heavens, the sun has gone in, and I don't have to go out and enjoy it. [Ib.]

Smith, Samuel Francis (1808–1895)

10 My country, 'tis of thee, / Sweet land of liberty, / Of thee I sing. ['America']

Smith, Stevie (1902–1971)

11 I was much further out than you thought / And not waving but drowning. ['Not Waving But Drowning']

Smith, Sydney (1771–1845)

12 The moment the very name of Ireland is mentioned, the English seem to bid adieu to common feeling, common prudence, and common sense, and to act with the barbarity of tyrants, and the fatuity of idiots. [*Peter Plymley's Letters*]

13 Where etiquette prevents me from doing things

disagreeable to myself, I am a perfect martinet.
[*Letters*, To Lady Holland]

1 I look upon Switzerland as an inferior sort of
Scotland. [Ib. To Lord Holland]

2 I am convinced digestion is the great secret of
life. [Ib. To Arthur Kinglake]

3 There are three sexes — men, women, and
clergymen. [Lady Holland, *Memoirs*, I]

4 It requires a surgical operation to get a joke well
into a Scotch understanding. Their only idea of
wit...is laughing immoderately at stated
intervals. [Ib.]

5 [Scotland] That knuckle-end of England — that
land of Calvin, oat-cakes, and sulphur. [Ib.]

6 I have, alas, only one illusion left, and that is the
Archbishop of Canterbury. [Ib.]

7 Deserves to be preached to death by wild
curates. [Ib.]

8 He [Macaulay] has occasional flashes of silence,
that make his conversation perfectly delightful.
[Ib.]

9 —'s idea of heaven is, eating *pâtés de foie gras*
to the sound of trumpets. [Pearson, *The Smith of
Smiths*]

10 Death must be distinguished from dying, with
which it is often confused. [Ib.]

11 I am just going to pray for you at St. Paul's, but
with no very lively hope of success. [Ib.]

12 I never read a book before reviewing it; it
prejudices a man so. [Ib.]

13 Poverty is no disgrace to a man, but it is
confoundedly inconvenient. [*His Wit and
Wisdom*]

Smith, Sir Sydney (1883–1969)

1 No child is born a criminal: no child is born an angel: he's just born. [*Remark*]

Smollett, Tobias (1721–1771)

2 Hark ye, Clinker, you are a most notorious offender. You stand convicted of sickness, hunger, wretchedness, and want. [*Humphrey Clinker*, Letter to Sir Watkin Phillips]

3 The painful ceremony of receiving and returning visits. [*Peregrine Pickle*, 5]

4 Some folks are wise, and some are otherwise. [*Roderick Random*, 6]

5 I consider the world as made for me, not me for the world. It is my maxim therefore to enjoy it while I can, and let futurity shift for itself. [Ib. 45]

6 True Patriotism is of no party. [*Sir Lancelot Greaves*, 9]

7 Too coy to flatter, and too proud to serve, / Thine be the joyless dignity to starve. ['Advice']

Snow, C.P. (1905–1980)

8 The Corridors of Power [Title of novel]

9 The Two Cultures [Title of lecture series]

Socrates (469–399 B.C.)

10 [Looking at goods for sale] How many things I have no need of! [Diogenes Laertius, *Lives of the Eminent Philosophers*]

Solon (c. 638–c. 559 B.C.)

11 Laws are like spider's webs, which stand firm when any light, yielding object falls upon them, while a larger thing breaks through them and escapes. [Diogenes Laertius, *Lives of the Eminent Philosophers*]

1 Call no man happy until he is dead, but only lucky. [Herodotus, *Histories*]

Solzhenitsyn, Alexander (1918–)

2 You only have power over people so long as you don't take *everything* away from them. But when you've robbed a man of everything he's no longer in your power — he's free again. [*The First Circle*, 17]

Sontag, Susan (1933–)

3 Interpretation is the revenge of the intellect upon art. [*Against Interpretation*]

Sophocles (495–406 B.C.)

4 Life is short but sweet. [*Alcestis*]

5 Marvels are many, but man is the greatest. [*Antigone*]

6 Not to be born is best. The second best is to have seen the light and then to go back quickly whence we came. [*Oedipus at Colonus*]

Soule, John Babsone Lane (1815–1891)

7 Go west, young man. [*Terre Haute* (Indiana) *Express*, 1851]

Southey, Robert (1774–1843)

8 'But what good came of it at last?' / Quoth little Peterkin. / 'Why, that I cannot tell,' said he, / 'But 'twas a famous victory.' ['The Battle of Blenheim']

9 Curses are like young chickens, they always come home to roost. [*The Curse of Kehama*, motto]

10 You are old, Father William, the young man cried, / The few locks which are left you are grey; / You are hale, Father William, a hearty old man, / Now tell me the reason, I pray. ['The Old Man's Comforts, and how he Gained them']

1 In the days of my youth I remembered my God! / And He hath not forgotten my age. [Ib.]

Spark, Muriel (1918–)

2 If only you small girls would listen to me, I would make of you the crème de la crème. [*The Prime of Miss Jean Brodie*, 1]

Spencer, Herbert (1820–1903)

3 Science is organized knowledge. [*Education*, 2]

4 The Republican form of Government is the highest form of government; but because of this it requires the highest type of human nature − a type nowhere at present existing. [*Essays*, 'The Americans']

5 The survival of the fittest. [*Principles of Biology*]

6 No one can be perfectly free till all are free; no one can be perfectly moral till all are moral; no one can be perfectly happy till all are happy. [*Social Statics*]

7 It was remarked to me ... that to play billiards well was a sign of an ill-spent youth. [Duncan, *Life and Letters of Spencer*]

Spender, Stephen (1909–)

8 I think continually of those who were truly great − / The names of those who in their lives fought for life, / Who wore at their hearts the fire's centre. ['I Think Continually of Those']

9 Born of the sun they travelled a short while towards the sun, / And left the vivid air signed with their honour. [Ib.]

Spenser, Edmund (c. 1522–1599)

10 Most glorious Lord of life, that on this day / Didst make thy triumph over death and sin: / And, having harrow'd hell, didst bring away / Captivity thence captive, us to win. [*Amoretti*, Sonnet 68]

1 So let us love, dear love, like as we ought, / —
Love is the lesson which the Lord us taught. [Ib.]

2 One day I wrote her name upon the sand / But
came the waves and washed it away: / Again I
wrote it with a second hand / But came the tide,
and made my pains his prey. [Ib. 75]

3 Open the temple gates unto my love, / Open
them wide that she may enter in. [*Epithalamion*]

4 Fierce wars and faithful loves shall moralize my
song. [*The Faerie Queen*, I]

5 A gentle knight was pricking on the plain. [Ib.]

6 Her angel's face / As the great eye of heaven
shined bright, / And made a sunshine in the
shady place. [Ib.]

7 A cruel crafty Crocodile, / Which in false grief
hiding his harmful guile, / Doth weep full sore,
and sheddeth tender tears. [Ib.]

8 Sleep after toil, port after stormy seas, / Ease
after war, death after life, does greatly please.
[Ib.]

9 And all for love, and nothing for reward. [Ib. II]

10 A monster, which the Blatant beast men call, / A
dreadful fiend of gods and men ydrad. [Ib. V]

11 What man that sees the ever-whirling wheel / Of
Change, the which all mortal things doth sway /
But that thereby doth find, and plainly feel, /
How Mutability in them doth play / Her cruel
sports, to many men's decay? [Ib. VII]

12 Sweet Thames, run softly, till I end my song.
['Prothalamion']

13 So now they have made our English tongue a
gallimaufry or hodgepodge of all other speeches.
[*The Shepherd's Calendar*, Letter to Gabriel
Harvey]

Spinoza, Baruch (1632–1677)

1 One and the same thing can at the same time be good, bad, and indifferent, for example, music is good to the melancholy, bad to those who mourn, and neither good nor bad to the deaf. [*Ethics*, IV]

2 We feel and know that we are eternal. [Ib. V]

Spooner, William (1844–1930)

3 Kinquering Congs their titles take. [Announcing hymn in chapel]

4 Let us drink to the queer old Dean. [Attr.]

Sprat, Thomas (1635–1713)

5 Poetry is the mother of superstition. [*History of the Royal Society*]

Spring-Rice, Arthur Cecil (1859–1918)

6 I vow to thee, my country — all earthly things above — / Entire and whole and perfect, the service of my love. ['Last Poem']

7 Her ways are ways of gentleness and all her paths are peace. [Ib.]

Squire, J.C. (1884–1958)

8 It did not last: the devil howling 'Ho! / Let Einstein be!' restored the status quo. ['Answer to Pope's Epitaph on Sir Isaac Newton']

Stalin, Joseph (1879–1953)

9 The Pope! How many divisions has *he* got? [Remark, 1935]

Stanley, Sir Henry Morton (1841–1904)

10 Dr. Livingstone, I presume? [*How I found Livingstone*, 2]

11 The Dark Continent [Africa] [Title of book]

Steele, Sir Richard (1672–1729)

12 Women dissemble their Passions better than

Men, but Men subdue their Passions better than Women. [*The Lover*, 9]

1 No Woman of spirit thinks a Man hath any Respect for her 'till he hath played the Fool in her Service. [Ib.]

2 The insupportable labour of doing nothing. [*Tatler*, 54]

3 Reading is to the mind what exercise is to the body. [Ib. 54]

Steffens, Lincoln (1866–1936)

4 I have seen the future, and it works. [Remark after visiting Russia in 1919]

Stein, Gertrude (1874–1946)

5 Rose is a rose is a rose is a rose. [*Sacred Emily*]

6 What is the answer?... [On receiving no response] In that case, what is the question? [Last words]

Stendhal (1783–1842)

7 A novel is a mirror walking along the highway. [*Le Rouge et le Noir*, 49]

Sterne, Laurence (1713–1768)

8 There are worse occupations in the world than feeling a woman's pulse. [*A Sentimental Journey*, 'The Pulse']

9 So that when I stretched out my hand, I caught hold of the fille de chambre's [Ib. 'The Case of Delicacy', last words]

10 I wish either my father or my mother, or indeed both of them, as they were in duty both equally bound to it, had minded what they were about when they begot me. [*Tristram Shandy*, I, 1]

11 Writing, when properly managed (as you may be sure I think mine is), is but a different name for conversation. [Ib. II, 11]

1 'Tis known by the name of perseverance in a
good cause, — and of obstinacy in a bad one. [Ib.
II, 17]

2 Whenever a man talks loudly against religion, —
always suspect that it is not his reason, but his
passions which have got the better of his creed.
[Ib.]

3 Digressions, incontestably, are the sunshine; —
they are the life, the soul of reading! — take
them out of this book for instance, — you might
as well take the book along with them. [Ib. II, 22]

4 Heat is in proportion to the want of true
knowledge. [Ib. IV, Slawkenbergius's Tale]

5 The nonsense of the old women (of both sexes).
[Ib. V, 16]

6 You forget the great Lipsius, quoth Yorick, who
composed a work the day he was born; — they
should have wiped it up, said my uncle Toby,
and said no more about it. [Ib. VI, 2]

7 The excellency of this text is that it will suit any
sermon, — and of this sermon, — that it will suit
any text. [Ib. VI, 11]

8 Said my mother, 'what is all this story about?' —
'A Cock and a Bull', said Yorick. [Ib. IX, 33]

Stevens, Wallace (1879–1955)

9 Poetry is the supreme fiction, madame. ['A High-
Toned old Christian Woman']

10 Oh! Blessed rage for order, pale Ramon. ['The
Idea of Order at Key West']

11 They said, 'You have a blue guitar / You do not
play things as they are.' / The man replied,
'Things as they are / Are changed upon a blue
guitar.' [*The Man with the Blue Guitar*]

Stevenson, Adlai (1900–1965)

1 A lie is an abomination unto the Lord, and a very present help in trouble. [Speech, 1951]

2 Making peace is harder than making war. [Address, 1946]

3 [Of Eleanor Roosevelt] She would rather light a candle than curse the darkness. [Speech, 1962]

Stevenson, Robert Louis (1850–1894)

4 In winter I get up at night / And dress by yellow candle-light. / In summer, quite the other way, — / I have to go to bed by day. [*A Child's Garden of Verses*, 'Bed in Summer']

5 O Leerie, I'll go round at night and light the lamps with you. [Ib. 'The Lamplighter']

6 The world is so full of a number of things, / I'm sure we should all be as happy as kings. [Ib. 'Happy Thought']

7 All I seek, the heaven above / And the road below me. [*Songs of Travel*, 'The Vagabond']

8 Be it granted to me to behold you again in dying, / Hills of home! [Ib. 'To S.R. Crockett']

9 Under the wide and starry sky / Dig the grave and let me lie / Glad did I live and gladly die, / And I laid me down with a will. / This be the verse you grave for me: / 'Here he lies where he longed to be; / Home is the sailor, home from sea, / And the hunter home from the hill.' [*Underwoods*, 'Requiem']

10 'Am I no a bonny fighter?' [*Kidnapped*, 10]

11 'I've a grand memory for forgetting, David.' [Ib. 18]

12 I regard you with an indifference closely bordering on aversion. [*New Arabian Nights*, 'The Rajah's Diamond']

13 Fifteen men on the dead man's chest / Yo-ho-ho,

and a bottle of rum! / Drink and the devil had done for the rest — / Yo-ho-ho, and a bottle of rum. [*Treasure Island*, 1]

1 Pieces of eight! [Ib. 10]

2 Many's the long night I've dreamed of cheese — toasted, mostly. [Ib. 15]

3 Even if we take matrimony at its lowest, even if we regard it as no more than a sort of friendship recognized by the police. [*Virginibus Puerisque*, 1]

4 Marriage is like life in this – that it is a field of battle and not a bed of roses. [Ib.]

5 To marry is to domesticate the Recording Angel. Once you are married, there is nothing left for you, not even suicide, but to be good. [Ib.]

6 Man is a creature who lives not upon bread alone, but principally by catchwords. [Ib.]

7 To travel hopefully is a better thing than to arrive, and the true success is to labour. [Ib. 6]

Stone, Samuel John (1839–1900)

8 The Church's one foundation / Is Jesus Christ her Lord. [Hymn]

Stoppard, Tom (1937–)

9 To sum up: your father, whom you love, dies, you are his heir, you come back to find that hardly was the corpse cold before his younger brother popped on to his throne and into his sheets, thereby offending both legal and natural practice. Now why exactly are you behaving in this extraordinary manner? [*Rosencrantz and Guildenstern Are Dead*, I]

10 The bad end unhappily, the good unluckily. That is what tragedy means. [Ib. II]

Stowe, Harriet Beecher (1812–1896)

11 'Do you know who made you?' 'Nobody, as I

knows on,' said the child, with a short laugh ... 'I 'spect I grow'd.' [*Uncle Tom's Cabin*, 20]

Suckling, Sir John (1609–1642)

1 I prithee send me back my heart, / Since I cannot have thine: / For if from yours you will not part, / Why then shouldst thou have mine? ['Song']

2 Out upon it, I have lov'd / Three whole days together; / And am like to love three more, / If it prove fair weather. ['Song']

3 Why so pale and wan, fond lover? / Prithee, why so pale? / Will, when looking well can't move her, / Looking ill prevail? ['Song']

Suetonius (fl. A.D. 75–150)

4 *Festina lente.* Hasten slowly. [*Divus Augustus*]

5 *Ave, Imperator, morituri te salutant.* Hail, Emperor, those about to die salute thee. [*Life of Claudius*]

Swift, Jonathan (1667–1745)

6 Satire is a kind of glass, wherein beholders do generally discover everybody's face but their own. [*Battle of the Books*, Preface]

7 And he gave it for his opinion, that whoever could make two ears of corn or two blades of grass to grow upon a spot of ground where only one grew before, would deserve better of mankind, and do more essential service to his country than the whole race of politicians put together. [*Gulliver's Travels*, 'Brobdingnag']

8 Monday is parson's holiday. [*Journal to Stella*, 1712]

9 Proper words in proper places, make the true definition of a style. ['Letter to a Young Clergyman']

1 Promises and pie-crust are made to be broken. [*Polite Conversation*, 1]

2 Bachelor's fare; bread and cheese, and kisses. [Ib.]

3 Why, every one as they like; as the good woman said when she kissed her cow. [Ib.]

4 I won't quarrel with my bread and butter. [Ib.]

5 Faith, that's as well said, as if I had said it myself. [Ib. 2]

6 Books, like men their authors, have no more than one way of coming into the world, but there are ten thousand to go out of it, and return no more. [*A Tale of a Tub*, Dedication]

7 Satire, by being levelled at all, is never resented for an offence by any. [Ib. Preface]

8 Last week I saw a woman flayed, and you will hardly believe how much it altered her person for the worse. [Ib. 9]

9 This is the sublime and refined point of felicity, called, the possession of being well deceived; the serene peaceful state of being a fool among knaves. [Ib.]

10 When a true genius appears in the world, you may know him by this sign, that the dunces are all in confederacy against him. ['Thoughts on Various Subjects']

11 I never wonder to see men wicked, but I often wonder to see them not ashamed. [Ib.]

12 We have just enough religion to make us hate, but not enough to make us love one another. [Ib.]

13 Every man desires to live long; but no man would be old. [Ib.]

14 When men grow virtuous in their old age, they only make a sacrifice to God of the devil's leavings. [Ib.]

15 The stoical scheme of supplying our wants by

lopping off our desires is like cutting off our feet when we want shoes. [Ib.]

1 So, naturalists observe, a flea / Hath smaller fleas that on him prey; / And these have smaller fleas to bite 'em, / And so proceed *ad infinitum*. [*On Poetry: A Rhapsody*]

2 He gave the little wealth he had / To build a house for fools and mad; / And show'd, by one satiric touch, / No nation wanted it so much. ['Verses on the Death of Dr. Swift']

3 [Of *A Tale of a Tub*] Good God! what a genius I had when I wrote that book. [Scott, *Life of Swift*]

4 *Ubi saeva indignatio ulterius cor lacerare nequit.* Where fierce indignation can no longer tear his heart. [Epitaph]

Swinburne, Algernon Charles (1837–1909)

5 Sleep; and if life was bitter to thee, pardon, / If sweet give thanks; thou hast no more to live; / And to give thanks is good, and to forgive. ['Ave atque Vale']

6 But sweet as the rind was the core is; / We are fain of thee still, we are fain, / O sanguine and subtle Dolores, / Our Lady of Pain. [*Dolores*]

7 For the crown of our life as it closes / Is darkness, the fruit thereof dust; / No thorns go as deep as a rose's, / And love is more cruel than lust. [Ib.]

8 Come down and redeem us from virtue, / Our Lady of Pain. [Ib.]

9 In a coign of the cliff between lowland and highland, / At the sea-down's edge between windward and lee, / Walled round with rocks as an inland island, / The ghost of a garden fronts the sea. ['The Forsaken Garden']

10 Stretched out on the spoils that his own hand

spread, / As a god self-slain on his own strange altar, / Death lies dead. [Ib.]

1 We thank with brief thanksgiving / Whatever gods may be / That no man lives forever, / That dead men rise up never; / That even the weariest river / Winds somewhere safe to sea. ['The Garden of Proserpine']

2 Thou has conquered, O pale Galilean; the world has grown grey from Thy breath; / We have drunken of things Lethean, and fed on the fullness of death. ['Hymn to Proserpine']

3 I will go back to the great sweet mother, / Mother and lover of men, the sea. / I will go down to her, I and no other, / Close with her, kiss her and mix her with me. ['The Triumph of Time']

Synge, J. M. (1871–1909)

4 A man who is not afraid of the sea will soon be drownded, he said, for he will be going out on a day he shouldn't. But we do be afraid of the sea, and we do only be drownded now and again. [*The Aran Islands*]

5 I have put away sorrow like a shoe that is worn out and muddy, for it is I have had a life that will be envied by great companies. [*Deirdre of the Sorrows*, III]

6 A daring fellow is the jewel of the world, and a man did split his father's middle with a single clout should have the bravery of ten, so may God and Mary and St. Patrick bless you, and increase you from this mortal day. [*The Playboy of the Western World*, III]

7 I've lost the only playboy of the western world. [Ib., final words]

Syrus, Publilius (fl. 1st century B.C.)

1 *Bis dat qui cito dat.* He gives twice who gives soon. [Attr. proverb]

2 *Necessitas non habet legem.* Necessity has no law. [Ib.]

Tacitus (A.D. c. 55–c. 120)

3 *Ubi solitudinem faciunt pacem appellant.* They create desolation, and call it peace. [*Agricola*]

Talleyrand, Charles-Maurice de (1754–1838)

4 *Voilà le commencement de la fin.* This is the beginning of the end. [Comment on Napoleon's defeat at Borodino, 1812]

5 War is much too serious to be left to the generals. [Attr.]

Tarkington, Booth (1869–1946)

6 An ideal wife is any woman who has an ideal husband. [Attr.]

Tate, Nahum (1652–1715) and Brady, Nicholas (1659–1726)

7 As pants the hart for cooling streams / When heated in the chase. [*New Versions of the Psalms*]

8 While shepherds watch'd their flocks by night, / All seated on the ground, / The Angel of the Lord came down, / And glory shone around. [Ib.]

Tawney, R. H. (1880–1962)

9 It is a commonplace that the characteristic virtue of Englishmen is their power of sustained practical activity, and their characteristic vice a reluctance to test the quality of that activity by reference to principles. [*The Acquisitive Society*]

Taylor, Jane (1783–1824)

10 Twinkle, twinkle, little star, / How I wonder

what you are! / Up above the world so high, /
Like a diamond in the sky. ['The Star']

Taylor, Bishop Jeremy (1613–1667)

1 As our life is very short, so it is very miserable,
and therefore it is well it is short. [*Holy Dying*]

2 Every school boy knows it. [*On the Real Presence*]

Taylor, John (1580–1653)

3 'Tis a mad world, my masters. [*Western Voyage, 1*]

Temple, Sir William (1628–1699)

4 When all is done, human life is, at the greatest
and the best, but like a froward child, that must
be play'd with and humoured a little to keep it
quiet till it falls asleep, and then the care is over.
['Of Poetry']

Tennyson, Alfred, Lord (1809–1892)

5 Break, break, break, / On thy cold grey stones, O
Sea! / And I would that my tongue could utter /
The thoughts that arise in me. ['Break, Break, Break']

6 I come from haunt of coot and hern, / I make a
sudden sally / And sparkle out among the fern, /
To bicker down a valley. ['The Brook']

7 For men may come and men may go, / But I go
on for ever. [Ib.]

8 Half a league, half a league, / Half a league
onward, / All in the valley of Death / Rode the
six hundred. ['The Charge of the Light Brigade']

9 'Forward the Light Brigade!' / Was there a man
dismay'd? / Not tho' the soldier knew / Some
one had blunder'd: / Their's not to make reply, /
Their's not to reason why, / Their's but to do
and die. [Ib.]

10 He is all fault who hath no fault at all: / For

who loves me must have a touch of earth. [*The Idylls of the King*, 'Lancelot and Elaine']

1 His honour rooted in dishonour stood, / And faith unfaithful kept him falsely true. [Ib.]

2 It is the little rift within the lute, / That by and by will make the music mute, / And ever widening slowly silence all. [Ib. 'Merlin and Vivien']

3 An arm / Clothed in white samite, mystic, wonderful. [Ib. 'The Passing of Arthur']

4 Men may rise on stepping-stones / Of their dead selves to higher things. [*In Memoriam*]

5 For words, like Nature, half reveal / And half conceal the Soul within. [Ib.]

6 And ghastly thro' the drizzling rain / On the bald streets breaks the blank day. [Ib.]

7 I hold it true, whate'er befall; / I feel it, when I sorrow most, / 'Tis better to have loved and lost / Than never to have loved at all. [Ib.]

8 Who trusted God was love indeed / And love Creation's final law — / Tho' Nature, red in tooth and claw / With ravine, shriek'd against his creed. [Ib.]

9 There lives more faith in honest doubt, / Believe me, than in half the creeds. [Ib.]

10 Ring out the old, ring in the new / . . . Ring out the false, ring in the true. [Ib.]

11 The gardener Adam and his wife / Smile at the claims of long descent. ['Lady Clara Vere de Vere']

12 Kind hearts are more than coronets, / And simple faith than Norman blood. [Ib.]

13 'Tirra lirra,' by the river / Sang Sir Lancelot. ['The Lady of Shalott']

14 The mirror crack'd from side to side; / 'The

curse is come upon me,' cried / The Lady of Shalott. [Ib.]

1 In the Spring a young man's fancy lightly turns to thoughts of love. [*Locksley Hall*]

2 He will hold thee, when his passion shall have spent its novel force, / Something better than his dog, a little dearer than his horse. [Ib.]

3 Music that gentlier on the spirit lies, / Than tir'd eyelids upon tir'd eyes. ['The Lotos-Eaters']

4 I hate that dreadful hollow behind the little wood. [*Maud*, I, 1]

5 Gorgonized me from head to foot / With a stony British stare. [Ib. I, 13]

6 Come into the garden, Maud, / For the black bat, night, has flown. / Come into the garden, Maud, / I am here at the gate alone. [Ib. I, 22]

7 The splendour falls on castle walls / And snowy summits old in story: / The long light shakes across the lakes, / And the wild cataract leaps in glory.
Blow, bugle, blow, set the wild echoes flying, / Blow, bugle; answer, echoes dying, dying, dying.
O hark, O hear! how thin and clear, / And thinner, clearer, farther going! / O sweet and far from cliff and scar / The horns of Elfland faintly blowing! [*The Princess*, IV]

8 Tears, idle tears, I know not what they mean, / Tears from the depth of some divine despair. [Ib.]

9 Man is the hunter; woman is his game: / The sleek and shining creatures of the chase, / We hunt them for the beauty of their skins; / They love us for it, and we ride them down. [Ib. V]

10 At Flores in the Azores Sir Richard Grenville lay. ['The Revenge']

11 It little profits that an idle king, / By this still hearth, among these barren crags, / Match'd

with an aged wife, I mete and dole / Unequal
laws unto a savage race. ['Ulysses']

1 I will drink / Life to the lees: all times I have
enjoy'd / Greatly, have suffer'd greatly. [Ib.]

2 Far on the ringing plains of windy Troy. [Ib.]

3 Some work of noble note may yet be done, / Not
unbecoming men that strove with Gods. [Ib.]

4 That which we are, we are; / One equal temper
of heroic hearts, / Made weak by time and fate,
but strong in will / To strive, to seek, to find,
and not to yield. [Ib.]

5 Every moment dies a man, / Every moment one
is born. [*The Vision of Sin*]

6 [Of a critic] A louse in the locks of literature.
[Charteris, *Life of Gosse*]

Terence (c. 190–159 B.C.)

7 *Amantium irae amoris integratio est.* The
quarrels of lovers are the renewal of love.
[*Andria*]

8 *Modo liceat vivere, est spes.* While there's life,
there's hope. [*Heauton Timoroumenos*]

9 *Homo sum; humani nil a me alienum puto.* I am
a man, I count nothing human indifferent to me.
[Ib.]

10 *Fortis fortuna adiuvat.* Fortune helps the brave.
[*Phormio*]

Tertullian (c. A.D. 160–c. 225)

11 *Semen est sanguis Christianorum.* The blood of
the martyrs is the seed of the church.
[*Apologeticus*]

12 *De calcaria in carbonarium.* Out of the frying pan
into the fire. [*De Carne Christi*]

13 *Certum est quia impossibile est.* It is certain
because it is impossible. [Ib.]

Thackeray, William Makepeace (1811–1863)

1 'Tis not the dying for a faith that's so hard, Master Harry — every man of every nation has done that — 'tis the living up to it that is difficult. [*Henry Esmond*, 6]

2 'Tis strange what a man may do, and a woman yet think him an angel. [Ib. 7]

3 And this I set down as a positive truth. A woman with fair opportunities, and without an absolute hump may marry *whom she likes*. [*Vanity Fair*, 4]

4 Some cynical Frenchman has said that there are two parties to a love transaction; the one who loves and the other who condescends to be so treated. [Ib. 13]

5 Whenever he met a great man he grovelled before him, and my-lorded him as only a free-born Briton can do. [Ib.]

6 Them's my sentiments! [Ib. 21]

7 I think I could be a good woman if I had five thousand a year. [Ib. 36]

8 Ah! *Vanitas Vanitatum!* Which of us is happy in this world? Which of us has his desire? or, having it, is satisfied? — Come, children, let us shut up the box and the puppets, for our play is played out. [Ib. 67]

Thatcher, Margaret (1925–)

9 [Of her economic policy] There is no alternative. [Said on several occasions]

Thayer, W.M. (c. 1820–1898)

10 From Log Cabin to White House [Title of biography of President Garfield]

Thomas à Kempis, *see* KEMPIS.

Thomas, Brandon (1856–1914)

1 I'm Charley's aunt from Brazil — where the nuts come from. [*Charley's Aunt*, I]

Thomas, Dylan (1914–1953)

2 Though lovers be lost love shall not; / And death shall have no dominion. ['And death shall have no dominion']

3 Do not go gentle into that good night, / Old age should burn and rave at close of day; / Rage, rage against the dying of the light. ['Do not go gentle']

4 The force that through the green fuse drives the flower / Drives my green age; that blasts the roots of trees / Is my destroyer. ['The force that through the green fuse drives the flower']

5 It was my thirtieth year to heaven / Woke to my hearing from harbour and neighbour wood / And the mussel pooled and the heron / Priested shore. ['Poem in October']

6 After the first death, there is no other. ['A refusal to mourn the death, by fire, of a child in London']

7 And before you let the sun in, mind it wipes its shoes. [*Under Milk Wood*]

8 Nothing grows in our garden, only washing. And babies. [Ib.]

9 Organ Morgan, you haven't been listening to a word I said. It's organ organ all the time with you . . . [Ib.]

10 Seventeen and never been sweet in the grass ho ho. [Ib.]

Thompson, Francis (1859–1907)

11 I fled Him, down the nights and down the days; / I fled Him, down the arches of the years; / I fled

Him, down the labyrinthine ways / Of my own mind; and in the mist of tears / I hid from Him, and under running laughter. [*The Hound of Heaven*]

Thompson, Hunter S. (1939–)

1 Fear and Loathing in Las Vegas [Title of book]

Thomson, James (1700–1748)

2 Rule, Britannia, rule the waves; / Britons never will be slaves. [*Alfred: a Masque*, II]

3 An elegant sufficiency, content, / Retirement, rural quiet, friendship, books. [*The Seasons*, 'Spring']

Thomson, James (1834–1882)

4 The City is of Night; perchance of Death, / But certainly of Night; for never there / Can come the lucid morning's fragrant breath / After the dewy dawning's cold grey air. [*The City of Dreadful Night*, I]

5 The vilest thing must be less vile than Thou / From whom it had its being, God and Lord! [Ib. VIII]

Thomson, Roy, Lord (1894–1977)

6 [Commercial television] A licence to print your own money. [Attr.]

Thoreau, Henry David (1817–1862)

7 The mass of men lead lives of quiet desperation. [*Walden*]

8 I would rather sit on a pumpkin and have it all to myself than be crowded on a velvet cushion. [Ib.]

9 Things do not change; we change. [Ib. conclusion]

10 Poetry is nothing but healthy speech. [*Journal*, 1841]

Thorpe, Jeremy (1929–)

1 Greater love hath no man than this, that he lay down his friends for his life. [Remark on Macmillan's Cabinet purge, 1962]

Thucydides (c. 460–c. 395 B.C.)

2 To great men the whole world is a sepulchre. [*History of the Peloponnesian War*, II]

Thurber, James (1894–1961)

3 Well, if I called the wrong number, why did you answer the phone? [Cartoon caption]

4 Perhaps *this* will refresh your memory. [Cartoon caption; remark by lawyer producing kangaroo in court]

5 It's a naïve domestic Burgundy, without any breeding, but I think you'll be amused by its presumption. [Cartoon caption]

6 All right, have it your way — you heard a seal bark. [Cartoon caption]

7 You wait here and I'll bring the etchings down. [Cartoon caption]

8 Progress was all right; only it went on too long. [Attr.]

Thurlow, Edward, First Baron (1731–1806)

9 Did you ever expect a corporation to have a conscience, when it has no soul to be damned, and no body to be kicked? [Attr.]

Tolstoy, Leo (1828–1910)

10 Pure and complete sorrow is as impossible as pure and complete joy. [*War and Peace*, XV, 1]

11 I sit on a man's back, choking him and making him carry me, and yet assure myself and others that I am very sorry for him and wish to ease his lot by all possible means — except by getting off his back. [*What Then Must We Do?*]

Toplady, Augustus Montague (1740–1778)

1 Rock of Ages, cleft for me, / Let me hide myself in Thee. [Hymn]

Tree, Herbert Beerbohm (1853–1917)

2 My poor fellow, why not carry a watch? [Remark to a man carrying a grandfather clock in the street]

3 He is an old bore; even the grave yawns for him. [Attr.]

Trollope, Anthony (1815–1882)

4 Of all the needs a book has the chief need is that it be readable. [*Autobiography*, 19]

5 It has been the great fault of our politicians that they have all wanted to do something. [*Phineas Finn*, 13]

6 The tenth Muse, who now governs the periodical press. [*The Warden*, 14]

Truman, Harry S. (1884–1972)

7 A statesman is a politician who's been dead ten or fifteen years. [Attr.]

8 The buck stops here. [Sign on his desk]

9 It's a recession when your neighbour loses his job: it's a depression when you lose yours. [*Observer*, 'Sayings of the Week', 1958]

Tucker, Sophie (1884–1966)

10 [Asked, when 80, the secret of longevity] Keep breathing. [Attr.]

11 I've been poor and I've been rich. Rich is better. [Quoted in Cowan, *The Wit of Women*]

Tupper, Martin (1810–1889)

12 Well-timed silence hath more eloquence than speech. [*Proverbial Philosophy*, 'Of Discretion']

Turgenev, Ivan (1818–1883)

1 The boldness to believe in nothing. [*Fathers and Sons*, 14]

2 Whatever a man prays for, he prays for a miracle. Every prayer reduces itself to this: 'Great God, grant that twice two be not four.' ['Prayer']

Tusser, Thomas (c. 1524–1580)

3 A fool and his money be soon at debate. [*Five Hundred Points of Good Husbandry*]

4 Make hunger thy sauce, as a medicine for health. [Ib.]

5 At Christmas play and make good cheer, / For Christmas comes but once a year. [Ib.]

6 Who goeth a borrowing / Goeth a sorrowing. / Few lend (but fools) / Their working tools. [Ib.]

Twain, Mark (1835–1910)

7 I have been told that Wagner's music is better than it sounds. [*Autobiography*]

8 [Definition of a classic] Something that everybody wants to have read and nobody wants to read. ['The Disappearance of Literature']

9 Man is the only animal that blushes. Or needs to. [*Following the Equator*]

10 Persons attempting to find a motive in this narrative will be prosecuted; persons attempting to find a moral in it will be banished; persons attempting to find a plot in it will be shot. [*Huckleberry Finn*, Introduction]

11 There was things which he stretched, but mainly he told the truth. [Ib. 1]

12 All kings is mostly rapscallions. [Ib. 23]

13 Hain't we got all the fools in town on our side? and ain't that a big enough majority in any town? [Ib. 26]

1 When angry count four; when very angry swear.
[*Pudd'nhead Wilson's Calendar*]

2 The English are mentioned in the Bible: Blessed
are the meek for they shall inherit the earth. [Ib.]

3 Don't part with your illusions. When they are
gone, you may still exist, but you have ceased to
live. [Ib.]

4 As to the Adjective: when in doubt, strike it out.
[Ib.]

5 The holy passion of Friendship is of so sweet and
steady and loyal and enduring a nature that it
will last through a whole lifetime, if not asked to
lend money. [Ib.]

6 Work consists of whatever a body is obliged to
do . . . Play consists of whatever a body is not
obliged to do. [*Tom Sawyer*, 2]

7 To promise not to do a thing is the surest way in
the world to make a body want to go and do that
very thing. [Ib. 22]

8 The report of my death was an exaggeration.
[Cable, 1897]

9 I can live for two months on a good compliment.
[Attr.]

10 Most people are bothered by those passages in
Scripture which they cannot understand; but as
for me, I always noticed that the passages in
Scripture which trouble me most are those that I
do understand. [Quoted in Simcox, *Treasury of
Quotations on Christian Themes*]

11 When I was a boy of 14 my father was so
ignorant I could hardly stand to have the old
man around. But when I got to be 21, I was
astonished at how much he had learned in 7
years. [Quoted in Mackay, *The Harvest of a
Quiet Eye*]

Tynan, Kenneth (1927–1980)

1 What, when drunk, one sees in other women, one sees in Garbo sober. [Quoted in Halliwell, *Filmgoer's Book of Quotes*]

Unamuno, Miguel de (1864–1937)

2 Faith which does not doubt is dead faith. [*The Agony of Christianity*]

3 Man, by the very fact of being man, by possessing consciousness, is, in comparison with the ass or the crab, a diseased animal. Consciousness is a disease. [*The Tragic Sense of Life*, 1]

4 It is not usually our ideas that make us optimists or pessimists, but it is our optimism or pessimism, of physiological or pathological origin... that makes our ideas. [Ib.]

5 To believe in God is to yearn for His existence and, furthermore, it is to act as if He did exist. [Ib. 8]

Upton, W. (fl. 18th century)

6 I'd crowns resign to call thee mine, / Sweet lass of Richmond Hill. ['The Lass of Richmond Hill']

Urey, Harold (1893–1981)

7 The next war will be fought with atom bombs and the one after that with spears. [*Observer*, 'Sayings of the Week', 1946]

Ustinov, Peter (1921–)

8 A diplomat these days is nothing but a head-waiter who's allowed to sit down occasionally. [*Romanoff and Juliet*, I]

9 ... the great thing about history is that it is adaptable. [Ib. II]

Valéry, Paul (1871–1945)

1 A poem is never finished, only abandoned. [Quoted in Auden, *A Certain World*]

2 A man is infinitely more complicated than his thoughts. [Ib.]

3 Consciousness reigns but does not govern. [Ib.]

Vanbrugh, Sir John (1664–1726)

4 The want of a thing is perplexing enough, but the possession of it is intolerable. [*The Confederacy*, I.2]

5 Much of a muchness. [*The Provok'd Husband*, I.1]

6 *Belinda:* Ay, but you know we must return good for evil.
Lady Brute: That may be a mistake in the translation. [Ib.]

Vaughan, Henry (1622–1695)

7 They are all gone into the world of light! / And I alone sit lingering here. [*Silex Scintillans*, 'Ascension-Hymn']

8 Dear, beauteous death! the Jewel of the Just. [Ib.]

9 Man is the shuttle, to whose winding quest / And passage through these looms / God order'd motion, but ordain'd no rest. [Ib. 'Man']

10 My soul, there is a country / Far beyond the stars, / Where stands a winged sentry / All skilful in the wars. [Ib. 'Peace']

11 Happy those early days! when I / Shin'd in my Angel-infancy. [Ib. 'The Retreat']

12 And in those weaker glories spy / Some shadows of eternity. [Ib.]

13 I saw Eternity the other night, / Like a great ring of pure and endless light, / All calm, as it was bright. [Ib. 'The World']

Veblen, Thorstein (1857–1929)

1 Conspicuous consumption of valuable goods is a means of reputability to the gentleman of leisure. [*The Theory of the Leisure Class*, 4]

Vegetius Renatus, Flavius (fl. c. A.D. 375)

2 *Qui desiderat pacem, praeparet bellum.* Let him who desires peace, prepare for war. [*Epitome Institutionum Rei Militaris*]

Venantius Fortunatus (c. 530–c. 610)

3 *Pange, lingua, gloriosi / Proelium certaminis.* Sing, tongue, of battle in the glorious conflict. [Hymn]

Vergniaud, Pierre (1753–1793)

4 It was possible to fear that the Revolution might, like Saturn, devour each of her children one by one. [Remark, attr. at his trial, 1793]

Verlaine, Paul (1844–1896)

5 *Prends l'éloquence et tords-lui son cou!* Take eloquence and wring its neck. ['L'Art poétique']

6 *Les sanglots longs / Des violons / De l'automne / Blessent mon coeur / D'une langueur / Monotone.* The long sobbings of autumn violins wound my heart with a monotonous languor. ['Chanson de l'automne']

7 *Et, O ces voix d'enfants chantants dans la coupole!* And oh those voices of children, singing in the cupola! ['Parsifal, A Jules Tellier']

8 *Il pleure dans mon coeur / Comme il pleut sur la ville.* There is weeping in my heart as it rains on the city. ['Romances sans paroles']

Vespasian (A.D. 9–79)

9 *Vae, puto deus fio.* Oh dear, I must be turning into a god. [Last words]

Victoria, Queen (1819–1901)

1 [Of Gladstone] He speaks to me as if I was a public meeting. [Attr.]

2 We are not amused. [Attr.]

3 We are not interested in the possibilities of defeat. [Attr. remark to A.J. Balfour, 1899]

Vidal, Gore (1925–)

4 He will lie even when it is inconvenient, the sign of the true artist. [*Two Sisters*]

5 American writers want to be not good but great; and so are neither. [*Ib.*]

Villiers de l'Isle-Adam, Philippe-Auguste (1838–1889)

6 *Vivre? les serviteurs feront cela pour nous.* Live? Our servants will do that for us. [*Axel*, IV, 2]

Villon, François (1431–c. 1484)

7 *Mais où sont les neiges d'antan?* But where are the snows of yesteryear? ['Ballade des Dames du Temps Jadis'; trans. D.G. Rossetti]

8 *Frères humains qui après nous vivez, / N'ayez les cuers contre nous endurcis.* Brother humans who live after us, do not harden your hearts against us. ['Ballade des pendus']

Virgil (70–19 B.C.)

9 *Arma virumque cano.* Arms and the man I sing. [*Aeneid*, I, opening words]

10 *Sunt lacrimae rerum.* Events have tears. [*Ib.*]

11 *Quidquid id est, timeo Danaos et dona ferentis.* Whatever it is, I fear the Greeks even when they bring gifts. [*Ib.*II]

12 *Dis aliter visum.* Heaven thought otherwise. [*Ib.*]

13 *Auri sacra fames!* Detestable desire for gold! [*Ib.* III]

1 *Varium et mutabile semper / Femina*. Woman is always fickle and changeable. [Ib. IV]

2 *Facilis descensus Averni: / Noctes atque dïes patet atri ianua Ditis; / Sed revocare gradum superasque evadere ad auras, / Hoc opus, hic labor est*. The way to Hell is easy: night and day the gates of black Dis stand open; but to retrace the step and reach the breezes above, this is the task, and in it the labour. [Ib. VI]

3 *Procul, o procul este, profani*. Far, far from me, let all profane ones be. [Ib.]

4 *Experto credite*. Believe one who knows by experience. [Ib. XI]

5 *Deus nobis haec otia fecit*. A god has made this peace for us. [*Eclogues*, I]

6 *Latet anguis in herba*. A snake lurks in the grass. [Ib. III]

7 *Omnia vincit Amor: et nos cedamus Amori*. Love conquers all: and we succumb to love. [Ib. X]

8 *Ultima Thule*. Farthest Thule. [*Georgics*, I]

9 *Labor omnia vincit*. Work conquers all. [Ib.]

10 *Imponere Pelio Ossam*. To heap Ossa on Pelion. [Ib.]

11 *Sed fugit interea, fugit inreparabile tempus*. Time meanwhile flies, flies never to return. [Ib. II]

Voltaire (1694–1778)

12 *Tout est pour le mieux dans le meilleur des mondes possibles*. All is for the best in the best of all possible worlds. [*Candide*, 1 (and elsewhere)]

13 *Dans ce pays-ci il est bon de tuer de temps en temps un amiral pour encourager les autres*. In this country [England] it is considered good to kill an admiral from time to time, to encourage the others. [Ib. 23]

1 *Il faut cultiver notre jardin — Quand l'homme fut mis dans le jardin d'Eden, il y fut mis pour qu'il travaillât; ce qui prouve que l'homme n'est pas né pour le repos. — Travaillons sans raisonner, c'est le seul moyen de rendre la vie supportable.* We must cultivate our garden. When man was put in the garden of Eden, he was put there to work; that proves that man was not born for rest. Let us work without question, that is the only way to make life tolerable. [Ib. 30]

2 *Le mieux est l'ennemi du bien.* The best is the enemy of the good. [*Dictionnaire philosophique*, 'Art dramatique']

3 *Si Dieu n'existait pas, il faudrait l'inventer.* If God did not exist, it would be necessary to invent him. [*Epîtres*, 96]

4 *Ce corps qui s'appelait et qui s'appelle encore le saint empire romain n'était en aucune manière ni saint, ni romain, ni empire.* This body, which was called and still calls itself the Holy Roman Empire was not Holy, nor Roman, nor an Empire. [*Essai sur les Moeurs*]

5 *En effet, l'histoire n'est que le tableau des crimes et des malheurs.* Indeed, history is nothing but a tableau of crimes and misfortunes. [*L'Ingénu*, 10]

6 *La Liberté est née en Angleterre des querelles des tyrans.* Liberty was born in England from the quarrels of tyrants. [*Lettres philosophiques*]

7 No one will ever make me believe that I think all the time. [Ib.]

8 *On doit des égards aux vivants; on ne doit aux morts que la vérité.* We owe respect to the living; to the dead we owe nothing but truth. [*Lettres sur Oedipe*, 1]

9 *La crainte suit la crime, et c'est son châtiment.*

Fear follows crime, and is its punishment. [*Semiramis*, V]

1 *Le secret d'ennuyer est ... de tout dire.* The secret of being boring is to say everything. ['Sept Discours en verse sur l'Homme']

2 *Si Dieu nous a fait à son image, nous le lui avons bien rendu.* If God has created us in his image, we have repaid him well. [*Le Sottisier*]

3 *Dieu n'est pas pour les gros bataillons, mais pour ceux qui tirent le mieux.* God isn't on the side of the big batallions, but of the best marksmen. [*Notebooks*]

4 *Ecrasez l'infâme.* Wipe out the infamous. [Letter to d'Alembert, 1760 (Voltaire's motto)]

5 I have never made but one prayer to God, a very short one: 'O Lord, make my enemies ridiculous.' And God granted it. [Letter, 1767]

6 I am very fond of truth, but not at all of martyrdom. [Letter to d'Alembert, 1776]

7 I disapprove of what you say, but I will defend to the death your right to say it. [Attr.]

Vulgate

8 *Dominus illuminatio mea.* The Lord is my light. [Psalms, 26:1]

9 *Cantate Dominum canticum novum.* Sing unto the Lord a new song. [Ib. 97:1]

10 *Non nobis, Domine, non nobis.* Not unto us, Lord, not unto us. [Ib. 113:9]

11 *Laudate Dominum, omnes gentes.* Praise the Lord, all nations. [Ib. 116:1]

12 *De profundis clamavi ad te, Domine.* Out of the depths I have cried to thee, Lord. [Ib. 129:1]

13 *Vanitas vanitatum, et omnia vanitas.* Vanity of vanities, and all things are vanity. [Ecclesiastes, 1:2]

1 *Magnificat anima mea Dominum.* My soul magnifies the Lord. [Luke, 1:46]

2 *Nunc dimittis servum tuum, Domine, secundum verbum tuum in pace.* Lord, now lettest thou thy servant depart in peace: according to thy word. [Ib. 2:29; trans. Book of Common Prayer]

3 *Pax Vobis.* Peace be unto you. [Ib. 24:36]

4 *Quo vadis?* Where are you going? [John, 16:5]

5 *Ecce homo.* Behold the man. [Ib. 19:5]

6 *Consummatum est.* It is finished. [Ib. 19:30]

7 *Noli me tangere.* Do not touch me. [Ib. 20:17]

Wallace, William Ross (c. 1819–1881)

8 The hand that rocks the cradle / Is the hand that rules the world. [*John o' London's Treasure Trove*]

Wallas, Graham (1858–1932)

9 The little girl had the makings of a poet in her who, being told to be sure of her meaning before she spoke, said: 'How can I know what I think till I see what I say?' ['The Art of Thought']

Waller, Edmund (1606–1687)

10 Go, lovely Rose! / Tell her, that wastes her time and me, / That now she knows, / When I resemble her to thee, / How sweet and fair she seems to be. ['Song']

Walpole, Horace (1717–1797)

11 Our supreme governors, the mob. [Letter, 1743]

12 One of the greatest geniuses that ever existed, Shakespeare, undoubtedly wanted taste. [Letter, 1764]

13 Everybody talks of the constitution, but all sides forget that the constitution is extremely well, and would do very well, if they would let it alone. [Letter, 1770]

1 [Of the East] It was easier to conquer it than to know what to do with it. [Letter, 1772]

2 Old age is no such uncomfortable thing if one gives oneself up to it with a good grace, and don't drag it about 'To midnight dances and the public show'. [Letter, 1774]

3 This world is a comedy to those that think, and a tragedy to those that feel. [Letter, 1776]

4 They who cannot perform great things themselves may yet have a satisfaction in doing justice to those who can. [Attr.]

Walpole, Sir Robert (1676–1745)

5 Madam, there are fifty thousand men slain this year in Europe, and not one Englishman. [Remark to the Queen, 1734]

6 The balance of power. [Speech, House of Commons, 1741]

7 All those men have their price. [Attr.]

Walton, Izaak (1593–1683)

8 As no man is born an artist, so no man is born an angler. [*The Compleat Angler*, Epistle to the Reader]

9 We may say of angling as Dr. Boteler said of strawberries: 'Doubtless God could have made a better berry, but doubtless God never did'; and so (if I might be judge) God never did make a more calm, quiet, innocent recreation than angling. [Ib. 4]

10 I love such mirth as does not make friends ashamed to look upon one another next morning. [Ib. 5]

Warburton, William (1698–1779)

11 Orthodoxy is my doxy; heterodoxy is another man's doxy. [Remark]

Ward, Artemus (1834–1867)

1 I girdid up my Lions & fled the Seen. [*Artemus
  Ward His Book*]

2 He [Brigham Young] is dreadfully married. He's
  the most married man I ever saw in my life.
  [*Artemus Ward's Lecture*]

3 Why is this thus? What is the reason of this
  thusness? [Ib.]

4 Let us all be happy, and live within our means,
  even if we have to borrer the money to do it
  with. ['Science and Natural History']

Ward, Nathaniel (1578–1652)

5 The world is full of care, and much like unto a
  bubble; / Women and care, and care and women,
  and women and care and trouble. [Epigram]

Warhol, Andy (1931–)

6 In the future everyone will be famous for fifteen
  minutes. [Attr. remark]

Warner, Anna (1820–1915)

7 Jesus loves me! this I know, / For the Bible tells
  me so; / Little ones to Him belong, / They are
  weak, but He is strong. [Hymn]

Washington, George (1732–1799)

8 Few men have virtue to withstand the highest
  bidder. [*Moral Maxims*]

9 Influence is not government. [*Political Maxims*]

10 The very idea of the power and the right of the
  People to establish Government, presupposes the
  duty of every individual to obey the established
  Government. [Farewell Address, 1796]

11 Be courteous to all, but intimate with few, and
  let those few be well tried before you give them
  your confidence. True friendship is a plant of
  slow growth, and must undergo and withstand

the shocks of adversity before it is entitled to the appellation. [Letter, 1783]

1 Mankind, when left to themselves, are unfit for their own government. [Letter, 1786]

2 Liberty, when it begins to take root, is a plant of rapid growth. [Letter, 1788]

3 [On being accused of chopping down a cherry tree] Father, I cannot tell a lie; I did it with my little hatchet. [Attr., probably apocryphal]

Watts, Isaac (1674–1748)

4 Birds in their little nests agree / And 'tis a shameful sight, / When children of one family / Fall out, and chide, and fight. [*Divine Songs for Children*, 'Love between Brothers and Sisters']

5 How doth the little busy bee / Improve each shining hour, / And gather honey all the day / From every opening flower! [Ib. 'Against Idleness and Mischief']

6 For Satan finds some mischief still / For idle hands to do. [Ib.]

7 Time, like an ever-rolling stream, / Bears all its sons away; / They fly forgotten, as a dream / Dies at the opening day. [Psalm 90]

8 When I survey the wondrous Cross / On which the Prince of Glory died, / My richest gain I count but loss, / And pour contempt on all my pride. [Hymn]

Waugh, Evelyn (1903–1966)

9 I expect you'll be becoming a school-master, sir. That's what most of the gentlemen does, sir, that gets sent down for indecent behaviour. [*Decline and Fall*]

10 We can trace almost all the disasters of English history to the influence of Wales. [Ib.]

11 I came to the conclusion many years ago that

almost all crime is due to the repressed desire for aesthetic expression. [Ib.]

1 When Lord Copper was right he said, 'Definitely, Lord Copper'; when he was wrong, 'Up to a point'. [*Scoop*, I,1]

2 All this fuss about sleeping together. For physical pleasure I'd sooner go to my dentist any day. [*Vile Bodies*]

Webb, Sidney (1859–1947)

3 Marriage is the waste-paper basket of the emotions. [Bertrand Russell, *Autobiography*]

Webster, Daniel (1782–1852)

4 The people's government, made for the people, made by the people, and answerable to the people. [Speech, 1830]

5 Fearful concatenation of circumstances. ['Argument on the murder of Captain White']

6 There is always room at the top. [Remark]

Webster, John (c. 1580–1625)

7 I am Duchess of Malfi still. [*The Duchess of Malfi*, IV.2]

8 I know death hath ten thousand several doors / For men to take their exits. [Ib.]

9 Cover her face; mine eyes dazzle; she died young. [Ib.]

10 Physicians are like kings — they brook no contradiction. [Ib. V.2]

11 We are merely the stars' tennis-balls, struck and bandied, / Which way please them. [Ib. V.4]

12 I saw him even now going the way of all flesh. [*Westward Hoe*, II.2]

13 A mere tale of a tub, my words are idle. [*The White Devil*, II.1]

14 Call for the robin redbreast and the wren, /

Since o'er shady groves they hover, / And with
leaves and flowers do cover / The friendless
bodies of unburied men. [Ib. V.4]

1 But keep the wolf far thence that's foe to men, /
For with his nails he'll dig them up again. [Ib.]

2 My soul, like to a ship in a black storm, / Is
driven, I know not whither. [Ib. V.6]

3 I have caught / An everlasting cold; I have lost
my voice / Most irrecoverably. [Ib.]

Wedgwood, Josiah (1730–1795)

4 Am I not a man and a brother? [Motto adopted
by Anti-Slavery Society]

Weiss, Peter (1916–   )

5 *Denn was wäre schon dies Revolution / ohne
eine allgemeine Kopulation.* What's the use of a
revolution without general copulation! [*Marat/
Sade*, II]

Welles, Orson (1915–   )

6 In Switzerland they had brotherly love, five
hundred years of democracy and peace, and what
did they produce? The cuckoo clock! [*The Third
Man*]

7 He has Van Gogh's ear for music. [Variously
attr.]

Wellington, Arthur Wellesley, Duke of (1769
–1852)

8 The battle of Waterloo was won on the playing
fields of Eton. [Attr.]

9 Up guards and at 'em! [Attr. remark during
Battle of Waterloo (but see below)]

10 What I must have said and possibly did say was,
Stand up, Guards! and then gave the
commanding officers the order to attack. [Letter
to J.W. Croker]

1 It has been a damned nice thing — the nearest run thing you ever saw in your life. [Remark on Waterloo]

2 The next greatest misfortune to losing a battle is to gain such a victory as this. [Ib.]

3 Publish and be damned. [Attr.]

4 [On his troops] I don't know what effect these men will have on the enemy, but, by God, they frighten me. [Attr.]

5 The mere scum of the earth. [Remark, on his troops]

6 [To a man who approached him saying, 'Mr. Jones, I believe?'] If you believe that, you'll believe anything. [Attr.]

Wells, H.G. (1866–1946)

7 Every time Europe looks across the Atlantic to see the American eagle, it observes only the rear end of an ostrich. [*America*]

8 How d'you like her? Puts old Velasquez in his place. A young mistress is better than an old master, eh? [*Autocracy of Mr. Parham*, 3]

9 In the Country of the Blind the One-eyed Man is King. ['The Country of the Blind']

10 [Of the British officer] He muffs his real job without a blush, and yet he would rather be shot than do his bootlaces up criss-cross. [*Mr. Britling Sees It Through*, II, 4]

11 Human history becomes more and more a race between education and catastrophe. [*The Outline of History*]

12 Moral indignation is jealousy with a halo. [*The Wife of Sir Isaac Harman*, 9]

13 In England we have come to rely upon a comfortable time-lag of fifty years or a century intervening between the perception that something ought to be done and a serious

attempt to do it. [*Work, Wealth and Happiness of Mankind*]

1 The Shape of Things to Come [Title of book]

Wesley, Charles (1707–1788)

2 Gentle Jesus, meek and mild, / Look upon a little child. [Hymn]

3 Hark! the herald angels sing, / 'Glory to the new-born King. / Peace on earth, and mercy mild, / God and sinners reconciled!' [Hymn]

Wesley, John (1703–1791)

4 I look upon all the world as my parish. [*Journal*, 1739]

Wesley, Samuel (1662–1735)

5 The poet's fate is here in emblem shown, / He asked for bread, and he received a stone. ['Epigram on Butler's Monument in Westminster Abbey']

West, Mae (1892–1980)

6 Is that a gun in your pocket or are you just pleased to see me? [*My Little Chickadee*]

7 'Goodness, what beautiful diamonds!' 'Goodness had nothing to do with it!' [*Night After Night*]

8 Come up and see me sometime. [*She Done Him Wrong* (attr. version)]

Westcott, E.N. (1846–1898)

9 A reasonable amount o' fleas is good fer a dog — keeps him from broodin' over *bein'* a dog. [*David Harum*]

Wharton, Edith (1862–1937)

10 Mrs. Ballinger is one of the ladies who pursue Culture in bands, as though it were dangerous to meet it alone. [*Xingu*, 1]

Whately, Richard (1787–1863)

1 Happiness is no laughing matter. [*Apophthegms*]

2 It is a folly to expect men to do all that they may reasonably be expected to do. [Ib.]

Whistler, James McNeil (1834–1903)

3 [To a lady who said that a landscape reminded her of his work] Yes, madam, Nature is creeping up. [D.C. Seitz, *Whistler Stories*]

4 [To a lady who said the two greatest painters were himself and Velasquez] Why drag in Velasquez? [Ib.]

5 [Replying to the question 'For two days' labour, you ask two hundred guineas?'] No, I ask it for the knowledge of a lifetime. [Ib.]

6 *Oscar Wilde:* I wish I had said that.
Whistler: You will, Oscar, you will. [Ingleby, *Oscar Wilde*]

White, William Allen (1868–1944)

7 All dressed up with nowhere to go. [Remark, 1916]

Whitehead, A.N. (1861–1947)

8 It is more important that a proposition be interesting than that it be true. [*Adventures of Ideas*]

9 It is the essence of life that it exists for its own sake. [*Nature and Life*]

10 The history of Western philosophy is, after all, no more than a series of footnotes to Plato's philosophy. [Attr.]

Whiting, William (1825–1878)

11 Eternal Father, strong to save, / Whose arm hath bound the restless wave / ... O hear us when we cry to Thee / For those in peril on the sea. [Hymn]

Whitman, Walt (1819–1892)

1 O Captain! My Captain! our fearful trip is done. ['O Captain! My Captain!']

2 Out of the cradle endlessly rocking, / Out of the mocking bird's throat, the musical shuttle. ['Out of the Cradle endlessly Rocking']

3 I celebrate myself, and sing myself, / And what I assume you shall assume. [*Song of Myself*]

4 I loafe and invite my soul. [Ib.]

5 I believe a leaf of grass is no less than the journey-work of the stars. [Ib.]

6 [Of animals] They do not sweat and whine about their condition, / They do not lie awake in the dark and weep for their sins, / They do not make me sick discussing their duty to God, / Not one is dissatisfied, not one is demented with the mania of owning things, / Not one kneels to another, nor to his kind that lived thousands of years ago. [Ib.]

7 Do I contradict myself? / Very well then I contradict myself / (I am large, I contain multitudes). [Ib.]

8 I sound my barbaric yawp over the roofs of the world. [Ib.]

9 When lilacs last in the dooryard bloom'd, / And the great stars early droop'd in the western sky in the night, / I mourn'd, and yet shall mourn with ever-returning spring. ['When Lilacs Last in the Dooryard Bloom'd']

Whittier, John Greenleaf (1807–1892)

10 'Shoot if you must, this old grey head, / But spare your country's flag,' she said. ['Barbara Frietchie']

11 Dear Lord and Father of mankind, / Forgive our foolish ways. [Hymn]

Whittington, Robert (fl. 1520)

1 [Of Sir Thomas More] As time requireth, a man of marvellous mirth and pastimes, and sometimes of as sad gravity, as who say: a man for all seasons. [*Vulgaria*, II]

Wilbur, Richard (1921–)

2 We milk the cow of the world, and as we do / We whisper in her ear, 'You are not true.' ['Epistemology']

Wilcox, Ella Wheeler (1855–1919)

3 Laugh and the world laughs with you; / Weep, and you weep alone; / For the sad old earth must borrow its mirth, / But has trouble enough of its own. ['Solitude']

4 So many gods, so many creeds, / So many paths that wind and wind. ['The World's Need']

Wilde, Oscar (1854–1900)

5 That little tent of blue / Which prisoners call the sky. [*The Ballad of Reading Gaol*, I]

6 Yet each man kills the thing he loves, / By each let this be heard, / Some do it with a bitter look, / Some with a flattering word, / The coward does it with a kiss, / The brave man with a sword! [Ib.]

7 To give an accurate description of what has never occurred is not merely the proper occupation of the historian, but the inalienable privilege of any man of parts and culture. [*The Critic as Artist*, I]

8 Education is an admirable thing, but it is well to remember from time to time that nothing that is worth knowing can be taught. [Ib.]

9 As long as war is regarded as wicked, it will always have its fascination. When it is looked upon as vulgar, it will cease to be popular. The

change will, of course, be slow, and people will not be conscious of it. [Ib. II]

1 Most people are other people. Their thoughts are someone else's opinions, their lives a mimicry, their passions a quotation. [*De Profundis*]

2 Art never expresses anything but itself. [*The Decay of Lying*]

3 The final revelation is that Lying, the telling of beautiful untrue things, is the proper aim of Art. [Ib.]

4 [Of Wordsworth] He found in stones the sermons he had already hidden there. [Ib.]

5 No, my Lord Cardinal, I weary of her! / Why, she is worse than ugly, she is good. [*The Duchess of Padua*, II]

6 Men can be analysed, women ... merely adored. [*An Ideal Husband*, I]

7 Questions are never indiscreet. Answers sometimes are. [Ib.]

8 Morality is simply the attitude we adopt towards people whom we personally dislike. [Ib. II]

9 To love oneself is the beginning of a lifelong romance, Phipps. [Ib. III]

10 Really, if the lower orders don't set us a good example, what on earth is the use of them? They seem, as a class, to have absolutely no sense of moral responsibility. [*The Importance of Being Earnest*, I]

11 The truth is rarely pure and never simple. Modern life would be very tedious if it were either, and modern literature a complete impossibility. [Ib.]

12 You don't seem to realize, that in married life three is company and two is none. [Ib.]

13 To lose one parent, Mr. Worthing, may be

regarded as a misfortune; to lose both looks like carelessness. [Ib.]

1 All women become like their mothers. That is their tragedy. No man does. That's his. [Ib.]

2 The good ended happily, and the bad unhappily. That is what Fiction means. [Ib. II]

3 I never travel without my diary. One should always have something sensational to read in the train. [Ib.]

4 *Cecily:* When I see a spade I call it a spade.
Gwendolen: I am glad to say that I have never seen a spade. It is obvious that our social spheres have been widely different. [Ib.]

5 On an occasion of this kind it becomes more than a moral duty to speak one's mind. It becomes a pleasure. [Ib.]

6 Three addresses always inspire confidence, even in tradesmen. [Ib. III]

7 Never speak disrespectfully of Society, Algernon. Only people who can't get into it do that. [Ib.]

8 Please do not shoot the pianist. He is doing his best. [*Impressions of America*, 'Leadville']

9 It is absurd to divide people into good and bad. People who are either charming or tedious. [*Lady Windermere's Fan*, I]

10 I couldn't help it. I can resist everything except temptation. [Ib.]

11 *Cecil Graham:* What is a cynic?
Lord Darlington: A man who knows the price of everything and the value of nothing. [Ib. II]

12 We are all in the gutter, but some of us are looking at the stars. [Ib. III]

13 There is no such thing as a moral or an immoral book. Books are well written or badly written. [*Picture of Dorian Gray*, Preface]

14 There is only one thing in the world worse than

being talked about, and that is not being talked about. [Ib.]

1 A man cannot be too careful in the choice of his enemies. [Ib.]

2 The only way to get rid of a temptation is to yield to it. [Ib. 2]

3 It is better to be beautiful than to be good. But... it is better to be good than to be ugly. [Ib. 17]

4 Wickedness is a myth invented by good people to account for the curious attractiveness of others. [*Phrases and Philosophies for the Use of the Young*]

5 Nothing that actually occurs is of the smallest importance. [Ib.]

6 If one tells the truth, one is sure, sooner or later, to be found out. [Ib.]

7 The old believe everything: the middle-aged suspect everything: the young know everything. [Ib.]

8 It is only by not paying one's bills that one can hope to live in the memory of the commercial classes. [Ib.]

9 The only way to atone for being occasionally a little over-dressed is by being always absolutely over-educated. [Ib.]

10 Experience, the name men give to their mistakes. [*Vera, or The Nihilists*]

11 One should never trust a woman who tells one her real age. A woman who would tell one that would tell one anything. [*A Woman of No Importance*, I]

12 The English country gentleman galloping after a fox — the unspeakable in full pursuit of the uneatable. [Ib.]

13 Twenty years of romance make a woman look

like a ruin; but twenty years of marriage make her something like a public building. [Ib.]

1 Children begin by loving their parents. After a time they judge them. Rarely, if ever, do they forgive them. [Ib.]

2 You should study the Peerage, Gerald. It is the one book a young man about town should know thoroughly, and it is the best thing in fiction the English have done. [Ib. III]

3 Moderation is a fatal thing, Lady Hunstanton. Nothing succeeds like excess. [Ib.]

4 Those things which the English public never forgives — youth, power, and enthusiasm. [Lecture, 'The English Renaissance']

5 I must decline your invitation owing to a subsequent engagement. [Attr.]

6 Work is the curse of the drinking classes. [Pearson, *Life of Wilde*]

7 [Wilde was to be charged a large fee for an operation] 'Ah, well, then,' said Oscar, 'I suppose that I shall have to die beyond my means.' [R.H. Sherard, *Life of Oscar Wilde*]

8 [At the New York Customs] I have nothing to declare except my genius. [F. Harris, *Oscar Wilde*]

9 A thing is not necessarily true because a man dies for it. [*Sebastian Melmoth* and *Oscariana*]

Wilhelm II, Kaiser (1859–1941)

10 A contemptible little army. [Of the British Expeditionary Force in 1914]

Wilkes, John (1727–1797)

11 [Told by Lord Sandwich that he would die either on the gallows or of the pox] That must depend on whether I embrace your lordship's principles or your mistress. [Attr.]

Williams, Harry (1874–1924) and Judge, Jack (1878–1938)

1 Good-bye Piccadilly, Farewell Leicester Square; /
It's a long, long way to Tipperary, but my heart's
right there. ['It's a Long Way to Tipperary']

Williams, Tennessee (1912–1983)

2 Knowledge–Zzzzzp! Money — Zzzzzzp! —
Power! That's the cycle democracy is built on!
[*The Glass Menagerie*]

3 I have always depended on the kindness of
strangers. [*A Streetcar Named Desire*, II]

Williams, William Carlos (1883–1963)

4 . . . no ideas but in things. [*Paterson*, I, 1]

5 no woman is virtuous / who does not give
herself to her lover / —forthwith. [Ib. VI, 3]

Wilson, Charles E. (1890–1961)

6 What is good for the country is good for General
Motors, and vice versa. [Remark to
Congressional Committee, 1953]

Wilson, Harold (1916–   )

7 The little gnomes of Zurich. [Speech, 1956]

8 It does not mean, of course, that the pound here
in Britain, in your pocket or purse or in your
bank, has been devalued. [T.V. broadcast, 1967]

9 A week is a long time in politics. [Remark, 1965]

Wilson, Woodrow (1856–1924)

10 No nation is fit to sit in judgement upon any
other nation. [Address, 1915]

11 Armed neutrality. [Address, 1917]

12 It must be a peace without victory. [Address,
1917]

13 The world must be made safe for democracy.
[Address, 1917]

1 Open covenants of peace, openly arrived at, after which there shall be no private international understandings of any kind, but diplomacy shall proceed always frankly and in the public view. [Speech ('Fourteen Points'), 1918]

Wittgenstein, Ludwig (1889-1951)

2 The solution of the problem of life is seen in the vanishing of the problem. [*Tractatus Logico-Philosophicus*]

3 Whereof one cannot speak, thereon one must be silent. [Ib.]

4 The world is everything that is the case. [Ib.]

5 Everything that can be said can be said clearly. [Ib.]

Wodehouse, P.G. (1881-1975)

6 He spoke with a certain what-is-it in his voice, and I could see that, if not actually disgruntled, he was far from being gruntled. [*The Code of the Woosters*]

7 She fitted into my biggest armchair as if it had been built round her by someone who knew they were wearing armchairs tight about the hips that season. ['Jeeves and the Unbidden Guest']

8 I spent the afternoon musing on Life. If you come to think of it, what a queer thing Life is! So unlike anything else, don't you know, if you see what I mean. ['Rallying Round Old George']

9 'That,' I replied cordially, 'is what it doesn't do anything else but.' [*Ukridge*]

Wolfe, Charles (1791-1823)

10 Not a drum was heard, not a funeral note, / As his corse to the rampart we hurried. ['The Burial of Sir John Moore at Corunna']

Wolfe, Humbert (1886-1940)

11 You cannot hope / to bribe or twist, / thank

God! the / British journalist. / But, seeing what / the man will do / unbribed, there's / no occasion to. [*The Uncelestial City*]

Wolfe, Tom (1931–   )

1 Radical chic. [Title of essay]

Wollstonecraft, Mary (1759–1797)

2 [Of women] I do not wish them to have power over men; but over themselves. [*A Vindication of the Rights of Women*, 4]

3 When a man seduces a woman, it should, I think, be termed a *left-handed* marriage. [Ib.]

Wolsey, Thomas, Cardinal (c. 1475–1530)

4 Father Abbot, I am come to lay my bones amongst you. [Remark at Leicester Abbey, 1529]

5 Had I but served God as diligently as I have served the King, he would not have given me over in my grey hairs. [Attr.]

Wood, Mrs. Henry (1814–1887)

6 Dead! and ... never called me mother. [*East Lynne* (stage adaptation)]

Woolf, Virginia (1882–1941)

7 In or about December, 1910, human character changed. ['Mr. Bennett and Mrs. Brown']

8 A Room of One's Own [Title of essay]

Wordsworth, William (1770–1850)

9 I wandered lonely as a cloud / That floats on high o'er vales and hills, / When all at once I saw a crowd, / A host of golden daffodils. ['Daffodils']

10 On Man, on Nature and on Human Life, / Musing in solitude. [*The Excursion*, Preface]

11 Wisdom is ofttimes nearer when we stoop / Than when we soar. [Ib. III]

1 The wiser mind / Mourns less for what age takes away / Than what it leaves behind. ['The Fountain']

2 I have learned / To look on nature, not as in the hour / Of thoughtless youth; but hearing oftentimes / The still, sad music of humanity. ['Lines composed a few miles above Tintern Abbey']

3 And I have felt / A presence that disturbs me with the joy / Of elevated thoughts; a sense sublime / Of something far more deeply interfused, / Whose dwelling is the light of setting suns, / And the round ocean and the living air, / And the blue sky, and in the mind of man, / A motion and a spirit, that impels / All thinking things, all objects of all thought, / And rolls through all things. [Ib.]

4 My heart leaps up when I behold / A rainbow in the sky. ['My heart leaps up']

5 The Child is father of the Man; / And I could wish my days to be / Bound each to each by natural piety. [Ib.]

6 There hath passed away a glory from the earth. ['Ode: Intimations of Immortality']

7 Not in entire forgetfulness, / And not in utter nakedness, / But trailing clouds of glory do we come / From God, who is our home: / Heaven lies about us in our infancy! / Shades of the prison house begin to close / Upon the growing boy. [Ib.]

8 Though nothing can bring back the hour / Of splendour in the grass, of glory in the flower. [Ib.]

9 To me the meanest flower that blows can give / Thoughts that do often lie too deep for tears. [Ib.]

10 The harvest of a quiet eye, / That broods and sleeps on his own heart. ['A Poet's Epitaph']

1 Fair seed-time had my soul, and I grew up /
Fostered alike by beauty and by fear. [*The
Prelude*, I]

2 Dust as we are, the immortal spirit grows / Like
harmony in music; there is a dark / Inscrutable
workmanship that reconciles / Discordant
elements, makes them cling together / In one
society. [Ib.]

3 The unfetter'd clouds, and region of the Heavens,
/ Tumult and peace, the darkness and the light /
Were all like workings of one mind, the features
/ Of the same face, blossoms upon one tree, /
Characters of the great Apocalypse, / The types
and symbols of Eternity, / Of first and last, and
midst, and without end. [Ib. VI]

4 Bliss was it in that dawn to be alive, / But to be
young was very heaven. [Ib. XI]

5 We poets in our youth begin in gladness; / But
thereof comes in the end despondency and
madness. ['Resolution and Independence']

6 We feel that we are greater than we know. ['The
River Duddon']

7 She dwelt among the untrodden ways / Beside
the springs of Dove, / A maid whom there were
none to praise / And very few to love. ['She
Dwelt among the Untrodden Ways']

8 A slumber did my spirit seal; / I had no human
fears: / She seemed a thing that could not feel /
The touch of earthly years.
No motion has she now, no force; / She neither
hears nor sees; / Rolled round in earth's diurnal
course, / With rocks, and stones, and trees. ['A
Slumber did My Spirit Seal']

9 The music in my heart I bore, / Long after it
was heard no more. ['The Solitary Reaper']

10 Earth has not anything to show more fair; / Dull
would he be of soul who could pass by / A sight

so touching in its majesty. [*Sonnets*: 'Sonnet composed upon Westminster Bridge']

1 Dear God! the very houses seem asleep; / And all that mighty heart is lying still. [Ib.]

2 It is a beauteous evening, calm and free, / The holy time is quiet as a nun, / Breathless with adoration. [Ib. 'It is a beauteous evening']

3 Surprised by joy — impatient as the Wind / I turned to share the transport — Oh! with whom / But Thee, deep buried in the silent tomb. [Ib. 'Surprised by joy']

4 The world is too much with us; late and soon, / Getting and spending, we lay waste our powers. [Ib. 'The world is too much with us']

5 Milton! thou should'st be living at this hour: / England hath need of thee. [*Sonnets Dedicated to Liberty*, 14]

6 One impulse from a vernal wood / May teach you more of man, / Of moral evil and of good, / Than all the sages can. ['The Tables Turned']

7 Sweet is the lore which Nature brings; / Our meddling intellect / Misshapes the beauteous forms of things: / We murder to dissect. [Ib.]

8 I have said that poetry is the spontaneous overflow of powerful feelings: it takes its origin from emotion recollected in tranquillity: the emotion is contemplated till, by a species of reaction, the tranquillity gradually disappears, and an emotion, kindred to that which was before the subject of contemplation, is gradually produced, and does itself actually exist in the mind. [*Lyrical Ballads*, Preface]

Wotton, Sir Henry (1568–1639)

9 Virtue is the roughest way, / But proves at night a bed of down. ['Upon the Imprisonment of the Earl of Essex']

1 *Legatus est vir bonus peregrare missus ad mentiendum rei publicae causae.* An ambassador is an honest man sent to lie abroad for the good of the state. [Written in the Album of Christopher Fleckamore, 1604]

Wren, Sir Christopher (1632–1723)

2 *Si monumentum requiris, circumspice.* If you would see his monument look around. [Inscription, St. Paul's Cathedral, London]

Wright, Frank Lloyd (1869–1959)

3 Give me the luxuries of life and I will willingly do without the necessities. [Attr.]

4 The truth is more important than the facts. [Quoted in Simcox, *Treasury of Quotations on Christian Themes*]

Wyatt, Sir Thomas (c. 1503–1542)

5 They flee from me, that sometime did me seek / With naked foot, stalking in my chamber. ['They flee from me']

6 When her loose gown from her shoulders did fall, / And she me caught in her arms long and small, / Therewith all sweetly did me kiss / And softly said, 'Dear heart how like you this?' [Ib.]

Wycherley, William (c. 1640–1716)

7 With faint praises one another damn. [*The Plain Dealer*, Prologue]

Xenophon (c. 430–355 B.C.)

8 The sea! The sea! [*Anabasis*]

Yeames, W.F. (1835–1918)

9 And when did you last see your father? [Title of painting]

Yeats, W. B. (1865–1939)

10 O chestnut-tree, great-rooted blossomer, / Are

you the leaf, the blossom or the bole? / O body swayed to music, O brightening glance, / How can we know the dancer from the dance? ['Among School Children']

1 The fury and the mire of human veins. ['Byzantium']

2 That dolphin-torn, that gong-tormented sea. [Ib.]

3 The intellect of man is forced to choose / Perfection of the life, or of the work. ['The Choice']

4 Now that my ladder's gone, / I must lie down where all the ladders start, / In the foul rag-and-bone shop of the heart. ['The Circus Animals' Desertion']

5 But Love has pitched his mansion in / The place of excrement. / For nothing can be sole or whole / That has not been rent. ['Crazy Jane talks with the Bishop']

6 He knows death to the bone — / Man has created death. ['Death']

7 I am content to live it all again / And yet again, if it be life to pitch / Into the frog-spawn of a blind man's ditch / A blind man battering blind men. ['A Dialogue of Self and Soul' II]

8 Down by the salley gardens my love and I did meet; / She passed the salley gardens with little snow-white feet. / She bid me take love easy, as the leaves grow on the tree; / But I, being young and foolish, with her would not agree. ['Down by the Salley Gardens']

9 He, too, has resigned his part / In the casual comedy; / He, too, has been changed in his turn, / Transformed utterly. ['Easter 1916']

10 MacDonagh and MacBride / And Connolly and Pearse / Now and in time to be, / Wherever green is worn, / Are changed, changed utterly: / A terrible beauty is born. [Ib.]

1 The second best's a gay goodnight and quickly turn away. ['From "Oedipus at Colonus"']

2 I have spread my dreams under your feet; / Tread softly because you tread on my dreams. ['He wishes for the Cloths of Heaven']

3 The years to come seemed waste of breath, / A waste of breath the years behind / In balance with this life, this death. ['An Irish Airman foresees his Death']

4 I will arise and go now, and go to Innisfree, / And a small cabin build there, of clay and wattles made. ['The Lake Isle of Innisfree']

5 A shudder in the loins engenders there / The broken wall, the burning roof and tower / And Agamemnon dead. ['Leda and the Swan']

6 O heart, we are old; / The living beauty is for younger men: / We cannot pay its tribute of wild tears. ['The Living Beauty']

7 We had fed the heart on fantasies, / The heart's grown brutal from the fare; / More substance in our enmities / Than in our love. ['Meditations in Time of Civil War', VI]

8 How can I, that girl standing there, / My attention fix / On Roman or on Russian / Or on Spanish politics? ['Politics']

9 An intellectual hatred is the worst, / So let her think opinions are accursed. ['A Prayer for my Daughter']

10 That is no country for old men. ['Sailing to Byzantium']

11 An aged man is but a paltry thing, / A tattered coat upon a stick, unless / Soul clap its hands and sing / For every tatter in its mortal dress. [Ib.]

12 Turning and turning in the widening gyre / The falcon cannot hear the falconer; / Things fall

apart; the centre cannot hold; / Mere anarchy is loosed upon the world, / The blood-dimmed tide is loosed, and everywhere / The ceremony of innocence is drowned; / The best lack all conviction, while the worst / Are full of passionate intensity. ['The Second Coming']

1 And what rough beast, its hour come round at last, / Slouches towards Bethlehem to be born? [Ib.]

2 Was it for this the wild geese spread / The grey wing upon every tide; / For this that all that blood was shed . . . / All that delirium of the brave? / Romantic Ireland's dead and gone, / It's with O'Leary in the grave. ['September, 1913']

3 Those dancing days are gone. ['Those Dancing Days are Gone']

4 But was there ever dog that praised his fleas? ['To a Poet, who would have me Praise certain Bad Poets, Imitators of His and Mine']

5 What shall I do with this absurdity − / O heart, O troubled heart −this caricature, / Decrepit age that has been tied to me / As to a dog's tail? ['The Tower', I]

6 Death and life were not / Till man made up the whole, / Made lock, stock and barrel / Out of his bitter soul. [Ib. III]

7 Cast your mind on other days / That we in coming days may be / Still the indomitable Irishry. ['Under Ben Bulben', V]

8 *Cast a cold eye / On life, on death. / Horseman, pass by!* [Ib. VI (Yeats' epitaph)]

9 Why should not old men be mad? ['Why Should not Old Men be Mad?']

10 Out of the quarrel with others we make rhetoric; out of the quarrel with ourselves we make poetry. [Essay]

Young, Andrew (1807–1889)

1 There is a happy land, / Far, far away, / Where saints in glory stand, / Bright, bright as day. [Hymn]

Young, Edward (1683–1765)

2 By night an atheist half believes a God. [*The Complaint: Night Thoughts*, V]

3 You are so witty, profligate, and thin, / At once we think thee Milton, Death and Sin. [Epigram on Voltaire]

4 Be wise with speed; / A fool at forty is a fool indeed. [*Love of Fame*, II]

Young, George W. (1846–1919)

5 The lips that touch liquor must never touch mine! [Temperance verse]

Zangwill, Israel (1864–1926)

6 America is God's Crucible, the great Melting-Pot where all the races of Europe are melting and re-forming! [*The Melting Pot*]

Zola, Emile (1840–1902)

7 *J'accuse.* I accuse. [Title of open letter to the President of the Republic, 1898 (on the Dreyfus Affair)]

Zukor, Adolph (1873–1976)

8 The public is never wrong. [Quoted in Halliwell, *Filmgoers' Book of Quotes*]

INDEX

A. was not Adamant 163:3
gardener A. and his wife
  317:11
When A. delved 10:4
Adamant: Adam was not A.
  163:3
adapt: persists in trying to a. the
  world 290:1
address: a. will soon be
  Annihilation 105:10
addresses: Three a. always
  inspire 346:6
Adjective: A.: when in doubt,
  strike it out 326:4
admiral: kill an a. from time to
  time 331:13
admiration: from a. to love 15:13
admired: a. through being
  misunderstood 95:3
adored: women . . . merely a.
  345:6
adorn: a. a tale 172:10
adulteration: Not quite adultery,
  but a. 75:3
adultery: a., / Is much more
  common 73:9
  Do not a. commit 94:2
  Not quite a., but adulteration
    75:3
  Thou shalt not commit a.
    30:14
advantage: a. both of Eyes and
  Voice 207:8
  A. rarely comes of it 94:2
adventure: awfully big a. 23:6
Adversity: A. doth best discover
  Virtue 17:7
  A.'s sweet milk, philosophy
    283:8
  uses of a. 265:10
  withstand the shocks of a.
    336:11
advertisement: a. that will take
  in 168:3
Advertisements: A. contain the
  only truths 171:2
Advice: A. is seldom welcome
  87:10
  A. to persons about to marry
    247:7

ask a. is . . . to tout for flattery
  97:4
aesthetic: crime . . . desire for a.
  expression 337:11
  high a. band 143:11
aesthetics: long-haired a. 143:10
affair: never had a love a. 191:2
affairs: Nothing in the a. of men
  237:2
affection: a. beaming in one eye
  111:4
  more a. than she feels 16:6
affinity: betray a secret a. 154:6
Affluent: A. Society 139:10
afford: morals . . . Can't a. them
  291:1
afraid: be not a. 43:11
  not afraid of God, a. of me
    242:7
  they were sore a. 45:2
  Who's A. of Virginia Woolf
    3:7
Africa: Ex A. semper aliquid
  novi 237:5
  something new out of A. 237:5
again: ye no come back a. 162:2
against: a. everything all the
  time 184:11
  not with me is a. me 43:9
  who can be a. us 46:15
Agamemnon: And A. dead 357:5
Age: A. cannot wither her
  264:15
  A. shall not weary them 50:4
  a. that has been tied to me
    358:5
  a., which forgives itself
    anything 290:2
  Another a. shall see 240:5
  grey with a. becomes religion
    258:8
  if a. only could 130:10
  not of an a. 176:5
  Old a. is no such
    uncomfortable 335:2
  Old a. should burn and rave
    321:3
  what a. takes away 352:1
  woman who tells her real a.
    347:11

worth an a. without a name
222:2
aged: a. man is but a paltry
357:11
  deliciously a. and sad 288:10
a-gley: Gang aft a. 69:4
Agnus: A. Dei 210:2
agree: world and I shall ne'er a.
101:10
a-hunting: daren't go a., / For
fear 4:9
ail: what can a. thee 179:5
aim: a. I never fash 66:11
air: castles . . . built with a. 176:2
  left the vivid a. 304:9
  planted in the a. 252:5
  'twixt A. and Angels' purity
115:13
Alas: History . . . may say A. 14:6
Albert: take a message to A.
115:8
ale: no more cakes and a. 285:15
  Spicy Nut-brown A. 214:11
Alexander: A. wept 237:9
Alice: went down with A. 213:10
alien: amid the a. corn 181:14
alive: Officiously to keep a. 94:3
  still a. at twenty-two 185:10
  that dawn to be a. 353:4
All: A. for one 122:10
  a. is vanity 37:4
  a. shall be well 178:1
  a. things to all men 46:18
  take him for a. in all 267:5
allegory: headstrong as an a.
296:11
  Shakespeare led a life of a.
184:2
alley: she lives in our a. 78:6
Allons: A., enfants de la patrie
254:3
almighty: a. dollar, that great
object 169:9
  A.'s orders to perform 1:6
alms: a. for oblivion 285:5
Alone: A., alone, all, all alone
95:13
  embarrassment on being left a.
together 188:9
  fastest who travels a. 187:14

I want to be a. 140:1
  less a. than when completely
92:7
  man should be a. 29:7
  mortal millions live a. 12:10
  now God a. knows 188:3
aloud: denied none of it a. 15:6
Alph: A., the sacred river 96:6
Alpha: A. and Omega 49:7
alphabet: got to the end of the a.
112:8
alternative: There is no a. 320:9
alternatives: exhausted all other
a. 123:9
alters: a. when it alteration
287:8
altissimo: a. poeta 105:7
always: a. a gentleman 111:3
amateurs: disease that afflicts a.
89:8
  Hell is full of musical a. 289:6
  nation of a. 253:3
ambassador: a. is an honest man
355:1
Ambition: A. should be made of
sterner 273:7
  Lowliness is young a.'s ladder
272:13
  Vaulting a., which o'erleaps
276:5
Amen: sound of a great A. 247:1
america: a. i / love you 104:6
  A. is a land where boys refuse
203:7
  A. is God's Crucible 359:6
  A. is the only nation in history
93:5
  A. was thus clearly top 263:9
  A. . . . where law and custom
255:9
  business of A. 100:1
  my A.! my new-found-land
116:12
  woman governs A. 203:7
  Young man, there is A. 64:9
American: A. writers want 330:5
  see the A. eagle, it observes
only 340:7
Americanism: only hundred per
cent A. 252:2

Americans: A. and nothing else
252:8

amiability: gained in a. 72:3

amiable: a. weakness 133:2

ammunition: Lord and pass the
a. 135:10

Amor: *Omnia vincit A.* 331:7

amphibious: a., ill-born mob
107:9

amused: We are not a. 330:2

Analytics: Sweet A. 204:8

Anarch: Thy hand, great A.
239:3

anarchy: a. . . . the laws of death
255:7

Mere a. is loosed 357:12

ancestors: a. are very good
296:12

glory belongs to our a. 237:10

Ancestral: A. voices prophesying
war 96:8

ancestry: a. back to a
protoplasmal 143:1

ancient: It is an a. Mariner 95:8

praise of a. authors 161:7

ancients: a. without idolatry
87:11

ancre: *levons l'a.* 24:5

anecdotage: man fell into his a.
114:7

Angel: A. of the Lord came
down 315:8

a. of the Lord came upon them
45:2

a.'s face / As the great eye
305:6

beautiful and ineffectual a.
13:9

domesticate the Recording A.
310:5

In heaven an a. is nobody
290:7

Look homeward, A., now
215:6

no child is born an a. 302:1

woman ye think him an a.
320:2

Angel-infancy: Shin'd in my A.
328:11

Angels: A. affect us oft, and
worship'd 115:12

A. fear to tread 241:5

a. of God ascending 30:5

entertained a. unawares 48:15

Four a. to my bed 8:2

herald a. sing 341:3

little lower than the a. 34:2

on the side of the a. 115:2

they have the countenance of
a. 148:9

'twixt Air and A.' purity
115:13

Anger: A. is a brief madness
164:11

A. is one of the sinews 139:5

mistress some rich a. shows
181:4

monstrous a. of the guns 230:2

angler: no man is born an a.
335:8

Angles: they were called A.
148:9

angling: innocent recreation than
a. 335:9

angry: a. at a slander 175:13

a. with my friend 53:1

Be ye a., and sin not 48:2

When a. count four 326:1

anguis: *a. in herba* 331:6

animal: a. is very wicked 5:11

poor, bare, forked a. 274:10

tool-making a. 137:12

animals: All a. are equal 229:2

[a.] do not sweat and whine
343:6

distinguish us from the other
a. 24:10

Animula: *A. vagula blandula*
150:1

Anna: great A.! whom three
realms obey 242:11

annals: Happy the people whose
a. 79:1

Annihilating: A. all that's made
208:1

Annihilation: A.. As for my
name 105:10

annoy: He only does it to a. 80:4

Answer: A. a fool 36:16

a. came there none 259:7
a. is blowin' in the wind 123:3
dusty a. gets the soul 211:9
more than the wisest man can
a. 97:10
not stay for an a. 17:1
What is the a. 307:6
wrong number, why did you a.
323:3
answerable: a. to the people
338:4
Answers: A. sometimes
[indiscreet] 345:7
ante: *qui a. nos* 115:11
ant-hill: epoch of the a. 5:1
Anthropophagi: A., and men
whose heads 280:16
antic: dance the a. hay 205:8
put an a. disposition 267:13
anti-everythings: hungry, savage
a. 162:5
antipathies: a. . . . betray a secret
affinity 154:6
ants: If a. are such busy workers
120:2
anxiety: Nothing . . . worthy of
great a. 237:2
anybody: Then no one's a. 142:6
anything: doesn't do a. else but
350:9
Remembering him like a. 89:4
you'll believe a. 340:6
ape: Jesus and a nameless a.
202:2
man an a. or an angel 115:2
Naked A. 222:6
apes: a. and peacocks 209:4
aphrodisiac: Power . . . ultimate
a. 188:1
Apocalypse: Characters of the
great A. 353:3
Apollo: after the songs of A.
275:11
A.'s . . . Priest 78:2
burnéd is A.'s laurel bough
205:6
apostle: a. in the high aesthetic
band 143:11
apostolic: a. blows and knocks
70:12

apothecary: ounce of civet, good
a. 274:17
apparel: a. oft proclaims the
man 267:6
appetite: a. may sicken, and so
die 285:9
appetites: cloy / The a. they feed
264:15
Apply: know my methods. A.
them 119:5
April: A. is the cruellest 127:6
A.'s in the west wind 209:7
Now that A.'s there 60:7
April: Whan that A. with his
shoures 84:7
Aquitaine: *Le prince d'A.* 225:4
Arabia: perfumes of A. will not
277:9
Arabs: tents, like the A. 197:6
Arcadia: *Et in A. ego* 6:8
Archbishop: that is the A. of
Canterbury 301:6
arches: down the a. of the years
321:11
Architecture: A. is frozen music
145:10
are: That which we a., we are
319:4
argue: as absurd to a. men
225:10
argument: All a. is against it
174:13
a. of the broken pane 231:6
a. of the stronger man 134:10
staple of his a. 275:7
Arguments: A. out of a pretty
mouth 2:8
a. which influenced my
opinion 132:2
arise: I will a. and go now 357:7
aristocracy: a. . . . government by
the badly educated 90:2
A. of the Money bag 79:7
a. the most democratic 200:7
Arma: *A. virumque* 330:9
armchair: fitted into my biggest
a. 350:7
armies: ignorant a. clash by
night 12:6
invasion of a. is resisted 167:1

armour: a. of light 245:6
whole a. of God 48:3

armourer: a.'s iron brace 50:10

Arms: A. and the man 330:9
laid down his a. 162:12
Roman's a., / Take thou 200:4

army: a. marches on its stomach 5:7

a-roving: go no more a. 75:14

arrive: a. where we started 126:7

arrived: I've a., and to prove it 72:6

arrows: a. of outrageous fortune 268:1

Ars: A. longa 160:6

arsenal: great a. of democracy 252:6

art: a. constantly aspires 233:2
A. does not reproduce 188:2
a. for art's sake 100:8
A. . . . God's grandchild 105:6
A. is a jealous mistress 129:3
A. is either a plagiarist 140:3
A. is science in the flesh 95:5
a. itself is nature 286:8
A. . . . makes us see 188:2
A. most cherishes 61:2
A. must be parochial 221:5
A. must then give way 258:10
A. never expresses anything but 345:2
a. pour l'art 100:8
a. that is interested in itself 257:6
clever, but is it A. 186:5
Dying is an a., like 236:9
how to live is . . . my a. 220:7
In a. the best is good 145:6
love of a. for art's sake 233:4
Lying . . . proper aim of a. 345:3
nature is but a. unknown 241:11
next to Nature, A. 190:1
responsibility is to his a. 131:11
revenge of the intellect upon a. 303:3
sacrificed to their a. 129:11
start on all this A. 158:2

work at anything but his a. 289:2

writing comes from a., not chance 241:2

you are only interested in a. 291:5

article: snuff'd out by an a. 75:2

artifex: Qualis a. pereo 225:2

artist: a. will let his wife starve 289:2
grant the a. his subject 170:5
Never trust the a. 192:6
sign of the true a. 330:4
What an a. dies 225:2

artistic: a. temperament is a disease 89:8

Artists: A. must be sacrificed 129:11

Arts: Murder . . . One of the Fine A. 109:4
spoiled by going into the a. 140:2

ashamed: a. of, the more respectable 289:1
mirth as does not make friends 335:10
wonder to see them not a. 312:11

ashes: a. to ashes 246:7

asinorum: Pons a. 131:2

Ask: A., and it shall be given 43:4
A. yourself whether 212:4

asked: glad to have been a. 229:11
Oliver Twist has a. for more 111:14

asking: first time of a. 245:9

asleep: a. before you finish saying 254:8
too young to fall a. for ever 258:3

aspires: While man a., he errs 145:1

assassination: absolutism moderated by a. 5:8
A. . . . extreme form of censorship 291:3

asses: bridge of a. 131:2

Assyrian: A. came down 73:8

astray: have gone a. 39:9

asunder: let no man put a. 246:3

asylum: Jerusalem of a lunatic a. 128:8

Atheism: inclineth Man's Mind to A. 18:4

atheist: a. . . . has no invisible means 62:4

a., thank God 63:3

By night an a. half believes 359:2

worst moment for the a. 253:12

Athens: Another A. shall arise 293:2

Maid of A., ere we part 75:10

sunrise from the sea, / A. arose 292:11

atom bombs: a. and the one after 327:7

attack: situation excellent. I shall a. 134:8

with his plan of a. 258:4

attacked: When . . . a. it defends 5:11

attaque: *situation excellente. J'a.* 134:8

attic: little brain a. 119:3

attire: Her rich a. creeps 179:11

attractiveness: account for the curious a. 347:4

Auchtermuchty: Tak' A. for a name 201:8

audace: *a., et toujours de l'audace* 105:9

augury: we defy a. 269:2

Auri: *A. sacra fames* 330:13

author: asked by an a. what he thinks 175:3

a. as you choose a friend 253:1

authority: little brief a. 278:2

authors: We a., Ma'am 115:6

Autumn: thou breath of A.'s being 294:3

Autumnal: seen in one A. face 116:7

availeth: struggle naught a. 94:4

Avarice: A., the spur of industry 167:6

Ave: *A., Imperator* 311:5

frater, a. atque vale 83:1

Avenge: A., O Lord, thy slaughtered 218:11

Averni: *Facilis descensus A.* 331:2

Avernus: fair are gone down to A. 244:1

aversion: a.; pleasure was his business 124:3

indifference closely bordering on a. 309:12

matrimony to begin with . . . a. 296:8

awake: man will lie a. thinking 254:8

one must stay a. all day 227:3

a-waltzing: You'll come a., Matilda 233:5

away: and quickly turn a. 357:1

awe: even kings in a. 106:4

power to keep them all in a. 161:4

awful: God! this is an a. place 259:3

awkward: Don't let the a. squad 69:11

awoke: a. one morning and found myself famous 76:4

axioms: not a. until they are proved 183:8

Azores: Flores in the A. 318:10

Baa: B.! Baa! Baa 186:9

Babes: B. reduced to misery 52:13

babies: only washing. And b. 321:8

baboon: bred out / Into b. and monkey 284:10

baby: When the first b. laughed 23:4

Babylon: By the rivers of B. 36:4

Bacchus: B. and his pards 181:11

Bachelor: B.'s fare 312:2

bachelors: reasons for b. to go out 125:7

back: b. the world 178:9

except by getting off his b. 323:11

beak: Take thy b. from out my heart 238:3

be-all: b. and the end-all 276:4

beaming: affection b. in one eye 111:4

beamish: my arms, my b. boy 81:2

beams: Dim, as the borrowed b. 121:14

Bear: B. of Very Little Brain 213:8
b. with a sore head 206:10
Exit, pursued by a b. 286:6
gave pain to the b. 200:8
How a b. likes honey 213:7
oft outwatch the B. 214:6

bear-baiting: Puritan hated b. 200:8

Beard: singeing of the King of Spain's B. 119:8

beast: any b. of the field 29:8
Blatant b. men call 305:10
making the b. with two backs 280:14
maw-crammed b. 61:11
what rough b. 358:1
wild B., or a God 18:6

beastie: cow'rin', tim'rous b. 69:3

beasties: ghosties and long leggety b. 7:1

beastly: b. the bourgeois is 192:1
b. to the Germans 101:4

beautiful: b. and therefore to be woo'd 271:12
b. is as useful as 167:2
B. Railway Bridge 202:7
b. than to be good 347:3
good is the b. 236:11
Oysters are more b. 256:9
Small is B. 259:1
When a woman isn't b. 87:3

beauty: b. . . . best thing God invents 60:5
B. in things exists in the mind 167:7
B. is truth 180:1
b. without a fortune 131:8
daily b. in his life 281:12
Everything has its b. 98:10
flaw in b. 128:7

Fostered alike by b. 353:1

living b. is for younger 357:6

no b. that we should desire him 39:8

no Excellent B. 18:10

No Spring, nor Summer B. 116:7

soon as b. dies 116:6

terrible b. is born 356:10

thing of b. is a joy 179:6

walks in b., like the night 75:13

Became: B. him like the leaving it 275:14

because: b. – after all we do think 297:7

Becket: [B.] this turbulent priest 156:9

becomes: woman, one b. one 25:6

bed: and so to b. 234:9
B. be blest that I lie on 8:2
Early to b. 137:6
go to b. by day 309:4
go to b. in another world 157:6
I in my b. again 10:1
take up thy b. 46:2
used to go to b. early 247:4

bedfellows: strange b. 284:2

bee: b. sucks, there suck I 284:7
How doth the little busy b. 337:5

beef: island of b. flesh 204:4
roast b. of England 132:6

been: b. and gone and done 142:3

beer: all b. and skittles 166:9
only a b. teetotaller 288:3

Beer-sheba: Dan even to B. 32:4

before: I have been here b. 253:11
said our remarks b. us 115:11

beg: law . . . forbids the rich . . . to b. 136:3

begat: fathers that b. us 41:1

begetter: only b. of these ensuing 286:12

beggary: b. in the love 264:9

Begin: B. at the beginning 80:14

b. with a single step 190:9
b. with doubts 16:8
vee may perhaps to b. 254:2

beginning: b. and the ending 49:7
b. of the end 315:4
In my b. is my end 126:5
In the b. 29:3
In the b. was the Word 45:15
not even the b. of the end 91:6
was in the b. 244:7

beginnings: great things in their b. 190:7

Begone: B., dull Care 5:10

begot: when they b. me 307:10

begotten: b. by despair 207:5

behaving: b. in this extraordinary manner 310:9

behind: led his regiment from b. 142:4

behold: granted to me to b. you 309:8
thou mayst in me b. 287:5

being: have our b. 46:11

belief: all b. is for it 174:13
b. is not true 5:2

believe: b., because they so were bred 121:7
B. it or not 250:11
B. one who knows by experience 331:4
b. that what is true for you 129:6
boldness to b. in nothing 325:1
I b. in God the Father 244:9
I don't b. in fairies 23:5
If you b. that 340:6
If you don't b. it 14:11
must b. in God 177:2
one *can't* b. impossible things 81:7

believed: understood, and not be b. 52:7

believers: earnest b. in the world 20:5

believes: man wishes he generally b. 108:9

believing: torture them, into b. 225:10

Bell: B., book, and candle 273:13

for whom the b. tolls 116:5
sexton toll'd the b. 163:1
surly sullen b. 287:4
Who will b. the cat 109:6

bells: b. of Hell go ting 8:6
From the b., bells 237:12
liked the ringing of church b. 87:4

belly: Jonah was in the b. 40:12
something of a round b. 270:7

beloved: Dearly b. 245:10

belt: b. without hitting below 13:10

belts: Fasten your seat b. 107:1

bely: wombe! O b.! O stynking cod 86:2

benevolence: question whether the b. of mankind 20:8

Berliner: *Ich bin ein B.* 184:10

Berries: pluck your B., harsh and crude 215:1

berry: better b., but doubtless God never 335:9
sweeter than the b. 140:7

best: All is for the b. 331:12
b. and happiest moments 296:2
b. is the best 248:10
b. is the enemy of the good 332:2
b. words in their best 97:3
criticism . . . to learn and propagate the b. 13:8
In art the b. is good enough 145:6
It was the b. of times 112:12
live in the b. of all possible worlds 76:5

bestride: Why, man, he doth b. 272:7

Bethlehem: Slouches towards B. 358:1

betimes: to be up b. 285:12

betray: guts to b. my country 135:11

betray'd: b. me into common sense 238:11

better: even from worse to b. 163:6
for b. for worse 245:13

books: attention to the inside of
b. 88:3
B. and the Man 238:8
B. are well written 346:13
b. by which the printers have
lost 139:6
B., like men their authors
312:6
B. think for me 189:6
but his b. were read 27:4
God has written all the b.
71:10
making many b. there is no
end 37:9
Some B. are to be tasted 19:2
stranger commodity . . . than b.
194:8
study of mankind is b. 168:2
Wherever B. are burned 155:4
boot: b. in the face 236:7
b. stamping on a human face
229:6
Boots: B. — boots — boots 186:4
booze: reliefs we ha'e in b. 202:1
Border: Night Mail crossing the
B. 14:4
Bore: *B.*: A person who talks
50:1
b.; even the grave yawns 324:3
hero becomes a b. 130:3
Bored: tribes, the *Bores* and *B.*
75:6
boredom: Sooner barbarity than
b. 140:4
boring: b. is to say everything
333:1
Life, friends, is b. 28:7
born: All men are b. good 98:1
b. about three of the clock
270:7
b. out of my due time 222:8
die as to be b. 17:5
Every moment one is b. 319:5
he's just b. 302:1
Man is b. free 254:4
not b. for death 181:14
Not to be is b. best 303:6
one and one-sixteenth is b.
16:7
powerless to be b. 12:9

some are b. great 285:17
some are b. posthumously
226:9
When we are b., we cry
274:19
borrer: b. the money to do it
336:4
borrower: Neither a b. 267:7
borrowing: b. / Goeth a
sorrowing 325:6
b. only lingers 270:8
goes a b. goes a sorrowing
137:3
bosom: not a b. to repose upon
111:2
botched: b. civilization 243:8
boue: *nostalgie de la b.* 14:8
Bough: beneath the B. 133:6
on a wet, black b. 243:9
boughs: which shake against
the cold 287:5
Bountiful: My Lady B. 131:7
bourgeois: beastly the b. is 192:1
épater le b. 24:6
Bourgeoisie: British B. / Is not
born 298:8
bourgeois-smug: trend is towards
the b. 148:1
bourn: from whose b. / No
traveller 268:3
boutique: *réserver une arrière b.*
220:6
Bow: B., bow, ye lower middle
classes 142:10
b. of burning gold 52:1
bowels: in the b. of Christ
103:11
Bowl: inverted B. they call the
Sky 133:9
Love in a golden b. 51:3
boy: b. my greatness 265:3
b. playing in the b. of the
seashore 226:3
b. stood on the burning deck
155:9
b.'s will is the wind's 197:8
mad about the b. 101:5
Speak roughly to your little b.
80:4

Britain: B. a fit country 196:9
  B. has lost an Empire 1:2
Britannia: B., rule the waves
  322:2
brithers: b. be for a' that 67:4
British: ridiculous as the B.
  public 200:11
  stony B. stare 318:5
Briton: grovelled . . . as only a
  free-born B. 320:5
Britons: B. never will be slaves
  322:2
brittle: most b. of all human
  things 65:8
broken: argument of the b. pane
  231:6
broodin': b. over bein' a dog
  341:9
brothels: b. with bricks of
  Religion 52:5
Brother: Big B. is watching you
  229:3
  B. humans who live after us
  330:8
  man and a b. 339:4
  my b.'s keeper 30:1
  white man's b., not 185:7
brother-in-law: not his b. 185:7
brotherly: Let b. love continue
  48:14
brothers: men will be b. 258:6
Brüder: *Menschen werden B.*
  258:6
Brute: B. heart of a brute 236:7
  Et tu, B. 76:10
  Et tu, B. 273:2
  Feed the b. 122:11
brutish: nasty, b., and short
  161:5
Brutus: B. is an honourable man
  273:6
bubble: b. winked at me 159:4
  now a b. burst 241:8
  world's a b. 19:7
bubbles: With headed b. 181:8
buck: b. stops here 324:8
buds: shake the darling b. of
  May 286:13
bug: b. with gilded wings 240:1
  snug / As a b. in a rug 137:9

bugles: b., over the rich Dead
  57:5
build: b. your ship of death
  192:2
  Except the Lord b. 36:3
  think that we b. for ever 255:6
builders: stone which the b.
  refused 35:7
building: Light . . . principal
  beauty of b. 139:4
  something like a public b.
  347:13
built: we have b. Jerusalem 52:2
Bull: Cock and a B. 308:8
  milk the B. 173:10
bullet: ballot is stronger than the
  b. 195:2
bully: Like a tall b. 240:3
bump: things that go b. 7:1
bumpy: going to be a b. night
  107:1
bundle: b. of contradictions
  97:11
  b. of prejudices 189:3
bunk: History is b. 135:7
Burden: White Man's B. 187:13
Burg: *Ein feste B.* 199:5
buried: b. in so sweet a place
  291:7
  But Thee, deep b. 354:3
Burke: [B.] rose like a rocket
  230:10
burned: men too are eventually
  b. 155:4
burning: boy stood on the b.
  deck 155:9
burnt: Christians have b. each
  other 73:10
burnt-out: b. ends of smoky days
  127:4
bury: come to b. Caesar 273:5
  We will b. you 185:3
bus: not even a b., I'm a tram
  152:3
bush: aims but at a b. 297:8
  common b. afire with God
  59:1
business: about my Father's b.
  45:6
  b. in great waters 35:6

b. of America 100:1
B. was his aversion 124:3
Christianity; it is good b.
196:10
No praying, it spoils b. 229:10
true b. precept 111:5
Busy: B. old fool 118:3
thou knowest how b. 13:11
but: doesn't do anything else b.
350:9
butler: inspired b. 154:1
butter: b. will only make us fat
144:9
like a little bit of b. 213:11
buttered: always on the b. side
233:8
butterfly: breaks a b. upon a
wheel 239:14
buttress: regarded as a b. of the
church 211:2
buy: Do not b. what you want
82:6
Byron: [B.] Mad, bad and
dangerous 189:2
B. they drew a system 200:12
cabbages: Of c. — and kings 81:5
Cabin: Log C. to White House
320:10
cacoethes: *Scribendi c.* 178:6
Caesar: *C. aut nihil* 54:7
C.'s self is God's 103:8
C.'s wife must be above
suspicion 76:7
loved C. less 273:4
things which are C.'s 44:5
where some buried C. bled
133:8
Cage: Iron bars a C. 198:9
Cain: and the first city C. 101:8
cake: Let them eat c. 204:7
Cakes: Hear, Land o' C.
manufacture of little c. 136:1
no more c. and ale 285:15
Calais: find 'C.' lying in my heart
209:3
calculation: c. shining out the
other 111:4
Caledonia: C.! stern and wild
260:2
calf: fatted c., and kill 45:12

Call: C. me Ishmael 211:3
C. of the Wild 197:5
c. ye upon him 39:10
Go, for they c. you 13:1
Callay: Callooh! C. 81:2
called: many are c., but 44:4
calm: c. of mind 218:7
Calvin: land of C., oat-cakes
301:5
Cambridge: put back at Oxford
or C. 25:11
came: I c., I saw, I conquered
76:9
camel: easier for a c. 44:16
camera: I am a c. 169:10
can: He who c., does 290:3
You c., for you must 145:8
candid: be c. where we can
241:7
save me, from the c. friend
77:10
candle: c. to the sun 134:4
light such a c. 191:8
little c. throws his beams
279:8
Out, out, brief c. 277:13
rather light a c. 309:3
candlesticks: stately and daintily
as c. 17:2
candles: Night's c. are burnt out
283:9
Candy: C. / Is dandy 224:5
cannikin: why clink the c. 60:4
cannon: Even in the c.'s mouth
266:1
Cantate: *C. Dominum* 333:9
capability: world of c. / Of taking
joy 59:13
capacity: Genius . . . of taking
trouble 78:10
infinite c. for taking pains
164:6
comparisons: No c., miss 297:1
Cape St. Vincent: nobly C. to the
North-west 60:9
capitaine: *Mort, vieux c.* 24:5
Capital: high C., where kingly
Death 291:8
capitalism: unacceptable face of
c. 154:10

Capitol: ruins of the C. 141:6
capitulate: I will not c. 175:6
Captain: C.! My Captain 343:1
  c. of my soul 156:4
captains: All my sad c. 264:16
  C. and the Kings depart 187:6
  c. couragous 21:5
  C. of industry 79:10
Capten: C., art thou sleepin'
  225:5
Captivity: bring away / C.
  thence captive 304:10
carbonarium: De calcaria in c.
  319:12
card: cheery old c.,' grunted
  Harry 258:4
Care: Begone, dull C. 5:10
  c. and women 336:5
  don't c. what is written about
  me 157:7
  full of c., / We have no 106:9
  ravell'd sleave of c. 276:9
  Take c. of the sense 80:10
  took c. of number one 206:9
  wrinkled C. derides 214:9
careful: c. indeed what we say
  98:9
carelessness: lose both looks like
  c. 345:13
cares: c. that infest the day
  197:6
Carew: grave of Mad C. 153:6
cargo: c. of ivory 209:4
caricature: this c., / Decrepit age
  358:5
carlin: ilka c. swat and reekit
  68:8
carnal: wun at times in c. states
  202:1
Carpe: C. diem 165:4
Carthage: C. must be destroyed
  82:5
case: everything that is the c.
  350:4
  heard only one side of the c.
  71:10
  nothing to do with the c. 143:7
casement: Full on this c. 179:13
casements: Charm'd magic c.
  181:14

Cash: C. payment is not the sole
  nexus 79:9
  hand to hand of c. 297:6
castle: c. hath a pleasant seat
  276:2
  house . . . is . . . as his c. 95:7
Castlereagh: had a mask like C.
  293:10
castles: c. I have, are built with
  air 176:2
casualty: first c. when war
  comes 171:9
cat: bell the C. 109:6
  c. may look at a king 80:7
  consider my C. Jeoffry 299:2
  Touch not the c. 261:1
cataract: wild c. leaps in glory
  318:7
catastrophe: c. of the old
  comedy 274:4
  race between education and c.
  340:11
Catch-22: C., which specified
  155:6
catchwords: Man . . . lives . . . by
  c. 310:6
caterpillars: two religious c.
  205:13
catharsis: c. of such emotions
  11:15
Catherine the Great: illegitimate
  child of . . . C. 13:12
Cats: C. is 'dogs' 247:10
cattle: these who die as c. 230:2
caught: c. hold of the fille 307:9
cauldron: Fire burn and c.
  bubble 277:3
cause: c. that perishes with them
  93:7
  effect, / Whose c. is God
  103:1
  it is the c., my soul 281:13
  one can discover the c. 238:5
causes: any good, brave c. left
  229:8
  dire offence from am'rous c.
  242:9
cavaliero: perfect c. 72:8
Cavaliers: C. (Wrong but
  Wromantic) 263:6

Cave: *C. canem* 235:2

caverns: c. measureless to man 96:6

Cease: C.! must men kill 293:3
that I may c. to be 183:2
Wonders will never c. 122:4

ceasing: Pray without c. 48:6

celebrate: c. myself, and sing 343:3

celebrity: c. . . . for his well-knownness 54:5

celibacy: c. has no pleasures 172:8

cenotaph: laugh at my own c. 292:3

censorship:
Assassination . . . extreme form of c. 291:3

centre: c. cannot hold 357:12

ceremony: painful c. of receiving . . . visits 302:3

Ceres: laughing C. reassume the land 240:2

certain: A lady of a 'c. age,' 74:12
c. because it is impossible 319:13
However c. our expectation 127:2
nothing can be said to be c., except 137:10

certainties: begin with c. 16:8
hot for c. 211:9

Certum: *C. est* 319:13

chaff: c. is printed 166:8

chains: c. and calls them Liberty 62:5
everywhere is in c. 254:4
nothing to lose but their c. 208:10

chaise-longue: hurly-burly of the c. 77:2

chambermaid: c. as of a Duchess 174:14

chambre: *demeurer en repos dans une c.* 232:6

champagne: c. teetotaller 288:3

chance: care o' th' main c. 71:4
c., direction which thou canst not see 241:11

C. is perhaps God's pseudonym 136:2

in nativity, c. or death 279:13

marriage . . . a matter of c. 15:12

right, by c. 101:12

chang'd: loves are but c. sorts of meat 116:3

Change: C. is not made without 163:6
ever-whirling wheel / Of C. 305:11
I would c. still less 59:4
often c. who would be constant 98:11
Plus ça c. 178:11
point, however, is to c. it 208:13
small c. of silence 211:12
state without . . . means of . . . c. 64:2
Things do not c.; we change 322:9
wind of c. is blowing 203:5

changed: c., changed utterly 356:10
human character c. 351:7
we shall all be c. 47:3

changing: stress on not c. one's mind 210:6

chantant: *c. mes vers* 251:11

chante: *dit, on le c.* 24:9

Chaos: C. and old Night 216:4
C. is come again 281:4
dread Empire, C.! is restor'd 239:3

Chaos-like: Not C. together crush'd 242:14

chapels: c. had been churches 278:8

chaps: Biography is about c. 28:3

chapter: c. of accidents 88:5

character: c. in the current of affairs 145:7
Fate and c. are the same 228:1

characters: c. . . . result of our conduct 11:14
man has three c. 179:1

charged: c. with the grandeur 164:1

chariot: c. so long in coming 32:1
my c. of fire 52:1
Time's wingèd C. hurrying 208:4

charioted: Not c. by Bacchus 181:11

charity: greatest of these is c. 47:1

Charlie: C. he's my darling 66:3
C. is my darling 162:1

Charm: [C.]...don't need...anything else 23:8

Charm'd: C. magic casements 181:14

charming: People are either c. 346:9

charms: acres o' c. 66:13
Do not all c. fly 180:7

Chartreuse: religious system that produced green C. 256:10

chassis: terr...ible state o'...c. 228:5

Chaste: C. to her Husband 239:7
English text is c. 141:7

chasteneth: loveth he c. 48:13

chastity: Give me c. 14:9

chatter: Love is only c. 63:13

cheap: c. and chippy chopper 143:4

cheat: life, 'tis all a c. 121:7
sweet c. gone 108:4

cheating: c. of our friends 90:6

cheeks: crack your c. 274:6
scarce forbear to c. 200:5

cheer: Be of good c. 43:11

cheerful: c. look makes a dish 159:2

cheerfulness: c. was always breaking in 124:8

cheese: dreamed of the c.—toasted, mostly 310:2

Chequer'd: Dancing in the C. shade 214:11

cherche: Je ne c. pas 235:6

Cherchez: C. la femme 122:9

cherish: love, c. and to obey 246:1

Cherry: 'C. ripe' themselves do cry 77:9
ruddier than the c. 140:7

Cherry-ripe: C., ripe, ripe I cry 159:5
c. themselves do cry 4:5

chess-board: We called the c. white 59:8

chestnut: c. casts his flambeaux 165:9

chestnut-tree: c., great-rooted blossomer 355:10

Chevalier: the young C. 66:3
young C. 162:1

chicken: c. in his pot every Sunday 156:8
Some c.! Some neck 91:5

chieftain: c. o' the puddin'-race 69:7

chield: c.'s amang you taking notes 68:5

Child: C.! Do not throw this book 26:10
c. imposes on the man 121:7
C. is father of the Man 352:5
every formal visit a c. 16:4
life is...like a froward c. 316:4
no c. is born a criminal 302:1
Train up a c. 36:13
Tuesday's c. is full of grace 8:3
unto us a c. is born 38:9

childhood: c. shews the man 218:2

childishness: Second c. and mere oblivion 266:3

Children: C. begin by loving 348:1
c. cried in the streets 223:2
c. died in the streets 14:1
c....hostages to fortune 17:8
c. of a larger growth 88:2
c. of a larger growth 121:2
devour each of her c. 329:4
dogs than of their c. 234:8
not much about having c.; 197:3
Parents...last people...to have c. 71:13

Suffer the little c. 44:15

chill: bitter c. it was 179:8

chimes: heard the c. at midnight 270:12

CHIMNEY: HORSES WEDGED IN A C. 223:1

chivalrie: He loved c. 84:8

chivalry: age of c. is gone 64:1

choice: you takes your c. 10:6

choirs: Bare ruined c. 287:5

choose: c. a member indeed 64:5
c. / Perfection of the life 356:3

chord: struck one c. 247:1

chosen: few are c. 44:4

Christ: all things through C. 48:5
C. the tiger 126:8
C. were to come to-day 79:16
in the bowels of C. 103:11
See see where C.'s blood 205:5

Christe: C. receive thy saule 21:4

Christendom: wisest fool in C. 156:6

Christian: C. ideal has not been tried 89:11
Onward! C. soldiers 23:2

Christianity: C. is part of the Common Law 150:2
decay of C. 256:10
local cult called C. 151:6
loving C. better than Truth 96:9
not merely sound C. 196:10

Christians: C. have burnt each other 73:10

Christmas: C. comes but once a year 325:5
C. Day in the Workhouse 298:6
C. is coming 6:2
night before C. 221:3

chronicle: c. of wasted time 287:6

church: As some to c. repair 241:1
buttress of the c. 211:2
C.'s one foundation / Is Jesus 310:8
I will build my c. 43:14
martyrs is the seed of the c. 319:11

no salvation outside the c. 14:10

no salvation outside the C. 105:1

churches: chapels had been c. 278:8
C. built to please the priest 67:10

cigar: good c. is a Smoke 186:2
good five-cent c. 207:2

Cinara: dear C. was my queen 165:7

Cinema: C. is truth twenty-four times 144:7

circenses: Panem et c. 178:7

circle: God . . . a c. of which the centre 9:8

Circumlocution: C. Office was beforehand 110:13

circumspice: requiris, c. 355:2

circumstances: concatenation of c. 338:5

circuses: Bread and c. 178:7

cities: hum / Of human c. torture 73:4

citizen: c. of no mean city 46:13
c. of the world 114:1

citizens: fat and greasy c. 265:11
and the first c. Cain 101:8

city: and the first c. Cain 101:8
as it rains on the c. 329:8
C. is of Night 322:4
crowded c.'s horrible street 60:3
long in c. pent 183:1
long in populous C. pent 217:13
no mean c. 46:13
populous and a smoky c. 294:7
Unreal C. 127:8

civilization: botched c. 243:8
can't say c. don't advance 251:5
C. degrades the many 3:5
elements of modern c. 78:9
usual interval of c. 93:5
[Western c.] an excellent idea 139:12

civilized: force another to be c. 213:1
last thing c. by Man 211:10

colour: any c., so long as it's black 135:8

colours: All c. will agree 17:6
coat of many c. 30:6

column: fifth c. 219:4
London's c., pointing at the skies 240:3

come: ain't much dat don't c. out 152:6

Cannot c., lie follows 247:6

C. up and see me 341:8

men may c. and men may go 316:7

slow, or c. he fast 260:6

Comedies: C. of manners swiftly become obsolete 101:3

comedy: All I need to make a c. 84:2

catastrophe of the old c. 274:4

C. is medicine 149:3

c. to those that think 335:3

In the casual c. 356:9

comeliness: no form nor c. 39:4

cometh: no man c. unto the Father 46:7

comfort: a' the c. we're to get 69:6

Be of good c., Master Ridley 191:8

cold c. 273:15

comfortable: something more c. 152:5

coming: as their c. hither 275:2
cold c. they had 5:4
cold c. we had 126:11

commandments: perfectly to keep the c. 82:4

commencement: c. de la fin 315:4

commend: thy hands I c. my spirit 45:14

Comment: C. is free 259:2

commerce: equal to the whole of that c. 64:9
honour sinks where c. 146:8

commercial: memory of the c. classes 347:8

commit: c. his body to the ground 246:7
loves to c. eating 254:9

common: hard to say c. things 164:7

Commons: C., faithful to their system 202:9

common sense: betray'd me into c. 238:11

C. is the collection of prejudices 125:2

English ... bid adieu to ... c. 300:12

organized c. 168:9

Communism: C. is the illegitimate child 13:12

community: c. has a right to force 213:1

company: bear him c. 198:3
Crowds without c. 141:5
three is c. and two 345:12

compare: c. thee to a summer's day 286:13

c. / The prison where I live 282:9

not Reason and C. 51:5

Comparisons: C. are odorous 280:12

competition: c., the laws of death 255:7

complains: c. of his memory 191:5

complexion: Mislike me not for my c. 278:11

compliance: by a timely c., prevented 132:7

compliment: two months on a good c. 326:9

composed: Lipsius ... who c. a work 308:6

compromises: one finds certain c. 220:1

compulsion: fools by heavenly c. 274:3

concatenation: Fearful c. of circumstances 338:5

conceal: woman ... should c. 15:8

Conceit: Riches ... but C. 18:8

concentrates: c. his mind wonderfully 174:11

conclusion: could but spot a c. 224:1

conclusions: art of drawing
sufficient c. 72:1
jump to c. rarely alight 149:5

Concordia: C. discors 164:13

Condemn: C. the fault 278:1

condescends: loves and the other
who c. 320:4

conditions: sorts and c. of men
245:5

conduct: characters . . . result of
our c. 11:14

confederacy: dunces are all in c.
312:10

conference: naked into the c.
chamber 29:1

conflict: field of human c. 91:2
in armed c. 124:1

Confound: C. their politics 78:5

confounded: Confusion worse c.
217:3

Confusion: C. now hath made
276:14
C. worse confounded 217:3

congregation: face of this c.
245:10
latter has the largest c. 107:8

Congs: Kinquering C. 306:3

conjuring: Pason left c. 262:6

conquer: c. it than to know what
335:1
In this sign thou shalt c. 99:16

conquered: c. and peopled half
the world 262:3
c., O pale Galilean 314:2
I came, I saw, I c. 76:9
I will be c. 175:6
not yet c. one 237:9
perpetually to be c. 64:10
You have c., Galilean 177:11

conquering: See, the c. hero
comes 222:4

Conquerors: madmen . . . C. and
Kings 73:2

conquers: Love c. all 331:7

Conquest: Roman C. was,
however, a Good 263:4

conscience: catch the c. of the
king 267:21
c. doth make cowards 268:4
c. that it is wrong 20:5

c., when it has no soul 323:9
good c. on the proceeds 300:3
Science without c. 220:11
uncreated c. of my race 177:5

conscientious: c. man, when I
throw rocks 224:3

Consciousness: C. is a disease
327:3
C. reigns but does not govern
328:3

consent: 'I will ne'er c.' —
consented 73:12

consequences: there are c. 169:7

conservation: without the means
of its c. 64:2

Conservatism: C. discards
Prescription 114:4

Conservative: C. government is
an organized hypocrisy
114:13
C. government . . . Tory men
and Whig measures 114:5
c. when old 138:5
else a little C. 142:11

Conservatives: C. . . . the
stupidest party 212:5

consider: c. the end 135:3

considérer: c. la fin 135:3

consistency: c. is the hobgoblin
129:8

conspicuous: c. by its presence
256:2
C. consumption 329:1

Conspiracy: Indecency's C. of
Silence 290:9

constitution: c. is extremely well
334:13
genius of the C. 236:3
higher law than the C. 264:1

construe: c. things after their
own fashion 272:11

consume: c. happiness without
288:2

consummation: And c. comes
151:3

Consummatum: C. est 334:6

consumption: Conspicuous c.
329:1

contagion: c. of the world's slow
stain 291:9

contain: I c. multitudes 343:7

contemporaries: we shall all of us be c. 2:7

contempt: Silence is the supreme c. 256:5

contemptible: c. little army 348:10

content: lot is happy if you are c. 53:7

contests: mighty c. rise from trivial 242:9

contract: verbal c. isn't worth 147:1

contradict: Do I c. myself? / Very well then 343:7

contradiction: Physicians . . . brook no c. 338:10

contradictions: bundle of c. 97:11

contraries: Without c. is no progression 51:8

Contrariwise: C.,' continued Tweedledee 81:4

controversy: c. is either superfluous 225:11

Conventionality: C. is not morality 56:8

conversation: silence, that makes his c. 301:8

war: it ruins c. 135:4

Writing . . . different name for c. 307:11

convicted: c. of sickness, hunger 302:2

conviction: best lack all c. 357:12

convince: persuading others, we c. ourselves 178:3

cook: c. was a good cook 257:1

cookery: c. do 211:11

cooks: Many excellent c. are spoiled 140:2

Cool'd: C. a long age 181:7

cooperation: c. . . . the laws of life 255:7

coot: haunt of c. and hern 316:6

copier: mere c. of nature 250:6

Copper: Definitely, Lord C. 338:1

copulation: Birth, and c. and death 127:5

Let c. thrive 274:16

revolution without general c. 339:5

coral: bones are c. made 284:1

India's c. strand 154:11

corbies: I heard twa c. 22:2

cormorant: c. devouring Time 275:5

corn: amid the alien c. 181:14

make two ears of c. 311:7

corner: Sits the wind in that c. 280:11

world in ev'ry c. sing 158:4

Cornishmen: twenty thousand C. 153:4

coronets: Kind hearts are more than c. 317:12

corporation: expect a c. to have a conscience 323:9

corpse: make a lovely c. 111:6

correct: do the perfectly c. thing 288:8

Corridors: C. of Power 302:8

corroborative: Merely c. detail 143:6

corrupt: appointment by the c. few 289:14

Power tends to c. 1:3

Corruption: C., the most infallible symptom 141:10

corse: his c. to the rampart 350:10

Cortez: like stout C. 182:8

cosmopolitan: c. in the end 221:5

cottage: not his visage from our c. 286:10

cottages: c. princes' palaces 278:8

counsel: Dost sometimes c. take 242:11

counsellors: wisest of c., Time 235:1

count: Let me c. the ways 59:2

counted: stand up and be c. 227:6

countenance: damned disinheriting c. 297:3

counters: words are wise men's
c. 161:3
country: best c. ever is, at home
146:6
choose between . . . betraying
my c. 135:11
c. / Far beyond the stars
328:10
c. in town 207:4
c. is good for General Motors
349:6
C. of the Blind 340:9
die for one's c. 165:5
God made the c. 102:10
King and C. need you 10:8
my c. – all earthly things 306:6
My c. is the world 231:1
My c., 'tis of thee 300:10
no c. for old men 357:10
nothing good to be had in the
c. 154:2
our c., right or wrong 107:5
save in his own c. 43:10
Saviour of 'is c. 187:11
coupole: chantants dans la c.
329:7
Courage: C., brother 203:1
[C.] Grace under pressure
156:2
c. never to submit 216:1
screw your c. 276:7
courageous: captains c. 21:5
course: c. of true love 279:14
finished my c. 48:10
Court: C. of King's Bench, Den
of Thieves 94:6
courted: never be c. at all 77:5
Courts: C. for cowards were
erected 67:10
Courtship: C. to marriage 99:8
Covenants: C. without the sword
161:6
Cover: C. her face 338:9
covet: c. thy neighbour's house
30:17
coveted: c. his neighbour's goods
185:9
cow: milk the c. of the world
344:2
till the c. comes home 25:5

when she kissed her c. 312:3
coward: c. does it with a kiss
344:6
c. on instinct 269:18
c. towards Men 17:4
No c. soul is mine 57:2
cowards: conscience doth make
c. 268:4
Courts for c. were erected
67:10
C. die many times 273:1
cowslip: In a c.'s bell 284:7
coxcomb: c. ask two hundred
guineas 255:3
coyness: This c., Lady 208:2
Crabbed: C. age and youth
cannot 286:11
crack: c. of doom 277:8
c. your cheeks 274:6
cradle: c. endlessly rocking 343:2
rocks the c. . . . rules the world
334:8
craft: c. so long to lerne 86:6
Crafty: C. men contemn Studies
19:1
crainte: c. suit la crime 332:9
crawl: slimy things did c. 95:12
cream: queen of curds and c.
286:9
Create: my business is to C. 51:5
created: God c. the heaven and
the earth 29:3
Man has c. death 356:6
Creation: consulted me . . . upon
C. 4:3
opposition / To the facts of c.
138:10
creations: acts his own c. 61:4
creature: Not a c. was stirring
221:3
creatures: All c. great and small
3:10
credideritis: Nisi c. 14:11
Creditors: C. have better
memories 137:7
creeds: dust of c. outworn 295:2
so many c. 344:4
strewn with c. 20:6
Creeps: C. in this petty pace
277:13

crème: c. de la crème 304:2
crew: admit me of thy c. 214:10
cricket: c. on the hearth 214:5
cried: c. all the way to the bank
194:7
  when he c. the little children
died 14:1
crime: c. . . . desire for aesthetic
expression 337:11
  c. of being a young man 236:1
  c. to love too well 239:4
  Fear follows c. 332:9
  Lady, were no c. 208:2
  old Custom, legal C. 292:9
  punishment fit the c. 143:5
crimes: c., follies, and
misfortunes 141:9
  C., like virtues 131:9
  liberty! what c. are committed
251:10
  tableau of c. and misfortunes
332:5
  tissue of c. 145:12
criminal: c. class I am of it
107:4
  No child is born a c. 302:1
Crispin: upon Saint C.'s Day
271:8
critic: [c.] louse in the locks
319:6
critical: nothing if not c. 281:3
criticism: c.; a disinterested
endeavour 13:8
  People ask you for c. 210:5
criticize: don't c. / What you
can't understand 123:8
criticizing: c. takes away from
us 189:1
Critics: C. like me shall make it
Prose 239:1
  lot of c. is to be remembered
221:6
  Turn'd C. next 240:9
Crocodile: cruel crafty C. 305:7
Cromwell: [C.] a brave bad man
92:15
  C. guiltless of his country's
148:4
  C. knocked about 196:6

crooked: should I strive to set
the c. 222:8
Cross: survey the wondrous C.
337:8
crowd: crucified, the c. will
always save 95:4
  madding c.'s ignoble strife
148:6
  Out of the c. a mistress 292:6
crowded: c. on a velvet cushion
322:8
Crowdieknowe: men o' C. 201:4
Crowds: C. without company
141:5
crown: fruition of an earthly c.
206:4
  head that wears a c. 270:10
crowns: c. resign to call thee
mine 327:6
Crucible: America is God's C.
359:6
Crucified: c. 'twixt a smile and
whimper 294:8
cruel: c. only to be kind 269:2
cruellest: c. month, breeding /
Lilacs 127:6
cruelty: full / Of direst c. 276:1
crumb: craved no c. 144:3
cry: too old to c. 196:2
crying: no use c. over spilt milk
210:7
Crystal: Ring out ye C. spheres
215:9
cuccu: Lhude sing c. 9:4
cuckold: whore and a c. 285:3
cuckoo: c.: O word of fear 275:9
  c. shouts all day 165:10
  what did they produce? The c.
clock 339:6
Cui: *C. bono* 92:11
culpa: *felix* c. 219:3
  Mea c. 209:9
cult: local c. called Christianity
151:6
Cultivate: C. simplicity,
Coleridge 189:8
cultiver: *c. notre jardin* 332:1
culture: great aim of c. 13:7
  hear anyone talk of C. 144:10
  ladies who pursue C. 341:10

Cultures: Two C. 302:9

cunningly: little world made c. 117:4

cup: let this c. pass 44:9
Life's enchanted c. 72:12

Cupid: wing'd C. painted blind 279:15

cupiditas: *Radix malorum est c.* 85:12

curate: sit upon the c.'s knee 88:11

curates: preached to death by wild c. 301:7

cure: kings can cause or c. 146:7
labour against our own c. 58:9
no c. for birth and death 257:8

curfew: c. tolls the knell 148:3

curious: c. habits of man 243:10
Tammie glowr'd, amaz'd, and c. 68:8

Curiouser: C. and curiouser 80:1

currency: Debasing the moral c. 125:8

currite: *c., noctis equi* 205:4

curs: common cry of c. 266:11

curse: bless them that c. 42:2
C. God, and die 33:8
c. is come upon me 317:14
c. the darkness 309:3
I know how to c. 283:15

Curses: C. are like young chickens 303:9

curtain: Draw the c. 249:2
Iron C. has descended 91:7

curteisie: honour, fredom and c. 84:8

Curtsied: C. when you have 283:16

custodiet: *quis c. ipsos / Custodes* 178:5

custom: c. / More honoured 267:9
c. stale / Her infinite variety 264:15
C., that unwritten law 106:4
old C., legal Crime 292:9
Without the aid of ... c. 154:3

customer: c. is always right 263:2

Cut: C. is the branch 205:6

most unkindest c. of all 273:9

Cutty-sark: Weel done, C. 68:9

cynic: c. . . . knows the price 346:11

Cynicism: C. is intellectual dandyism 211:13

cypress: sad c. let me be laid 285:16

Daddy: D., daddy, you bastard 236:8

Daffodil: D. bulbs instead of balls 127:12

daffodils: host of golden d. 351:9

daft: thinks the tither d. 261:4

dagger: d. which I see before me / The handle toward my hand? 276:8

dalliance: silken d. in the wardrobe 271:1

dammed: saved by being d. 163:4

Damn: D. braces 52:10
I don't give a d. 139:8
praises one another d. 355:7

damn'd: Faustus must be d. 205:4

damned: Better be d. than mentioned not 235:8
D. from here to Eternity 186:9
d. if I see how the helican 212:1
d. nice thing 340:1
must be d. perpetually 205:3
one d. thing after another 166:7
Out, d. spot 277:7

Dan: D. even to Beer-sheba 32:4

Danaos: *timeo D.* 330:11

dance: best d. e'er cam to the Land 66:6
d. in the old dame yet 206:8
dancer from the d. 355:10
will you join the d. 80:12

danced: d. by the light 193:3

dancer: know the d. from the dance 355:10

dances: No sober man 92:12

dancing: d. days are gone 358:3
D. . . . of savage origin 65:7
manners of a d. master 173:3

dandyism: Cynicism is intellectual d. 211:13

danger: conquer without d. 100:2

this nettle, d. 269:17

dangerous: bad, and d. to know 189:2

d. to meet it alone 341:10

such men are d. 272:9

dangerously: Live d. 227:1

Daniel: D. come to judgement 279:4

dappled: for d. things 164:3

dare: d. do all that may 276:6

d. to eat a peach 127:1

Love that I d. not speak 118:8

dares: Who d. do more is none 276:6

Darien: upon a peak in D. 182:8

daring: d. fellow is the jewel 314:6

d. is to know how far 95:1

d. young man 194:6

dark: colours . . . agree in the d. 17:6

D. Continent 306:11

go home in the d. 157:2

great leap in the d. 161:8

O d., dark, dark 218:6

darker: Do not let us speak of d. days 91:4

Darkling: D. I listen 181:13

on a dark plain 12:6

darkness: candle than curse the d. 309:3

cast away the works of d. 245:6

d. comprehended it not 45:16

encounter d. as a bride 278:4

life as it closes / Is d. 313:7

Lighten our d. 245:2

people that walked in d. 38:8

prince of d. is a gentleman 274:11

rather d. visible 215:13

Universal D. buries All 239:3

world to d. and to me 148:3

darling: Charlie he's my d. 66:3

Charlie is my d. 162:1

date: keep them up to d. 288:7

daughter: Don't put your d. 101:7

O my d. 278:14

daughters: O ye d. of Jerusalem 38:1

dauntless: so d. in war 260:7

dauphin: daylight's d. 164:4

lichter nor a d. 55:2

David: D. his ten thousands 32:11

dawn: d. comes up like thunder 187:5

Rosy-fingered d. 162:8

day: every dog has his d. 54:8

what a d. may bring 37:2

Without all hope of d. 218:6

daylight: naked and open d. 17:2

days: d. of our glory 76:1

d. of wine and roses 118:11

lov'd / Three whole a. together 311:2

not dark d.; these are great 91:4

Ten D. that Shook 249:10

Thirty d. hath November 147:7

daysyes: Swiche as men callen d. 86:5

dazzle: mine eyes d. 338:9

dead: besides, the wench is d. 206:1

bugles over the rich D. 57:5

D.! and . . . never called 351:6

d. ere his prime 215:2

D. for a ducat 268:13

d. selves to higher things 317:4

d. we owe nothing but truth 332:8

Down among the d. men 123:2

Either he's d. or my watch 208:7

good Indian is a d. Indian 296:4

happy until he is d. 303:1

I am d. and opened 209:3

Mistah Kurtz—he d. 99:13

never know that he is d. 72:4

number of the d. 106:6

quick and the d. 244:9

saw a d. man win a fight 20:9

sea shall give up her d. 246:8

talk with the departed d. 293:5

when you're d. 159:4

you remind me of the d. 258:3

deadly: more d. than the male 186:8

deal: new d. for the American people 252:1

death: afraid of d., as ashamed 58:7

Any man's d. diminishes me 116:5

back resounded D. 217:2

Be absolute for d. 278:3

Brought D. into the World 215:11

build your ship of d. 192:2

but D. who comes 260:6

come away, d. 285:16

competition, the laws of d. 255:7

cry'd out D. 217:2

Dear, beauteous d. 328:8

d. after life, does greatly please 305:8

D. and life were not 358:6

D. be not proud 117:5

d. does not surprise 135:1

D. goes dogging 156:5

d. had undone so many 127:8

D. has a thousand doors 210:4

d. hath ten thousand several doors 338:8

D. — / He kindly stopped 113:2

D. in the front 72:10

d. is slumber 294:1

d. is the cure of all diseases 58:9

D. is the privilege 254:7

D. is the veil 295:4

d. lie heavily 263:11

D. lies dead 313:10

D. . . . like a mole 158:8

d. must be distinguished from dying 301:10

d. reveals the eminent 290:8

d. shall be no more 117:6

d. shall have no dominion 321:2

d., the destroyer of worlds 29:2

d. they were not divided 32:12

d. to the bone 356:6

D. tramples it to fragments 291:11

d., where is thy sting 47:4

D., where is thy sting-a-ling-a-ling 8:6

enormously improved by d. 256:8

except d. and taxes 137:10

Fear d.? — to feel the fog 61:10

fed on the fullness of d. 314:2

first d., there is no other 321:7

half in love with easeful D. 181:13

in love with d., to think 291:7

kingly D. / Keeps his pale court 291:8

kiss of d. 300:1

last enemy . . . is d. 47:2

liberty, or give me d. 157:4

my d. was an exaggeration 326:8

never taste of d. but once 273:1

new terrors of d. 10:11

not born for d. 181:14

Pale D., with impartial foot 165:1

perchance of D., / But certainly 322:4

rendezvous with D. 262:2

sat on him was D. 49:9

thick shapes of human d. 294:9

This fell sergeant, d. 269:10

This is d., / To die 199:1

till d. us do part 245:13

up the line to d. 258:1

valley of the shadow of d. 34:3

wages of sin is d. 46:14

way to dusty d. 277:13

we are in d. 246:6

with this life, this d. 357:3

wonderful is D. 292:4

Debasing: D. the moral currency 125:8

debonaire: kaught is d. 86:10

Debt: National D. is a very Good 263:7

debtors: better memories than d. 137:7

decay: human things are subject to d. 121:10
muddy vesture of d. 279:6
our love hath no d. 116:1
pale court in beauty and d. 291:8

deceitful: d. above all things 40:4

deceive: d. one's self 108:9
first we practise to d. 260:8
Oh, don't d. me 6:5

deceived: possession of being well d. 312:9

deceiver: gay d. 97:8

deceivers: Men were d. ever 280:10

Decencies: Content to dwell in D. 239:8

Decency: D. is Indecency's Conspiracy 290:9
want of d. is want of sense 253:2

decent: d. means poor 234:2
d. obscurity of a learned 141:7

declare: d. except my genius 348:8

decline: idea of writing the d. and fall 141:6

declined: d. / Into the vale of years 281:7

decorous: monotony of a d. age 129:4

decorum: Dulce et d. 165:5

decoyed: fools d. into our condition 234:10

deed: clears us of this d. 276:11
d. without a name 277:5
get the d. 223:5
shines a good d. 279:8
thought, word, and d. 82:4

deep: commit his body to the d. 246:8
D. calleth unto deep 34:7
D. in the shady sadness 180:4
lie too d. for tears 352:9
upon the face of the d. 29:3

deep-delved: d. earth 181:7

deer: a-chasing the d. 68:2

defeat: possibilities of d. 330:3

defeated: History to the d. 14:6

defect: chief d. of Henry King 27:1

defend: d. to the death your right 333:7
on l'attaque il se d. 5:11

definite: maybe 146:13

deform: d. the human race 50:10

degeneration: from barbarism to d. 93:5

degree: Take but d. away 285:2

deid: lang time d. 5:9
they're a' d. 7:5

delay: sweet reluctant amorous d. 217:7

Delenda: D. est Carthago 82:5

deliberate: both d., the love is slight 205:9

deliberates: woman that d. is lost 1:8

deliciously: d. aged and sad 288:10

Delight: comest thou, / Spirit of D. 295:8
Energy is Eternal D. 51:9
give d. and hurt not 284:3
Shepherd's d. 5:5
very temple of D. 181:5

delights: To scorn yet 215:4

delirium: d. of the brave 358:2

deliver: d. / Their land from error's 154:11
pestilence, good Lord, d. us 224:8

déluge: Après nous le d. 238:7

demented: d. with the mania of owning 343:6

democracies: d. against despots — suspicion 108:10

democracy: cycle d. is built on 349:2
D. . . . government by the uneducated 90:2
d. in order to have a revolution 89:10
D. substitutes election by the incompetent 289:14

despots: democracies against
d. — suspicion 108:10

Destiny: belief in a brute Fate or
D. 130:2

Character is d. 228:1

d.. And it is white 131:6

destroy: whom God wishes to d.
131:3

destroyer: death, the d. of worlds
29:2

D. and preserver; hear 294:4

destruction: All other things, to
their d. 116:1

D. in the rear 72:10

D. with destruction to destroy
217:17

Pride goeth before d. 36:12

detail: corroborative d., intended
143:6

determined: d. to prove a villain
282:12

detest: but they d. at leisure 75:4

deus: *puto d. fio* 329:9

deviates: never d. into sense
121:12

Devil: And the D. did grin 96:3

apology for the d. 71:10

A walking the D. is gone 96:2

D. always builds a chapel
107:8

d. can cite Scripture 278:10

d. damn thee black 277:10

d. should have all the good
tunes 160:4

d.'s leavings 312:14

D. with Devil damn'd 216:11

renounce the d. and all his
works 82:3

world, the flesh and the d.
245:3

devilish: most d. when
respectable 58:11

Devils: at liberty when of D.
51:10

dewdrop: d. on its perilous way
182:3

diamond: Better a d. with a flaw
98:14

d. . . . lasts forever 198:5

Diana: burnt the Temple of D.
58:6

diary: never travel without my d.
346:3

dice: never believe that God
plays d. 125:1

dickens: cannot tell what the d.
279:11

dictatorship: d. of the proletariat
209:1

did: But he d. for them both
258:4

die: and gladly d. 309:9

as natural to d. 17:5

bad d. late 107:6

believe they d. to vex me
210:11

Curse God, and d. 33:8

Death, thou shalt d. 117:6

depart is to d. a little 150:7

d. . . . an awfully big adventure
23:6

d., and go we know not where
278:5

d. before they sing 96:5

d. beyond my means 348:7

d. for one's country 165:5

d. is cast 76:8

D., my dear Doctor 231:5

for to-morrow we shall d.
38:11

If I should d. 57:9

Lives to d. another day 166:1

love one another or d. 14:5

not altogether d. 165:6

should d. before I wake 8:5

someday d., which is not so
192:10

Their's but to do and d. 316:9

those about to d. salute thee
311:5

To d. and know it 199:1

To d.: to sleep 268:1

we d. in earnest 249:7

We shall d. alone 232:9

died: d. the little children cried
223:2

dog it was that d. 146:3

I had d. for thee 32:15

Men have d. from time 266:6

should have d. hereafter 277:13

diem: *Carpe d.* 165:4

dies: artist d. with me 225:2
d. to himself unknown 263:11
Every moment d. a man 319:5
gods love d. young 211:4
not necessarily true because a man d. 348:9
young person who ... d. 15:4

dieted: not be d. with praise 181:2

Dieu: *D. est mort* 225:3
D. et mon droit 225:1
Si D. n'existait pas 332:3
Verbe, c'est 166:10

differ: all things d., all agree 242:14

difficult: d.; and left untried 89:11
D. do you call it 175:8
D. things take a long time 6:4
it is d. to speak 65:3

difficulties: Ten thousand d. do not make 225:9

digest: learn and inwardly d. them 245:7

digestion: d. is the great secret of life 301:2
prove in d. sour 282:1

dignity: joyless d. to starve 302:7

Digressions: D., incontestably, are the sunshine 308:3

diminishes: death d. me 116:5

dimittis: *Nunc d.* 334:2

dine: gang and d. the day 22:2
jury-men may d. 242:12

dinner: pleased when he has a good d. 175:9
want d. do not ring 20:3

dinner-bell: tocsin of the soul — the d. 74:10

diplomacy: d. shall proceed always frankly 350:1

diplomat: d. ... nothing but a head-waiter 327:8

dire: *ennuyer est ... de tout d.* 333:1

direction: chance, d. which thou canst not see 241:11

directions: rode madly off in all d. 192:9

dirt: painted child of d. 240:1

Dis: *D. aliter visum* 330:12

disagreeable:
Matrimony ... always d. 15:2
things d. to myself 300:13

disappointing: As for d. them 146:4

disapprove: d. of what you say 333:7

disbelief: willing suspension of d. 96:10

discontent: d. / Made glorious summer 282:10

discord: d., harmony not understood 241:11
hark what d. follows 285:2
Harmony in d. 164:13

discors: *Concordia* 164:13

discourse: child ... provision for d. 16:4

discoverers: ill d. that think 16:11

discretion: Philosophy is nothing but d. 262:8

disdain: little d. is not amiss 99:10
more love or more d. 78:3

disease: Consciousness is a d. 327:3
d. is incurable 270:8
d. of modern life 13:2

diseased: minister to a mind d. 277:12

diseases: death is the cure of all d. 58:9
d. require desperate remedies 131:12

disgrace: d. and ignominy of our natures 58:7

disgruntled: if not actually d. 350:6

disguise: naked is the best d. 99:3

dish: makes a d. a feast 159:2

disinheriting: damned d. countenance 297:3

dislike: people whom we
personally d. 345:8

disliked: get ourselves rather d.
244:2

dislikings: of likings and d. 189:3

Dismal: [Economics] The D.
Science 79:8

disobedience: By one man's d.
lost 218:1

Of Man's First D. 215:11

disorder: sweet d. in the dress
159:6

disposes: God d. 184:7

dispraised: d., is the most perfect
praise 175:14

disputed: Facts ... down a be d.
66:8

Disraeli: [D.] ... worships his
creator 56:4

dissatisfied: Not one is d. 343:6

dissect: murder to d. 354:7

dissent: protestantism ... a sort
of d. 64:11

dissidence: d. of dissent 64:11

dissimilar: For one another,
though d. 292:5

dissipation: d. without pleasure
141:5

dissociation: d. of sensibility
127:13

dissolve: d., and quite forget
181:9

distance: d. lends enchantment
to the view 77:6

distinguished: d. thing 170:7

distressful: most d. country 9:2

distribution: same d. of the
necessities 299:6

ditch: blind man's d. 356:7

great d. from all the world
104:4

divided: death they were not d.
32:12

house be d. against itself 44:13

dividing: by d. we fall 113:5

divine: human form d. 53:4

some are fou o' love d. 67:1

to forgive, d. 241:3

divinity: d. doth hedge a king
269:4

d. in odd numbers 279:13

d. that shapes our ends 269:7

surely a piece of d. in us 58:8

divisions: How many d. has *he*
got 306:9

Do: D. as I say, not as I do
263:1

D. other men, for they 111:5

I am to do what I please
137:14

not as we d. 53:6

doctors: drunkards than old d.
137:13

doctrine: Not for the d. 241:1

prove their d. orthodox 70:12

Dodger: The artful D. 111:15

dog: As to a d.'s tail 358:5

beaten d. beneath the hail
235:4

better than his d. 318:2

Beware of the d. 235:2

called a d. because I fawn
114:2

d. it was that died 146:3

d. starv'd at his master's gate
51:1

d.'s walking on his hinder
173:7

every d. has his day 54:8

fleas is good fer a d. 341:9

To his d., every man is
Napoleon 168:7

very flea of his d. 176:3

whose d. are you? 240:6

doggedly: set himself d. to it
173:1

dogs: curious habits of d. 243:10

let slip the d. of war 273:3

straw d. 190:8

doing: see what she's d. 248:1

what everyone is d. 158:1

dollar: almighty d. 169:9

almighty d. 9:5

Dolores: sanguine and subtle D.
313:6

dolphin-torn: d., that gong-
tormented 356:2

dome: d. of many-coloured glass
291:11

Domestic: D. happiness, thou only bliss 102:13

dominion: death shall have no d. 321:2

dominions: d., on which the sun never 227:9

Dominus: D. vobiscum 209:8

dona: d. ferentis 330:11

done: d., it is needless to speak about 98:3
d. when 'tis done 276:3
ever d. in this world 288:13
read, but what we have d. 184:6

Dong: D.! – the Dong 192:12

Donne: D.'s verses are like the peace 170:3

donnée: his idea, his d 170:5

doom: crack of d. 277:6

Doon: braes o' bonny D. 69:10

door: Get up and bar the d. 21:2
knock at the d. 189:5

doors: d. to let out life 210:4
ten thousand several d. 338:8
ye everlasting d. 34:5

double: deep peace of the d. bed 77:2
D., double, toil and trouble 277:3

Doublethink: D. means the power of holding 229:4

doubt: difficulties do not make one d. 225:9
d. diversified by faith 59:8
d., to prove that faith exists 59:9
more faith in honest d. 317:9
No possible d. whatever 142:5
not d. is dead faith 327:2
speak out and remove all d. 196:1
troubled with religious d. 88:11

doubted: Never d. clouds would break 61:15

doubts: end in d. 16:8

dove: gently as any sucking d. 279:16
wings like a d. 35:1

down: at night a bed of d. 354:9

D. among the dead men 123:2
d. need fear no fall 63:9
d. to the seas again 209:5

downstairs: you kick me d. 49:14

doxy: another man's d. 335:11

drag: Why d. in Velasquez 342:4

Drake: D. he's in his hammock 225:5

Drama: D. is life with the dull bits 160:8

Drang: Sturm und D. 179:2

drappie: d. in our e'e 69:9

draught: d. of vintage 181:7

draw: can ye d. but twenty miles 206:6
d. more than a hundred 166:4

drawers: d. of water 31:11

dreadfully: [Brigham Young] is d. married 336:2

Dreadnoughts: two D.; and dukes are 196:8

dream: beyond the shadow of a d. 179:7
dream'd a dreary d. 20:9
d. that I am home 134:2
if I d. I have you 116:8
If you can d. 187:1
I have a d. 185:5
love's young d. 221:8
old men shall d. dreams 40:11
say what d. it was 280:4
To sleep: perchance to d. 268:1
vision, or a waking d. 182:1
wrecks of a dissolving d. 293:1

dreamer: d. of dreams 31:10
D. of dreams 222:8
poet and the d. 180:3

dreams: d., wherewith they weave 180:1
Real are the d. of Gods 180:6
stuff / As d. are made on 284:4
tread on my d. 357:2

dress: Language is the d. of thought 172:5

dressed: d. up with nowhere to go 342:7

Drink: D. deep, or taste not 240:10

d. of a hundred good
  symptoms 243:2
forgive my friends for d. 300:7
I am d., Egypt 265:1
immortality . . . by not d. 4:8
in d., / Hills of home 309:8
it had a d. fall 285:10
lips of d. men 13:5
not the d. for a faith 320:1
unconscionable time d. 84:5
each: From e. according to his
  abilities 208:11
ear: e. / Of him that hears it
  275:8
reasonable good e. in music
  280:3
right sow by the e. 156:10
with a flea in's e. 25:3
early: e. to rise 137:6
e. I seek thee 35:2
good die e. 107:6
ears: bless our human e. 215:9
Jug' to dirty e. 127:9
lend me your e. 273:5
earth: All people that on e.
  184:13
deep-delved e. 181:7
E. bless the Lord 244:8
E. felt the wound 217:14
E. has not anything to show
  353:10
e. is the Lord's 34:4
e. must borrow its mirth 344:3
e. shall be filled with the glory
  3:4
E.'s the right place for love
  138:1
E., thou bonnie broukit bairn
  201:3
e. to earth 246:7
e. was without form 29:3
e. will hold us also 7:2
faults . . . the e. covereth 248:7
girdle round about the e. 280:2
I will move the e. 11:1
let the e. rejoice 33:3
new heaven and a new e.
  49:11
nor e. two masters 3:9
replenish the e. 29:6

Rolled round in e.'s diurnal
  353:8
salt of the e. 42:1
scum of the e. 340:5
snug little farm the E. 96:2
touch of e. 316:10
two paces of the vilest e.
  270:5
way of all the e. 31:12
While the e. remaineth 30:2
earthly: all e. things above 306:6
earthquake: Lord was not in the
  e. 33:1
ease: e. his lot by all possible
  323:11
e. in writing comes from art
  241:2
take mine e. at mine inn 270:2
easier: e. to conquer it than
  335:1
East: [E.] easier to conquer
  335:1
E. is East 186:1
gorgeous E. with richest hand
  216:6
It is the E. 283:2
Easy: E. live and quiet die
  260:11
If to do were as e. 278:8
rack of a too e. chair 238:12
eat: and I did e. 29:9
cannot e. that want it 67:6
Let us e. and drink 38:11
One should e. to live 219:5
Tell me what you e. 56:5
'eathen: 'e. in 'is blindness 186:6
eating: loves to commit e. 254:9
eats: Man is what he e. 132:3
whatever Miss T e. 108:6
Ecce: *E. homo* 334:5
Ecclefechan: kent that E. stood
  201:8
echo: Sound must seem an e.
  241:2
Eclipse: Irrecoverably dark, total
  E. 218:6
Economics: [E.] The Dismal
  Science 79:8
it is bad e. 252:3

economists: sophisters, e. and
calculators 64:1
Economy: E. is going without
163:8
fear of Political E. 263:7
wrote 'Principles of Political
E.' 28:4
Ecrasez: *E. l'infâme* 333:4
Eden: This other E. 282:3
Through E. took their solitary
217:18
Editor: E.: a person employed
166:8
education: By e. most have been
misled 121:7
E. . . . disguises from the
foolish 50:2
E. is an admirable thing 344:8
E. is what survives 299:1
E. makes a people easy to lead
58:1
e. of the heart 261:7
race between e. and
catastrophe 340:11
roots of e. are bitter 11:6
educe: e. the man 60:11
Edward: E.! Edward 21:1
effect: don't know what e. these
men 340:4
e., / Whose cause is God
103:1
effort: written without e. 175:10
Egalité: *Liberté E. Fraternité* 8:1
egg: e. without salt 187:9
Everything from an e. 153:2
got a bad e. 248:4
hairless as an e. 159:7
ego: *Et in Arcadia* e. 6:8
Egypt: dying, E., dying 265:1
eight: Pieces of e. 310:1
Eildon: riding down by the E.
tree 21:9
Einstein: Let E. be 306:8
Eisen: *Blut und E.* 50:6
election: e. by the incompetent
many 289:14
electric: touch was as e. poison
292:7
elegant: It's so e. / So intelligent
127:10

Elementary: E.,' said he 119:1
elements: e. / So mix'd in him
273:12
elephants: women and e. never
forget 257:2
Elfland: horns of E. faintly
blowing 318:7
Elginbrodde: Here lie I, Martin
E. 202:5
éloquence: *Prends l'é.* 329:5
silence hath more e. 324:12
Take e. and wring its neck
329:5
else: happening to someone e.
251:7
Elysium: *Tochter aus E.* 258:5
embarrassment: e. on being left
alone together 188:9
embrace: none I think do there
e. 208:5
whether I e. your lordship's
348:11
emotion: e. recollected in
tranquillity 354:8
escape from e. 128:1
emotions: e. from A to B 232:2
waste-paper basket of the e.
338:3
emperor: e. and clown 181:14
E. or nothing 54:7
Empire: Britain has lost an E.
1:2
found a great e. 299:8
empires: faiths and e. gleam
293:1
Hatching vain E. 216:10
Vaster than e., and more slow
208:3
employment: man who gives me
e. 141:4
enchantment: lends e. to the
view 77:6
encourage: to e. the others
331:13
encourager: *pour e. les autres*
331:13
encumbers: e. him with help
173:2
end: beginning of the e. 315:4
consider the e. 135:3

e. in certainties 16:8
e. of all our exploring 126:7
e. of the beginning 91:6
God be at my e. 7:3
In my beginning is my e. 126:5
Man's chief e. is to glorify God
82:2
there's an e. on't 174:1
world will e. in fire 138:4
world without e. 244:7
ended: good e. happily 346:2
ends: Everything is an e. 25:1
endure: better to e. it 172:11
e. / Their going mere 275:2
Youth's a stuff will not e.
285:14
endured: much is to be e. 172:7
enemies: choice of his e. 347:1
Love your e. 42:2
Love your e. 45:8
make my e. ridiculous 333:5
enemy: effect . . . on the e., but
340:4
e. you killed, my friend 230:5
last e. that shall be destroyed
47:2
Man is not the e. of Man
230:12
O mine e. 33:2
see / No e. / But winter
265:12
Energy: E. is Eternal Delight
51:9
enfants: *ces voix d'e.* 329:7
Les e. terribles 140:5
engagement: owing to a
subsequent e. 348:5
engine: e. that moves 152:3
Wit's an unruly e. 158:5
engineer: sometimes the e. 158:5
Engines: E. more keen than ever
207:9
England: always be an E. 232:4
Bible made E. 167:4
E. and Saint George 271:4
E. bore, shaped, made aware
57:10
E. . . . comfortable time-lag of
fifty 340:13
E. expects 224:12

E. has saved herself by 236:5
E. . . . hast been my cradle
292:1
E. hath need of thee 354:5
E., home and beauty 55:5
E. is a nation of shopkeepers
223:10
E. is a paradise for women
70:7
E. is merely an island of beef
204:4
E. is not all the world 209:2
E. is the paradise of women
134:7
[E.] it is considered good to
kill 331:13
E. . . . mother of Parliaments
56:3
E.'s green and pleasant 52:2
E.'s mountains green 51:11
E.'s roast beef 132:6
E. will have her neck wrung
91:5
gentlemen in E. now a-bed
271:8
in E. a particular bashfulness
2:3
In E., justice is open 7:8
King born of all E. 204:2
Liberty was born in E. 332:6
not suffer E. to be the
workshop 114:11
Oh, to be in E. 60:7
old E.'s winding sheet 51:2
only E. know 186:7
people of E. that never 89:3
perfidious E. 54:10
road that leads him to E.
173:6
Slaves cannot breathe in E.
102:12
That is for ever E. 57:9
That knuckle-end of E. 301:5
this realm, this E. 282:5
Ye Mariners of E. 77:7
English: breathing E. air 57:10
disasters of E. history 337:10
E. . . . act with the barbarity
300:12

E. are mentioned in the Bible
326:2

[E.] conquered . . . half the
world 262:3

E. . . . least . . . philosophers
19:12

E. . . . little . . . inferior to the
Scotch 227:8

E. . . . no respect for their
language 290:14

E. public never forgives 348:4

E. tongue a gallimaufry 305:13

rolling E. road 89:1

Englishman: E. as ever coveted
185:9

E. in the wrong 290:12

E. is to belong to 224:2

E. thinks he is moral 289:8

E. to open his mouth 290:14

in Europe, and not one E.
335:5

remains an E. 142:9

vain, ill-natur'd thing, an E.
107:9

Englishmen: characteristic virtue
of E. 315:9

enigma: mystery inside an e.
90:9

enjoy: better to e. life 172:11

don't have to go out and e.
300:9

e. it while I can 302:5

to e. him forever 82:2

enjoy'd: all times I have e. 319:1

warm and still to be e. 180:12

enjoyed: little to be e. 172:7

enmities: More substance in our
e. 357:7

enough: doesn't go far e. 111:9

enslave: but impossible to e.
58:1

enslaved: e. by another Man's
51:5

enthusiasm: forgives — youth,
power, and e. 348:4

épater: é. le bourgeois 24:6

Epigram: E.? a dwarfish whole
96:4

epigrams: tempered by e. 79:4

epitaphs: nice derangement of e.
296:10

of worms and e. 282:6

Eppur: E. si muove 139:11

equal: all men are created e.
195:5

all men are created e. 9:12

created free and e. 195:3

sees with e. eye as God 241:8

some animals are more e. than
229:2

equi: noctis e. 205:4

Eremite: patient, sleepless E.
182:5

err: e. as grossly as the few
120:9

prefer / to e. / with her 10:5

To e. is human 241:3

wise may e. 2:9

erred: We have e. 244:5

error: e. is immense 54:2

inherent power denied to e.
212:8

errs: man aspires, he e. 145:1

Esau: E. my brother is a hairy
30:4

E. selleth his birthright 6:7

escape: e. from emotion 128:1

Establishment: ideals is not the
E. 27:6

estate: fourth e. of the realm
200:6

relief of man's e. 16:9

État: L'É. c'est moi 198:6

etchings: I'll bring the e. down
323:7

eternal: e. in the human breast
241:9

e. triangle 9:7

know that we are e. 306:2

pairt o' an e. mood 201:8

with th'E. to be deem'd /
Equal 216:7

Eternity: Damned from here to
E. 186:9

E. in an Hour 50:8

I saw E. the other night
328:13

small parenthesis in e. 58:3

Exit: E., pursued by a bear 286:6
exits: e. and their entrances
265:15
   men to take their e. 338:8
expect: folly to e. men to do
342:2
expellas: *Naturam e. furca*
164:12
expenditure: annual e. nineteen
110:5
expense: e. damnable 88:8
experience: Believe one who
   knows by e. 331:4
   E. keeps a dear school 136:10
   E., the name men give 347:10
   knowledge . . . beyond his e.
   196:11
   triumph of hope over e. 174:2
experiment: desist from the e.
189:4
expert: e. . . . has made all the
   mistakes 53:9
   e. . . . knows more and more
   70:10
Experto: *E. credite* 331:4
explanation: inaccuracy . . . saves
   tons of e. 256:7
exploration: shall not cease from
   e. 126:7
express'd: ne'er so well e. 240:11
expression: not the e. of
   personality 128:1
extinguished: Nature
   is . . . seldom e. 18:9
extra: *Salus e. ecclesiam* 14:10
extraordinary: behaving in this e.
   manner 310:9
extreme: For e. illnesses 160:7
Extremes: aye be whaur / E.
   meet 201:5
exuberance: e. of his own
   verbosity 115:4
eye: beaming in one e., and
   calculation 111:4
   Cast a cold e. 358:8
   great e. of heaven shined
   305:6
   harvest of a quiet e. 352:10
   He had but one e. 111:7
   If thine e. offend thee 43:17

less in this than meets the e.
22:5
eye-ball: We're e. to eye-ball
255:2
Eyeless: E. in Gaza 218:5
eyelids: tir'd e. upon tir'd eyes
318:3
Eyes: Black E., red Lips 207:9
   e. to the blind 33:11
   Have e. to wonder 287:7
   Love looks not with the e.
   279:15
   Mine e. have seen 166:3
   My mistress' e. are nothing
   287:1
   only with thine e. 176:4
   proud of those two e. 159:8
   see the whites of their e.
   248:5
   things not seen with e. 222:5
   upon her peerless e. 181:4
   will lift up mine e. 36:1
fable: life's sweet f. ends 103:9
face: boot stamping on a human
   f. 229:6
   everybody's f. but their own
   311:6
   f. that launch'd a thousand
   205:2
features / Of the same f. 353:3
   one to f. the world with 61:3
   your honest sonsie f. 69:1
faces: apparition of these f.
243:9
   know the f. I shall see 253:10
   old familiar f. 189:7
   sighin', cantin', grace-proud f.
   69:5
fact: any irritable reaching after
   f. 183:4
   Here or nowhere is the whole
   f. 130:5
   hypothesis an ugly f. 168:8
Facts: F. are chiels that winna
   ding 66:8
   f. are sacred 259:2
   F. do not cease to exist 168:6
   imagination for his f. 297:4
   more important than the f.
   355:4

fantastic: Giddy f. Poets 117:14
    light f. round 214:2
    light f. toe 214:9
fantastical: joys are but f. 116:8
Far: F. and few 193:1
    f., far better thing 113:1
    f. from me, let all profane
        331:3
    f. one can go too far 95:1
    so f. as it goes 111:9
farce: f. is over 249:2
fare-weel: f., and then for ever
        65:11
farewell: brother, hail and f. 83:1
    F., a long farewell 272:3
farm: snug little f. the Earth 96:2
farms: lass wi' the weel-stockit f.
        66:13
farts: smell of their own f. 14:7
Fascist: Every woman adores a
        F. 236:7
fashion: faithful to thee . . . in my
        f. 118:10
fast: grew f. and furious 68:8
Fasten: F. your seat belts 107:1
faster: Will you walk a little f.
        80:11
fastest: f. who travels alone
        187:14
fat: f. of the land 30:7
    in every f. man a thin one
        99:12
    men about me that are f.
        272:9
fatal: first strange and f.
        interview 116:10
Fate: belief in a brute F. or
        Destiny 130:2
    F. and character are the same
        228:1
    fears his f. too much 221:2
    master of my f. 156:4
    trouncings at the hands of f.
        298:5
    when f. summons 121:10
fates: silly horrors o' oor f. 202:1
Father: about my F.'s business
        45:6
    Child is f. of the Man 352:5
    f. was so ignorant 326:11

F. which art in heaven 42:5
fathom five thy f. lies 284:1
folly without f. bred 214:3
Honour thy f. 31:6
It is the f. with his child
        144:11
last see your f. 355:9
Lord and F. of mankind
        343:11
man did split his f.'s middle
        314:6
no longer have a f. 225:3
Throw bricks at your f. instead
        26:5
wise f. that knows 278:12
fathers: God of your f. 30:11
    iniquity of the f. 31:4
    our f. that begat us 41:1
fathom: Full f. five thy father
        284:1
    many f. deep I am in love
        266:7
fatted: Bring hither the f. calf
        42:12
fatuity: f. of idiots 300:12
fault: all f. who hath no fault
        316:10
    f. and not the actor 278:1
    f., dear Brutus 272:8
    happy f. 219:3
    Through my f. 209:9
Faultless: F. to a fault 61:13
faults: f. they commit, the earth
        248:7
Faustus: F. must be damn'd
        205:4
favour: to this f. she must come
        269:6
fear: arousing pity and f. 11:15
    F. and Loathing in Las Vegas
        322:1
    F. follows crime 332:9
    f. in a handful of dust 127:7
    f. it would make me
        conservative 138:5
    f. of little men 4:9
    f. the Greeks even 330:11
    hate whom they f. 130:8
    have to f. is fear itself 252:2
    love casteth out f. 49:6

one universal passion: f.
290:11

so long as they f. 1:1

fearful: lovely and a f. thing 74:5

fears: f. that I may cease 183:2

feast: great f. of learning 275:6
makes a dish a f. 159:2

feather: Stuck a f. in his cap
22:4

feathers: owl, for all his f. 179:8

feed: f. deep, deep 181:4
F. the brute 122:11

feel: tragedy to those that f.
335:3

feeling: f. too falsely disdained
295:13

feels: more affection than she f.
16:6

feet: And did those f. 51:11
cutting off our f. 312:15
f. firmly planted in the air
252:5
f. of him that bringeth 39:7
f. was I to the lame 33:11

felicity: Absent thee from f.
269:11
perfect bliss and sole f. 206:4
refined point of f. 312:9

felix: f. culpa 219:3

fell: f. like the stick 230:10

female: f. of the species 186:8
some f. errors find 242:10

femme: *Cherchez la f.* 122:9
elle est f. 249:5

Festina: F. lente 311:4

fever: f. call'd 'Living' 238:2
life's fitful f. 277:1
weariness, the f. and the fret
181:9

few: f., and they're a' deid 7:5
f. are chosen 44:4
governed by the f. 167:5
grossly as the f. 120:9
so many to so f. 91:2
We f., we happy few 271:7

Fiat: F. justitia 132:1

fickle: Woman is always f. 331:1

fiction: best thing in f. the
English 348:2
improbable f. 286:2

Poetry is the supreme f. 308:9
truth . . . / Stranger than f.
75:7

what F. means 346:2

fictions: Who says that f. only
158:9

fide: *Punica f.* 257:3

fidg'd: f. fu' fain 68:9

field: some corner of a foreign f.
57:9
though the f. be lost 216:1

fiends: f. in upper air 260:9

Fifteen: F. men on the dead
man's 309:13

fifty-fifty: no f. Americanism
252:8

fig: f. for those by law protected
67:10

fight: don't want to f. 167:9
f. between you and the world
178:9
f. for an idea like a hero 289:9
f. in the fields and in 90:11
F. the good fight 220:4
F. the good fight 48:9
fly, may f. again 71:5

fighter: Am I no a bonny f.
309:10

fighting: f. for this woman's
honour 208:8

fights: f. you on patriotic
principles 290:12

figs: long life better than f.

fig-tree: Train up a f. in the way
110:9

figures: prove anything by f.
78:8

fill: Come f. up my cup 259:6

fille de chambre: caught hold of
the f.'s   307:9

film: f. should have a beginning
144:8

films: money to see bad f. 147:2

Finality: F. is not the language
of politics 115:1

find: f. out what everyone is
doing 158:1
I f. 235:6
not be able to f. my way 154:3

frog: like a f. / To tell your
name 113:4

frontier: edge of a new f. 184:9

frowning: Behind a f. providence
102:5

frowns: slowly killed by f. and
smiles 294:9

frozen: torrid or the f. zone 78:3

Fruit: F. / Of that Forbidden
Tree 215:11

Much f. of sense 240:12

fruitful: Be f., and multiply 29:6

fruitfulness: mellow f. 179:4

fruition: sweet f. of an earthly
crown 206:4

fruits: By their f. ye shall know
43:6

f. of the Spirit 245:4

fugit: f. inreparabile tempus
331:11

Führer: Ein F. 6:6

fulness: f. thereof 34:4

fum: Fie, foh, and f., / I smell
274:12

fun: I rhyme for f. 66:11

not here for f. 158:3

thought What Jolly F. 249:9

funeral: not a f. note 350:10

funny: Everything is f. as long as
251:7

funny-ha-ha: or f. 153:5

Funny-peculiar: F. or funny-ha-
ha 153:5

fur: Oh my f. and whiskers 80:2

on some other f. 10:5

furious: grew fast and f. 68:8

furnace: burning fiery f. 40:7

furnish: You f. the pictures 154:8

furor: Ira f. brevis 164:11

fury: full of sound and f. 277:13

f. and the mire 356:1

fuse: through the green f. drives
321:4

future: seen the f., and it works
307:4

time f. contained in time past
126:1

futurity: let f. shift for itself
302:5

Gaels: great G. of Ireland 88:9

gai: toujours g. 206:8

gaiety: eclipsed the g. of nations
172:6

gains: Light g. make heavy
purses 19:3

gaiters: gas and g. 111:11

galanterie: n'ont jamais eu de g.
191:2

Galilean: conquered, O pale G.
314:2

You have conquered, G.
177:11

gallant: very g. gentleman 5:6

gallantry: men call g., and gods
adultery 73:9

Gallia: G. est omnis divisa 76:6

gallimaufry: English tongue a g.
305:13

galloped: we g. all three 60:10

gambler: g., by the state /
Licensed 51:2

game: and play the g. 225:7

g. . . . never lost till won 103:4

plenty of time to win this g.
119:9

Gamesmanship: G. or, The Art
243:3

gamut: whole g. of the emotions
232:2

Garbo: one sees in G. sober
327:1

garden: Come into the g., Maud
318:6

cultivate our g. 332:1

first g. made, and the first city
101:8

ghost of a g. fronts 313:9

God Almighty first planted a
G. 18:11

I value my g. more 2:5

nearer God's Heart in a g.
149:8

Nothing grows in our g. 321:8

gardener: Adam was a g. 272:1

g. Adam and his wife 317:11

gardens: passed the salley s
356:8

garland: green willow is my g.
159:12

gas: g. and gaiters 111:11

gate: g. of the year 153:3

gates: heads, O ye g. 34:5

iron g. of life 208:6

temple g. unto my love 305:3

gathered: two or three are g. 43:18

we are g. together 245:10

Gaudeamus: G. igitur 7:2

Gaul: G. is divided into three parts 76:6

gave: g. my life for freedom 131:4

Lord g., and 33:6

gay: gallant g. Lothario 254:6

I'm a g. deceiver 97:8

gaze: g. for long into an abyss 226:7

geese: for this the wild g. spread 358:2

g. are getting fat 6:2

Geist: G. der stets verneint 145:2

gemlike: this hard, g. flame 233:3

General: G. Good is the plea 51:7

General Motors: country is good for G. 349:6

generals: bite . . . my other g. 141:3

G. Janvier and Février 226:5

left to the g. 315:5

generation: best minds of my g. 144:4

g. of leaves 162:11

generations: g. of the living 199:3

hungry g. tread thee 181:14

genius: Consult the g. of the place 240:4

declare except my g. 348:8

'G.' (which means transcendent capacity 78:10

G. . . . a greater aptitude for patience 62:9

g. and his money 296:3

G. does what it must 211:14

g. I had when I wrote that book 313:3

g. . . . infinite capacity for 164:6

G. is one per cent inspiration 124:4

g. of the Constitution 236:3

talent instantly recognizes g. 119:7

true for all men — that is g. 129:6

unseen G. of the Wood 214:7

was g. found respectable 58:10

When a true g. appears 312:10

gentil: parfit g. knyght 84:9

gentle: Do not go g. 321:3

gentleman: g.: I live by robbing 289:7

Once a g. 111:3

prince of darkness is a g. 274:11

very gallant g. 5:6

Who was then a g. 10:4

Gentleman-Rankers: G. out on the spree 186:9

Gentlemen: G. Prefer Blondes 198:4

while the G. go by 187:8

gentleness: ways are ways of g. 306:7

gently: shall g. lead those 39:4

geographical: Italy is a g. expression 212:3

Geography: G. is about Maps 28:3

geology: what happens to the world's g. 202:3

geometrical: looking so g. 138:12

geometry: no royal road to g. 130:11

George: [G. III] despised, and dying king 295:10

King G. will be able to read 150:6

Georges: praised, the G. ended 189:12

George the First: G. was always reckoned 189:12

George the Third: Any good of G. 189:12

G. — ['Treason,' cried 157:3

German: G. army was stabbed 160:5

wee G. lairdie 104:9

Germans: beastly to the G. 101:4

Germany: G. will claim me as a German 124:9

Get: G. you the sons 165:12

Ghost: G. in the Machine 256:4
 g. of a garden fronts 313:9
 some old lover's g. 117:10

ghosties: From ghoulies and g. 7:1

ghosts: g. from an enchanter 294:3
 yet a boy I sought for g. 293:5

giant: g.'s shoulder to mount on 96:13

giants: on the shoulders of g. 226:4

Giddy: G. fantastic Poets 117:14

Gift: G., like genius 164:6

giftie: some Power the g. gie us 69:2

gifts: presented unto him g. 41:5
 when they bring g. 330:11

gild: g. refined gold 273:14

gilding: great deal about g. the eastern 296:5

Gilead: no balm in G. 40:2

girdle: I'll put a g. round 280:2

girl: breaks just like a little g. 123:6
 that g. standing there 357:8

Gitche Gumee: By the shores of G. 198:1

give: to g. than to receive 46:12

gives: blesseth him that g. 279:3
 He g. twice who gives soon 315:1

Glad: G. did I live 309:9

gladly: g. wolde he lerne 84:11

gladness: begin in g. 353:5

Gladstone: [G.] grand old man 227:11

glass: g., wherein beholders do generally 311:6
 sound of broken g. 27:3

glasses: girls who wear g. 231:8

glean'd: g. my teeming brain 183:2

glisters: g. is not gold 278:13

global: image of a g. village 203:2

globe: great g. itself 284:4

gloire: g. des grands hommes 191:3
 jour de g. est arrivé 254:3

gloria: *Sic transit g. mundi* 184:8

glories: in those weaker g. spy 328:12

glorify: Man's chief end is to g. God 82:2

glorious: crowded hour of g. life 222:2
 many a g. morning 287:2

glory: count the g. of my crown 128:3
 g. belongs to our ancestors 237:10
 g. from the earth 352:6
 g. is departed 62:2
 g. is departed from Israel 32:6
 g. of great men 191:3
 g. of the coming 166:3
 g., or the grave 77:4
 g. that was Greece 238:4
 G. to God in the highest 45:4
 I felt it was g. 76:2
 paths of g. lead 148:5
 sea of g. 272:4
 to g. we steer 253:5
 triumph without g. when 100:2
 war as all g., but, boys 297:5

glotoun: g. of wordes 190:5

glove: cat but a g. 261:1
 iron hand in a velvet g. 84:6

glowr'd: Tammie g., amaz'd, and curious 68:8

glum: whose glance was g. 144:3

glut: g. thy sorrow 181:4

Glyn: With Elinor G. / On a tiger-skin 10:5

gnomes: g. of Zurich 349:7

go: In the name of God, g.! 104:2
 Time stays, *we* g. 115:10

Goats: G. and monkeys 281:11

God: am a jealous G. 31:4
 as it were, G.'s grandchild 105:5
 atheist, thank G. 63:3
 Beast, or a G. 18:6
 Beware of the man whose g. 289:11

brave towards G. 17:4

Chance is perhaps G.'s pseudonym 136:2

denied to G. 3:3

Doubtless G. could have made 335:9

flood, leads – G. knows where 74:11

G. Almighty first planted a Garden 18:11

G. be in my head 7:3

G. disposes 184:7

g. has made this peace 331:5

G. has written all the books 71:10

G. is a circle 9:8

G. is dead 226:10

G. is dead 225:3

G. is forgotten 176:9

G. is in heaven, and thou 37:6

G. is love 49:5

G. is Love, I dare say 71:11

G. is not mocked 47:7

G. is our refuge 34:9

G. is the perfect poet 61:4

G. is working His purpose out 3:4

G. made him 278:9

G. made the country 102:10

G. moves in a mysterious 102:4

G. of Isaac 30:11

G. only a blunder of man 227:4

G., / Or something very like 94:1

g. self-slain on his own strange 313:10

G.'s no blate gin he stirs up 201:4

G. the first garden made 101:8

G., thou art my God 35:2

G. wasn't too bad a novelist 24:1

G. will pardon me 155:5

G. will save the Queen 165:12

I am a G. and cannot find 295:1

If G. be for us 46:15

If G. did not exist 332:3

If G. has created us 333:2

I must be turning into a g. 329:9

I wad do, were I Lord G. 202:5

I who saw the face of G. 204:10

kills the image of G. 219:1

like a G. in pain 179:10

Lord G. made them all 3:10

man who said 'G. 188:6

nearer G.'s Heart in a garden 149:8

negation of G. 144:5

never believe that G. plays dice 125:1

'next to of course g. 104:6

Nor G. alone in the still 242:2

No sacrifice to G. more acceptable 263:10

not sing *G. Save the King* 66:7

now G. alone knows 188:3

observed by Yours faithfully, G. 6:3

One, on G.'s side 235:5

presume not G. to scan 242:1

served G. as diligently 351:5

Though G. cannot alter the past 71:7

three person'd G. 117:8

To believe in G. is to yearn 327:5

Verb is G. 166:10

vindicate the ways of G. to man 241:7

ways of G. to men 215:12

whole armour of G. 48:3

whom G. wishes to destroy 131:3

with G. all things are possible 44:2

Word was G. 45:15

youth I remembered my G. 304:1

Goddamn: Lhude sing G. 243:5

godly: g., righteous and sober life 244:5

gods: g. are just 275:3

g., but there ought to be 113:7

G. they had tried of every
shape 120:4
men that strove with G. 319:3
no other g. before me 31:3
should not resort to the g.
238:5
So many g. 344:4
stupidity the very g. contend
258:7
Thinking of his own G. 12:8
Twa g. guides us 55:2
wanton boys, are we to the g.
274:15
Whom the g. love 211:4
godsmiths: That g. could produce
120:4
goes: so far as it g. 111:9
going: g., / But go at once 277:2
gold: and next, my g. 176:7
Detestable desire for g. 330:13
fetch the age of g. 215:10
glisters is not g. 278:13
realms of g. 182:7
golden: did in the g. world 265:9
g. age never was the present
136:11
G. Road to Samarkand 134:3
g. rule is that there are no
290:4
G. slumbers kiss your eyes
108:3
poets only deliver a g. 298:1
The G. opes 215:5
gone: all g. into the world of
light 328:7
G. far away 253:7
gong-tormented: g. sea 356:2
good: all g. as another until
177:1
best is the enemy of the g.
332:2
but not religious g. 152:1
Evil be thou my G. 217:6
God saw that it was g. 29:4
g., bad, and indifferent 306:1
g. ended happily 346:2
g. [end] unluckily 310:10
g. in the worst 9:9
g. is oft interred 273:5
g. is the beautiful 236:11

g. men to do nothing 65:6
g. than to be ugly 347:3
g. time that was had by all
107:2
g. to be merry 7:9
g. woman if I had five
thousand 320:7
greatest g. 92:6
If one g. deed 284:12
must return g. for evil 328:6
my religion is to do g. 231:1
never had it so g. 203:4
nothing either g. or bad 267:17
Truth . . . the sovereign g. 17:3
worse than ugly, she is g.
345:5
would do g. to another 51:7
goodness: is in removing it from
them 132:8
g. springs from a man's own
heart 98:1
If g. lead him not 158:11
powerful g. want 294:10
Good-night: G.? ah! no; the hour
is ill 292:10
second best's a gay g. 357:1
goods: with all my worldly g.
246:2
Good Thing: Conquest was,
however, a G. 263:4
good will: peace, g. toward men
45:4
gorgeous: g. East with richest
hand 216:6
Gorgonized: G. me from head to
foot 318:5
gory: Welcome to your g. bed
68:7
gossip: to the town g. 251:8
govern: Consciousness reigns but
does not g. 328:3
difficult to drive; easy to g.
58:1
g. according to the common
weal 170:2
governed: g. by shopkeepers
299:8
many are g. by the few 167:5
nation is not g. 64:10

not so well g. as they ought
163:5
government: erected into a
system of g. 144:5
false system of g. 230:12
G. . . . a necessary evil 230:9
g. as with medicine 28:1
g. by the badly educated 90:2
G. . . . contrivance of human
wisdom 64:3
g. it deserves 203:10
g. of the people 195:6
g. shall be upon his shoulder
38:9
G. . . . the laws of life 255:7
g. to suffer so much poverty
234:7
Influence is not g. 336:9
just watch the g. 251:9
No G. can be long secure
114:3
obey the established G. 336:10
oppressive g. is more to be
feared 98:2
people's g., made for the
people 338:4
Republican . . . highest form of
g. 304:4
right . . . to establish G. 336:10
unfit for their own g. 337:1
governors: supreme g., the mob
334:11
gown: loose g. from her
shoulders 355:6
grace: But for the g. of God
there goes 55:3
g. of our Lord Jesus Christ
49:13
G. under pressure 156:2
Tuesday's child is full of g. 8:3
graces: half mile g. 69:5
gracious: God save our g. king
78:4
grammar: heedless of g. 22:6
Grammere: G., that grounde is of
alle 190:6
grand: That g. old man 227:11
grandchild: Art . . . God's g. 105:6
grandeur: g. he derived from
Heaven 121:6

g. of God 164:1
grano: *Cum g. salis* 237:7
grapes: eaten sour g. 40:5
g. of wrath 166:3
grapeshot: whiff of g. 79:5
Grasp: G. it like a man 160:2
reach should exceed his g.
59:3
grass: believe a leaf of g. 343:5
his days are as g. 35:5
splendour in the g. 352:8
two blades of g. to grow 311:7
gratuit: *acte g.* 142:2
grave: ayont the g., man 69:6
bore; even the g. yawns 324:3
dark inn, the g. 260:4
glory lead but to the g. 148:5
glory, or the g. 77:4
g. hides all things beautiful
295:1
G.'s a fine and private place
208:5
g., where is thy victory 47:4
O G., thy victoree 8:6
graves: Let's talk of g. 282:6
gravis: *Illi mors g.* 263:11
gravity: alters the centre of g.
79:15
gravy: gulf stream of g. 204:4
greasy: g. Joan doth keel 275:10
grey-green, g. Limpopo 187:2
great: age of g. men is going 5:1
but g.; and so are neither
330:5
cannot perform g. things 335:4
folly of the G. 135:2
glory of g. men 191:3
g. brake through 16:14
g., ere fortune made him so
121:6
history . . . biography of g. men
79:3
rising to G. Place 18:1
they are all g. 147:6
To g. men . . . world is a
sepulchre 323:2
who were truly g. 304:8
Greater: G. love hath no man
323:1
g. than we know 353:6

Guns: G. will make us powerful 144:9
  like loaded g. with boys 103:3
guts: sheep's g. should hale souls 280:9
gutter: all in the g., but some 346:12
gypsy: to the vagrant G. life 209:6
gyre: turning in the widening g. 357:12

Habit: H. with him was all the test 103:2
habitation: local h. and a name 280:6
habits: curious h. of dogs 243:10
  h. that carry them far apart 98:5
hail: brother, h. and farewell 83:1
hair: bright h. about the bone 117:13
  false h. / Become a verse 158:9
  h. of a woman can draw 166:4
  tangles of Neaera's h. 215:3
  you have lovely h. 87:3
hairless: h. as an egg 159:7
hairs: ill white h. become 270:14
hairy: my brother is a h. man 30:4
halcyon: h. days 271:11
half: ae h. the warld thinks 261:4
  dearer h. 217:8
  h. of the world cannot understand 15:3
  H. to remember days 134:2
  h. was not told me 32:17
half-a-dozen: h. of the other 206:12
Hallowed: H. be thy name 42:5
halo: h.? It's only one more 138:11
halt: h., and the blind 45:10
  How long h. ye between 32:18
Hamlet: good juggler to a bad H. 94:9
hammock: Drake he's in his h. 225:5

hand: h. into the hand of God 153:3
  h. that rocks the cradle 334:8
  led by an invisible h. 299:6
  sweeten this little h. 277:9
  This is the h. that wrote 103:5
handful: Just for a h. of silver 60:12
hands: their h. are blue 193:1
handwriting: sight of their own h. 14:7
hang: h. a man first 219:9
  We must all h. together 137:11
  wretches h. that jury-men 242:12
hang'd: h. my braw John Highlandman 67:7
hanged: h. in a fortnight 174:11
  not h. for stealing horses 150:3
hanget: he was h. 55:9
hangin': h. men an' women there 9:2
hanging: good h. prevents a bad marriage 285:11
  H. is too good for him 63:6
  nane the waur o' a h. 55:8
happiest: h. and best minds 296:2
  h. women, like the happiest nations 125:6
happiness: consume h. without producing it 288:2
  Domestic h., thou only bliss 102:13
  greatest h. of the greatest number 28:2
  h. destroyed by preparation 15:5
  H. in marriage 15:12
  H. is no laughing matter 342:1
  h.! no man alive could bear it 289:4
  h. of the greatest number 168:1
  Knowledge is not h. 75:12
  pursuit of h. 9:12
  result h. 110:5
  so much h. is produced 174:9
  state is the greatest h. 237:1
  Withdraws into its h. 207:10

more things in h. and earth
267:12

new h. and a new earth 49:11

One H., one Hell 292:8

open face of h. 183:1

some call it the road to h. 22:1

then — what pleases H. 260:3

thirtieth year to h. 321:5

what's a h. for 59:3

young was very h. 353:4

heavenly: from h. harmony 122:1

heavens: Hung be the h. with
black 271:10

Let the h. be glad 33:4

spangled h. a shining frame
2:4

though the h. fall 132:1

Heav'n: Down from the verge of
H. 217:10

make a H. of Hell 216:2

than serve in H. 216:3

Heav'n-borne: H. child 215:8

heels: Time wounds all h. 9:10

Helen: Dust hath closed H.'s eye
224:7

hell: all we need of h. 113:3

Better to reign in H. 216:3

boys, it is all h. 297:5

England . . . h. of horses 134:7

heaven in h.'s despair 52:12

Heaven, one H., one
immortality 292:8

h., even from the gates of
heaven 63:7

H. is a city 294:7

H. is full of musical amateurs
289:6

H. is other people 257:13

H. of Heav'n 216:2

h. of this world 25:8

H. raised a hoarse 106:7

h. shall not prevail against
43:14

H. trembl'd at the hideous
217:2

Italy . . . h. for women 70:7

Nor H. a fury, like a woman
99:6

out of H. leads up 217:1

this is h., nor am I out 204:10

way to H. is easy 331:2

where we are is H. 205:1

Which way I fly is H. 217:4

help: encumbers him with h.
173:2

in whom there is no h. 36:5

Since there's no h. 120:1

very present h. in trouble 34:9

help meet: h. for him 29:7

hemispheres: jars two h. 151:3

hemlock: h. I had drunk 181:6

hen: h. is only an egg's way 71·9

herald: Hark! the h. angels 341:3

herde: Oon ere it h. 87:2

herd-instinct: Morality is the h.
226:11

heresies: new truths to begin as
h. 168:11

Hermes: thrice great H. 214:6

hermitage: take / That for an h.
198:9

hero: fight for an idea like a h.
289:9

h. becomes a bore 130:3

h. must drink brandy 175:1

h. the Conqueror Worm 238:1

h. to his valet 100:5

very valet seem'd a h. 72:8

Herod: It out-herods H. 268:9

heroes: And speed glum h. 258:1

fit country for h. 196:9

land that is in need of h. 56:1

heroic: h. poem of its sort 78:7

heroine: h. goes mad she always
296:7

heron: h. / Priested shore 321:5

Herostratus: H. lives that burnt
58:6

hesitates: She wavers, she h.
249:5

Hesperus: schooner H. 198:3

heterodoxy: h. is another man's
doxy 335:11

heureux: *jamais si h. ni si
malheureux* 191:1

Hewers: H. of wood 31:11

hid: mist of tears / I h. from
Him 321:11

hierarchy: Olympus' faded h.
182:2

highbrow: h....looks at a sausage 157:10

higher: dead selves to h. things 317:4

    h. law than the Constitution 264:1

highest: h. type of human nature 304:4

Highlandman: hang'd my braw John H. 67:7

Highlands: heart's in the H. 68:2

    H. and ye Lawlands 20:10

Highness: his H.' dog at Kew 240:6

highway: h. for our God 39:2

hill: green h. far away 4:2

    H. will not come to Mahomet 18:2

    hunter home from the h. 309:9

    On a huge h., / Cragged 118:1

Hills: H. of home 309:8

    mine eyes unto the h. 36:1

    Over the h. and far away 140:9

him: all cried, 'That's h.!' 22:6

himself: superior man seeks is in h. 98:8

hindrances: h. to human improvement 213:3

hint: Just h. a fault 239:13

Hippocrene: blushful H. 181:8

hiss: dismal universal h. 217:16

historian: proper occupation of the h. 344:7

historians: alter the past, h. can 71:7

history: great deal of h. to produce 170:6

    happiest women . . . have no h. 125:6

    h. . . . biography of great men 79:3

    H. came to a 263:9

    h. in all men's lives 270:11

    H. is a nightmare 177:9

    H. is bunk 135:7

    H. is nothing but a tableau 332:5

    h. is on our side 185:3

    H. is Philosophy teaching 54:1

h. is that it is adaptable 327:9

h. is the world's judgement 258:9

H. . . . register of the crimes 141:9

H. to the defeated 14:6

Human h. . . . race between education 340:11

no h.; only biography 129:5

regard the h. of Europe 145:12

War makes rattling good h. 151:7

whole h. of civilization 20:6

whole h. of the world would 232:7

history-books: blank in h. 79:1

hit: Don't h. at all if 252:9

    h., a very palpable hit 269:9

hobgoblin: h. of little minds 129:8

hodgepodge: h. of all other speeches 305:13

Hoist: H. with his own petar 269:3

hold: To have and to h. 245:13

holiday: Butcher'd to make a Roman h. 73:6

    Monday is parson's h. 311:8

holidays: year were playing h. 269:14

Holiness: Go! put off H. 51:6

    h. of the heart's affections 183:5

    what he has lost in h. 72:3

Holland: H. . . . lies so low 163:4

hollow: I hate that dreadful h. 318:4

Hollywood: phony tinsel off H. 194:1

holy: Is this a h. thing 52:13

Holy Roman Empire: H. was not Holy, nor Roman 332:4

homage: h. that vice pays 191:4

    owes no h. unto the sun 58:8

home: best country ever is, at h. 146:6

    blest by the suns of h. 57:10

    burned / As h. his footsteps 259:10

dream that I am h. again 134:2

England, h. and beauty 55:5

go h. in the dark 157:2

H. is the sailor 309:9

H. . . . They have to take you in 138:2

no place like h. 234:1

till the cow comes h. 25:5

Homer: 'H. sometimes sleeps' 74:9

man who has not read H. 20:2

single exception of H. 208.0

worthy H. nods 164:9

homes: stately h. of England 156:1

Homesickness: H. for the gutter 14:8

homeward: Look h., Angel 215:6

homo: *Ecce h.* 334:5

H. sum 319:9

honest: good to be h. 7:9

h. by an act of parliament 176:1

h. God's the noblest work 71:8

h. Man's the noblest work 242:3

looking for an h. man 113:9

Necessity makes an h. man 108:1

honey: flowing with milk and h. 30:10

h. still for tea 57:8

How a bear likes h. 213:7

took some h. 193:2

Honi: *H. soit qui mal* 7:4

honied: h. indolence 181:1

honour: do h. the very flea 176:3

high h. / Bot wind 157:5

h., it is no longer peace 256:1

H. pricks me on 270:4

h. rooted in dishonour 317:1

h. sinks where commerce 146:8

H. the greatest poet 105:7

H. thy father and 31:6

idiot race, to h. lost 68:6

leap / To pluck bright h. 269:15

peace, I hope, with h. 115:3

peace with h. 83:8

signed with their h. 304:9

sin to covet h. 271:6

woman's h.; which is probably more 208:8

honourable: all h. men 273:6

strictly h., as the phrase is 133:3

honoured: more h. in the breach 267:9

hope: Abandon h., all ye who enter 105:4

Because I do not h. 125:9

fooled with h. 121:4

h. beyond the shadow 179:7

H. deferred maketh 36:10

H. is a good breakfast 16:13

H. springs eternal 241:9

life, there's h. 319:8

lives upon h. will die fasting 137:4

loving . . . when h. is gone 15:10

sure and certain h. 246:7

triumph of h. over experience 174:2

unconquerable h. 13:3

While there's tea there's h. 235:9

hoped: never h. can never despair 288:1

Hoping: H. it might be so 151:10

Hornie: Auld H., Satan, Nick 65:9

Horny-handed: H. sons of toil 179:3

horror: h.! The horror 99:14

horse: behold a pale h. 49:9

kingdom for a h. 282:14

little dearer than his h. 318:2

Never look a gift h. 171:6

Horseman: *H., pass by* 358:8

horses: England . . . hell for h. 70:7

hell of h. 134:7

h. of instruction 52:9

hostages: to fortune 17:8

hot: h. for certainties in this 211:9

hotch'd: h. and blew 68:9

hypocrisy: Conservative
government is an organized
h. 114:13

H. is the homage 191:4

hypocrite: h. in his pleasures
175:5

H. lecteur 24:3

hypothesis: slaying of a beautiful
h. 168:8

Iacta: *I. alea est* 76:8

ice: Some say in i. 138:4

Ichabod: I., Ichabod 62:2
named the child I. 32:6

idea: fight for an i. like a hero
289:9

pain of a new i. 20:7

would be an excellent i. 139:12

ideals: enemy of progressive i.
27:6

ideas: i. that make us optimists
327:4

no i. but in things 349:4

Ides: Beware the I. of March
272:6

idiot: law is a ass—a i. 111:16

Told by an i. 277:13

idle: i. as a painted ship 95:10
i. hands to do 337:6

less i. than when free from
work 92:7

more or less i. people 20:5

idleness: Love in i. 283:10

idol: one-eyed yellow i. 153:6

idolatry: honour his memory, on
this side i. 176:8

of the ancients without i.
87:11

if: much virtue in 'i.' 266:10

ifs: If i. and ands were pots
234:5

ignorance: i. is bliss 148:7

I. of the law excuses 262:5

no sin but i. 205:11

science . . . exchange of i. 75:12

ignorant: father was so i. 326:11

ignored: cease to exist
because . . . i. 168:6

Ignotus: I. moritur sibi 263:11

Ill: I. fares the land 145:13

Looking i. prevail 311:3

ony guid or i., / They've done
67:2

ill-favoured: i. thing, sir, but
mine own 266:9

ill-natur'd: vain, i. thing, an
Englishman 107:9

illnesses: extreme i. extreme
remedies 160:7

illogical: i. belief in
the . . . improbable 211:8

ills: nae real i. perplex them 69:7

illuminatio: Dominus i. mea
333:8

illusion: alas, only one i. left
301:6

only one i. . . . the Archbishop
301:6

illusions: Don't part with your i.
326:3

Image: Best I. of my self 217:8
graven i., or any likeness 31:4

in his i., we have repaid him
333:2

make man in our i. 29:5

imagination: i. amend them
280:8

i. bodies forth 280:6

i. for his facts 297:4

lady's i. is very rapid 15:13

of i. all compact 280:5

sweeten my i. 274:17

truth of i. 183:5

Were it not for i. 174:14

imagine: i. a vain thing 33:13

Imitation: I. is the sincerest form
97:9

i. of an action 11:15

Immodest: I. words admit of no
defence 253:2

immoral: moral or an i. book
346:13

immortal: His biting is i. 265:4

I. longings in me 265:6

in a long i. dream 180:6

make me i. with a kiss 205:2

not search for i. life 235:7

To himself every one is an i.
72:4

What i. hand or eye 53:2

immortality: achieve i. through
my work 4:8
just Ourselves — / And I. 113:2
one Hell, one i. 292:8
Immortals: President of the I.
151:11
Imparadis'd: I. in one another's
arms 217:5
impartial: Death, with i. foot
165:1
impatient: i. as the Wind 354:3
impediment: cause, or just i.
245:9
impediments: Admit i. 287:8
imperial: enslaves you on i.
principles 290:12
Imperialism: I. is a paper tiger
204:6
impertinence: variety of matter
to his i. 1.10
importance: Nothing ... of the
smallest i. 347:5
imposes: child i. on the man
121:7
Impossibility: by despair / Upon
I. 207:5
impossible: believed as many as
six i. things 81:7
certain because it is i. 319:13
eliminated the i. 119:4
i. takes a little longer 6:4
i. to be silent 65:3
I. venir, mensonge 247:6
not i. she 103:10
states that something is i. 93:1
wish it were i. 175:8
imprecision: i. of feeling 126:6
improbable: however i., must be
the truth 119:4
illogical belief in the ... i.
211:8
Impropriety: I. is the soul of wit
210:8
improved: enormously i. by
death 256:8
improvement: hindrances to
human i. 213:3
impulse: i. from a vernal wood
354:6
impune: Nemo me i. lacessit 8:4

impure: Puritan all things are i.
192:4
inaccessible: Remote, serene, and
i. 294:2
inaccuracy: i. sometimes saves
tons 256:7
lying, but I hate i. 71:14
inarticulate: raid on the i. 126:6
incapacity: old maid courted by
i. 52:6
incarnadine: multitudinous seas
i. 276:10
include: i. me out 146:12
income: Annual i. twenty pounds
110:5
live beyond its i. 72:2
Incorruptible: sea-green I. 79:6
increase: i. / The number of the
dead 106:6
incurable: Life is an i. disease
101:9
Indecency: I.'s Conspiracy of
Silence 290:9
indecent: sent down for i.
behaviour 337:9
independent: i. wish / E'er
planted 68:1
poor and i. 94:5
Indian: Like the base I. 281:16
only good I. is a dead 296:4
indifference: i. closely bordering
on aversion 309:12
indifferent: count nothing human
i. 319:9
good, bad, and i. 306:1
indignatio: Ubi saeva i. 313:4
indignation: fierce i. can no
longer 313:4
Moral i. is jealousy 340:12
Indignor: I. quandoque 164:9
indiscreet: Questions are never i.
345:7
inditing: My heart is i. 34:8
individualism: Rugged i. 163:7
individuality: crushes i. is
despotism 212:9
individuals: worth of the i.
composing it 213:2
indivisible: Peace is i. 196:4
indolence: honied i. 181:1

novel . . . that it be i. 170:4
interfused: something far more
  deeply i. 352:3
Intérieur: shouting: 'Vive l'I.
  263:8
Interpretation: I. is the revenge
  of the intellect 303:3
interpreted: only i. the world
  208:13
interrupt: i. my interruptions
  125:10
interview: strange and fatal i.
  116:10
intimate: i. with few 336:11
intolerable: possession of it is i.
  328:4
  worst state, an i. one 230:9
intoxication: best of life is but i.
  74:3
invasion: i. of ideas 167:1
invent: necessary to i. him 332:3
inviolable: clutching the i. shade
  13:3
invisible: led by an i. hand 299:6
  no i. means of support 62:4
Iona: warmer among the ruins of
  I. 172:4
Ireland: I. is mentioned, the
  English 300:12
  I. is the old sow 177:4
  [I.] most distressful country
  9:2
  Romantic I.'s dead 358:2
  the great Gaels of I. 88:9
Irish: I. question 114:12
Irishry: Still the indomitable I.
  358:7
iron: blood and i. 50:6
  I. bars a Cage 198:9
  I. Curtain has descended 91:7
  i. hand in a velvet 84:6
  I. shuts amain 215:5
Irony: I. is the essence . . . of
  Providence 22:3
irrelevant: i. to the world's
  geology 203:3
irrevocabile: Volat i. verbum
  164:14
Ishmael: Call me I. 211:3
Island: little, tight little I. 109:9

No man is an I. 116:4
isle: i. is full of noises 284:3
isolation: splendid i. 147:5
Israel: glory is departed from I.
  32:6
Italy: Graved inside of it, 'I..'
  60:2
  I. a paradise for horses 70:7
  I. is a geographical expression
  212:3
  Paradise of exiles, I. 293:6
itch: i. to write 178:6
itchez: When Ah i. 224:6
ivoire: tour d'i. 256:6
ivory: in his i. tower 256:6
Jabberwock: hast thou slain the
  J. 81:2
jades: pampered j. of Asia 206:6
jads: like the j. for a' that 67:9
jam: never j. to-day 81:6
James: Henry J. has always
  seemed divisible 149:4
Janvier: Generals J. and Février
  226:5
jardin: cultiver notre j. 332:1
jealousy: j.; / It is the green-ey'd
  281:6
  j. with a halo 340:12
jelly: Out, vile j. 274:13
jerks: bring me up by j. 110:10
Jerusalem: due to the absence
  from J. 128:8
  J. the golden 28:5
  O ye daughters of J. 38:1
  was J. builded here 51:12
jest: fellow of infinite j. 269:5
  j.'s prosperity lies 275:8
  Life is a j. 141:2
  that's no j. 249:7
jests: j. at scars 283:2
Jesus: Friend we have in J.
  261:8
  Gentle J., meek and mild 341:2
  J. and a nameless ape 202:2
  J. calls us 4:1
  J. loves me! this I know 336:7
  J. wept 46:5
  J. wept; Voltaire smiled 167:3
  more popular than J. Christ
  193:7

laugh: hurt too much to l. 196:2
L. and the world laughs 344:3
l. at them in our turn 16:3
L. where we must 241:7

laughed: first baby l. for the first
time 23:4
once heartily and wholly l.
79:11

laughing: Happiness is no l.
matter 342:1
l. immoderately at stated
intervals 301:4

laughs: Earth l. in flowers 129:10

laughter: ill-bred, as audible l.
87:5
L. holding both his sides 214:9
senators burst with l. 14:1

launch'd: face that l. a thousand
ships 205:2

laurel: burned is Apollo's l.
bough 205:6

laurels: once more, O ye L.
215:1

lave: Whistle owre the l. 67:8

law: become a universal l.
178:10
built with stones of L. 52:5
by the l. of the land 203:8
Christianity is part of the
Common L. 150:2
Ignorance of the l. excuses
262:5
l. ends, there tyranny begins
236:2
L. ends, Tyranny begins 197:1
l., in its majestic equality
136:3
l. is a ass—a idiot 111:16
l. is an infraction of liberty
28:1
Necessity has no l. 315:2
Necessity hath no l. 104:3
those by l. protected 67:10
ultimate l. 92:5
windward of the l. 90:5

lawe: Love is a gretter l. 85:6

lawful: that which is neither
quite l. 72:3

laws: bad or obnoxious l. 147:10

cooperation . . . the l. of life
255:7
L. are like spider's webs
302:11
l. were like cobwebs 16:14
L. were made to be broken
227:10
nothing to do with the l. 165:8
obedient to their l., we lie
298:4
That part which l. 146:7
Unequal l. unto a savage race
318:11
whatever the l. permit 221:1

Lawsuit: L.: A machine 50:3

Lay: L. your sleeping head 14:2

lays: ways of constructing tribal
l. 186:11

Lazy: L. fokes' stummucks don't
git tired 152:11

lea: and o'er the l. 161:11

Lead: L., kindly Light 226:1
L. us, heavenly Father 124:5

leader: one people, one l. 6:6

league: Half a l. onward 316:8

leak: One l. will sink a ship 63:8

lean: l. and hungry look 272:9

leap: giant l. for mankind 12:4
great l. in the dark 161:8

leaps: My heart l. up 352:4

Lear: pleasant to know Mr. L.
192:11

learn: something about
everything 169:2
season for the old to l. 3:1
through so much to l. so little
112:8
We live and l. 238:6

learned: how much he had l. in 7
years 326:11

learning: All Classic l. lost 239:2
a' the l. I desire 66:10
great feast of l. 275:6
L. hath gained most 139:6
l. is most excellent 136:5
l., like your watch 87:12
l. . . . makes a silly man 1:10
L. without thought 98:7
little l. is a dang'rous thing
240:10

where l. is more like life 228:4
life-insurance: I detest l. agents
192:10
lifetime: knowledge of a l. 342:5
l. of happiness! No man 289:4
Lift: L. not the painted veil 295:9
L. up your heads 34:5
light: against the dying of the l.
321:3
best is to have seen the l.
303:6
dusk with a l. behind her
144:2
gone into the world of l. 328:7
'Let there be l.!' said God
74:13
Let there be l.! said Liberty
292:11
L. (God's eldest daughter)
139:4
l. but the shadow of God 58:4
l. in the dust lies 293:9
l. shineth in darkness 45:16
l. such a candle 191:8
l. that I may tread 157:2
l. through yonder window
breaks 283:2
l. unto my path 35:8
Lord is my l. 333:8
More l. 145:11
Newton be! and all was l.
240:7
no object so foul that intense
l. 130:1
Put out the l. and then 281:14
ring of pure and endless l.
328:13
seen a great l. 38:8
lighted: l. fools / The way
277:13
Lighten: L. our darkness 245:2
lightning: Shakespeare by flashes
of l. 97:2
lights: l. around the shore 253:11
Turn up the l. 157:2
like: every one as they l. 312:3
find their l. agen 260:5
know what I l. 26:2
l. the jads for a' that 67:9
Love and do what you l. 14:12

not look upon his l. again
267:5
wha's l. us 7:5
liked: She l. whate'er / She
looked 60:15
likeness: after our l. 29:5
likewise: Go, and do thou l. 45:9
liking: saves me the trouble of l.
16:5
lilacs: l. last in the dooryard
343:9
L. out of the dead 17:6
lilac-time: down to Kew in l.
228:2
lilies: Consider the l. 42:8
lilting: heard them l. 128:5
lily: paint the l. 273:14
Piccadilly with a poppy or a l.
143:11
limbs: great smooth marbly l.
59:11
limit: act a slave to l. 285:4
limits: Hell hath no l. 205:1
limousine: All we want is a l.
203:6
Limpopo: greasy L. River 187:2
line: thin red l. 256:3
up the l. to death 258:1
lineaments: l. of gratified desire
52:4
Lines: As L. so Loves 207:6
l. and life are free 158:7
lingua: *Pange,* l. 329:3
lion: l. is the beast to fight 248:9
Lions: girdid up my L. 336:1
lip: stiff upper l. 82:1
lips: l. suck forth my soul 205:2
l. that touch liquor 359:5
on my l. ye'll heed nae mair
201:7
people of unclean l. 38:7
Truth sits upon the l. 13:5
liquefaction: l. of her clothes
159:10
liquor: l. / Is quicker 224:5
l.'s out, why clink 60:4
Livelier l. than the Muse 166:2
touch l. must never touch
359:5

lisp'd: I l. in numbers 239:11

men that God made m. 88:9
old, m., blind 295:10
old men be m. 358:9
professor, who became m.
231:4

Madam: M. Life's a piece in
bloom 156:5

madder: I cried for m. music
118:10

madding: Far from the m.
crowd's 148:6

made: know who m. thee 53:5

madman: difference between a
m. and me 105:2
m. who thought he
was... Hugo 95:2

madmen: m.... Conquerors and
Kings 73:2

madness: Anger is a brief m.
164:11
destroyed by m. 144:4
fine m. still he did retain
119:11
in the end despondency and m.
353:5
m., yet there is method in it
267:16
sure to m. near alli'd 120:5
that way m. lies 274:8
very midsummer m. 286:1

magazines: women's m.... may
not be subtle 139:9

Maggots: M. half-form'd in
rhyme 238:9

magic: rough m. / I here abjure
284:6

magistrate: m. as equally useful
141:8

Magnificat: *M. anima mea* 334:1

magnificent: m., but it is not war
54:9

magnifies: soul m. the Lord
334:1

magnifique: *m. mais ce n'est pas*
54:9

magnify: m. him for ever 244:8

Mahomet: M. will go to the Hill
18:2

maid: m. and her wight / Come
whispering 151:9

M. of Athens, ere we part
75:10

maiden: m. of bashful fifteen
297:2
m. with white fire laden 292:2
use a poor m. so 6:5

maids: Three little m. from
school 143:3

Mail: Night M. crossing the
Border 14:4

maimed: poor, and the m. 45:10
wants [anger] hath a m. mind
139:5

main: care o' th' m. chance 71:4

maison: *m. est une machine-à-
habiter* 193:5

majesty: ride on in m. 213:5
rounded them with m. 151:2
so touching in its m. 353:10

Major-General: model of a
modern M. 143:12

majority: big enough m. in any
town 201:5
damns the vast m. o' men
235:5
God's side, is a m. 235:5
great silent m. of Americans
227:6

Majors: live with scarlet M.
258:1

make: does not usually m.
anything 235:3
Scotsman on the m. 23:9

Maker: M. of heaven and earth
244:9

male: more deadly than the m.
186:8

malignity: motiveless m. 97:1

malt: m. does more than Milton
166:2

mammon: serve God and m.
42:7

man: Arms and the m. 330:9
childhood shews the m. 218:2
Child is father of the M. 352:5
Every m. has three characters
179:1
gently scan your brother m.
65:10

hour is come, but not the m.
261:2

let him pass for a m. 278:9

make m. in our image 29:5

m. and a brother 339:4

m., by possessing
consciousness 327:3

M. is . . . a political animal 12:3

M. is a tool-making animal
137:12

M. . . . is a tool-using animal 79:12

M. . . . is a wicked creature
220:2

M. is a wolf to man 237:4

M. is born unto trouble 33:9

M. is condemned to be free
257:12

m. is infinitely more
complicated 328:2

M. is not the enemy of Man
230:12

M. is only a reed 232:11

M. is something to be
surpassed 227:2

M. is the measure of all 247:2

M. is the shuttle 328:9

m. is the superior animal
243:10

M. is what he eats 132:3

M. . . . lives . . . by catchwords
310:6

M. . . . must get drunk 74:3

m. only a blunder of God
227:4

M. partly is 59:14

M. proposes 184:7

m.'s a man 67:3

m.'s bred out / Into baboon
284:10

m.'s [business] to keep
unmarried 289:5

m., take him for all 267:5

m. who wasn't there 210:9

m. . . . will fight for an idea
289:9

Marvels . . . m. is the greatest
303:5

Nothing links m. to man 297:6

only m. is vile 155:1

piece of work is a m. 267:18

strange what a m. may do
320:2

This was a m. 273:12

Thou art the m. 32:14

manacles: mind-forged m. I hear
53:3

Mandalay: road to M. 187:5

mandrake: Get with child a m.
root 118:2

mane: runs with all his m. 248:9

mangent: *Qu'ils m. de la brioche*
204:7

manger: rude m. lies 215:8

Manhood: M. a struggle 114:6

manhoods: hold their m. cheap
271:8

mankind: deserve better of m.
311:7

giant leap for m. 12:4

If all m. minus one 212:7

justified in silencing m. 212:7

M. . . . unfit for their own
government 337:1

study of M. is Man 242:1

manner: all m. of things shall be
well 178:1

manners: A good m. are made up
129:12

m. of a dancing master 173:3

no longer any m. 101:3

mansion: pitched his m. in 356:5

mansions: many m. 46:6

many: ease with which the m.
167:5

shortest way to do m. things
299:4

many-coloured: m. glass, /
Stains 291:11

map: Roll up that m. 236:6

Marathon: force upon the plain
of M. 172:4

M. looks on the sea 74:8

marble: m. to retain 72:9

Mariners: M. of England 77:7

Marlowe: M., bathed in the
Thespian 119:11

marriage: after m., he'll fall
asleep 254:8

Courtship to m. 99:8

fortune by way of m. 133:3

M., as the origin of change
15:2

m. . . . friendship recognized by
the police 310:3

m. to begin with . . . aversion
296:8

to m. in a moment 15:13

matter: Friends are all that m.
63:13

Matthew: M., Mark, Luke, and
John 8:2

Maud: Come into the garden, M.
318:6

maxim: m. by which I act 178:10
useless as a general m. 200:10

maxima: *mea m. culpa* 209:9

maximum: m. of temptation
289:13

May: darling buds of M. 286:13
leads with the flow'ry / The Flow'ry
M. 218:8

maybe: definite m. 146:13

maze: mighty m.! but not
without a plan 241:6

mazes: through m. running
214:13

mean: virtuous person with a m.
mind 20:4

meaning: m. to the utmost
possible 244:4
some faint m. make pretence
121:12

means: m., even if we have to
borrer 336:4
m. just what I choose 81:8
measured by the m. 191:3

measles: Love's like the m. 171:7

measure: m. of all things 247:2

meat: chang'd sorts of m. 116:3
eater came forth m. 32:3
Some have m. and cannot eat
67:6

méchant: *animal est très m.* 5:11
m. animal 220:2

meddle: Wha daur m. wi' me 8:4

Medes: given to the M. and the
Persians 40:9

medias: *In m. res* 164:8

medicine: Comedy is m. 149:3
[m.] so long to learn 160:6

medieval: lily in your m. hand
143:11

mediocre: Titles distinguish the
m. 290:6

Mediocrity: M. knows nothing
higher 119:7

medium: m. is the message
203:3

meek: Blessed are the m. 41:10
Jesus, m. and mild 341:2

meet: Though infinite can never
m. 207:6

meeter: therefore deemed it m.
234:6

meeting: as if I was a public m.
330:1
Journeys end in lovers m.
285:13
this m. is drunk 112:9

Mehr: *M. Licht* 145:11

meilleur: *m. des mondes
possibles* 331:12

Melancholy: Hail divinest M.
214:4
loathed M. 214:8
m. fit shall fall 181:4
M. has her sovran shrine
181:5
Naught so sweet as M. 70:2
suck m. out of a song 265:13

melodie: Luve's like the m. 68:3

melodies: Heard m. are sweet
180:10

melted: m. into air 284:4

melting: m. voice 214:13

Melting-Pot: M. where all the
races 359:6

member: not m. of Bristol 64:5
would have me as a m. 208:9

members: m. one of another 48:1

même: *plus c'est la m.* 178:11

memorial: which have no m.
41:2

memory: complains of his m.
191:5
grand m. for forgetting 309:11
liar should have a good m.
248:11
m. for his jests 297:4

m. of men without distinction
58:5

this will refresh your m. 323:4

Vibrates in the m. 295:12

men: England . . . purgatory of m.
134:7

may not be subtle but neither
are m. 139:9

M. are but children 121:2

M. can be analysed 345:6

m. . . . live in hatred, enmity
216:11

M. subdue their Passions
better 306:12

M. were deceivers ever 280:10

more I see of m. 76:3

most m. dread [Liberty] 290:10

power over m.; but over
themselves 351:2

Mens: *M. cuiusque* 92:8

m. sana in corpore sano 178:8

Mental: cease from M. Strife
52:2

mentioned: be damned than m.
not 235:8

mépris: *souverain m.* 256:5

mercenary: m., and the prudent
motive 16:1

Mercury: words of M. 275:11

mercy: have m. upon us 210:2

Justice with M. 217:15

M. has a human heart 53:4

m. o' my soul, Lord God 202:5

quality of m. is not strained
279:3

merry: all their wars are m. 88:9

good to be m. and wise 7:9

m. monarch 251:2

never m. when I hear sweet
279:7

never was a m. world since
262:6

merrygoround: no go the m.
203:6

merryman: song of a m. 144:3

mess: another fine m. 151:1

message: medium is the m.
203:3

take a m. to Albert 115:8

messages: fair speechless m.
278:6

M. are for Western Union
147:4

messing: simply m. about in
boats 147:9

met: Ill m. by moonlight 280:1

Metaphysics: M. . . . finding of
bad reasons 55:4

methods: know my m.. Apply
them 119:5

métier: *C'est son m.* 155:5

m. et mon art, c'est vivre
220:7

metuunt: *Quem m., oderunt*
130:8

mice: schemes o' m. an' men
69:4

Michelangelo: Talking of M.
126:13

microscopic: has not man a m.
eye 241:10

mid-day: out in the m. sun 101:6

Middle: it was / The M. of Next
Week 81:10

middle-aged: m. suspect
everything 347:7

midnight: and m. never come
205:3

blackest m. born 214:8

chimes at m. 270:12

m. oil 140:10

my Lamp at m. hour 214:6

'Tis the year's m. 117:11

midst: In the m. of life 246:6

there am I in the m. 43:18

midsummer: very m. madness
286:1

mid-winter: In the bleak m.
253:6

mieux: *Tout est pour le m.*
331:12

might: m. half slumb'ring 182:4

run with all your m. 248:9

With all thy m. 220:4

mighty: How are the m. fallen
32:13

Look on my works, ye M.
294:6

miles: m. to go before I sleep
138:7

milk: flowing with m. and honey
30:10

    gone to m. the bull 173:10

    m. of human kindness 275:15

    m. the cow of the world 344:2

    sincere m. of the word 49:3

    With m. and honey blest 28:5

Mill: at the M. with slaves 218:5

    M., / By a mighty effort of
will 28:4

Millennium: description of the
M. 154:5

miller: Than wots the m. of
284:11

millionaire: m. makes me less
forlorn 300:8

    M.. That is my religion 288:12

mills: dark Satanic m. 51:12

    m. of God grind slow 197:4

mill-stones: Turned to m. as they
fell 293:11

Milton: M., Death and Sin 359:3

    M.! thou should'st be living
354:5

    M. wrote in fetters 51:10

    more than M. can / To justify
166:2

    mute inglorious M. 148:4

mimicry: their lives a m. 345:1

mimsy: All m. were the
borogoves 81:1

mind: and in the m. of man
352:3

    but with the m. 279:15

    cannot get out of my m. 155:3

    concentrates his m.
wonderfully 174:11

    duty to speak one's m. 346:5

    healthy m. in a healthy body
178:8

    like workings of one m. 353:3

    M., from pleasure less 207:10

    m. has mountains 164:2

    m. is its own place 216:2

    m. is the man himself 92:8

    minister to a m. diseased
277:12

physicians of a m. diseased
3:2

    pleased to call his m. 28:8

    Reading is to the m. what
exercise 307:3

    which the m. knows nothing of
232:10

minded: had m. what they were
about 307:10

mind-forged: m. manacles I hear
53:3

minds: best m. of my generation
144:4

    in the m. of men that . . . peace
9:3

    lose myself in other men's m.
189:6

mine: Was ever grief like m.
158:12

minion: morning morning's m.
164:4

ministers: actions are my m.'
84:3

ministries: Times has made
many m. 19:8

ministry: marriage than a m.
19:9

minority: m. is always right
169:4

minstrel: wandering m. I 142:13

minutes: m. hasten to their end
287:3

    set with sixty diamond m.
204:3

miracle: prays for a m. 325:2

    to establish a m. 167:8

miraculous: more m. than the
fact 167:8

mirror: m. crack'd from side
317:10

    m. up to nature 268:10

    m. walking along the highway
307:7

mirth: Far from all resort of m.
214:5

    Him serve with m. 184:13

    M., admit me of thy crew
214:10

    m. as does not make friends
ashamed 335:10

very tragical m. 280:7

misanthropy: ethics,
    compounded of m. 200:12

mischief: some m. still / For idle
    hands 337:6

miserable: Nothing is m. unless
    you think 53:7
    short, so it is very m. 316:1

miserere: *m. nobis* 210:2

Misery: M. acquaints a man
    284:2
    result m. 110:5

misfortune: next greatest m. to
    losing 340:2

misfortunes: tableau of crimes
    and m. 332:5

Miss: M. T eats / Turns into
    108:6
    You'll me brother 159:4

missed: never would be m.
    143:2

missus: punctual snorin' m.
    201:6

mistaken: possible you may be
    m. 103:11

mistakes: all the m. which can
    be made 53:9
    makes no m. does not usually
    235:3

mistress: m. some rich anger
    shows 181:4
    principles or your m. 348:11
    young m. is better than an old
    340:8

mistresses: m. with great smooth
    marbly 59:11

mists: Season of m. 179:4

misunderstand: m. a lot 136:4

misunderstood: admired through
    being m. 95:3

mix: kiss her and m. her with
    me 314:3

mob: governors, the m. 334:11
    M., Parliament 94:6

mobs: Suppose there are two m.
    112:4

mock: m. on, Voltaire 52:3
    m. / The meat it feeds on
    281:6

mocked: God is not m. 47:7

mocking bird: Out of the m.'s
    throat 343:2

model: m. of a modern Major-
    General 143:12

moderation: m. even in excess
    114:10
    M. is a fatal thing 348:3

modern: disease of m. life 13:2
    M. life would be very tedious
    345:11

moderns: Speak of the m.
    without contempt 87:11

mole: still working like a m.
    158:8

moment: Every m. dies a man
    319:5

momentary: pleasure is m. 88:8

moments: lovely m. but awful
    quarters 254:1
    m. big as years 180:5
    m. of the happiest and best
    296:2

monarch: merry m., scandalous
    251:2
    m. of all I survey 102:7

monarchs: fate summons, m.
    must obey 121:10

Monarchy: M. is a strong
    government 19:10
    universal M. of wit 78:2

Monday: M.'s child is fair of face
    8:3

Money: Aristocracy of the M.
    bag 79:7
    fool and have m. . . . at debate
    325:3
    I love m. 300:8
    know the value of m. 137:3
    love of m. is the root 48:8
    M. doesn't talk, it swears
    123:5
    M. is indeed the most
    important 288:9
    M. is like muck 18:3
    m. of fools 161:3
    M. speaks sense 26:9
    not asked to lend m. 326:5
    only interested in m. 291:5
    parted . . . genius and his m.
    296:3

pretty to see what m. will do
234:12

print your own m. 322:6

Put m. in thy purse 281:2

rub up against m. long enough
255:1

than in getting m. 174:5

time is m. 136:5

want of m. 71:6

wrote, except for m. 174:10

Zzzzzp! M. 349:2

monkey: into baboon and m.
284:10

monkeys: Goats and m. 281:11

monotony: m. of a decorous age
129:4

monster: green-ey'd m. 281:6

monstruosity: m. in love, lady
285:4

monument: would see his m.
355:2

monumentum: *Si m. requiris*
355:2

moon: auld m. in her arm 21:8

from the pale-faced m. 269:15

inconstant m., / That monthly
changes 283:5

m. / Walks the night 108:7

mortals call the M. 292:2

shone the wintry m. 179:13

moonlight: Ill met by m. 280:1

sweet the m. sleeps 279:5

moonshine: consider every thing
as m. 261:7

moping: m. mum, / Whose soul
143:3

moquer: *Se m. de la philosophie*
233:1

Moral: *dann Kommt die M.* 56:2

Debasing the m. currency
125:8

M. indignation is jealousy
340:12

m. when he is only
uncomfortable 289:8

perfectly m. till all are moral
304:6

persons attempting to find a
m. 325:10

To point a m. 172:10

moralitee: Goodbye, m. 158:2

morality: Conventiality is not m.
56:8

Fodder . . . then m. 56:2

Master m. 226:8

m., and some of religion 124:2

M. . . . attitude we adopt 345:8

m. for morality's sake 100:8

M. is the herd-instinct 226:11

periodical fits of m. 200:11

successful personal and
national m. 288:9

moralize: m. my song 305:4

morals: Have you no m., man
291:1

m. of a whore 173:3

More: M. light 145:11

M. will mean worse 5:3

Oliver Twist has asked for m.
111:14

mores: *tempora! O m.* 92:9

mori: *pro patria m.* 165:5

moriar: *Non omnis m.* 165:6

morituri: *m. te salutant* 311:5

morn: m., in russet mantle clad
266:14

m. to night, my friend 253:9

morning: Early one m., just as
6:5

Good m. to the day 176:7

many a glorious m. 287:2

Never glad confident m. 60:14

Bowl: Morning in the B. of Night
133:5

moron: wish I were a m. 9:1

morrow: m. shall take thought
43:1

mort: *m. ne surprend* 135:1

M., vieux capitaine 24:5

mortal: tatter in its m. dress
357:11

mortality: nothing serious in m.
276:15

Mortis: *Timor M. conturbat me*
122:12

most: m. may err 120:9

moth: m. and rust doth corrupt
42:6

m. in his brother's parachute
298:5

mother: great sweet m. 314:3
Honour . . . thy m. 31:6
like saying, 'My m., drunk 89:6
M. and lover of men 314:3
m. drudge for his living 289:2
m., / Who'd give her booby 141:1
never called me m. 351:6
Never throw stones at your m. 26:5

mothers: women become like their m. 346:1

motion: m. and a spirit, that impels 352:3
order'd m., but ordain'd no rest 328:9

motive: mercenary, and the prudent m. 16:1
Persons attempting to find a m. 325:10

motiveless: m. malignity 97:1

mountain: Land of the m. and the flood 260:2
tiptoe on the misty m. tops 283:9

mountains: beautiful upon the m. 39:7
faith . . . could remove m. 46:19
High m. are a feeling 73:4
men and m. meet 51:4
M. are . . . natural scenery 255:4
M. are the beginning 255:4
m. look on Marathon 74:8

mourn: m. with ever-returning spring 343:9
No longer m. for me 287:4

Mourns: M. less for what age takes 352:1

mouse: not even a m. 221:3

moustache: didn't wax his m. 187:9

mouth: false m. was like faint flowers 292:7

move: But it does m. 139:11
I will m. the earth 11:1

Much: M. of a muchness 328:5

Muchos: M. pocos hacen 83:4

muck: m., not good except it be spread 51:9

Muckle: M. he made o' that 55:9

mud: One sees the m. 190:3

muffs: m. his real job 340:10

multiply: Be fruitful, and m. 29:6

multitude: cover the m. of sins 49:4

multitudes: I am large, I contain m. 343:7

multitudinous: m. seas incarnadine 276:10

munch: So m. on, crunch on 61:8

mundi: peccata m. 210:2

Murder: I met M. on the way 293:10
love and m. will out 99:2
Macbeth does m. sleep 276:9
m. back into the home 160:9
M., like talent 194:4
M. most foul 267:11
M. . . . One of the Fine Arts 109:4
m. to dissect 354:7
once indulges himself in m. 109:3
What is slavery? . . . M. 247:3

murdered: Each one a m. self 253:10
m. both his parents 195:7

Murray: slain the Earl of M. 20:10

Muse: M. of fire 270:15
M., who now governs the periodical 324:6

music: Architecture is frozen m. 145:10
brave M. of a *distant* Drum 133:7
but the m. there 241:1
Fled is that m. 182:1
formed, as notes of m. are 292:5
how potent cheap m. 101:2
If m. be the food of love 285:9
I shall be made thy M. 117:9
know anything about m. 26:2
make the m. mute 317:2

merry when I hear sweet m.
279:7

M. and women I cannot but
234:11

M. has charms to soothe 99:5

M. helps not the toothache
159:3

. m. in my heart I bore 353:9

M. is essentially useless 257:7

m. is good to the melancholy
306:1

m. is the brandy of the
damned 289:6

M. shall untune the sky 122:2

M. that gentlier on the spirit
318:3

M., the greatest good 1:9

M., when soft voices die
295:12

m., yearning like a God 179:10

Poetry is . . . set
to . . . lascivious m. 211:7

read m. but can't hear 25:9

sounds of m. / Creep in 279:5

still, sad m. of humanity 352:2

stops when the m. stops 155:7

towards the condition of m.
233:2

Van Gogh's ear for m. 339:7

musicologist: m. is a man who
25:9

Musing: M. in solitude 351:10

Muss: *M. es sein* 26:4

Must: M.! is must a word 128:4

M. it be 26:4

You can, for you m. 145:8

mustn't: tell her she m. 248:1

mutabile: *m. semper / Femina*
331:1

Mutability: M. in them doth play
305:11

mutantur: *brevi spatio m.* 199:3

muttering: m. grew to a
grumbling 61:7

myriad-minded: m. Shakespeare
96:11

Myriads: outshine / M. though
bright 215:14

myrrh: frankincense, and m.
41:5

Myrtles: Ye M. brown 215:1

myself: and sing m. 343:3

been one m. for years 139:2

m. am Hell 217:4

mysterious: m. way / His
wonders 102:2

mystery: m. will lead millions
54:4

shew you a m. 47:3

mystic: white samite, m.,
wonderful 317:3

Nagasaki: ashamed of, even
in . . . N. 56:6

nail: want of a n., the shoe 137:5

nails: nineteen hundred and forty
n. 298:7

with his n. he'll dig them up
339:1

naïve: n. domestic Burgundy
323:5

naked: left me n. to mine
enemies 272:5

n. into the conference chamber
29:1

n. is the best disguise 99:3

seek / With n. foot 355:5

starving hysterical n. 144:4

nakid: n. as a worm was she
86:9

name: committed in thy n.
251:10

my good n. / Robs me 281:5

n. great in story 76:1

n. . . . in the Pantheon of
History 105:10

n. liveth for evermore 41:3

n. was writ in water 184:5

Thou shalt not take the n. 31:5

What's in a n. 283:4

wrote her n. upon the sand
305:2

Napoleon: dog, every man is N.
168:7

N. of crime 119:2

narrative: bald and unconvincing
n. 143:6

nasty: n., brutish, and short
161:5

n. in the woodshed 142:1

nation: n. of amateurs 253:3

oblique: As Lines so Loves o. 207:6

oblivion: alms for o. 285:5
commend / To cold o. 292:6
iniquity of o. 58:5

obscurity: decent o. of a learned 141:7

observance: breach than the o. 267:9

obstinacy: o. in a bad one 308:1

obstruction: lie in cold o. 278:5

occupation: Othello's o.'s gone 281:8

occupations: worse o. in the world 307:8

occurred: description of what has never o. 344:7

occurs: o. is of the smallest importance 347:5

ocean: great o. of truth lay 226:3
Mind, that O. where 207:10
round o. and the living air 352:3
Upon a painted o. 95:10
who has not seen the o. 20:2

oceans: Portable, and compendious o. 103:7

ocular: o. proof 281:9

odd: divinity in o. numbers 279:13
How o. / Of God 131:5
think it exceedingly o. 188:6

Ode on a Grecian Urn: 'O.' is worth any number 131:11

Oderint: O. dum metuant 1:1

odorous: Comparisons are o. 280:12

o'erthrown: noble mind is here o. 268:6

Off: O. with his head 80:6
O. with his head – so much for 92:2

offence: Satire . . . never . . . an o. 312:7

offend: If thine eye o. thee 43:17

offer: o. he can't refuse 55:6

Officiously: strive / O. to keep alive 94:3

oil: midnight o. 140:10

old: I grow o. 127:1

no country for o. men 357:10

no man would be o. 312:13

off with the o. love 7:9

O. Age a regret 114:6

o. believe everything 347:7

penny in the o. man's hat 6:2

redress the balance of the O. 78:1

Ring out the o. 317:10

season for the o. to learn 3:1

should not o. men be mad 358:9

tell an o. soldier by 287:13

They shall grow not o. 50:4

too o. to cry 196:2

virtuous in their o. age 312:14

When you are very o. 251:11

woman as o. as she looks 97:5

You are o., Father William 303:10

oldest: in literature, the o. 63:1
o. hath borne most 275:4

Olympus': O. faded hierarchy 182:2

one: do only o. thing at once 299:4
o. for all 122:10
O., on God's side 235:5

one-eyed: o. yellow idol 153:6

one up: How to be o. 243:4

onions: eyes smell o.; I shall weep 264:7

Onward: O.! Christian soldiers 23:2

open: o. face of heaven 183:1
O. Sesame 10:10
O. them wide that she 305:3

openly: o. arrived at 350:1

opinion: minus one, were of one o. 212:7

opinions: halt ye between two o. 32:18
think o. are accursed 357:9
thoughts are someone else's o. 345:1
wish to punish o. 20:5

opium: just, subtle, and mighty o. 109:2
Religion . . . is the o. 208:12

opportunity: man must make his
  o. 16:12
  maximum of o. 289:13
opposition: secure without a
  formidable o. 114:3
oppressive: o. government is
  more to be feared 98:2
optimism: o. . . . of
  physiological . . . origin 327:4
  pessimism . . . as agreeable as
  o. 27:9
optimist: o. proclaims . . . best of
  all possible worlds 76:5
opus: *Hoc o., hic labor est* 331:2
orare: *Laborare est o.* 7:11
order: Blessed rage for o. 308:10
  not necessarily in that o. 144:8
  o. in variety we see 242:14
  upon the o. of your going
  277:2
ore: your subject with o. 184:4
organ: organ o. all the time
  321:9
organized: o. common sense
  168:9
original: common things in an o.
  way 164:7
  Their great O. proclaim 2:4
orisons: patter out their hasty o.
  230:2
ornament: still deceived with o.
  278:17
orphan: grounds that he was an
  o. 195:7
orthodox: prove their doctrine o.
  70:12
Orthodoxy: O. is my doxy 335:11
Ossa: heap O. on Pelion 331:10
ostrich: rear end of an o. 340:7
Othello: O.'s occupation's gone
  281:8
other: I can do no o. 199:6
  no o. world 130:5
others: Do not do unto o. 289:12
otherwise: some are o. 302:4
otia: *haec o. fecit* 331:5
otiosus: *o., nec minus solum*
  92:7
ought: not what we o. to say
  275:4

perception that something o.
  to be done 340:13
WHERE O. I TO BE 90:3
  which we do to have done
  244:5
ourselis: see o. as others see us
  69:2
ourselves: do with o. this
  afternoon 133:13
  in o., are triumph 197:9
  in o. that we are thus 281:1
  love of power . . . love of o.
  154:7
out: at other o. it wente 87:2
outgrabe: mome raths o. 81:1
Outshone: O. the wealth of
  Ormus 216:6
outside: contempt for the o. 88:3
  I am just going to o. 228:3
outward: looketh on the o.
  appearance 32:9
  o. shows be least themselves
  278:17
over: oversexed, and o. here 8:7
overcomes: who o. his enemies
  11:8
over-dressed: occasionally a little
  o. 347:9
over-educated: always absolutely
  o. 347:9
Overpaid: O., overfed 8:7
overrated: much o. by the poets
  122:8
ovo: *Ex o. omnia* 153:2
owed: o. by so many to so few
  91:2
Owl: O. and the Pussy-Cat 193:2
  o., for all his feathers 179:8
  sings the staring o. 275:10
owls: couch when o. do cry
  284:7
own: but mine o. 266:9
oxen: see the o. kneel 151:10
  than a hundred pair of o.
  166:4
Oxford: nonsense . . . put back at
  O. 25:11
oyster: unselfishness of an o.
  256:9
  world's mine o. 279:9

oysters: first ventured on eating of o. 139:3
  Poverty and o. 112:5
Ozymandias: O., king of kings 294:6

pace: e nostra p. 105:8
pacem: Qui desiderat p. 329:2
Pacific: star'd at the P. 182:8
pack: revenged on the whole p. 286:4
paddle: p. his own canoe 207:1
pageant: insubstantial p. faded 284:4
paid: might as well get p. 123:1
Pain: Our Lady of P. 313:6
  p. of a new idea 20:7
  Sweet is pleasure after p. 121:1
pains: infinite capacity for taking p. 164:6
paint: looking as fresh as p. 299:3
  p. an inch thick 269:6
  p. in the public's face 255:3
  p. the lily 273:14
painted: p. ship / Upon a painted 95:10
  young as they are p. 25:10
painter: vast commendation of a p. 132:9
painters: bad [p.] vomit Nature 83:6
  Light is the first of p. 130:1
painting: Poetry is like p. 164:10
palaces: cottages princes' p. 278:8
pale: Prithee, why so p. 311:3
Palladium: P. of all the civil 178:2
palliate: neither attempt to p. nor deny 236:1
Pallida: P. Mors 165:1
palms: before my feet 88:10
pampered: p. jades of Asia 206:6
Pan: great god P. is dead 237:8
Panem: P. et circenses 178:7
Pange: P., lingua 329:3
pantaloon: lean and slipper'd p. 266:2
panteth: As the hart p. 34:6

Pantheon: P. of History 105:10
panting: For ever p. 180:12
parachute: moth in his brother's p. 298:5
parade: p. of riches 299:7
paradise: England . . . p. of women 134:7
  enjoy p. in the next 25:8
  hast the keys of P. 109:2
  p. for a sect 180:1
  sing / Recover'd P. 218:1
  Wilderness is P. enow 133:6
paradises: true p. . . . we have lost 247:5
Parallel: ours so truly P. 207:6
pardon: God will p. me 155:5
pardonnera: Dieu me p. 155:5
parent: object to an aged p. 110:11
  To lose one p. 345:13
parenthesis: small p. in eternity 58:3
parents: begin by loving their p. 348:1
  murdered both his p. 195:7
  P. are the last people 71:13
parfit: verray, p. gentil knyght 84:9
Paris: P. is well worth a mass 156:7
  When P. sneezes, Europe 212:2
parish: world as my p. 341:4
parliament: he is a member of p. 64:5
  honest by the act of p. 176:1
  Mob, P. 94:6
  P. is . . . a big meeting 20:1
  p. men o' our ain 261:3
Parliaments: England . . . mother of P. 56:3
parlour: walk into my p. 166:6
parochial: p. in the beginning to be cosmopolitan 221:5
parrot: sell the family p. 251:8
parson: Monday is p.'s holiday 311:8
  P. left conjuring 262:6
part: from yours you will not p. 311:1

heart ay's the p. 66:9
let us kiss and p. 120:1
parterre: nod on the p. 240:5
particle: mind, that very fiery p.
75:2
Particulars: must do it in Minute
P. 51:7
Parting: P. is all we know of
heaven 113:3
p. is such sweet sorrow 283:6
Partir: P. c'est mourir 150:7
Parts: P. of it are excellent 248:4
sum of the p. 11:9
party: Conservatives ... the
stupidest p. 212:5
of the Devil's p. 51:10
Patriotism is of no p. 302:6
Stick to your p. 115:5
pasarán: No p. 169:3
pass: They shall not p. 227:5
They shall not p. 169:3
passage: p. which you think is
particularly fine 174:4
passed: p. away a glory 352:6
So he p. over 63:12
passengers: we the p. 166:5
passer: laissez p. 248:8
P. mortuus est 82:7
passeront: Ils ne p. pas 227:5
passes: Men seldom make p.
231:8
passing: p. brave to be a King
206:3
passing-bells: p. for these who
die 230:2
passion: all p. spent 218:7
In her first p. woman 74:6
one universal p.: fear 290:11
P. for fame 64:7
p. shall have spent 318:2
ruling P. conquers Reason
240:2
tear a p. to tatters 268:8
tender p. is much overrated
122:8
Passions: dissemble their P.
better 306:12
not his reasons, but his p.
308:2
p. as it is with fire 193:8

p. ... bad masters 193:8
their p. a quotation 345:1
various ruling p. find 239:9
past: alter the p., historians can
71:7
p. is a foreign country 153:1
p., it is needless to blame 98:3
power to change the p. 3:3
remembrance of things p.
287:1
world is weary of the p. 293:3
Pastoral: Cold P. 180:13
Pastures: and P. new 215:7
pat: Now I might do it p. 268:12
P. he comes 274:4
patches: king of shreds and p.
269:1
pâtés: eating p. de foie gras to
the sound 301:9
path: That is the p. of
wickedness 22:1
paths: all her p. are peace 36:6
all her p. are peace 306:7
So many p. that wind 344:4
patience: Genius ... a greater
aptitude for p. 62:9
patria: pro p. mori 165:5
Patriot: Idea of a P. King 54:3
p.'s boast, where'er we roam
146:6
patriotic: fights you on p.
principles 290:12
Patriotism: P. is of no party
302:6
P. is the last refuge 174:6
whose p. would not gain 172:4
patriots: blood of p. and tyrants
171:1
Patron: is not a P. 173:2
Pax: P. Vobis 334:3
pays: You p. your money 10:6
peace: all her paths are p. 36:6
all her paths are p. 306:7
desires p., prepare for war
329:2
desolation, and call it p. 315:3
Give p. in our time 244:10
god has made this p. 331:5
hereafter forever hold his p.
245:11

Perdition: P. catch my soul 281:4

père: *vous n'avez plus de p.* 225:3

Pereant: *P. . . . qui ante nos* 115:11

Perfect: P. love casteth out fear 49:6

perfection: ascertain what p. is 13:7

heart contains p.'s germ 295:6

let us speak of p. 244:2

P. of the life 356:3

perfectly: be p. free till all 304:6

perfidious: in England 54:10

perform: cannot p. great things themselves 335:4

performance: desire . . . outlive p. 270:9

perfume: p. on the violet 273:14

perfumes: All the p. of Arabia 277:9

Perhaps: grand P. 59:6

seek a great p. 249:3

perish: not p. from the earth 195:6

p. with the sword 44:11

periwig-pated: robustious p. fellow 268:8

perpetual: p. light shine 210:1

persecution: truth put down by p. 212:8

Persepolis: ride in triumph through P. 206:3

perseverance: p. in a good cause 308:1

Persians: Medes and the P. 40:9

person: altered her p. for the worse 312:8

personality: not the expression of p. 128:1

persons: God is no respecter of p. 46:10

perspiration: ninety-nine per cent p. 124:4

persuading: p. others, we convince ourselves 178:3

pessimism: p. of . . . pathological origin 327:4

P., when you get used to it 27:9

pessimist: p. fears this is true 76:5

Petals: P. on a wet, black bough 243:9

petar: Hoist with his own p. 269:3

Peter: Thou art P. 43:14

pet-lamb: p. in a sentimental farce 181:2

Petrarch: if Laura had been P.'s wife 74:7

peur: *sans p. et sans reproche* 6:1

peut-être: *chercher un grand p.* 249:3

phantasma: Like a p. or a hideous 272:12

phenomenon: infant p. 111:10

Philadelphia: rather be in P. 133:4

Philistines: P. may jostle 143:11

philosopher: absurd but some p. has said 92:4

by the p. as equally false 141:8

great poet . . . profound p. 96:12

guide, p., and friend 242:4

p.; but, I don't know how 124:8

philosophers: least a nation of pure p. 19:12

p. have only interpreted 208:13

philosophy: Adversity's sweet milk, p. 283:8

dreamt of in your p. 267:12

high-rife / With old P. 180:8

History is P. teaching 54:1

history of Western p. is 342:10

little P. inclineth . . . to Atheism 18:4

P. is nothing but discretion 262:8

p. out of closets 2:1

p. to be substantially true 257:9

To ridicule p. is really 233:1

touch of cold p. 180:7

physic: Take p., pomp 274:9

Physician: P., heal thyself 45:7

Physicians: P. are like kings 338:10

P. of all men are most happy 248:7

p. of a mind diseased 3:2

physicists: p. have known sin 228:8

physiological: pessimism, of p. or pathological 327:4

pianist: do not shoot the p. 346:8

Picasso: sausage and thinks of P. 157:10

Piccadilly: Good-bye P. 349:1
walk down P. with a poppy 143:11

pictura: *Ut p. poesis* 164:10

pictures: cutting all the p. out 26:10
You furnish the p. 154:8

pie: p. in the sky 160:3

pie-crust: p. are made to be broken 312:1

piety: each to each by natural p. 352:5
p. would not grow warmer 172:4

pigs: as p. have to fly 80:8
whether p. have wings 81:5

Pilate: jesting P. 17:1

pilgrim: To be a p. 63:11

pillar: became a p. of salt 30:3
cannot be regarded as a p. 211:2
triple of the world 264:8

pillars: hewn out her seven p. 36:9

Pilot: P. of the Galilean lake 215:5

Pimpernel: demmed, elusive P. 228:9

pipe: drawn through a p. 189:11
p. . . . and smoke it 23:1

piping: p. time of peace 282:11

pissing: outside p. in 171:10

pistol: p. misses fire, he knocks 146:11

pistols: young ones carry p. 287:13

pitchfork: drive away Nature with a p. 164:12

pity: incidents arousing p. and fear 11:15
P. is but one remove 250:10
p. of it, Iago 281:10
Poetry is in the p. 230:6
to a woman's love / P.'s 134:6

place: genius of the p. 240:4
Men in Great P. 17:10
not love a p. the less 15:9
own p. in the sun 62:10
p. for everything 299:5

plagiarist: Art is either a p. 140:3

plague: instruments to p. us 275:3
p. o' both your houses 283:7
winter, p. and pestilence 224:8

plain: portion of that unknown p. 151:5

plains: ringing p. of windy Troy 319:2

plan: maze! but not without a p. 241:6

planet: new p. swims into 182:8

platitude: longitude with no p. 139:1

Plato: footnotes to P. 342:10
wrong with P. than right 92:13

play: before the p. be done 106:8
not p. things as they are 308:11
our p. is played out 320:8
P. . . . . not obliged to do 326:6
p.'s the thing 267:21
p. the man 191:8
P. up! play up 225:7
prologue to a very dull P. 99:8

playboy: p. of the western world 314:7

played: p. upon a stage now 286:2

player: poor p., / That struts and frets 277:13

players: men and women merely p. 265:15

playthings: Old boys have their p. 137:2

pleasance: Youth is full of p. 286:11

pleasant: castle hath a p. seat 276:2

lovely and p. in their lives 32:12

pleasantness: ways of p. 36:6

please: death after life, does greatly p. 305:8

hard to p. himself 121:3

I am to do what I p. 137:14

say what they p. 137:14

To tax and to p. 64:8

pleased: or are you just p. to see me 341:6

pleasing consists in being p. 154:4

pleases: Though every prospect p. 155:1

pleasing: p. consists in being pleased 154:4

pleasure: For physical p. . . . go to my dentist 338:2

gave p. to the spectators 200:8

hatred . . . becomes a p. 75:4

It becomes a p. 346:5

Love ceases to be a p. 26:6

love of p. 239:9

p. is momentary 88:8

p. of being moved 189:1

p. was his business 124:3

public stock of harmless p. 172:6

rich wot gets the p. 7:10

seize the p. at once 15:5

Sweet is p. after pain 121:1

Variety is the soul of p. 26:8

when Youth and P. meet 73:1

pleasure-dome: stately by decree 96:6

pleasures: all the p. prove 206:2

cannot understand the p. 15:3

Garden . . . purest of human P. 18:11

Heaven forbids certain p. 220:1

hypocrite in his p. 175:5

our p. with rough strife 208:6

unreproved free p. 214:10

plenty: wasna fou, but just had p. 66:5

pleure: *Il p. dans mon coeur* 329:8

Pleurez: *P.! enfants* 225:3

plight: I p. thee my troth 245:13

plods: ploughman homeward p. 148:3

plot: blessed p., this earth 282:5

find a p. in it will be shot 325:10

now the p. thickens 62:7

What the devil does the p. signify 62:6

plough: We p. the fields 93:2

plowshares: swords into p. 38:5

pluck: offend thee, p. it out 43:17

plumage: pities the p. 230:11

plump: Stately, p. Buck Mulligan 177:6

plurality: p. of loves no crime 116:11

poacher: p. a keeper turned 185:8

pocket: not scruple to pick a p. 108:11

poem: life of a man . . . a heroic p. 78:7

married to a p. 184:3

p. is never finished 328:1

p. may be worked over 138:8

poems: My p. are licentious 207:3

poesis: *Ut pictura p.* 164:10

poesy: p.; 'tis the supreme of power 182:4

viewless wings of P. 181:11

poet: flattery lost on p.'s ear 259:9

God is the perfect p. 61:4

great p. . . . profound philosopher 96:12

Honour the greatest p. 105:7

lunatic, the lover, and the p. 280:5

no person can be a p. 200:9

p. and the dreamer 180:3

p.'s fate is here 341:5

pomp: In lowly p. ride 213:5
   servile P. 216:9
   Take physic, p. 274:9
Pons: *P. asinorum* 131:2
poor: Decent means p. 234:2
   grind the faces of the p. 38:6
   live by robbing the p. 289:7
   p. and independent 94:5
   p. and I've been rich 324:11
   p. are the blacks of Europe
      83:10
   p.'s decay 146:2
   p. wot gets the blame 7:10
Pope: P.! How many divisions
      306:9
poppies: p. grow / In Flanders
      fields 201:2
poppy: oblivion blindly
      scattereth her p. 58:5
popular: more p. than Jesus
      Christ 193:7
populi: *Salus p. suprema* 262:7
Pornography: P. is the attempt
      to insult sex 192:5
port: p. after stormy seas 305:8
   p. for men 175:1
Portion: I become / P. of that
      around me 73:4
portrait: paint a p. I lose a friend
      257:10
   two styles of p. painting 111:8
position: p. ridiculous 88:8
possession: p. of it is intolerable
      328:4
possibilities: not interested in the
      p. 330:3
possibility: exhaust the
      boundaries of p. 235:7
   sceptic to deny the p. 169:1
possible: Politics ... art of the p.
      50:5
   p. as being probable 12:1
   states that something is p.
      93:1
   with God all things are p. 44:2
Posterity: see P. do something
      for us 2:6
posthumously: some are born p.
      226:9

pot: chicken in his p. every
      Sunday 156:8
   doth keel the p. 275:10
   flinging a p. of paint 255:3
   who the P. 133:10
potage: mess of p. 6:7
potent: how p. cheap music is
      101:2
Potomac: All quiet along the P.
      26:3
   quiet along the P. 201:1
pots: ands were p. and pans
      234:5
Potter: Who *is* the P. 133:10
pound: p. ... in your pocket
      349:8
Poverty: P. and oysters 112:5
   P. is an anomaly to rich
      people 20:3
   P. is no disgrace 301:13
   suffer so much p. and excess
      234:7
power: balance of p. 335:6
   Corridors of P. 302:8
   good want p. 294:10
   have p. over men 351:2
   Knowledge itself is p. 19:6
   Political p. grows 204:5
   P. dwells apart 294:2
   p. is the love of ourselves
      154:7
   P. is the ultimate aphrodisiac
      188:1
   p. over people so long 303:2
   P. tends to corrupt 1:3
   P. without responsibility
      187:15
   seek P. and to lose Liberty
      17:10
   shadow of some unseen P.
      293:4
   valued because they confer p.
      255:10
   Zzzzzzp! — P. 349:2
powerless: p. to be born 12:9
practical: power of sustained p.
      activity 315:9
practise: p. what you preach
      171:4

praise: but they only want p. 210:5

Damn with faint p. 239:13

dieted with p. 181:2

dispraised, is the most perfect p. 175:14

not to p. him 273:5

p. famous men 41:1

P. the Lord, all nations 333:11

P. the Lord and pass 135:10

praises: faint p. one another damn 355:7

pray: just going to p. for you 301:11

P. without ceasing 48:6

prayer: but one p. to God 333:5

Four spend in p. 95:6

God erects a house of p. 107:8

Work is p. 7:11

prayers: fall to thy p. 270:14

Robin is saying his p. 213:12

three mile p. 69:5

praying: No p., it spoils business 229:10

prays: Whatever a man p. for 325:2

preach: practise what you p. 171:4

preached: p. to death by wild curates 301:7

Preachers: P. say, Do as I 263:1

preaching: woman's p. is like a dog's 173:7

precious: so p. as the Goods 133:11

predestinate: In p. grooves 152:3

prejudice: popular p. runs in favour of two 111:7

Without the aid of p. 154:3

prejudices: bundle of p. 189:3

merely rearranging their p. 170:9

p. acquired by age eighteen 125:2

p. a man so 301:12

strengthen their own p. 122:7

preparation: happiness destroyed by p. 15:5

Prepare: P. ye the way 39:2

P. ye the way of the Lord 41:6

prerogative: p. of the harlot 187:15

presence: better than p. of mind 247:8

present: behold these p. days 287:7

golden age never was the p. 136:11

p. in time future 126:1

preserver: Destroyer and p.; hear 294:4

President: P. of the Immortals 151:11

press: Muse, who now governs . . . p. 324:6

p. is the *Palladium* 178:2

pressure: Grace under p. 156:2

presumption: amused by its p. 323:5

prêt: *toujours p. à partir* 135:1

Pretender: who P. is, or who is King 72:7

pretexts: Tyrants seldom want p. 65:5

pretty: Arguments out of a p. mouth 2:8

come to a p. pass when religion 210:10

prevail: cares whether it p. or not 233:7

price: peace at any p. 171:8

those men have their p. 335:7

prices: stroke, reduce the rise of p. 154:9

prick: if honour p. me off 270:4

p. us, do we not bleed 278:16

pricking: knight was p. on the plain 305:5

pricks: kick against the p. 46:9

pride: He that is low no p. 63:9

P. goeth before destruction 36:12

p. that apes humility 96:3

priest: entrails of the last p. 113:6

free me of this turbulent p. 156:9

p. continues what the nurse 121:7

true God's P. 78:2

priestcraft: ere p. did begin 120:3

priests: p. dare babble of a God 295:7

primrose: The p. way 276:13

prince: p. of Aquitaine 225:4
P. of Peace 38:9
Who made the a p. 30:8

princes: Put not your trust in p. 36:5

principle: does everything on p. 290:12
from some strong p. 211:1
rebels from p. 64:4

principles: activity by reference to p. 315:9
Damn your p. 115:5
p. or your mistress 348:11

printed: chaff is p. 166:8

printers: books by which the p. have lost 139:6

Printing: civilization, Gunpowder, P. 78:9

Prison: P. make / Nor Iron 198:9
p. where I live 282:9
Shades of the p. house 352:7
soul in p., I am not free 107:4

prisoners: blue / Which p. call the sky 344:5

Prisons: P. are built with stones 52:5

private: agreed to none of it in p. 15:6
fine and p. place 208:5
invade the sphere of p. life 210:10
public zeal to cancel p. crimes 120:7

privilege: Death is the p. 254:7

Privileged: P. and the People 114:9

prize: p. the thing ungained more 285:1

proba: vita p. 207:3

probable: possible as being p. 12:1

problem: solution of the p. of life 350:2

proceeds: good conscience on the p. 300:3

procrastinates: One yawns, one p. 88:7

procrastination: from that to incivility and p. 109:3

procul: p. este, profani 331:3

profane: far from me, let all p. ones be 331:3

profaned: word is too often p. 295:13

profani: procul este, p. 331:3

profession: It is his p. 155:5

professions: p. are conspiracies 288:5

profit: may p. by their example 157:3

profited: What is a man p. 43:16

profits: little p. that an idle king 318:11

profundis: De p. 333:12

Progress: calls each fresh link P. 62:5
'P.' is the exchange of one nuisance 128:6
p.... beyond its income 72:2
p. depends on the unreasonable 290:1
P., man's distinctive mark 59:14
P. was all right 323:8

progression: contraries is no p. 51:8

progressive: enemy of p. ideals 27:6

proletariat: dictatorship of the p. 209:1

prologue: witty p. to a very dull Play 99:8

promise: To p. not to do 326:7

promises: I have p. to keep 138:7
P.... made to be broken 312:1

promising: destroy they first call p. 99:11

proof: ocular p. 281:9

propaganda: peace p. makes war 192:3

Proper: P. words in proper places 311:9

realms: r. of gold 182:7
reap: r. the whirlwind 40:10
　　shall r. in joy 36:2
　　soweth, that shall he also r.
　　　47:7
rear: post lay in the r. 253:5
reason: finite r. reach Infinity
　　121:15
　　for the wrong r. 127:3
　　Is r. to the soul 121:14
　　I will not R. 51:5
　　kills r. itself 219:1
　　Language is... human r. 194:3
　　love, all r. is against it 71:12
　　not his r., but his passions
　　　308:2
　　reaching after fact and r.
　　　183:4
　　r. of this thusness 336:3
　　r. to strengthen... prejudices
　　　122:7
　　ruling Passion conquers R.
　　　240:2
　　Their's not to r. why 316:9
　　Will know the r. why 153:4
reasonable: r. / Is an invention
　　of man 138:10
　　r man adapts himself 290:1
　　What is r. is true 155:2
reasons: bad r. for what we
　　believe 55:4
　　heart has its r. 232:10
rebellion: little r. now and then
　　170:10
　　R. lay in his way 270:3
rebels: subjects are r. from
　　principle 64:4
recapture: never could r. 60:8
recession: r. when your
　　neighbour loses 324:9
recording: r., not thinking 169:10
recover: seldom or never r.
　　265:4
recreation: innocent r. than
　　angling 335:9
red: r. in tooth and claw 317:8
　　thin r. line 258:6
　　wine when it is r. 36:14
redbreast: Call for the robin r.
　　338:14

redeem: r. us from virtue 313:8
redeemer: my r. liveth 33:10
redress: r. the balance of the Old
　　78:1
reed: Man is only a r. 232:11
reflect: r. all objects without
　　being sullied 98:6
refuge: God is our r. 34:9
　　last r. of a scoundrel 174:6
refusal: great r. 105:5
refuse: offer he can't r. 55:6
refute: I r. it *thus* 173:12
Regiment: Monstrous R. of
　　Women 188:5
regret: I r. a little 59:4
　　Old Age a r. 114:6
Reich: *Ein R.* 6:6
reign: Better to r. in Hell 216:3
reigned: r. with your loves 128:3
reigneth: Lord r. 33:4
rejected: despised and r. of men
　　39:8
rejoice: Amazed to find it could
　　106:7
　　R. with them that do rejoice
　　　46:16
relations: r. between the two
　　sexes 213:3
relaxes: Bless R. 52:10
Religion: brothels with bricks of
　　R. 52:5
　　depth in Philosophy... to R.
　　　18:4
　　enough in r. to make us hate
　　　312:12
　　every thing that regards r. 2:3
　　grey with age becomes r.
　　　258:8
　　groans beneath r.'s iron age
　　　295:7
　　Millionaire. That is my r.
　　　288:12
　　more fierce in its r. 225:8
　　my r. is to do good 231:1
　　One r. is as true 70:8
　　Oysters... more beautiful
　　　than... r. 256:9
　　r. but a childish toy 205:11
　　r., but give me a little snug
　　　124:2

r. for religion's sake 100:8

R. . . . is the opium 208:12

R. [not] proper subject of
conversation 88:6

reproach to r. and government
234:7

rum and true r. 74:4

Self-righteousness is not r.
56:8

talks loudly against r. 308:2

There is only one r., though
290:13

when it is allowed to invade
210:10

religious: but not r. good 152:1
whole r. complexion 128:8

remain: let one r. above 244:1

remarks: said our r. before us
115:11

remedies: extreme r. are most
fitting 160:7
not apply new R. 18:5
require desperate r. 131:12

remedy: sovereign r. to all
diseases 70:6

remember: I r., I remember
163:2
Please to r. / The Fifth 8:8
R. me when I am gone 253:7
should r. and be sad 253:8
We will r. them 50:4

Remembering: R. him like
anything 89:4

remembrance: appear almost a r.
183:10
r. of things past 287:1

remembren: ben in prosperitee, /
And it r. 87:1

Reminiscences: R. make one feel
288:10

Render: R. therefore unto Caesar
44:5

rendezvous: r. with Death 262:2

rendu: lui avons bien r. 333:2

renounce: r. the devil and all his
works 82:3

rent: That has not been r. 356:5

repaid: image, we have r. him
333:2

repair: friendship in constant r.
173:4

repay: I will r., saith the Lord
46:17

repeal: r. of bad or obnoxious
laws 147:10

repent: r. at leisure 99:7
r. it from my very soul 284:12

repentance: sinners to r. 43:7

repenteth: one sinner that r.
45:11

report: r. of my death 326:8

reporters: gallery in which the r.
200:6

reprehend: If I r. anything in
296:10

representation: Taxation without
r. 229:9

representations: just r. of general
nature 172:9

reproach: towards heaven with
fierce r. 295:3

reproche: sans peur et sans r.
6:1

republican: king's head on r.
principles 290:12
R. form of Government is the
highest 304:4

reputation: act is all, the r.
nothing 145:4
bubble r. 266:1
delicate as the r. of a woman
65:8

reputations: home of ruined r.
125:5

Requiem: R. aeternam 210:1

Requiescant: R. in pace 210:3

require: men in women do r.
52:4

rerum: lacrimae r. 330:10

res: In medias r. 164:8

resemblance: straight its own r.
find 207:10

resist: r. everything except
temptation 346:10

resistance: r. against her is vain
207:8

resolution: native hue of r. 268:4

Respect: Man hath any R. for
her 307:1

owe r. to the living 332:8

respectable: ashamed of, the
more r. 289:1

most devilish when r. 58:11

R. means rich 234:2

was genius found r. 58:10

respecter: God is no r. of
persons 131:9

respice: *r. finem* 8:10

responsibility: no sense of moral
r. 345:10

Power without r. 187:15

r. is to his art 131:11

r. . . . most men dread it 290:10

rest: Grant them eternal r. 210:1

Keep it now, and take the r.
75:10

man was not born for r. 332:1

May they r. in peace 210:3

motion, but ordain'd no r.
328:9

she's at r., and so am I 121:5

result: r. happiness 110:5

Resurrection: R. to eternal life
246:7

return: I shall r. 200:1

unto dust thou shalt r. 29:11

reveal: half r. / And half conceal
317:5

revels: r. now are ended 284:4

Revenge: R. proves its own
executioner 135:9

study of r., immortal hate
216:1

wrong us, shall we not r.
278:16

revenged: r. on the whole pack
286:4

revenges: brings in his r. 286:3

reviewing: never read a book
before r. 301:12

révolution: *c'est une r.* 191:6

r. in order to establish a
democracy 89:10

R. might, like Saturn 329:4

r. without general copulation
339:5

Sire, it is a r. 191:6

revolutionary: Clemency is also
a r. measure 109:7

revolutionist: plagiarist or a r.
140:3

Revolutions: R. are not about
trifles 12:2

Women hate r. 211:6

reward: Desert and r., I can
assure 250:9

rewards: neither r. nor
punishments 169:7

their own r. 131:9

rhetoric: For r. he could not ope
70:11

quarrel with others we make r.
358:10

rhetorician: A sophistical r.,
inebriated 115:4

rhyme: I r. for fun 66:11

Maggots half-form'd in her
238:9

rich: forbids the r. as well as the
poor 136:3

Respectable means r. 234:2

r. in things or 169:6

R. is better 324:11

r. man's joys increase 146:2

r. man to enter 44:16

r. wot gets the pleasure 7:10

Sincerely Want to be R. 100:4

richer: for r. for poorer 245:13

R. than all his tribe 281:15

riches: Infinite r. in a little
205:12

r. consists in the parade of
299:7

R., there is no real use 18:8

Richesse: *Embarras de R.* 4:6

Richmond: Sweet lass of R. Hill
327:6

richt: curst conceit o' bein' r.
201:5

rickshaw: no go the r. 203:6

riddle: r. wrapped in a mystery
90:9

ride: r. on in majesty 213:5

we r. them down 318:9

rideau: *Tirez le r.* 249:2

rides: Who r. so late 144:11

ridiculous: make my enemies r.
333:5

position r. 88:8

Romantic: R. Ireland's dead 358:2

romanticism: r. is sickness 145:9

Rome: comes round by R. 61:12
falls the Coliseum, R. shall fall 73:7
grandeur that was R. 238:4
in R., live in the Roman 4:10
loved R. more 273:4
R. has spoken 15:1
R. in Tiber melt 264:10
R., on the 15th October 141:6

Romeo: wherefore art thou R. 283:3

Ronsard: R. sang of me 251:11

room: always r. at the top 338:6
coming to that Holy r. 117:9
riches in a little r. 205:12
R. of One's Own 351:8
stay quietly in a r. 232:6

roost: always come home to r. 303:9

rooster: Hongry r. don't cackle 152:10

rose: blossom as the r. 38:12
English unofficial r. 57:7
Go, lovely R. 334:10
last r. of summer 221:9
like a full-blown r. 179:12
luck to get / One perfect r. 231:9
Luve's like a red red r. 68:3
never blows so red / The R. 133:8
r. / By any other name 283:4
R. is a rose is 307:5
saw a wild r. growing 145:5

roseau: n'est qu'un r. 232:11

rose-buds: Gather ye r. 159:9

Rosencrantz: R. and Guildenstern are dead. 269:13

rose-red: r. city 'half as old 63:14

roses: Marriage ... not a bed of r. 310:4
r., roses, all the way 61:5

Röslein: R. auf der Heiden 145:5

Rosy-fingered: R. dawn 162:8

rot: cold obstruction and to r. 278:5
to hour we r. and rot 265:14

rotten: r. in the state of Denmark 267:10

rotting: rosing reid to r. sall retour 157:5

Rough-hew: R. them how we will 269:7

roundabouts: r. we pulls up on the swings 83:7

Roundheads: R. (Right but Repulsive) 263:6

Rousseau: mock on, Voltaire, R. 52:3

royal: r. road to geometry 130:11

Royalty: R. will be strong 19:11

rub: r. up against money 255:1
there's the r. 268:1

rubber: heart is like Indian r. 56:7

rubies: price is far above r. 37:3
ruddier: r. than the cherry 140:7

ruffian: r. on the stair 156:5

rugby: Nobody ever beats Wales at r. 223:4

Rugged: R. individualism 163:7

ruin: r. of the State 51:1
to r. or to rule the state 120:6
woman look like a r. 347:13

ruined: ever r. by trade 137:8

ruins: I'm one of the r. 196:6
musing amidst the r. 141:6
shored against my r. 127:11

rule: ruin or to r. the state 120:6
R., Britannia, rule the waves 322:2

rules: hand that r. the world 334:8
[r.] established without their consent 220:10
there are no golden r. 290:4

ruling: r. Passion, be it what it will 240:2

rum: r. and true religion 74:4
Yo-ho-ho, and a bottle of r. 309:13

rumours: wars and r. of wars 44:6

run: r. at least twice as fast 81:3
runcible: ate with a r. spoon
193:3
Runic: some fallen R. stone 12:8
runs: r. will never lack followers
122:6
Rus: *R. in urbe* 207:4
rushed: r. through life trying to
save 251:6
rushes: Green grow the r. O 7:7
rushy: Down the r. glen 4:9
russet: morn, in r. mantle clad
266:14
Russia: R. has two generals
226:5
R.. It is a riddle wrapped 90:9
rust: moth and r. doth corrupt
42:6
rustling: r. to her knees 179:11
ruth: melt with r. 215:6
sad heart of R. 181:14
rye: Coming through the r. 66:4
rymyng: drasty r. is nat worth a
toord 86:4
Sabbath: child that's born on the
S. 8:3
sacred: facts are s. 259:2
sacrifice: slain / No s. to God
263:10
sacrificed: Artists must be s.
129:11
sacrifices: Good
manners... petty s. 129:12
sad: all their songs are s. 88:9
every animal is s. 8:9
s. time we must obey 275:4
why I am so s. 155:3
saddest: I'm s. when I sing 24:8
sadness: s. of a vale 180:4
safely: But to be s. thus 276:16
safest: Just when we are s. 59:7
safety: pluck this flower, s.
269:17
public s. be the supreme 262:7
said: as if I had s. it myself
312:5
Everything that can be s.
350:5
sail: s. this ship of mine 21:7
saint: I may see my s. 16:7

Saints: S., whose bones / Lie
scattered 218:11
sais: *Que s.-je* 220:8
salad: My s. days 264:13
salley: Down by the s. gardens
356:8
sally: make a sudden s. 316:6
none like pretty S. 78:6
salt: pillar of s. 30:3
s. have lost his savour 42:1
With a grain of s. 237:7
saltus: *Natura non facit s.* 196:3
Salus: *S. extra ecclesiam* 105:1
S. populi suprema est lex 92:5
salute: those about to die s. thee
311:5
salvation: no s. outside the
Church 105:1
no s. outside the church 14:10
Samarkand: Golden Road to S.
134:3
same: s. things over and over
123:1
samite: Clothed in white s. 317:3
sana: *mens s. in corpore sano*
178:8
sancta: *s. simplicitas* 167:10
sand: name upon the s. 305:2
s. against the wind 52:3
World in a Grain of S. 50:8
Sandalwood: S., cedarwood and
sweet 209:4
sands: s. of time 197:10
saner: s. politics, / Whereof we
dream 151:4
sanglots: *s. longs / Des violons*
329:6
sans: sans taste, s. everything
266:3
sap: world's whole s. is sunk
117:12
sark: linket at it in her s. 68:8
sat: we s. down, yea 36:4
You have s. too long here
104:2
Satan: Even S. glowr'd 68:9
Get thee behind me, S. 43:15
S. exalted sat 216:6
S. finds some mischief 337:6
S., Nick, or Clootie 65:9

Satanic: dark S. mills 51:12

satin: goes into white s. 38:4

Satire: S., by being levelled at all 312:7

S. is a kind of glass 311:6

S. or sense, are 239:14

S. should, like a polished razor 220:5

satiric: show'd, by one s. touch 313:2

Saturn: Revolution might, like S., devour 329:4

Sat gray-hair'd S. 180:4

satyr: either a stoic or a s. 235:10

satyrs: like s. grazing on the lawns 205:8

sauce: best s. . . . is hunger 83:3

Make hunger thy s. 325:4

Saul: S. hath slain his thousands 32:11

saule: Christe receive thy s. 21:4

sausage: s. and thinks of Picasso 157:10

savage: laws unto a s. race 318:11

soothe a s. breast 99:5

save: time . . . trying to s. 251:6

Whenever you s. five shillings 185:2

saved: and we are not s. 40:1

England has s. herself 236:5

only s. by being dammed 163:4

Saviour: S. of 'is country 187:11

say: careful indeed what we s. 98:9

Do as we s. 53:6

I'll fear not what men s. 63:11

s., not as I do 263:1

s. the perfectly correct thing 288:8

see what I s. 334:9

They are to s. what they please 137:14

your right to s. it 333:7

saying: s. the same things over 123:1

something is not worth s. 24:9

scan: gently s. your brother man 65:10

scandal: Love and s. are the best sweeteners 133:1

scarlet: His sins were s. 27:4

sins be as s. 38:4

scatter: s. / The good seed 93:2

scene: tedious brief s. 280:7

scenery: end of all natural s. 255:4

S. is fine 183:7

scepter'd: this s. isle 282:3

sceptic: s. could inquire for 71:1

s. to deny the possibility 169:1

schemes: best laid s. o' mice an' men 69:4

Scholar: humour of a S. 18:12

school: creeping like snail / Unwillingly to s. 265:15

school boy: Every s. knows it 316:2

whining s., with his satchel 265:15

schoolgirl: Pert as a s. 143:3

school-master: you'll be becoming a s. 337:9

schools: a' their colleges and s. 69:7

Public s. are the nurseries of all vice 132:10

science: Art is s. in the flesh 95:5

destiny of s. to exterminate 234:4

great tragedy of S. 168:8

In s., read . . . the newest 63:1

s. . . . . exchange of ignorance 75:12

S. has nothing to be ashamed 56:6

S. is for those who learn 254:5

S. is nothing but trained 168:9

S. is organized knowledge 304:3

S. without conscience 220:11

this newe s. that men lere 86:7

score: just s. more points 223:4

scorn: little s. is alluring 99:10

sound / Of public s. 217:16

seduces: When a man s. a woman 351:3

see: s. oursels as others see us 69:2
  Shall never s. so much 275:4
  think till I s. what I say 334:9

seed: s. o' a' the men 201:7
  s. of the church 319:11

seed-time: Fair s. had my soul 353:1
  s. and harvest 30:2

seek: All I s., the heaven above 309:7
  s., and ye shall find 43:4
  S. ye the Lord 39:10
  to s., to find, and not 319:4
  We s. him here 228:9

seeks: small man s. is in others 98:8

seems: I know not 's.' 267:1

seeth: Lord s. not as man 32:9

sein: Es muss s. 26:4

self: Each one a murdered s. 253:10

self-interest: s. was bad morals 252:3

selfish: s. affairs is a coward 289:9

self-made: s. man, and worships 56:4

self-protection: sole end . . . is s. 212:6

Self-righteousness: S. is not religion 56:8

Semen: S. est sanguis 319:11

sensational: something s. to read 346:3

sensations: s. rather than of thoughts 183:6

Sense: Batteries of alluring S. 207:7
  echo to the s. 241:2
  fruit of s. beneath 240:12
  Nature, for it is not s. 90:4
  never deviates into s. 121:12
  s., and the sounds will take care 80:10
  want of decency is want of s. 253:2

sensibility: dissociation of s. 127:13

sentiment: marriage . . . as a mere matter of s. 56:11

sentimental: pet-lamb in a s. farce 181:2

sentiments: Them's my s. 320:6

sentry: Where stands a winged s. 328:10

sepulchre: whole world is a s. 323:2

sera: Che s., sera 204:9

sergeant: fell s., death 269:10

serious: nor trusts them with, s. matters 87:9
  nothing s. in mortality 276:15
  s. attempt to do it 340:13

sermon: s., – that it will suit any text 308:7

Sermons: S. and soda water 74:2
  s. he had already hidden 345:4

serpent: s. beguiled me 29:10
  s. of old Nile 264:12
  s. subtlest beast 217:12
  s. was more subtil 29:8

servant: for thy s. heareth 32:5
  s. depart in peace 334:2
  thy s. depart in peace 45:5

servants: both good s. 149:1
  good s., but bad masters 193:8
  Live? Our s. will do that 330:6
  Men in Great Place are thrice S. 17:10

serve: also s. who only stand 218:12
  s. two masters 42:7
  than s. in Heav'n 216:3
  too proud to s. 302:7

served: as I have s. the King 351:5
  despised as well as s. it 71:15
  Had I but s. my God 272:5

service: more essential s. to his country 311:7

Sesame: Open S. 10:10

sessions: s. of sweet silent thought 287:1

seul: On mourra s. 232:9

seven: acts being s. ages 265:15

some false impossible s. 13:6
shored: fragments have I s.
127:11
shores: earth's human s. 182:5
short: lyf so s. 86:6
s. and long of it 279:10
s., sharp shock 143:4
shortest: s. way to do many
things 299:4
shot: s. than do his bootlaces
340:10
should: no better than you s. be
25:2
shoulder: government shall be
upon his s. 38:9
shoulders: grow beneath their s.
280:16
Shout: S. with the largest 112:4
shower: drainless s. / Of light
182:4
shows: my s. are great 147:6
shreds: thing of s. and patches
142:13
shrine: Open the s. that I may
see 176:7
shudder: s. in the loins 357:5
shut: One cannot s. one's eyes
222:5
shuttle: s., to whose winding
quest 328:9
sick: I am s., I must die 224:7
never s. at sea 142:7
on our hands a s. man 226:6
s., and ye visited me 44:8
s. that surfeit with too much
278:7
were you not extremely s.
246:10
sicklied: s. o'er with the pale
cast 268:4
sickness: convicted of s., hunger
302:2
in s. and in health 245:13
Sieve: went to sea in a S. 193:1
sigh: s., and so away 103:9
sighing: plague of s. 270:1
Sighs: S. are the natural
language 264:3
sight: in the s. of God 245:10

sign: In this s. thou shalt
conquer 99:16
signal: do not see the s. 224:10
signo: In hoc s. vinces 99:16
silence: eternal s. of these
infinite 232:8
man's s. is wonderful 152:2
occasional flashes of s. 301:8
rest is s. 269:12
s. and slow time 180:9
s. éternel de ces espaces 232:8
S. is as full of potential
wisdom 168:4
S. is the supreme contempt
256:5
S. is the virtue of fools 16:10
small change of s. 211:12
there was s. in heaven 49:10
Well-timed s. hath more
eloquence 324:12
silencing: justified in s. mankind
212:7
silent: impossible to be s. 65:3
into the s. land 253:7
s. and be thought a fool 196:1
S., upon a peak in Darien
182:8
thereon one must be s. 350:3
silks: in s. my Julia goes 159:10
silvas: inter s. Academi 164:15
silver: handful of s. he left us
60:12
simple: beauty and nought
else 60:5
simpler: recommended
something s. 4:3
simplicitas: sancta s. 167:10
sed sancta 171:5
simplicity: Cultivate s., Coleridge
189:8
simulacrum: sun itself is but the
dark s. 58:4
sin: Be sure your s. will find you
out 31:8
Be ye angry, and s. not 48:2
He that is without s. 46:3
like to s. / With Elinor Glyn
10:5
Milton, Death and S. 359:3
no s. but ignorance 205:11

We shall not s. 201:2

sleepers: s. in that quiet earth 57:4

    snorted we in the Seven S. 117:3

sleepin': Capten, art tha' s. there 225:5

sleeping: fuss about s. together 338:2

    S. is no mean art 227:3

sleeps: s. feels not the toothache 266:13

sleping: nought good a s. hound 86:11

slept: thought he thought I s. 233:6

slice: how thin you s. it 300:2

slid: s. into my soul 96:1

slimy: legs / Upon the s. sea 95:12

slip: Excuse me while I s. into 152:5

Slit: S. your girl's, and swing 185:15

sloth: cares and woe of s. 295:5

Slough: fall on S. 28:9

    s. was Despond 63:4

Slowly: S., silently, now 108:7

slumber: s. did my spirit seal 353:8

slumbers: Golden s. kiss your eyes 108:3

Small: S. have suffered 135:2

    S. is Beautiful 259:1

    so s. a thing 12:7

smell: I s. the blood 274:12

smile: vain tribute of a s. 259:9

Smiles: S. awake you when you rise 108:3

smiling: hides a s. face 102:5

smirk: serious and the s. 111:8

Smoke: good cigar is a S. 186:2

smooth: I am a s. man 30:4

    never did run s. 279:14

smote: When 'Omer s. 187:12

smylere: s. with the knyf 85:9

snail: creeping like s. /
    Unwillingly 265:15

snake: s. lurks in the grass 331:6

snapper-up: s. of unconsidered trifles 286:7

snarling: silver, s. trumpets 179:9

snatches: Of ballads, songs and s. 142:13

Sneering: S. doesn't become ... the ... face 291:2

    without s., teach the rest to sneer 239:13

sneezed: Not to be s. at 97:7

sneezes: beat him when he s. 80:4

    When Paris s. 212:2

snorted: s. we in the Seven Sleepers 117:3

snotgreen: s. sea 177:7

snows: where are the s. 330:7

snug: s. / As a bug 137:9

    s. little Island 109:9

soap: used your s. two years 248:3

soar: stoop / Than when we s. 351:11

soaring: s. ever singest 295:15

sober: My mother, drunk or s. 89:6

    one sees in Garbo s. 327:1

    s. as a judge 132:5

    s., as a Scot ne'er was 201:6

sobers: drinking largely s. us 240:10

Socialism: S. with a human face 122:3

Society: speak disrespectfully of S. 346:7

Socrates: wisest who, like S. 236:10

soda: Sermons and s. water 74:2

soft: but *never* hit s. 252:9

    s. was the stone 190:4

sojourne: tyme, that may not s. 86:8

soldier: British s. can stand up to 288:4

    Drinking is the s.'s pleasure 121:1

    God and s. we alike 176:9

    old s. by the inside 287:13

soldiers: s. of the Cross 122:5

solitary: Eden took their s. way
    217:18
life of man, s., poor 161:5
solitude: Musing in s. 351:10
    s.! where are the charms 102:8
    Whosoever is delighted in s.
        18:6
solitudinem: s. faciunt pacem
    315:3
sollst: kannst, denn du s. 145:8
solution: s. of the problem of life
    350:2
somebodee: everyone is s. 142:6
somebody: dreary to be s. 113:4
somer: In a s. seson 190:4
something: everything about s.
    169:2
    s. very like Him 94:1
    Time for a little s. 213:9
somewhere: s., if we knew but
    where 102:2
Son: gave his only begotten S.
    46:1
    This is my beloved S. 41:7
song: end of ane old s. 228:7
    Lord a new s. 35:4
    melancholy out of a s. 265:13
    Perhaps the self-same s.
        181:14
    shall moralize my s. 305:4
    till I end my s. 305:12
    unto the Lord a new s. 333:9
songs: Come, my s., let us speak
    244:2
    Everything ends in a s. 25:1
    fruit for their s. 2:5
son-in-law: s. also rises 188:4
sonnets: ten passably effective s.
    168:3
    written all his life 74:7
sons: s. your fathers got 165:12
soon: gives twice who gives s.
    315:1
sop: body gets its s. 59:5
sorrow: complete s. is as
    impossible 323:10
    glut thy s. 181:4
    parting is such sweet s. 283:6
    s. like a shoe 314:5

sorry: having to say you're s.
    262:4
sottises: s. des Grands 135:2
soul: captain of my s. 156:4
    half conceal the S. 317:5
    if I have a s. 250:2
    knock and enter in our s. 59:7
    leaves s. free a little 59:5
    lips suck forth my s. 205:2
    loafe and invite my s. 343:4
    Lord my s. to keep 8:5
    lose his own s. 43:16
    my s. drew back 158:10
    my s. thirsteth for thee 35:2
    No coward s. is mine 57:2
    Out of his bitter s. 358:6
    real dark night of the s. 133:12
    reason to the s. 121:14
    single s. dwelling in two 11:7
    Sneering doesn't
        become ... human s. 291:2
    so panteth my s. 34:6
    S. clap its hands 357:1
    s., do not search for immortal
        235:7
    s. is not a clod 180:2
    s. lies buried in the ink 92:14
    s., like to a ship 339:2
    s. of man, like unextinguished
        295:3
    s. that knew not fear 106:7
    S. visits the National Gallery
        300:5
    stormy working s. 158:6
    sweet and virtuous s. 158:13
    try the s.'s strength on 60:11
    What of s. was left 62:1
souls: fame ... instinct of all
    great s. 64:7
    hale s. out of men's bodies
        280:9
    Love's mysteries in s. 117:1
    sell their s. and live 300:3
    s. but the shadows 58:4
    s. with but a single thought
        198:10
    times that try men's s. 230:8
    two s., and vapours both
        116:13

soul-sides: creatures / Boasts
    two s. 61:3
sound: s. must seem an echo
    241:2
sounds: better than it s. 325:7
    S. and sweet airs 284:3
    s. will take care of themselves
    80:10
soupe: *Je vis de bonne s.* 219:8
sovereynetee: Wommen desiren
    to have s. 85:10
sow: Ireland is the old s. 177:4
    right s. by the ear 156:10
    s. in tears 36:2
    s., you are like to reap 71:4
soweth: s., that shall he also
    reap 47:7
sown: s. the wind 40:10
space: more than time and s.
    189:10
Spaniards: thrash the S. too
    119:9
Spare: S., woodman, spare 77:3
    s. your country's flag 343:10
spark: ae s. o' Nature's fire
    66:10
sparkle: star-like s. in their skies
    159:8
sparks: as the s. fly upward 33:9
sparrow: My lady's s. is dead
    82:7
    providence in the fall of a s.
    269:8
Spartans: Go, tell the S. 298:4
speak: it is difficult to s. 65:3
    Let him now s. 245:11
    S., Lord 32:5
    s. out and remove all doubt
    196:1
    S. softly and carry 252:11
    S. what we feel 275:4
    Whereof one cannot s. 350:3
speaks: her foot s. 285:7
spears: [war] after that with s.
    327:7
spectacle: no s. so ridiculous
    200:11
spectre-thin: s., and dies 181:10
speech: more eloquence than s.
    324:12

Poetry is . . . healthy s. 322:10
    Speak the s., I pray 268:7
    S. is the small change 211:12
speechless: receive fair s.
    messages 278:6
speed: s. the parting guest 242:8
spheres: ever-moving s. of
    heaven 205:3
    Ring out ye Crystal s. 215:9
spice: Variety's the very s. of life
    102:11
spider: said a s. to a fly 166:6
spilling: bent on s. it 210:7
spin: neither do they s. 42:8
Spinner: S. of the Years 151:3
spinsters: dreams of s. 255:9
Spirit: Ah fleeting S. 150:1
    And with thy s. 209:8
    Blessed are the poor in s.
    41:10
    blithe S. 295:14
    body did contain a s. 270:5
    expense of s. 287:10
    fruits of the S. 245:4
    s. giveth life 47:5
    s. indeed is willing 44:10
    s. that forever denies 145:2
spiritu: *Et cum s. tuo* 209:8
spit: s. on his hands 211:5
spitefully: pray for them which
    s. use 42:2
spits: soul s. lies and froth 158:6
splendid: Between a s. and a
    happy 146:2
    our s. isolation 147:5
splendour: Not in lone s. hung
    182:5
    s. falls on castle walls 318:7
    s. in the grass 352:8
    s. of a sudden thought 60:1
spoke: s. among your wheels
    25:4
spoken: never have s. yet 89:3
sport: ended his s. with Tess
    151:11
    for the s. of kings 106:6
    kill us for their s. 274:15
    s. for our neighbours 16:3
    S. that wrinkled Care 214:9
    s. with Amaryllis 215:3

stepping-stones: s. / Of their
dead selves 317:4

sterner: let us rather speak of s.
days 91:4
made of s. stuff 273:7

stick: carry a big s. 252:11

sticking-place: courage to the s.
276:7

Still: S. falls the Rain 298:7
s. point of a turning world
126:3

stilly: Oft, in the s. night 222:1
lives into the s. 129:11

sting: death, where is thy s. 47:4

sting-a-ling-a-ling: Death, where
is thy s. 8:6

stings: s. you for your pains
160:2

stinks: s. and stings 240:1

Stirred: S. for a bird 164:5

stirrup: I sprang to the s. 60:10

stocked: o'er s. with prudent
men 121:13

stoic: either a s. or a satyr
235:10

stole: he s. those tarts 80:13

Stolen: S. sweets are best 92:3

stomach: army marches on its s.
5:7
heart and s. of a king 128:2

stomachs: march on their s.
263:8

stone: bread, and he received a
s. 341:5
first cast a s. 46:3
quiet as a s. 180:4
s. which the builders refused
35:7
sword of this s. 204:2

stones: found in s. the sermons
345:4
Never throw s. at your mother
26:5
worshipped Stocks and S.
218:11

stop: Because I could not s.
113:2
come to the end: then s. 80:14
s. everyone from doing it
158:1

stops: not everything s. when the
music 155:7

storehouse: [Knowledge is] a
rich s. 16:9

stories: tell sad s. of the death
282:7

storm: directs the s. 1:6
He mounts the s. 242:2
lost in the s. 12:12
S. and stress 179:2
S. in a Teacup 28:6

stormy: s. working soul spits lies
158:6

story: Ere their s. die 151:9
name great in s. 76:1

straight: might have grown full
s. 205:6

strain: That s. again 285:10

strangeness: s. in the proportion
18:10

stranger: s. and ye took me in
44:8
s. in a strange land 30:9

strangers: forgetful to entertain
s. 48:15
kindness of s. 349:3

strangled: last king is s. 113:6

straw: all things as s. dogs 190:8

strawberries: s.: 'Doubtless God
could have made 335:9

strayed: s. from thy ways like
lost sheep 244:5

stream: s., / Bears all its sons
337:7

streams: cooling s. / When
heated 315:7

streets: bald s. breaks the blank
317:6
Down these mean s. 84:1

strength: deem'd / Equal in s.
216:7
roll all our s. 208:6

stretched: things which he s.
325:11

strife: burning and the s. 180:8
our pleasures with rough s.
208:6

strike: particularly fine, s. it out
174:4
when in doubt, s. it out 326:4

string: chewing little bits of s.
27:1
  heart and harp have lost a s.
  72:11

strings: Like untun'd golden s.
205:10
  s. . . . in the human heart 110:1

strive: s. / Officiously to keep
alive 94:3
  To s., to seek 319:4

stroke: at a s., reduce the rise
154:9

strokes: Little s. fell great oaks
137:1

strong: nor the battle to the s.
37:7
  Out of the s. . . . sweetness
  32:3
  S. shall thrive 263:12

stronger: argument of the s.
134:10

stronghold: safe s. our God
199:5

strove: men that s. with Gods
319:3
  s. with none; for none 190:1

struck: s. the board, and cry'd
158:7

struggle: s. for existence 106:2
  s. naught availeth 94:4

strumpet: transformed / Into a
s.'s fool 264:8

struts: s. and frets his hour
277:13

Studies: too much Time in S.
18:12
  wise men use [S.] 19:1

study: much s. is the weariness
of 37:9
  proper s. of Mankind 242:1
  s. of mankind is books 168:2

stuff: s. / As dreams are made
on 284:4
  written such volumes of s.
  192:11

stumble: do not s. 203:1

stummucks: s. don't git tired
152:11

Stung: S. by the splendour 60:1

stupidity: s. the very gods
contend 258:7

Sturm: S. und Drang 179:2

Style: S. is the man 62:8
  support his drooping s. 154:5
  true definition of a s. 311:9

sublime: elevated thoughts; a
sense s. 352:3
  make our lives s. 197:10
  My object all s. 143:5
  s. and the ridiculous 230:7

sublunary: Dull s. lovers 118:7

Submerged: S. Tenth 54:6

submission: Yielded with coy s.
217:7

submit: Must he s. 282:8
  never to s. or yield 216:1

subtle: may not be s. but neither
are men 139:9

subtlest: s. beast of all the field
217:12

succeed: first you don't s. 160:1

succeeds: Nothing s. like excess
348:3

Success: bitch-goddess, S. 170:8
  failure's no s. at all 123:7
  road to s. is filled with women
  109:8
  to maintain this ecstasy, is s.
  233:3
  true s. is to labour 310:7
  wisdom to vulgar
  judgements – s. 65:4

Suck-a-Thumb: naughty little S.
161:10

sucker: s. born every minute
23:3

sucklings: mouth of babes and s.
34:1

sucks: as a weasel s. eggs
265:13
  s. the nurse asleep 265:7
  s. two souls, and vapours
  116:13

suffer: Better one s. than 120:8
  nobler in the mind to s. 268:1
  S. the little children 44:15

suffer'd: have s. greatly 319:1

suffering: About s. they were
never wrong 14:3

nothing but s. 15:9
s. what they teach 293:7
sufficiency: elegant s. 322:3
Sufficient: S. unto the day 43:1
suicide: war . . . is s. 202:6
sultry: more common where the climate's s. 73:9
sum: more than the s. 11:9
summer: compare thee to a s.'s day 286:13
dewy Eve, / A S.'s day 216:5
Made glorious s. 282:10
s. is ended 40:1
S. is icumen in 23:7
Summum: S. bonum 92:6
sun: Born of the s. they travelled 304:9
burnished s. 278:11
by this s. of York 282:10
candle to the s. 134:4
gained both the Wind and S. 207:8
going down of the s. 50:4
I will sing of the s. 243:7
Juliet is the s. 283:2
let not the s. go down 48:2
let the s. in, mind it wipes 321:7
maketh his s. to rise 42:3
nothing like the s. 287:11
on which the s. never sets 227:9
out of my s. 113:8
own place in the s. 62:10
shoots at the mid-day s. 297:8
S. of righteousness 40:13
s. that shines upon his court 286:10
s. . . . the dark *simulacrum* 58:4
Thank heavens, the s. has gone 300:9
To have enjoy'd the s. 12:7
unruly S., / Why dost thou 118:3
sung: s. women in three cities 243:7
suns: dwelling is the light of setting s. 352:3
Heaven cannot brook two s. 3:9

Sunshine: On a S. Holyday 214:11
s. in the shady place 305:6
superexcellent: s. tobacco 70:6
superman: teach you the s. 227:2
superstition: Poetry . . . mother of s. 306:5
superstitions: to end as s. 168:11
superstitious: were it vastly more s. 225:8
supper: Hope . . . is a bad s. 16:13
support: I s. it from the outside 211:2
s. of the woman I love 124:7
suppose: round in a ring and s. 138:6
supreme: public safety be the s. law 262:7
surface: sick that s. with too much 278:7
surfeit: sick that s. with too much 278:7
surgical: s. operation to get a joke 301:4
surmise: wild s. 182:8
surprise: s. by a fine excess 183:10
Surprised: S. by joy 354:3
surquidrie: s. and foul presumpcion 86:10
surrender: we shall never s. 90:11
survey: monarch of all I s. 102:7
Survival: S. of the Fittest 106:3
s. of the fittest 304:5
survive: only the Fit s. 263:12
survived: I s. 298:3
suspension: willing s. of disbelief 96:10
suspicion: against despots — s. 108:17
swagman: Once a jolly s. camped 233:5
swain: dispossess the s. 146:1
Swan: Sweet S. of Avon 176:6
Swans: S. sing before they die 96:5
sway: love of s. 239:9
swayed: body s. to music 355:10

swear: s. not by the moon 283:5
s. to never kiss the girls 60:6
when very angry s. 326:1

sweat: blood, toil, tears, and s.
90:10

sweet: Life is short but s. 303:4
never been s. in the grass
321:10
S. are the uses of adversity
265:10
The s. cheat gone 108:4
Things s. to taste 282:1

sweeten: not s. this little hand
277:9

sweeteners: best s. of tea 133:1

sweeter: thereby be the s. 278:3

sweetness: Our s. up into one
ball 208:6
out of the strong came forth s.
32:3

sweets: Stolen s. are best 92:3

swift: race is not to the s. 37:7

swim: s. on bladders 272:4

swine: pearls before s. 43:3

swing: girl's, and s. for it 185:10

swings: pulls up on the s. 83:7

Switzerland: In S. they had
brotherly love 339:6
S. as an inferior sort of
Scotland 301:1

sword: more cruel the pen is
than the s. 70:4
pen is mightier than the s.
63:2
s. of this stone 204:2
S. sleep in my hand 52:2
they that take the s. 44:11
without the s. are but words
161:6

swords: beat their s. into
plowshares 38:5

swore: By the nine gods he s.
200:2

syllable: last s. of recorded time
277:13

symmetry: frame thy fearful s.
53:2

syntax: s. of things 104:8

System: must Create a S. 51:5

systems: Founders of sects and
s. 73:2
s. into ruin hurl'd 241:8

table: you cannot make a t.
173:5

tainted: t. wether of the flock
279:2

take: They have to t. you in
138:2

tale: adorn a t. 172:10
bodies must tell the t. 259:5
round unvarnish'd t. deliver
280:15
sad t.'s best for winter 286:5
t. of a tub 338:13
t. / Told by an idiot 277:13
thereby hangs a t. 265:14
Trust the t. 192:6

Talent: T. does what it can
211:14
T. grows in peace 145:7
t. instantly recognizes genius
119:7

talents: t., industry will improve
them 250:5

talk: high t. with the departed
293:5

talked: not being t. about 346:14

talkin': wimmin, dey does de t.
152:6

talking: ain't t. about him, ain't
listening 55:7
t.: ask is a t. ship 209:5

tangere: Noli me t. 334:7

Tao: method of T. 190:7

tapestry: rich t. as divers poets
298:1

Tara: once through T.'s halls
221:7

Tar-baby: T. ain't sayin' nuthin'
152:8

tarts: Hearts, she made some t.
80:13

Tarzan: Me T., you Jane 70:1

taste: Shakespeare, undoubtedly
wanted t. 334:12

tastes: t. may not be the same
289:12

taught: Tortoise because he t. us
80:9

worth knowing can be t. 344:8
taughte: He t., but first he
 folwed 85:3
Tautology: great Prophet of T.
 121:11
tavern: by a good t. or inn 174:9
tax: To t. and to please 64:8
Taxation: T. without
 representation 229:9
taxes: except death and t. 137:10
true . . . as t. is 110:7
Tay: Silv'ry T. 202:7
Tea: and sometimes T. 242:11
 makes t. I makes tea 177:8
 While there's t. there's hope
 235:9
teach: t. you more of man 354:6
 what they t. in song 293:7
teaches: He who cannot t. 290:3
Teacup: Storm in a T. 28:6
tear: t. our pleasures 208:6
 Thinking every t. a gem
 293:11
tears: lies too deep for t. 352:9
 sow in t. 36:2
 T., idle tears 318:8
 t., prepare to shed them 273:8
 tribute of wild t. 357:6
tease: fleas that t. 27:5
 t. us out of thought 180:13
teases: Because he knows it t.
 80:4
teche: and gladly t. 84:11
tedious: either charming or t.
 346:9
 t. brief scene 280:7
teeth: I set my t. in rascals 114:2
 t. are set on edge 40:5
teetotaller: beer t. 288:3
television: see bad t. for nothing
 147:2
 T. has brought murder back
 160:9
tell: How could they t. 232:3
 t. you who you are 87:8
 would t. one anything 347:11
temperament: artistic t. is a
 disease 89:8
temperate: more lovely and more
 t. 286:13

tempestuous: world's t. sea
 124:5
temple: t. half as old as time
 251:3
 very t. of Delight 181:5
tempora: t.! O mores 92:9
temptation: maximum of t.
 289:13
 oughtn't to yield to t. 163:9
 resist everything except t.
 346:10
 rid of a t. is to yield 347:2
 Yield not to t. 231:3
temptations: t. / To belong to
 other nations 142:9
tempus: fugit inreparabile t.
 331:11
 T. edax 229:13
ten: God Almighty has only t.
 93:6
tenant: She's the t. of the room
 156:5
tender: t. is the night 181:12
ténébreux: Je suis le t. 225:4
tennis-balls: merely the stars' t.
 338:11
tent: inside the t. pissing out
 171:10
Tenth: Submerged T. 54:6
tents: fold their t. 197:6
terminological: t. inexactitude
 90:8
terrible: t. beauty is born 356:10
terribles: Les enfants t. 140:5
territorial: last t. claim which I
 have 161:2
terror: fools of time and t. 75:11
terrorist: t. and the policeman
 both come 99:15
text: t. is that it will suit any
 sermon 308:7
Thames: Sweet T., run softly
 305:12
thankful: t. and has nobody to
 thank 253:12
thankit: let the Lord be t. 67:6
That: 1066, And All T. 263:3
theatre: all-night sitting in a t.
 291:4

torture: t. them, into believing
225:10

Tory: T. men and Whig
measures 114:5

toss: weariness / May t. him
158:11

touch: dare not put it to the t.
221:2

Do not t. me 334:7

must never t. mine 359:5

One t. of nature 285:6

toujours: à la t. audace 105:9

t. gai 206:8

tour: à la t. abolie 225:4

tower: burning roof and t. 357:5

towers: burnt the topless t. 205:2

town: country in t. 207:4

man made the t. 102:10

toy: religion but a childish t.
205:11

toys: All is but t. 276:15

Trade: T.'s unfeeling train 146:1

t. to make tables 173:5

was ever ruined by t. 137:8

tradesmen: confidence, even in t.
346:6

traffic: two hours' t. of our stage
282:16

tragedies: two t. in life 289:10

tragedy: great t. of Science 168:8

That is their t. 346:1

That is what t. means 310:10

t. is the noblest production 2:2

t. . . . the imitation of an action
11:15

t. to those that feel 335:3

tragic: bitterest t. element in life
130:2

tragical: very t. mirth 280:7

Trahison: T. des Clercs 27:7

Train: T. up a child 36:13

tram: not even a bus, I'm a t.
152:3

trampling: t. out the vintage
166:3

tranquillity: emotion recollected
in t. 354:8

transcendent: Worship is t.
wonder 79:2

transit: Sic t. gloria mundi 184:8

translation: mistake in the t.
328:6

translunary: those brave t. things
119:11

trapeze: on the flying t. 194:6

traurig: ich so t. bin 155:3

travel: t. hopefully is a better
310:7

travell'd: Much have I t. 182:7

traveller: bourn / No t. returns
268:3

travels: the fastest 187:14

Tread: T. softly because 357:2

treading: he's t. on my tail 80:11

treason: If this be t. 157:3

temptation is the greatest t.
127:3

t. doth but peep 269:4

treasures: t. upon earth 42:6

tree: blossoms upon one t. 353:3

gave me of the t. 29:9

t. of liberty must be refreshed
171:1

t. of life is green 145:3

Woodman, spare that t. 222:7

woodman, spare the beechen t.
77:3

trees: t. were bread and cheese
7:6

Trelawney: shall T. die 153:4

tremble: Let Sporus t. 239:14

trembling: t. shivr'ing, dying
150:1

trespass: we forgive them that t.
244:6

triangle: eternal t. 9:7

tribute: t. of wild tears 357:6

vain t. of a smile 259:9

trick: pleasing to t. the trickster
134:9

when the long t.'s over 209:6

trickster: trick the t. 134:9

trifles: snapper-up of
unconsidered t. 286:7

trip: t. it as ye go 214:9

tristesse: Adieu t. 129:1

triumph: in ourselves, are t. and
197:9

ride in t. through 206:3

t. of hope over experience
174:2
trivial: contests rise from t.
things 242:9
tromper: *t. le trompeur* 134:9
trope: out there flew a t. 70:11
trouble: double, toil and t. 277:3
  Man is born unto t. 33:9
  saves me the t. of liking 16:5
  Scripture which t. me most
326:10
  women and care and t. 336:5
troubles: arms against a sea of t.
268:1
  nothing t. me less 189:10
  t. of men are caused 232:6
trousers: bottoms of my t. rolled
127:1
trouve: *je t.* 235:6
trovato: molto ben t. 8:11
trowel: lays it on with a t. 99:1
Troy: cornfield where T. once
was 229:12
  plains of windy T. 319:2
true: as long as it isn't t. 157:7
  her ear, 'You are not t.' 344:2
  interesting than that it be t.
342:8
  long enough it *will* be t. 27:11
  not necessarily t. because a
man dies 348:9
  not t. because it is useful 5:2
  not t., it is a happy 8:11
  philosophy to be substantially
t. 257:9
  to thine own self be t. 267:8
  t. . . . as taxes is 110:7
  what is t. is reasonable 155:2
trumpets: *foie gras* to the sound
of t. 301:9
  silver, snarling t. 179:9
  t. sounded for him 63:12
trust: never t. a woman who
tells 347:11
  Put not your t. in princes 36:5
  T. the tale 192:6
Truth: and steep, T. stands 118:1
  beauty must be t. 183:5
  dead we owe nothing but t.
332:8

grope for T. 106:5
however improbable, must be
the t. 119:4
Is there in t. no beauty 158:9
lie? 'Tis but / The t. in
masquerade 75:1
love Scotland better than t.
172:3
loving Christianity better than
T. 96:9
mainly he told the t. 325:11
ocean of t. lay all
undiscovered 226:3
Plain t. will influence 54:4
tells the t. . . . found out 347:6
test of t., / 'It must be right
103:2
t. above our friends 11:11
t. beauty 180:14
t., has any inherent power
212:8
T. . . . is daylight 17:2
t. is great, and shall prevail
233:7
T. is in wine 237:6
t. is more important 355:4
t. is rarely pure 345:11
t. lies somewhere, / If we
knew 102:2
T. lies within a little 54:2
t. shall make thee free 46:4
T., Sir, is a cow 173:10
t. sits upon the lips of dying
13:5
T. . . . so as to be understood
52:7
t. . . . / Stranger than fiction
75:7
T. that peeps / Over the edge
59:5
t. that's told with bad 50:9
t. twenty-four times a second
144:7
t. universally acknowledged
15:11
T., which is the love-making
17:3
very fond of t. 333:6
way, the, t., and the life 46:7
What is T. 17:1

what they failed to u. 221:6
When men u. what each
225:11
you won't u. it 14:11
understanding: Donne's
verses . . . pass all u. 170:3
get u. 36:7 '
God be . . . in my u. 7:3
passeth all u. 48:4
passeth all u. 245:8
understood: three men who have
ever u. 231:4
u., and not be believed 52:7
undesirable: u. character / When
I see one 139:2
undiscover'd: u. country 268:3
undone: death had u. so many
127:8
for I am u. 38:7
left u. those things 244:5
Uneasy: U. lies the head 270:10
uneatable: pursuit of the u.
347:12
uneducated: government by the
u. 90:2
u. man to read books of
quotations 92:1
unexpected: u. / When it arrives
127:2
unfaithful: faith u. kept him
falsely 317:1
ungained: prize the thing u.
more 285:1
unhappily: bad [ended] u. 346:2
bad end u. 310:10
unhappiness: Man's u., as I
construe 79:14
unhappy: so u. as one thinks
191:1
unheard: u. / Are sweeter
180:10
unhonour'd: Unwept, u. and
unsung 260:1
unimportance: u. of events
125:11
unite: Workers of the world, u.
208:10
united: u. voice of myriads
cannot 146:10
uniting: By u. we stand 113:5

universal: become a u. law
178:10
u. frame began 122:1
universe: u. is not hostile 162:3
u. next door 104:7
u. were bent on spilling 210:7
unjust: also on the u. fella 55:1
u. and wicked king 263:10
unknown: dies to himself u.
263:11
safely into the u. 153:3
unluckily: good [end] u. 310:10
unmarried: keep u. as long as
289:5
unplumb'd: u., salt, estranging
sea 12:11
unquiet: ever imagine u.
slumbers 57:4
unravish'd: still u. bride 180:9
Unreal: U. City 127:8
unreasonable: progress depends
on the u. 290:1
unseen: Floats though u. among
us 293:4
unselfishness: u. of an oyster
256:9
Unsex: U. me here 276:1
unsoundness: certain u. of mind
200:9
unspeakable: u. in full pursuit
347:12
unstoned: leave no tern u. 224:3
unsung: unhonour'd and u. 260:1
Untimely: mother's womb / U.
ripp'd 277:15
untouch'd: long time lie u.
205:10
untried: difficult and left u. 89:11
untrodden: dwelt among the u.
ways 353:7
untun'd: u. golden strings all
women 205:10
untune: Music shall u. the sky
122:2
u. that string 285:2
unvarnished: round u. tale
deliver 280:15
Unwashed: great U. 58:2
Unwept: U., unhonour'd, and
unsung 260:1

weasel: w. under the cocktail cabinet 235:11

weather: and rough w. 265:12
different kinds of good w. 255:8
no such thing as bad w. 255:8
three more, / If it prove fair w. 311:2

web: tangled w. we weave 260:8

webs: Laws are like spider's w. 302:11

Webster: W. was much possessed 127:12

wedding: wife, as she did her w. gown 146:9

wedlock: Consented together in holy w. 246:4

weed: w.? A plant whose virtues 129:9

week: w. is a long time 349:9

weep: smell onions; I shall w. 264:7
W., and you weep alone 344:3
w. with them that weep 46:16

weeping: w. in my heart 329:8

weighed: w. in the balances 40:8

welcome: And yet be w. home 261:6
Love bade me w. 158:10

well: all shall be w. 178:11
And did it very w. 142:12
Faith, that's as w. said 312:5

Weltgeschichte: *W. ist das Weltgericht* 258:9

wen: great w. of all 94:7

wench: joly w. in every toun 86:1

went: as cooks go she w. 257:1

wept: Jesus w. 46:5
w. when we remembered Zion 36:4

west: Go w., young man 303:7
Go W., young man 148:8
W. is West 186:1
w. wind but tears 209:7

Western: Quiet on the W. Front 250:1
W. wind, when wilt thou blow 10:1

Westminster: peerage or W. Abbey 224:9

wether: tainted w. of the flock 279:2

wheel: breaks a butterfly upon a w. 239:14
Upon a w. of fire 275:1

wheels: spoke among your w. 25:4
tarry the w. of his chariots 32:1

wherefore: every why he had a w. 71:1

whiff: w. of grapeshot 79:5

Whig: Tory men and W. measures 114:5

whimper: bang but a w. 126:10
'twixt a smile and a 294:8

whining: saying so / In w. Poetry 118:5

whipping: who would 'scape w. 267:19

whirligig: w. of time brings 286:3

whirlwind: reap the w. 40:10
Rides in the w. 1:6

whiskers: Oh my fur and w. 80:2

whisky: Freedom and w. gang 66:2

Whisper: W. who dares 213:12

whistle: w., and I'll come 69:8
W. owre the lave 67:8

white: w. man's brother 185:7
W. Man's Burden 187:13

White House: Log Cabin to W. 320:10

whitewash: no w. at the White House 227:7

whiting: said a w. to a snail 80:11

Whittington: Turn again, W. 9:11

whole: greatest happiness of the w. 237:1
nothing can be sole or w. 356:5
w. is more than the sum 11:9

wholly: w. hopes to be 59:14

whooping: out of all w. 266:5

whore: argument is a w. 285:3

w. and women, mirth and
  laughter 74:2
wine-dark: w. sea 162:10
wing: joy is ever on the w. 218:4
Winged: W. words 162:9
wings: beating . . . his luminous
  w. 13:9
  healing in his w. 40:13
  shade of your soft w. 258:6
  viewless w. of Poesy 181:11
  w. like a dove 35:1
Winkie: Wee Willie W. 213:4
winter: English w. – ending in
  July 75:5
  It was the W. wild 215:8
  sad tale's best for w. 286:5
  w. and rough weather 265:12
  w. I get up at night 309:4
  W. is icummen in 243:5
  w. of our discontent 282:10
wiped: should have w. it up
  308:6
wipes: sun in, mind it w. its
  shoes 321:7
wisdom: bettre than w.?
  Womman 86:3
  criterion of w. to vulgar
    judgements 65:4
  Government . . . contrivance of
    human w. 64:3
  greatness of thy w. 33:5
  palace of w. 52:8
  realizes that his w. is
    worthless 236:10
  therefore get w. 36:7
  W. be put in a silver rod 51:3
  w. even from a foe 11:3
  W. hath builded her house
    36:9
  W. is humble 102:14
  W. is ofttimes nearer 351:11
  W. is the principal thing 36:7
  w. of the fool 175:11
wise: ever did a w. one 251:1
  folly of the w. 175:11
  folly to be w. 148:7
  Some folks are w. 302:4
  w., like a mirror 98:6
  w. man . . . always ready to
    leave 135:1

w. men from the east 41:4
w. men use [Studies] 19:1
w. want love 294:10
wisely: nations behave w. once
  123:9
  not w. but too well 281:15
  w. worldly, not worldly wise
    248:6
wiser: not the w. grow 238:6
wisest: That man is w. who
  236:10
  w. fool in Christendom 156:6
  w. . . . may err 2:9
wish: I w. he'd stay away 210:9
  w. I liked the way it walks
    249:9
  w. was father 270:13
wishes: what a man w. he
  generally believes 108:9
wit: at thirty, the w. 136:9
  baiting-place of w. 297:9
  brevity, and w. its soul 96:4
  Brevity is the soul of w.
    267:15
  cause that w. is in other 270:6
  dream, past the w. of man
    280:4
  Impropriety is the soul of w.
    210:8
  Monarchy of w. 78:2
  W. is Nature to advantage
    240:11
  W.'s an unruly engine 158:5
  w.'s the noblest frailty 264:5
witch: suffer a w. to live 31:2
withers: state . . . w. away 130:6
witness: Thou shalt not bear
  false w. 30:16
Wits: first for W. then Poets
  240:9
  Great w. are sure to madness
    120:5
witty: not only w. in myself
  270:6
  so w., profligate, and thin
    359:3
wives: Old w.' fables 48:7
woe: and all our w. 215:11
  balm of w. 297:9
  W. to the vanquished 196:5

wolf: keep the w. far thence 339:1
  like the w. on the fold 73:8
Man is a w. to man 237:4
  w. also shall dwell 38:10
Wolf's-bane: neither twist / W. 181:3
WOLVERHAMPTON: AM IN W. STOP 90:3
wolves: ravening w. 43:5
woman: delicate as the reputation of a w. 65:8
  divine in w. / Grows cruel 294:8
  Every w. adores a Fascist 236:7
  every w. should marry — and no man 114:8
  Fortune is a w. 202:8
  Frailty, thy name is w. 267:4
  fury, like a w. scorn'd 99:6
  hair of a w. 166:4
  in a word, she is a w. 249:5
  just like a w. 123:6
  Look for the w. 122:9
  not born a w. 25:6
  One to show a w. 61:3
  silliest w. can manage 187:10
  weak and feeble w. 128:2
  Who can find a virtuous w. 37:3
  w. as old as she looks 97:5
  w. governs America 203:7
  w. had better show 16:6
  w. has her way 162:4
  W.! in our hours of ease 260:10
  W. is always fickle 331:1
  w. is at heart a Rake 239:10
  w. is his game 318:9
  w. is only a woman 186:2
  w. loves her lover 74:6
  w.? — only one of Nature's agreeable 101:11
  w. oweth to her husband 283:13
  w.'s business to get married 289:5
  w. . . . should conceal 15:8
  w.'s preaching 173:7

w.'s whole existence 74:1
w. that deliberates is lost 1:8
w., therefore to be won 271:12
w. who has had only one 191:2
w. who lives for others 194:5
w. whom thou gavest 29:9
W. who runs 122:6
W. will be the last thing civilized 211:10
w. yet think him an angel 320:2
womb: from his mother's w. 277:15
  teeming w. of royal kings 282:5
wombe: w.! O bely! O stynking cod 86:2
women: Alas! the love of w. 74:5
  Bah! I have sung w. 243:7
  could but say so of w. too 76:3
  England . . . paradise of w. 134:7
  In the room the w. come 126:13
  In w., two almost divide 239:9
  Italy . . . hell for w. 70:7
  Like untun'd . . . strings all w. are 205:10
  Monstrous Regiment of W. 188:5
  Most w. are not so young 25:10
  old w. (of both sexes) 308:5
  proper function of w. 125:7
  tide in the affairs of w. 74:11
  W. and care 336:5
  W. and elephants never forget 257:2
  w. are glad to have been asked 229:11
  w. become like their mothers 346:1
  W. . . . care . . . more for a marriage 19:9
  W. dissemble their Passions better 306:12
  w. do in men require 52:4
  W. hate revolutions 211:6

w. I cannot but give way to
234:11

[w.] . . . man of sense only
trifles 87:9

w. . . . married to a poem 184:3

w. . . . merely adored 345:6

W. . . . off the pedestal 250:7

[w.] power . . . over themselves
351:2

w. pushing their husbands
109:8

W. . . . refuse the rules of life
220:10

W., then, are only children
88:2

Woman: bettre than wisdom?
W. 86:3

in humblesse . . . As w. 85:11

Wommen: W. desiren to have
sovereynetee 85:10

won: never lost till w. 103:4
woman, therefore to be w.
271:12

wonder: Have eyes to w. 287:7
w. to see them not ashamed
312:11

w. why he does 213:7

wonderful: w., and most
wonderful 266:5

wonders: His w. to perform
102:4

W. will never cease 122:4

woo'd: beautiful and therefore to
be w. 271:12

Genius of the W. 214:7

impulse from a vernal w.
354:6

wooden: This w. O 270:16

Woodman: W., spare that tree
222:7

w., spare the beechen tree
77:3

Wood-notes: native W. wild
214:12

Woods: fresh W., and Pastures
new 215:7

pleasure in the pathless w.
73:5

w. are lovely, dark, and deep
138:7

woodshed: nasty in the w. 142:1

Woolf: Who's Afraid of Virginia
W. 3:7

word: doers of the w. 49:1
For one w. a man is 98:9

Thy w. is a lamp 35:8

w. flies 164:14

w. is the Verb 166:10

w. is too often profaned
295:13

w. . . . means just what I
choose 81:8

w. no man relies on 251:1

W. was made flesh 45:17

W. was with God 45:15

wordes: glotoun of w. 190:5

wording: w. of his own highest
thoughts 183:10

words: He w. me 265:2
knowing the force of w. 98:12

let thy w. be few 37:6

not fine w. 219:8

Proper w. in proper places
311:9

Winged w. 162:9

without the sword are but w.
161:6

W. are like leaves 240:12

w. are my own 84:3

W. are the physicians 3:2

W. are wise men's counters
161:3

w. but wind 71:3

w. in their best order 97:3

w., like Nature, half reveal
317:5

W. may be false 264:3

w. shall not pass away 44:7

Wordsworth: [W.] found in
stones 345:4

[W.] shows / That prose is
verse 75:8

W. sometimes wakes 74:9

work: as tedious as to w. 269:14
I like w.; it fascinates 171:3

let the toad w. 191:7

man out of w. for a day 185:2

too warm w., Hardy, to last
224:11

worms: graves, of w. and
epitaphs 282:6
made w.' meat of me 283:7
worried: poem . . . not be w. into
being 138:8
worse: fear of finding something
w. 27:2
More will mean w. 5:3
person for the w. 312:8
w. than being talked about
346:14
worship: modes of w., which
prevailed 141:8
with my body I thee w. 246:2
W. is transcendent wonder
79:2
worships: Everybody w. me, it's
nauseating 101:1
he w. in his way 299:2
worst: it was the w. of times
112:12
This is the w. 274:14
w. are no worse 280:8
w. kinde of infortune 87:1
worth: thing is w. doing 90:1
w. of the individuals 213:2
Worthington: on the stage, Mrs.
W. 101:7
worthy: w. o' the flatterer 284:9
wottehell: but w. 206:8
would: what a man w. do 61:14
wound: Earth felt the w. 217:14
never felt a w. 283:2
Willing to w., and yet 239:13
W. with a touch 220:5
Wounded Knee: heart at W. 27:8
wounds: Time w. all heels 9:10
Wrapped: W. up in a five-pound
193:2
wrath: eternal. / Burnt after
them 217:10
grapes of w. 166:3
my w. did end 53:1
sun go down upon your w.
48:2
tigers of w. are wiser 52:9
wreathing: w. his body seven
times round 299:2
writ: name was w. in water
184:5

write: itch to w. 178:6
read a novel I w. one 115:7
w. at any time 173:1
writer: w. has to rob his mother
131:11
writers: American w. want to be
not good 330:5
writing: only end of w. is 172:11
w. comes from art, not chance
241:2
W. . . . . different name for
conversation 307:11
written: until he has w. a book
177:1
well w. or badly written
346:13
w. by people who don't
understand 194:8
w. in wind and running water
82:10
w. without effort 175:10
wrong: Fifty million Frenchmen
can't be w. 149:6
One w. more to man 60:13
rather be w. with Plato 92:13
w. number, why did you
answer 323:3
w. us, shall we not revenge
278:16
wrote: genius I had when I w.
that book 313:3
never w., except for money
174:10
wysest: clerkes been noght the
w. 85:9
Xanadu: In X. did Kubla Khan
96:6
Yankee: Y. Doodle came to town
22:4
yawp: barbaric y. over the roofs
343:8
year: gate of the y. 153:3
That time of y. thou mayst
287:5
'Tis the y.'s midnight 117:11
yearn: y. for His existence 327:5
yearning: music, y. like a God
179:10
years: moments big as y. 180:5
vale of y. 281:7

y. to come seemed waste
357:3

yell: such a y. was there 260:9

yellow: Come unto these y.
sands 283:16

sear, the y. leaf 277:11

When y. leaves, or none 287:5

Y. God forever gazes 153:6

Yes: able to say Y. 11:13

y. I said yes I will Yes 177:10

yesterdays: all our y. 277:13

yesteryear: snows of y. 330:7

yield: find, and not to y. 319:4

Yielded: Y. with coy submission
217:7

Yo-ho-ho: Y., and a bottle of
rum 309:13

Yorick: Alas! poor Y. 269:5

young: and we were y. 165:11

crime of being a y. man 236:1

Fortune . . . friendly to the y.
202:8

gods love dies y. 211:4

if he be *caught* y. 174:3

seventy years y. 162:6

she died y. 338:9

world and love were y. 249:6

y. as they are painted 25:10

y. can do for the old 288:7

y. know everything 347:7

youth: done it from my y. 103:2

If y. only knew 130:10

public never forgives — y. 348:4

red / Sweet wine of y. 57:6

sign of an ill-spent y. 304:7

thoughts of y. are long 197:8

Time, the subtle thief of y.
218:9

when Y. and Pleasure meet
73:1

y. are the days of our glory
76:1

y. grows pale 181:10

y. I remembered my God
304:1

Y. is a blunder 114:6

y. of England are on fire 271:1

Y.'s a stuff will not endure
285:14

Y., which is forgiven
everything 290:2

Y. will be served 54:8

Yukon: Law of the Y. 263:12

zeal: holy mistaken z. in politics
178:3

Zenith: Dropt from the Z. 216:5

Zenocrate: fair Zenocrate, divine
Z. 206:5

Zion: wept when we
remembered Z. 36:4

zone: torrid or the frozen z. 78:3

Zzzzzp: Knowledge — Z.! — Money
349:2